D1233048

introduction to GUIDANCE

introduction to
GUIDANCE

Robert L. Gibson
Marianne H. Mitchell

Indiana University

Macmillan Publishing Co., Inc.
New York
Collier Macmillan Publishers
London

Copyright © 1981, Macmillan Publishing Co., Inc.
Printed in the United States of America

Macmillan Publishing Co., Inc.
866 Third Avenue, New York, New York 10022
Collier Macmillan Canada, Ltd.

Library of Congress Cataloging in Publication Data

Gibson, Robert Leone (date)
  Introduction to guidance.

  Bibliography: p.
  Includes index.
  1. Personnel service in education. I. Mitchell, Marianne, joint author. II. Title.
LB1027.5.G459   371.4   79–25788
ISBN 0–02–341730–7

Printing: 1 2 3 4 5 6 7 8   Year: 1 2 3 4 5 6 7

To Our Parents—for a lifetime of guidance

Flora Lewis Gibson

Alva Jason Gibson

Helen Metzger Mitchell

Frank Henry Mitchell

Preface

This book is primarily designed for use in introductory guidance courses and in related fields for those who seek a comprehensive overview of guidance and counseling. The reader will find here a broad general discussion rather than the in-depth treatment that students majoring in counseling and guidance can anticipate later in their specialized preparatory courses.

The objectives of this book are to provide the reader an overview and general understanding of (1) historical perspectives and current activities of counselors; (2) the role and function of the counselors in a variety of settings; (3) techniques utilized by counselors; and (4) organization of programs of counseling and guidance.

Because schools and school systems are the largest single employer of counselors, considerable attention is given to counselors and their activities in the school setting. Although counselors in both school and nonschool settings adhere to basically the same principles and practices, it is recognized, through special attention in Chapter 4 and discussions in the other chapters, that counselors are increasingly functioning in a variety of nonschool settings. We, therefore, believe that those interested in counseling in nonschool settings will also find this book an appropriate introduction.

The initial chapters lead the reader from the historical background of the guidance movement through traditional and current activities. These activities are then translated into the counselor's role and function in both school and nonschool settings (Chapters 3 and 4). Chapters 5 through 11 discuss the basic activities in which counselors engage (assessment through standardized, nonstandardized, and values clarification techniques; career guidance and placement; individual and group counseling; and consultation). Chapter 7 includes a number of exercises which allow students to explore themselves and their values through group discussion and games. The final chapters deal with the developing and managing of counseling and guidance programs and their improvement through accountability, evaluation, and research.

Finally as an introductory text we have tried to write this book in a relatively informal style in the hope that it may be readable and enjoyable as well as informative. Your comments, suggestions, and reactions will be most welcome.

Finally, we would like to acknowledge all of those who have contributed directly and indirectly to the undertaking and completion of this book. These include, of course, the helpful staff of the Macmillan Publishing Company, particularly our editor, Mr. Lloyd Chilton and our persistent, good-natured production supervisor, Mr. Hurd Hutchins. We would also like to acknowledge the valuable comments of our anonymous reviewers, and we are extremely grateful to the many considerate authors and publishers who granted us permission to quote from their publications. It is also appropriate to acknowledge the many useful suggestions from our departmental colleagues at Indiana University and our fellow counselor educators who volunteered their time and comments for our guidance. We have also been appreciative of the critical comments of our graduate students (who undoubtedly had in mind the well-being of their counterparts of the future). In conclusion, we would like to acknowledge our close friends and families who have endured "the worst of times" and are now looking forward to "the best of times."

R. L. G.
M. H. M.

Contents

Chapter **3.** The School Counselors' Role and Function   51

Chapter **4.** Counselors in Other Settings   78

Chapter **10.** **Group Guidance and Counseling**   295

Chapter **11.** **The Counselor As Developmental and Educational Consultant**   322

List of Examples

List of Exercises

introduction to
GUIDANCE

Historical Perspectives 1

INTRODUCTION: COUNSELING—A RESPONSE TO HUMAN NEEDS

Many of you have recently made a decision to prepare for careers as counselors, others may be considering such a decision, and still others are interested in the field of guidance and counseling because you are in or are preparing to enter various careers in education. In the process you have probably asked yourself, why have I selected this field or this career? Your friends and family may have asked similar questions of you. Too, on occasion, you may have even thought, why do I have to work? Both are age-old questions that are vital to society and that have been discussed and researched extensively over the years. Perhaps an equally important question, but one that is not raised quite as frequently or researched as extensively, is, why do certain occupations exist? What were the factors that led to their demand and creation? The answers to these questions are fairly obvious concerning such occupational fields as medicine and law, for their need and role in society have been clearly and universally recognized since the earliest recordings of civilizations. Less clear to many, however, are the need and role for such less well-known occupations as ornithologists, demographers, and cytotechnologists. Although popular understandings and acceptance of the need and

1

role of all occupations are not necessary or expected, it would appear helpful to those studying the broad general areas encompassed by counseling and guidance to understand the nature of societal need to which counseling and guidance are responding and, in turn, to understand the nature of those responsibilities and responses. It is, therefore, appropriate in an introduction to guidance and counseling to begin by examining some of the historical antecedents leading to the development of guidance and counseling programs and the professional careers they represent. You, the reader, may determine whether counseling and counselors are a response to human needs or just another fancy that will pass when the need is examined more closely and critically.

OUR HERITAGE FROM THE PAST

It is quite possible that the historically earliest, although unconfirmed, occasion in which humankind went in search of a counselor could have been when Adam reaped the consequences of his eating the apple in the Garden of Eden. There is no proof of this early beginning to counseling, but there is an abundance of evidence that humankind has throughout the ages sought the advice and counsel of others believed to possess superior knowledge, insights, or experiences.

Perhaps the first counterparts of the present-day counselor were the chieftains and elders of the ancient tribal societies to whom youth turned or were often sent for advice and guidance. In these primitive societies the tribal members shared fundamental economic enterprises such as hunting, fishing, and agriculture. No elaborate career guidance programs were developed—or needed—as occupational limitations are usually determined by two criteria: age and sex. Later, as skills became more recognizable and important to societies, the occupational determinant of inheritance became common. Thus, potters passed on the secrets and skills of their trade to their sons, as did the smiths and carpenters. Women passed on their skills to their daughters; however, their occupational opportunities were limited. A study of early primitive life can lead one to conclude that most of the conflicts existing in present-day society regarding career decision making were absent. However, this absence of career decision-making dilemma should not be interpreted to mean that workers did not enjoy or take pride in a "job well done." Even from those earliest evidences of humankind's existence, it appears that pride and pleasure resulted from developing and demonstrating one's skills—in developing one's "human potential."

In the early civilizations, the philosophers, priests, or other representatives of the gods and religions assumed the function of advising and offering counsel. The historical origins of guidance may be identified in the early Grecian societies with their emphasis on developing and strengthening the individual through education so that each could fulfill roles reflecting their greatest potential for themselves and their society. It was believed that within the individual there were forces that could be stimulated and guided toward goals beneficial to both the individual and the community. Of these early Greek "counselors," Plato more than any other individual is generally recognized as one of the first to organize psychological insights into a systemic theory. As has been frequently noted, his interests

> were varied, and he examined the psychology of the individual in all of its ramifications: in moral issues, in terms of education, in relation to society, in theological perspective, and so on. He dealt with such questions as "What makes a man virtuous—his inheritance, his upbringing, or his formal education" (Meno), "How can children be most effectively taught" (Republic), and "Which techniques have been successfully used in persuading and influencing people in their decisions and beliefs" (Gorgias). But it is not the specific questions themselves that prove important to counselors, but, rather, the method that Plato used to deal with these questions, a method which, more than any other in the history of human thought, sets the way for the counseling relationship. It is a dramatic method, in which profound questions are dealt with through the dynamics of very real human interactions, a method in which the characters are as important as the things they say.[1]

The second great counselor of the early civilizations was Plato's student Aristotle, who made numerous and various significant contributions to what was to become the field of psychology. One of these major contributions was his studies of people interacting with their environment and with others.

Later, in ancient Hebrew society, individuality and the right of self-determination were assumed. The early Christian societies emphasized, at least in theory if not always in practice, many of the humanistic ideals that later became basic to democratic societies and, in this century, to the counseling movement. Philosophers, who were also educators, such as Luis Vives (1492–1540), recognized the need to guide each person according to his/her attitudes and aptitudes. Foreshadowing the recent women's equity and earlier women's liberation movements, "Vives in his *De subventione pauperum* (Bruges, 1526) even demanded that girls should be prepared for useful occupations."[2]

"By the early Middle Ages the duty of advising and directing youth had become centered in the parish priest. At that time education was largely

---

[1] Gary S. Belkin, *Practical Counseling in the Schools* (Dubuque, Iowa: William C. Brown Company, Publishers, 1975), p. 5.
[2] Robert King Hall and J. A. Lauwerys, eds. *Yearbook of Education—1955,* (Cleveland: William Collins & World Publishing Co., Inc., 1955). Chapter 3, "The History of the Guidance Movement: Western Civilization—Spanish Origins," by José Mallart, p. 75.

under church jurisdiction. Sporadic efforts at placement of youth in appropriate vocations occurred during the rise of European kingdoms and the subsequent expansion of the colonial empires."[3] For example, as early as the ninth century, the emperor Charlemagne sought to identify the mentally talented in his kingdom and to utilize their talents to strengthen his rule. Books stating that they were to be used to help youth in the choice of an occupation began to appear in the seventeenth century.[4] One notable effort by the Italian Tomaso Garzoni was nearly 1,000 pages and treated various professions and occupations in great detail. His publication *La Piazza Universale ai Tutti le Professioni del Mundo* (The Universal Plaza of all the Professions of the World) had twenty-four Italian editions, as well as being translated into Latin, German, and Spanish. Zytowski labels it the Occupational Outlook Handbook of the sixteenth and seventeenth centuries.[5]

In the seventeenth century a number of picture books also appeared depicting different occupations. One of the more popular publications was Powell's *Tom of All Trades; Or the Plain Pathway to Preferment,* published in 1631 in London. "Powell gives much information on the professions and how to gain access to them, even suggesting sources of financial aid and the preferred schools in which to prepare."[6]

In 1747, an anonymously authored English book, *A General Description of all Trades,* and *The London Tradesman* by R. Campbell were published. Career guidance books also began to appear on the American scene. Among these were the anonymously authored *The Book of Trades: Or Library of Useful Arts* (Philadelphia, 1807), and *The Complete Book of Trades* (Edward Hazen, Philadelphia, 1836).[7]

Among those who expressed a guidance point of view in the eighteenth century was Jean Jacques Rousseau (1712–78) who "suggested that the growing individual can best learn when he is free to develop according to his natural impulses; he advocated permissiveness in learning and learning through doing."[8] At approximately the same time, the famous Swiss educator Johann Pestalozzi (1746–1827) "expressed the belief that society could be reformed only to the extent that the individual in that society was helped to help *himself* develop."[9]

Nor was the newly independent United States without its counselors, as "one of its most versatile citizens, Thomas Jefferson, called for a plan to

---

[3] Robert L. Gibson and Robert E. Higgins, *Techniques of Guidance: An Approach to Pupil Analysis* (Chicago: Science Research Associates, Inc., 1966), p. 4.
[4] Donald G. Zytowski, "Four Hundred Years Before Parsons," *Personnel and Guidance Journal,* **50**:448 (Feb. 1972).
[5] Ibid., p. 448.
[6] Ibid., p. 447.
[7] Ibid., p. 444.
[8] Robert L. Gibson and Robert E. Higgins, op. cit., p. 4.
[9] Ibid., p. 4.

recognize and educate its male youth as a source of national leadership."[10]
The second president of the United States, John Adams, called for laws for
the liberal education of youth, especially of the lower class of people, as so
extremely wise and useful that to a humane and generous mind, no expense
for this purpose would be thought extravagant.

The most famous American educator of the nineteenth century, Horace
Mann, included in his *Twelfth Annual Report* a notation of the advantages
of the American common school system, advantages that were to be conducive
to the development of guidance in American education in the next century.
Mann reported that "in teaching the blind and the deaf and dumb, in kindling
the latent spark of intelligence that lurks in an idiot's mind, and in the
more holy work of reforming abandoned and outcast children, education
has proved what it can do by glorious experiments."[11] Horace Mann also
believed that education should have as one of its objectives the reform of
society, and he continuously stressed this view in his reports to the Massachusetts Board of Education.

Later, in the wake of the political scandals of the Grant administration
and other evidences of the decay of Christian morals, methods of moral
instruction and moral education became significant in the later 1800s. In
1872, the noted educator A. D. Mayo stated that morality and good citizenship
were indistinguishably intermingled and that moral education in the public
schools should be based on concepts, principles, and models drawn from
the Christian tradition of American society.[12]

Also during this period, the biologist Herbert Spencer (1820–1903) set
forth his concept of *adjustment.* This biological concept was that forms of
life that would not adapt to their environment eventually become extinct.
From this, Spencer concluded that perfect life consisted of perfect adjustment.
In other words, biological adjustment is a criterion of life. Adaptive behavior
is that which maintains life.[13]

In the nineteenth century other experts in the art of "predicting and
guiding human behavior" also were active. As those who had practiced the
ancient arts of fortunetelling, palmistry, and astrology were joined by the
relatively new science of graphology, all flourished. A brief examination of
these may help us to understand their continuing attraction in the twentieth
century.

Fortunetellers, since ancient times, have proclaimed their ability to analyze an individual's character and to predict the future. Historically, fortune-

[10] Ibid., p. 4.

[11] John H. Johansen, Harold W. Collins, and James A. Johnson, *American Education,* 2nd ed.
(Dubuque, Iowa: William C. Brown Company, Publishers, 1975), p. 280.

[12] A. D. Mayo, *National Education Association Journal of Addresses and Proceedings,* 1872.

[13] Robert P. Hinshaw, "The Concept of Adjustment and the Problems of Norms," *Psychological
Review,* **49**:284–292 (1942) in Stanley S. Marzolf, *Psychological Diagnosis and Counseling in
the Schools* (New York: Holt, Rinehart and Winston, 1956), pp. 60–61.

telling included a wide variety of techniques—palmistry, graphology, and astrology, but these latter fields in the seventeenth and eighteenth centuries developed and refined their own areas of specialization. In addition to these other popular methods of fortunetelling in the nineteenth century was the reading of playing cards, coffee grounds, and tea leaves. These readings were based on interpretations of the arrangements and configurations over which, theoretically at least, the interpreter had no control. Another historically popular method of fortunetelling was crystal gazing, by which fortunetellers used their special powers to bring forth knowledge and predictions of future events. Although modern societies frequently associate fortunetelling with sideshows and gypsy caravans, its appeal has never been limited to the uneducated, and today, as in the past, many descendents of these fortunetellers write columns in daily newspapers, make annual New Year's predictions, and seemingly guide the destinies of many well-known personalities around the world.

Palmistry based its claim to forecasting on an assessment of the lines and configurations of the palm of the hand. These interpretations were used for both character analysis and predictions of the future. Today, according to *The Complete Encyclopedia of Practical Palmistry,* "the study of the hand can analyze abnormal mentality, health, happiness, success, and any mental or physical shortcoming."[14]

Historically, the study of astrology can be traced back to the civilization of Babylonia and Chaldea in 5000 B.C. By the nineteenth century it was well accepted as a predictive "science." Over these centuries, astrology was developed as an approach to understand those human characteristics and traits that permitted astrologers to make future predictions. Astrology's near-acceptance from time to time as a predictive science may also be noted in the historical interest of the medical profession in astrology up to and into the nineteenth century. Perhaps more than any other of these ancient approaches to understanding human behavior, astrology continues to be extremely popular in today's American culture, as verified by an estimated 5,000 working astrologers in the United States, turning out zodiac forecasts for 10 million people.[15]

Although one's "mark" has always been recognized as one's own individually, the earliest attempts to relate handwriting and personality were noted in the seventeenth century. It was not until the 1800s that the interpretation of handwriting began to reach some degree of popularity. In the latter part of the 1800s and the early part of the 1900s, this art, now labelled graphology, flourished throughout Europe and reached university status as a subject for study. Today, graphology still holds some appeal as a means of personality

[14] Marcel Broekman, *The Complete Encyclopedia of Practical Palmistry.* (Englewood Cliffs, N.J.: Prentice-Hall, Inc., 1972), pp. 5, 58, 63, 65.
[15] Bruce King, *The History of Astrology* (New York: Arco Publishing Co., Inc., 1972), p. 285.

assessment. Some psychologists have suggested that handwriting is a type of projective technique.

In the period following the Civil War through the turn of that century, a number of school systems also developed plans for recognizing individual differences, especially in terms of individual pupil performance. Typical of these were the plans of the St. Louis schools for quarterly promotions, which enabled successful pupils to progress more rapidly, and the Pueblo, Colorado schools, in which multiple curricula tracks enabled students to complete similar units of study at different rates of speed.

As the United States entered the 1900s, it could be noted that more than a century of public education had emphasized educational opportunity for all citizens without cost; the relationship between the educational opportunity for all citizenry and the well-being of the society; the desirability of recognizing and providing for individual differences; the responsibility of the schools to be concerned with public morality, good citizenship, and other societal problems; and an awakening concern for the more adequate preparation of youth to enter the job market.

While the schools were evidencing more concern in societal problems, the American society of the early 1900s was growing more complex, and finding one's appropriate place within it was becoming increasingly complicated. As a result, many adults were turning to such traditional sources of advice, guidance, and counsel as their family physician, minister, or employer. At the same time, it was increasingly evident that many young people needed but were failing to receive assistance in decision making and preparation preliminary to entering the world of work. Further, there were few mature adults trained to specifically assist youth in coping with these needs.

Reflecting the latter concern was Theodore Roosevelt, probably the first president to indirectly support the development of at least the vocational aspects of what would later be identified as guidance services. Although Roosevelt was a graduate of the classical, nonvocational schools of his era, he nevertheless was a vigorous supporter of vocational education and vocational direction (which might be translated as vocational guidance). He noted in a 1908 article

> (We) have to deal now, and will have to deal in the future, with a nation of families on the land; and our system of public education should be so broadened in its scope as to include not merely the traditional cultural studies, excellent and indispensable in their way, but also instruction relative to the farm, the trades and the home. Our immediate purpose is to take the first steps in providing for the ninety-five per cent who are not now trained for a vocational advantage corresponding to those enjoyed by the relatively few who are trained in the professional and technical schools.[16]

[16] Theodore Roosevelt, *Good Housekeeping* (Nov. 12, 1908).

It would appear that the twentieth century was ripe for a considered and genuinely scientific approach to youth guidance.

THE DEVELOPMENT OF GUIDANCE IN AMERICAN EDUCATION

History is often made when an individual with an idea coincides with a need and an opportunity. In 1908, Frank Parsons organized the Boston Vocational Bureau to provide vocational assistance to young people and to train teachers to serve as vocational counselors. These teachers were to aid in the selection of students for vocational schools and were to assist students in choosing a vocation wisely and making the transition from school to suitable work. Soon thereafter (1909) Parsons published *Choosing a Vocation,*[17] a predecessor to this and other basic guidance texts. In this publication he discussed the role of the counselor and techniques that might be employed in vocational counseling. This first guidance text was divided into three areas: personal investigation, industrial investigation, and the organization and the work. Parson's book is interesting reading even today, and few would find fault with his suggestions that three factors necessary to the wise choice of a vocation are as follows:

> (1) a clear understanding of yourself, your aptitudes, abilities, interests, ambitions, resources, limitations, and other causes; (2) a knowledge of the requirements and conditions of success, advantages and disadvantages, compensation, opportunities, and prospects in different lines of work; and (3) true reasoning on the relations of these two groups of facts.[18]

Parsons goes on to suggest that in initiating the personal investigation, the client should first make an extensive study of himself/herself by answering questions on a "schedule of personal data." The counselor then fills in the details by reading between the lines. Parsons suggests that this will give clues to possible defects such as defective verbal memory and slow auditory reactions. Such a client would make a poor stenographer, or as he puts it, "would have difficulty becoming an expert stenographer."[19] The inventory suggested by Parsons includes items such as "how far can you walk? Habits as to smoking? drinking? use of drugs? other forms of dissipation? How often do you bathe?" An unusual feature of the intake interview was the observations Parsons suggested regarding the physical appearance of the client:

[17] Frank Parsons, *Choosing a Vocation,* (Boston: Houghton Mifflin Company, 1909).
[18] Ibid., p. 5.
[19] Ibid., p. 7.

While I am questioning the applicant about his probable health, education, reading, experience, etc., I carefully observe the shape of his head, the relative development above, before, and behind the ears, his features and expression, color, vivacity, voice, manner, pose, general air of vitality, enthusiasm, etc.

If the applicant's head is largely developed behind the ears, with big neck, low forehead, and small upper head, he is probably of an animal type, and if the other symptoms coincide, he should be dealt with on that basis.[20]

Parsons advocates getting the client to see oneself exactly as others see the individual and to give the client recommendations about methods that can be used for self-improvement—for example, reading suitable books to develop analytical power. Parsons also recommended using biographies of famous people and finding commonalities with the client in biographical details as a form of inspiration.

Parsons also insisted that counselors be thoroughly familiar with all relevant details concerning job opportunity, the distribution of demand in industries, and courses of study. A detailed analysis should be made of industrial opportunities for men and women. This would include location and demand, work conditions, and pay. A similar detailed approach was to be given to opportunities in vocational schools.

Parsons also explained the need to train vocational counselors. This training was to be accomplished in one to three terms, and the applicants should have had some relevant occupational background and maturity. In addition to sound judgment, character, and maturity, Parsons believed the vocational counselor should have the following:

1. A practical working knowledge of the fundamental principles and methods of modern psychology.
2. An experience involving sufficient human contact to give him an intimate acquaintance with human nature in a considerable number of its different phases; he must understand the dominant motives, interests, and ambitions that control the lives of men, and be able to recognize the symptoms that indicate the presence or absence of important elements of character.
3. Ability to deal with young people in a sympathetic, earnest, searching, candid, helpful, and attractive way.
4. A knowledge of requirements and conditions of success, compensation, prospects, advantages, and disadvantages, etc., in the different lines of industry.
5. Information relating to courses of study and means of preparing for various callings and developing efficiency therein.
6. Scientific method—analysis and principles of investigation by which laws and causes are ascertained, facts are classified, and correct

[20] Ibid., p. 21.

conclusions drawn. The counselor must be able to recognize the essential facts and principles involved in each case, group them according to their true relations, and draw the conclusions they justify.[21]

Parsons' pioneer efforts and publications were popular and succeeded in identifying and launching a new helping profession—the guidance counselor. Today, Parsons is generally referred to as the "father of the guidance movement in American education," but he probably did not envision the growth of the movement from the several dozen counselors he trained to the more than 50,000 guidance counselors functioning in schools alone seventy years later.

By 1913, the fledgling guidance movement had grown sufficiently in numbers and specialization to warrant the organization of the National Vocational Guidance Association and to initiate, two years later, the publication of the first guidance journal, appropriately titled *Vocational Guidance*. The early years of the movement had a vocational orientation that was primarily concerned with those aspects of youth guidance dealing with vocational choice, preparation, and placement. (Sixty years later, many of the same characteristics would once again be reasserted in the career education and guidance movements.)

In addition to Parsons, other early leaders in the guidance movement in America were Jessie B. Davis, Anna Y. Reed, Eli W. Weaver, and David S. Hill.[22] Their contributions should also be noted.

Davis' approach to guidance was based on self-study and the study of occupations. His descriptions of counseling seemed to suggest that students should be "preached to" about the moral value of hard work, ambition, honesty, and the development of good character as assets to any person who planned to enter the business world.[23] In their discussion of early pioneers of the guidance movement, Rockwell and Rothney suggested that

Davis' position within the social gospel philosophy was enhanced by his use of the "call" concept of the ministry in relation to the way one should choose a vocation. When an individual was "called," he would approach it with the noblest and highest ideals which would serve society best by uplifting humanity.[24]

In the same era, Anna Reed was an admirer of the then prevailing concepts and ethics of the business world and the free enterprise system. She believed that guidance services could be important to the Seattle school

---

[21] Ibid., pp. 94–95.
[22] Perry J. Rockwell and John W. M. Rothney, "Some Social Ideas of Pioneers in the Guidance Movement," *Personnel and Guidance Journal,* 11:349 (Dec. 1961).
[23] Ibid., p. 350.
[24] Ibid., p. 351.

system as a means of developing the best possible educational "product."[25] Contrary to today's philosophy, she placed the system's (business world) needs above those of the individual. As a result, the guidance programs she developed were designed to judge an individual's worth by the employability of the individual.

Another early leader, Eli Weaver, succeeded in establishing teacher guidance committees in every high school in New York City. These committees worked actively to help boys and girls discover their capabilities and how to use these capabilities to secure the most appropriate employment.[26]

The fourth of these early pioneers, David S. Hill, was a researcher in the New Orleans school system who used scientific methods to study individuals. Because his research studies pointed out the wide diversity in student populations, he advocated and worked for a diversified curriculum complemented by vocational guidance. He viewed this model as most appropriate if the individual student was to develop fully.

In the first quarter of the twentieth century, two other significant developments profoundly influenced the guidance movement. These were the introduction and development of standardized, group-administered psychological tests and the mental health movement.

The French psychologist Alfred Binet and his associate Theodore Simon introduced the first general intelligence test to the public in 1905. In 1916, a translated and revised version was introduced in the United States by Lewis M. Terman and his colleagues at Stanford University and it enjoyed widespread popularity in the schools. However, when the United States entered World War I and the armed services sought a measure that would enable them to screen and classify inductees, the first so-called group intelligence measure, the Army Alpha Test, was developed and subsequently administered to thousands of draftees. The possibilities of applying these and other psychometric techniques to pupil assessment resulted in the rapid development and expansion of standardized testing in education in the decade immediately following World War I.

The mental health movement, like the vocational guidance movement, owed much of its impetus in the early 1900s to the efforts of one man. This man was Clifford Beers who was neither a physician nor a psychologist, but was, for a number of years, a patient in a mental institution suffering from schizophrenia. During his confinement Beers wrote as follows:

> I soon observed that the only patients who were not likely to be subjected to abuse were the only ones least in need of care and treatment. The violent, noisy, and troublesome patient was abused because he was violent, noisy, and troublesome. The patient too weak, physically or mentally, to attend to his own wants was frequently abused because of

[25] Ibid., p. 351.
[26] Ibid., p. 352.

that very helplessness which made it necessary for the attendants to wait upon him. Usually a restless or troublesome patient placed in the violent ward was assaulted the very first day. This procedure seemed to be a part of the established code of dishonor. The attendants imagined that the best way to gain control of a patient was to cow him from the first. In fact, these fellows—nearly all of them ignorant and untrained—seemed to believe that "violent cases" could not be handled in any other way.[27]

In another statement, Beers noted:

Most sane people think that no insane person can reason logically. But that is not so. Upon unreasonable premises I made most reasonable deductions, and at that time when my mind was in its most disturbed condition. Had the newspapers which I read on that day which I supposed to be February 1st borne a January date, I might not then, for so long a time, have believed in special editions. Probably I should have inferred that the regular editions had been held back. But the newspapers I had were dated about two weeks *ahead.* Now if a sane person on February 1st receives a newspaper dated February 14th, he will be fully justified in thinking something wrong, either with the publication or with himself. But the shifted calendar which had planted itself in my mind meant as much to me as the true calendar does to any sane businessman. During the seven hundred and ninety-eight days of depression I drew countless incorrect deductions. But, such as they were, they were deductions, and essentially the mental process was not other than that which takes place in a well-ordered mind.[28]

These and similar descriptions aroused the public to initiate humanitarian reforms and scientific inquiry into the problems of mental illnesses and their treatment. With the help of a few psychologists of the time, such as William James and Adolf Meyer, the mental hygiene movement was launched to educate the general public toward a better appreciation of the plight and treatment of disturbed persons.[29] During this time community efforts also increased to raise the standards of treatment and prevention of mental disorders and to establish local clinics for disturbed children. As the American public became increasingly aware of the extent and impact of mental illness, the possibility of preventive or early treatment in schools began to be discussed and made an impact on the growing guidance movement.

The 1920s was a lively decade in many ways. That noble experiment, prohibition, was launched which, in turn, presented such names as Al Capone

[27] Clifford Beers, *A Mind That Found Itself* (New York: Longmans Green and Co., 1908, and republished by Doubleday & Company, Inc., 1953), pp. 164–165.
[28] Ibid., pp. 57–58.
[29] June G. Shane, Harold G. Shane, Robert L. Gibson, and Paul F. Munger, *Guiding Human Development* (New York: Wadsworth Publishing Co., Inc., 1971), p. 39.

and "Baby Face" Nelson across the nation's newspaper headlines, while socially, the jazz age, flappers, and bathtub gin were in vogue. For the professional educator, the progressive movement ensured a lively educational era as well. This movement, whose thinking would influence the further development of a guidance philosophy, stressed the uniqueness and dignity of the individual pupil, emphasized the importance of humanistic (current label) classroom environment, and suggested that learning occurred in many ways. Many of today's counselors would have embraced the progressive education suggestions that pupils and teachers should plan together, that the child's social environment should be improved, that the developmental needs and purposes of the student should be considered, and that the psychological environment of the classroom should be a positive, encouraging one.

Organized guidance programs began to emerge with increasing frequency in secondary schools in the 1920s and more often than not modelled themselves after college student personnel programs with titles of deans—separately for boys and girls, of course—and with similar accompanying functions of discipline, school attendance, and related administrative responsibilities. As a result, many programs of this decade began to have a remedial emphasis as pupils who experienced academic or personal difficulties were sent to their deans who sought to help them modify their behavior or correct their deficiencies. Nevertheless, the counselor of the mid-1920s, if projected by a time capsule into a school counselor's meeting fifty years later, could have conversed easily with his or her present-day counterpart—at least to the point of their concern and involvement in vocational or career guidance, the use of standardized testing instruments, assistance to pupils with their educational planning, the need for a more humanistic school environment, and their role as disciplinarians and quasi-administrators.

It is also probable that the elementary school counseling movement had its beginnings in the mid-1920s and early 1930s, stimulated by the writings and efforts of William Burnham. Burnham emphasized the important role of the teacher in the mental health of the child in the elementary school.[30] Efforts to develop guidance in elementary schools during this period were scarcely noticeable, but a few notable programs were undertaken. One of these, in Winnetka, Illinois, established a department of elementary counseling with resource personnel for guidance. These personnel included (although not all on a full-time basis) psychiatrists, psychometrists, psychologists, an educational counselor, psychiatric social worker, and supporting clerical services. Their basic responsibilities were counseling, child study, psychotherapy, pupil analysis, parental assistance, and referrals.

Two acts significant in the development of rehabilitation counseling also occurred in the early 1920s. The Civilian Vocational Rehabilitation Act (Pub-

---

[30] Verne Faust, *The History of Elementary School Counseling: Overview and Critique* (Boston: Houghton-Mifflin Company, 1968), pp. 12–13.

lic Law 236, 1920) was followed in 1921 by Public Law 47. The latter created the Veteran's Bureau and provided, among other benefits, a continuation of vocational rehabilitation services for veterans, including counseling and guidance. As Obermann noted

> The counseling provided for veterans was one of the most important features of the Veterans Administration's vocational rehabilitation and education program. It had been observed early in the vocational rehabilitation program for the disabled veterans of World War I that good vocational counseling and guidance was of crucial importance. The lesson was not overlooked in the legislation for World War II veterans and in the implementation of that legislation. All Public Law 16 trainees were required to select their vocational objectives only after formal vocational evaluation and counseling. Those training under Public Law 346 could receive counseling services if they requested them.[31]

By the end of the 1920s it was evident that the early guidance pioneers believed there was a need for guidance services and believed that the school was the proper institution for the delivery of these services. Some even believed that pupil guidance should encompass all grades.

While in the 1930s the American public debated the policies of F.D.R. and the threat of Hitler to world peace, the guidance movement continued to develop to the point that it was becoming increasingly popular as a topic for discussions and debate in educational circles. Questions and criticisms concerning guidance activities were increasingly noted in the professional literature of the era. Educational associations appointed committees to study the movement, and many issued reports with descriptions and definitions of guidance and guidance services. One such report defined guidance as "the process of assisting individuals in making life adjustment. It is needed in the home, school, community, and in all other phases of the individual's environment."[32]

As today when concern is often expressed about the interchangeability of the words *guidance* and *counseling,* in the 1930s a similar concern was expressed over the interchangeability of the terms *student personnel* and *guidance.* Adding further to the confusion, leading spokespeople for the movement during that period, such as John Brewer, spoke of *education* as *guidance,* using the terms synonomously.[33]

---

[31] C. Esco Obermann, *A History of Vocational Rehabilitation in America.* (Minneapolis: T. S. Denison & Co., Inc., 1965), p. 190.

[32] *Guidance in the Secondary School,* Report of a subcommittee of the Committee on Secondary School Problems of the Associated Academic Principals, educational monograph of the New York State Teachers Association, #3 (Albany, N.Y.: New York State Teachers Association, 1935), p. 10.

[33] John M. Brewer, *Education as Guidance* (New York: Macmillan Publishing Co., Inc., 1932).

Sarah M. Sturtevant[34] sought to deal with some of these growing concerns by addressing herself to some questions regarding the developing secondary school guidance movement. These included What do we mean by the guidance movement? What are the essentials of a functioning guidance program? What personnel and what qualifications should guidance workers have for a good guidance program? and the inevitable question, What are the costs of individualizing education?—questions that would not be outdated more than forty years later.

During the late 1930s and early 1940s, the trait-factor approach to counseling became increasingly recognized and popular. This often-labelled "directive" theory received stimulus from the writings of E. G. Williamson (*How to Counsel Students: A Manual of Techniques for Clinical Couselors,* McGraw-Hill Book Company, 1939), and others. Whereas critics of this measurement-oriented approach claimed it was rigid and dehumanizing, Williamson (1975) noted that

You are trying to improve your understanding by using data with a smaller probable error of estimate, such as test data—instead of judgments, which have a much larger probable error of estimate: variability.[35]

During the 1930s, possible directions for guidance in the elementary school were also put forth by the child study movement, which suggested that it was the teacher's role to provide guidance for each pupil in the self-contained classroom. Publications by Zirbes[36] and others described the ways in which children's learning experiences could be guided. The intensive study of each child was recommended with the objective of understanding how children achieved or failed to achieve certain developmental tasks. This approach was a popular one that found some following at the secondary school level and ultimately led to the suggestion of "every teacher a guidance worker."

As the country emerged from World War II, the guidance movement appeared to be taking on new vitality and direction. A significant contributor to this new direction was Carl Rogers, who had set forth a new counseling theory in two significant books, *Counseling and Psychotherapy*[37] and a refinement of his early position, *Client-Centered Therapy.*[38] In his publication *Counseling and Psychotherapy,* Rogers offered nondirective counseling as an alternative to the older, more traditional methods. Rogers also stressed the

[34] Sarah M. Sturtevant, "Some Questions Regarding the Developing Guidance Movement," *School Review,* **14:**347–356 (May 1937).
[35] Dorlesa Barmettler Ewing, "Direct from Minnesota—E. G. Williamson," *Personnel and Guidance Journal,* **54:**84 (Oct. 1975).
[36] June G. Shane, Harold Shane, Robert L. Gibson, and Paul F. Munger, op. cit., p. 16.
[37] Carl R. Rogers, *Counseling and Psychotherapy* (Cambridge, Mass.: The Riverside Press, 1942).
[38] Carl R. Rogers, *Client-Centered Therapy* (Boston: Houghton-Mifflin Company, 1951).

client's responsibility in reperceiving the individual's problem and enhancing the client's "self." This self theory soon was labelled nondirective because it appeared to be the opposite of the traditional counselor-centered approach for dealing with client problems. Rogers' suggestion that the client assume the major responsibility for solving one's own problem rather than the therapist solving the client's problem provoked the first serious theoretical controversies in the school guidance movement. Rogers' follow-up publication of *Client-Centered Therapy* was the result of his continued research and application efforts. This book promoted the semantic change from nondirective to client-centered counseling, but, more importantly, indicated increasing emphasis on the growth-producing possibilities of the client. Perhaps more than any other individual, Rogers has influenced the way in which the American counselor interacts with the client. Further, his view of the client as an equal and his positive view of the individual's potential seemed more consistent with the American way of life and democratic traditions than did the European-based theories.

> The extent of [Rogers'] influence was most marked by the overnight replacement of testing by counseling as the key guidance function. In turn, counseling would rise to such eminence in the next few years that it would compete and contend with guidance in regard to the use of counselor's time and the overall purpose of counseling and guidance. *What began as an adjunct tool of guidance would now raise a challenge for ascendency in its own right.*[39]

Over the years Rogers has continued to research, test, revise, and challenge others to test his theory. In summary, it might be analagous to compare Carl Rogers' impact and contributions to the counseling movement in this century with Henry Ford's contribution to the development of the automotive industry.

Another dimension to the school counselors' technique of the late 1940s and one to which Rogers, again, was a significant contributor was *group counseling*. Others, utilizing research data gathered by the armed services and their investigations into small group dynamics, developed a theoretical framework within which school counselors could integrate the skills and processes of individual counseling with the dynamic roles and interactions of the individual in the group setting.

During and immediately following World War II, counselors again found increasing opportunities in the Veterans Administration vocational rehabilitation and educational services as these were rapidly expanded to accommodate the needs of U.S. Armed Service personnel and ex-service personnel.

Other opportunities also appeared on the horizon for the guidance move-

---

[39] Roger F. Aubrey, "Historical Development of Guidance and Counseling and Implications for the Future," *Personnel and Guidance Journal* (Feb. 1977), p. 292.

ment. Feingold, writing in *School Review,*[40] called for a new approach to guidance. He indicated that the guidance counselor cannot stop with mere educational direction—he must go beyond that goal—he must also provide guidance, "not only for the annointed, but for those pupils who really need it—the pupils who run afoul of rules and regulations."[41] Feingold and others also called for "guidance of the whole child," an outgrowth of the child study movement of the 1930s. Three years later, Traxler, writing in the same publication, identified emerging trends in guidance:[42]

1. More adequate training of guidance personnel.
2. Guidance as an all-faculty function.
3. Closer cooperation with home and community agencies.
4. Orderly accumulation and recording of individual information.
5. Use of objective measures.
6. Differential prediction of success on the basis of test batteries that yield comparable scores in broad areas.
7. Increased interest in improved techniques in the appraisal of personal qualities of pupils and the treatment of maladjustment.
8. Trend toward "eclectic" guidance (rather than directive/nondirective).
9. Recognition of relationship between remedial work and guidance.
10. Improved case study techniques.
11. Availability and better use of occupational-educational information.

In 1957, the Soviet Union made headlines around the world by its successful launching of the first earth satellite, Sputnik I. An indirect, but nevertheless significant, result of this accomplishment, was the lift off of the guidance movement into orbit in the United States. This came about through legislation resulting from the public's criticism of education and its failure to supply trained personnel vital for careers and deemed vital for the national well-being. This legislation, labelled the National Defense Education Act, passed in September 1958, became a most important landmark in American education, as well as of great significance to the guidance movement, for its acknowledgement of the vital linkages between our national well-being, personnel needs, and education. This act provided special benefits for youth guidance in five of its ten titles or sections. Of these, perhaps Title V was the key to the upsurge that was to follow in guidance program development. This title provided for "(1) grants to states for stimulating the establishment and maintenance of local guidance programs and (2) grants to institutions of higher education for the training of guidance personnel to staff local programs."[43]

[40] Gustave A. Feingold, *School Review* **4:**542–550 (Nov. 1947).
[41] Ibid., p. 550.
[42] Arthur E. Traxler, *School Review,* "Emerging Trends in Guidance," **58:**14–15 (Jan. 1950).
[43] Robert L. Gibson and Robert E. Higgins, op. cit., p. 7.

Six years later (September 1964), the impact of the act could be noted by announcements from the United States Department of Health, Education, and Welfare, pointing out that the act had, in that short period of time, achieved the following:

1. Made grants to states of approximately $30 million, thereby helping bring the number of full-time high school counselors from 12,000 (one for every 960 students) in 1958 to 30,000 (one for every 510 students) in 1964.
2. Through the end of the 1964–65 academic year, supported 480 institutes designed to improve counseling capabilities, which were attended by more than 15,700 secondary school counselors and teachers preparing to become counselors.
3. From 1959 to 1964, made it possible for 109 million scholastic aptitude and achievement tests to be given to public secondary school students and over 3 million to private secondary school students.
4. Helped 600,000 students obtain or continue their college education with federal loans.
5. Trained 42,000 skilled technicians to meet critical manpower needs.
6. Granted 8,500 graduate fellowships, a first step toward meeting the need for many more college teachers.[44]

Stimulated by this resulting rapid growth in counseling and guidance, standards for the certification and performance of school counselors were developed and upgraded; the criteria used by accrediting associations for school guidance program evaluation were strengthened; and noticeable progress was made in counselor training. Many writers in the field were to note that guidance had come of age . . . that there was a "new era."

For example, Donovan wrote about a new era for guidance, in which he pointed out that "the testing expert and professional counselor enter the picture to give scientific aid in getting each child in touch with those teachers and courses best calculated to free his abilities."[45] His and other writings further suggested the movement from an era of mass education to one in which each child is treated as an individual with "counseling personnel becoming indispensable auxiliaries to administrators and teachers."[46]

The following year (1960), Klopf called for an expanding role for the high school counselor. He pointed out that "as populations increase, schools will become larger and taxes become greater in most communities. Instructional services will increase in communities, but guidance programs may not increase accordingly."[47] He suggested that new uses and approaches to homeroom group guidance, small discussion groups, and group counseling

[44] Ibid., p. 7.
[45] Rev. Charles F. Donovan, S. J. *School and Society* **87**:241 (May 23, 1959).
[46] Ibid., p. 241.
[47] Gordon Klopf, *School and Society* **88**:418 (Nov. 5, 1960).

needed to be explored. He also suggested that the guidance worker should view himself/herself not only as a counselor but as one concerned with total learnings, including the personal and social relations of the student.

> If he has a knowledge of individual behavior, the social structure of the school and the community, and the awareness of the world of today and the future, this in all the ongoing activities of the school he should share.[48]

The 1960s were viewed and labelled by many in education, including guidance counselors, as the decade of innovation. Experimentations and innovations were called for and, often with substantial federal funding, initiated in schools and school systems across the country. Among the more popular were team teaching, modular scheduling, nongraded schools, open-planned schools, alternative schools, colleges without walls, programmed learning, and computer-assisted instruction. A Ford Foundation study concluded that these and other changes and innovations had little or no lasting effect on the content of school programs or the quality of teaching and learning.[49]

In the 1960s one of the most important developments for the school guidance movement was the "Statement of Policy for Secondary School Counselors" (1964), developed and approved as an official policy statement by the American School Counselors Association (ASCA). This effort to specify the role and function of the school counselor involved more than 6,000 school counselors plus teachers, school administrators, and other educators.

C. Gilbert Wrenn's classic contribution of the 1960s, *The Counselor in a Changing World,* also examined the counselor's role in a changing society with changing ideas about human behavior and changing schools. He noted the growing complexity of the counselor's task:

> It is not enough for the counselor to understand youth in isolation, as it were. More than ever before, the counselor must understand not only the student, but himself and his adult contemporaries as they attempt to adjust to a rapidly changing technology and world order.[50]

C. Harold McCulley suggested that if the school counselor was to move toward bona fide professionalization, "he cannot afford to define his functions on the basis of a retrospective analysis of what counselors have done in the past as technicians."[51] He forecast needed new directions in which the coun-

---

[48] Ibid., p. 418.

[49] *A Foundation Goes to School.* (New York: Ford Foundation, 1972), p. 3.

[50] C. Gilbert Wrenn, *The Counselor in a Changing World* (Washington, D.C.: American Personnel and Guidance Association, 1962), p. 8.

[51] C. Harold McCulley, "The Counselor: Instrument of Change," *Teachers College Record,* **66:**405 (Feb. 1965).

selor functioned as a consultant and agent for change, directions which would require substantive study of the dynamics of cultural and social change.

Munson[52] suggested that by the 1970s the school guidance counselor had inherited a series of stereotypes whose value and validity had to be determined. He suggested that what historians record about guidance in the 1970s will attest to their concern for these stereotypes and their behavior in dealing with them. They were as follows:

The Stereotype of Responsibility. The belief by parents and others that counselors have certain responsibilities such as ensuring that the student takes the "right" courses, selects the appropriate college, takes necessary standardized examinations, meets application deadlines, and so forth.

The Stereotype of Failure. The belief that the counselor is responsible for keeping individuals from failing—that the counselor is a buffer between success and failure. As a predictor of outcomes that determine decisions, the counselor can assess risks and chances for success or failure.

The Stereotype of Occupational Choice. Perhaps more consistent and widespread than another is the view of the counselor as the person who can tell a student what occupation to enter—who can make this "once-in-a-lifetime" decision for individuals. After all, the counselor is the one with the various interest and aptitude tests and occupational files—and one is constantly referred to as the person to see about industrial, armed services, and educational recruitment materials.[53]

In 1973 the Report of the National Commission on the Reform of Secondary Education[54] published its report with thirty-two recommendations for the improvement of secondary education. Although the majority of these held implications for the functioning of the secondary school counselor, the following were of particular importance:

Recommendation Number 6: Bias in Counseling
Counselors should insure that all students regardless of sex or ethnic background are afforded equal latitude and equally positive guidance in making educational choices.
Recommendation Number 9: Career Education
Career education advisory councils, including representatives of labor, business, community, students, and former students, should be established to assist in planning and implementing career education programs in comprehensive high schools.

---

[52] Harold L. Munson, *Foundations of Developmental Guidance* (Boston: Allyn & Bacon, Inc., 1971), pp. 16–17.
[53] Ibid., pp. 16–17.
[54] *The Reform of Secondary Education, A Report of the National Commission on the Reform of Secondary Education* (New York: McGraw-Hill Book Company, 1973), pp. 15–17.

Career awareness programs should be initiated as an integral part of the curriculum to assure an appreciation of the dignity of work.

Opportunities for exploration of a variety of career clusters should be available to students in grades eight to ten.

In grades eleven and twelve, students should have opportunities to acquire hard skills in a career area of their choice. This training should involve experience in the world outside school and should equip the student with job-entry skills.

Recommendation Number 10: Job Placement

Suitable job placement must be an integral part of the career education program for students planning to enter the labor force upon leaving school. Secondary schools should establish an employment office staffed by career counselors and clerical assistants. The office should work in close cooperation with the state employment services. Agencies certifying counselors for secondary schools should require such counselors to show experience in job placement as a condition for granting initial certification.

Recommendation Number 12: Alternative Paths to High School Completion

A wide variety of paths leading to completion of requirements for graduation from high school should be made available to all students. Individual students must be encouraged to assume major responsibility for the determination of their educational goals, the development of the learning activities needed to achieve those goals, and the appraisal of their progress.[55]

SUMMARY: IMPLICATIONS OF THE PAST FOR THE PRESENT AND FUTURE

In retrospect, we have examined the need for humankind from the time of Adam down through the ages for advice and counsel, to understand themselves and their relationships to their fellow human beings, and to recognize and develop one's potential. In responding to these needs, the chieftains and elders of the ancient tribal societies were perhaps the first forerunners, the ancient counterpart, of the present-day counselor. Later, in the early civilizations, the philosophers, priests, or other representatives of the gods were seen in roles offering advice and counsel. Religion's role in the counsel and advice of the young in particular, but not exclusively, continued through the Middle Ages, supplemented by sporadic efforts at talent identification and development and even planned career placement. From the Middle Ages onward, teachers also were increasingly expected to provide guidance for their pupils—often of the most directive kind. To supplement these efforts, books began to appear with increasing frequency from the eighteenth century

---

[55] Ibid., pp. 15–17.

onward, focusing on providing advice and counsel to youth in meeting many of the problems of the times, especially those concerning occupational choice. Meanwhile, many leading statesmen, philosophers, scientists, and educators were laying a philosophical groundwork that would eventually support and nurture an embryonic guidance movement.

This movement, unique for many years to American education, in its beginnings had a vocational guidance emphasis but was shortly to be influenced by a multitude of other movements, especially psychological testing, mental health, and progressive education. Later in the twentieth century, the interdisciplinary character of the movement was further emphasized with influences from the group dynamics, counseling psychology, education of the gifted, career education, and placement movements. Nor has the movement been without pioneers and heroes. Of course, the great humanistic teachers of history—Christ, Mohammed, Buddha, philosophers, and far-sighted leaders such as Plato, Aristotle, Pestalozzi, Rousseau, and Charlemagne would have been charter members and undoubtedly elected officers of any counseling and guidance associations of their times in history. In the United States, one can easily envision the Franklins, Jeffersons, Lincolns, and Roosevelts receiving honorary life memberships in the American Personnel and Guidance Association for their contributions to the eventual growth of the movement. The real heroes have been individuals such as Parsons, Davis, Reed, Weaver, and Hill—those early, persistent, and farsighted pioneers of the movement, whose efforts were later recognized and advanced, and then further enriched by the giants of the last half of the twentieth century, such as Carl Rogers, Ed Williamson, and C. Gilbert Wrenn.

It is said that a movement must have a cause and leadership to survive. This brief review of some historical highlights of the development of counseling and guidance in American education should indicate to you that neither has been lacking. As the past illuminates the future, it is possible to predict that regardless of the wonderful scientific and technological advances that await humankind in the generations ahead, many individuals, young and old, will search out the counsel and advice of the trained, while others will still seek self and other understandings for the development of their potential and/or the solution of their problems.

Traditional and Current Activities in Schools

INTRODUCTION

Schools throughout history have been mirrors of the societies they have served, reflecting the needs of those societies and responding in accordance with their perceived societal role in meeting these needs. Throughout the ages, this role has been the education of the citizenry of the society—and modern societies are no exceptions. In schools today, then, the instructional program— the teaching-learning activities—is central, with other programs and activities serving important support roles designed to ensure, insofar as possible, the fullest development of the individual's human potential. These support roles include, among others, administration and supervision and, of course, counseling and guidance. Despite the relatively short period of time that counseling and guidance has been in this support role, certain basic principles, identifiable patterns of program organization, and traditional activities have emerged. An understanding of these can provide some insights into the not infrequently asked question, "How come guidance counselors do what they do the way they do it?"

BASIC PRINCIPLES

Principles tend to form a philosophical framework within which programs
are organized and activities are developed. They are guidelines that are derived
from the experiences and values of the profession, and they are representative
of the views of the majority of the profession's membership. As such, they
become fundamental assumptions or a system of beliefs regarding a profession
and its role, function, and activities. Here are some principles that suggest
the school guidance program can make its contributions more effectively
when:

1. School guidance programs are designed to serve the developmental and
   adjustment needs of *all* youth.
2. Pupil guidance is viewed as a process that is continuous from the time
   of the pupil's initial entry into the educational system and throughout
   the child's formal education.
3. Trained guidance personnel are essential for ensuring professional competencies, leadership, and direction. (This does not imply that paraprofessionals cannot make worthwhile contributions.)
4. Certain basic guidance activities are essential to program effectiveness,
   and these must be specifically planned and developed if they are to be
   effective.
5. The school guidance program must reflect the uniqueness of the population it serves and the environment in which it seeks to render this
   service; thus, like individuals, each school guidance program will be
   different from other programs.
6. Relevant to the preceding, the school guidance program bases its uniqueness on a regular and systematic assessment of the needs of the student
   clientele and of the characteristics of environmental setting for the program.
7. The school guidance program is concerned with the total development
   of the individual.
8. An effective instructional program in the school requires an effective
   program of pupil guidance. Good education and good guidance are
   interrelated. They support and complement each other to the student's
   advantage.
9. Relevant to (7), teacher understanding and support of the school guidance program is significant to the success of such programs.
10. The school guidance program is accountable. It recognizes the need
    to provide objective evidence of accomplishments and their worthwhile-
    ness.
11. The school counselor is a team member. The counselor shares a concern
    and programs for youth with psychologists, social workers, teachers,
    administrators, and other educational professionals and staff.

12. The school guidance program recognizes the right and capability of the individual to make decisions and plans.
13. The school guidance program recognizes and respects the worth and dignity of the individual—*every* individual.
14. The school guidance program recognizes the uniqueness of the individual and the individual's right to that uniqueness.
15. The school counselor is a role model of positive human relations—of unbiased, equal treatment behavior.

TRADITIONAL ACTIVITIES

The historical review of guidance in Chapter 1 noted the contributions of many disciplines to a movement that has consistently been adding and expanding its areas of emphasis. Noted were eras of vocational guidance, mental health guidance, standardized testing for guidance purposes, education as guidance, group activities as guidance, and the identification and college placement of the gifted as guidance. Out of these various emphases has come a traditional view of guidance as a constellation of services, described as basic to any fully functioning program. More than twenty years ago, Froehlich[1] discussed services to pupils in groups and individually, services to the instructional staff, services to the administration and research services. Hatch and Costar noted that "it seems more desirable to think of the guidance program as a program of services—services which can be defined, recognized, administered, and evaluated. It is then possible to define a guidance program as a program of services specifically designed to improve the adjustment of the individual pupil for whom it was organized."[2] They went on to suggest that

Guidance services are for all concerned.
Guidance services are for all school levels.
Guidance services are primarily preventive in nature.
The teacher plays a major role in the guidance program.
The program of guidance services needs trained personnel.
The program of guidance services requires coordination.
The guidance program uses and improves on present practices.
Guidance services are not an added activity.
Guidance services are a group of facilitating services.
The training background of guidance workers presupposes certain elements.

[1] Clifford P. Froehlich, *Guidance Services in Schools* (New York: McGraw-Hill Book Company, 1958), pp. 13–21.
[2] Raymond N. Hatch and James W. Costar, *Guidance Services in the Elementary School* (Dubuque, Iowa: William C. Brown Company, Publishers, 1961), p. 14.

They concluded their first chapter by identifying the following services as desirable for a school guidance program:

Pupil inventory service.
Information service.
Counseling service.
Placement service.
Follow-up and evaluation service.

Zeran and Riccio in 1962 identified basic services as analysis of the individual, counseling, placement, and follow-up and informational services.[3]

Gibson and Higgins noted in 1966 that although semantics and labels varied, the basic services were usually identified as pupil analysis, individual counseling, informational activities, group guidance, placement and follow-up, and evaluation and research.[4]

Shertzer and Stone (1976) discussed individual counseling, counseling in groups, student appraisal, the information service, career development planning, and placement and evaluation.[5]

In summary, these and numerous other authors point toward five traditional or basic activities. These services, individual analysis, individual counseling, group guidance and counseling, occupational and educational information, and placement and follow-up are discussed briefly in the paragraphs that follow. It should be noted that these are discussed as they have traditionally been provided over the years with no attempts to modernize them at this point. The later chapters, which discuss some of these and related activities in greater detail, will bring you up to date.

Individual Analysis

Individual analysis is that activity of the school guidance program which seeks, through systematic assessment efforts, to identify the characteristics and potential of every student. This activity is based on the fundamental premises that individuals are similar in some ways but different in others and that techniques for assessing these similarities and differences should be a part of the counselor's professional repertoire. This activity is often referred to as the primary activity of the school guidance program because

---

[3] Franklin R. Zeran and Anthony C. Riccio, *Organization and Administration of Guidance Services,* (Skokie, Ill.: Rand McNally & Company, 1962), pp. 3–5.
[4] Robert L. Gibson and Robert E. Higgins, *Techniques of Guidance: An Approach to Pupil Analysis* (Chicago: Science Research Associates, Inc., 1966), p. 8.
[5] Bruce Shertzer and Shelley C. Stone, *Fundamentals of Guidance,* 3rd ed. (Boston: Houghton Mifflin Company, 1976).

it provides a data base for more readily understanding the individual in the counseling setting, the effective planning of group guidance and counseling activities which reflect student interests and needs, the development of responsive career guidance programs, and organization of systematic placement and follow-up programs. Often referred to as individual inventory, assessment, or appraisal, this basic service promotes the student's self-understanding, as well as better understandings by teachers and counselors. This activity first developed as a basic service as a result of the standardized testing movement in education. Even today, standardized test results and school records are the most frequently utilized objective data in individual analysis. Other popular and traditional techniques are observation and observation reports, self-reporting techniques such as the autobiography and, in recent years, an increasing use of values clarification techniques. It should be noted that other helping professional specialists in the school setting also have diagnostic skills and responsibilities. The school counselor will therefore often consult with school psychologists and psychometrists as specialists in psychological assessment, including individual testing and, with school social workers as specialists in environmental and case study analysis. Chapters 5, 6, and 7 will discuss these and other techniques for human resource assessment in greater detail.

Counseling

Individual counseling, since the early days of the school guidance movement, has been identified as the heart of the guidance program. It is the core activity, through which all the other activities become meaningful. Counseling is a one-to-one helping relationship which focuses upon the individual's growth and adjustment, and problem-solving and decision-making needs. It is a client-centered process that demands confidentiality. This process is initiated by establishing a state of psychological contact or relationship between the counselor and the counselee and will progress as certain conditions, essential to the success of the counseling process, prevail. These include counselor genuineness or congruence, respect for the client, and an empathic understanding of the counselee's internal frame of reference. Although each counselor will, in time, develop his or her own personal theory to guide his or her practice, established theories provide a basis for examination and learning. It must also be mentioned that effective counseling not only requires counselors with the highest levels of training and professional skills, but a certain type of person as well. Counseling programs will suffer in effectiveness and credibility unless counselors exhibit the traits of understanding, warmth, humaneness, and positive attitudes toward humankind. Chapter 9 will discuss individual counseling and its significance for the school guidance program in greater detail.

Group Guidance and Counseling

Students have been organized into groups for what might be called guidance purposes since long before there was the bestowing of any guidance label on the activity. The organization of courses and group meetings to dispense primarily occupational information can be traced back before evolution of the guidance movement. The homeroom also has served a guidance as well as an administrative function long before being labelled as such. However, in 1934, a textbook by H. C. McKown[6] bore the title *Home Room Guidance.* With the increasing importance and attention given to extracurricular activities in schools in the 1920s and 1930s, there were some who suggested those were a type of group guidance experience also. Although varying activities, from time to time, have been given the label *group guidance,* the most consistent definition of this service is one that views it as an activity designed to provide students information or experiences that promote their occupational or educational understandings and personal, social growth and adjustment. Some traditional group guidance activities that have become familiar to most high school students are career days, college days, and orientation days.

In recent generations, group counseling has also been viewed as a basic, but different, activity than group guidance. Whereas group guidance focuses on providing information and developmental experiences, group counseling tends to focus more on problem solving and adjustment needs of students through a process very similar to individual counseling. Gazda[7] makes three distinctions between group guidance and group counseling:

> First, group guidance is recommended for ALL school students on a regularly scheduled basis; group counseling is recommended only for those who are experiencing continuing or temporary problems that information alone will not resolve. Secondly, group guidance makes an INDIRECT attempt to change attitudes and behaviors through accurate information or an emphasis on cognitive or intellective functioning; group counseling makes a DIRECT attempt to modify attitudes and behaviors by emphasizing affective involvement. Finally, group guidance is applicable to classroom-size groups, whereas group counseling is dependent upon the development of strong group cohesiveness and the sharing of personal concerns which are most applicable to small, intimate groups.

Group counseling and other group responsibilities of the counselor will be discussed in greater detail in Chapter 10.

---

[6] H. C. McKown, *Home Room Guidance* (New York: McGraw-Hill Book Company, 1934).
[7] George M. Gazda, *Group Counseling: A Developmental Approach* (Boston: Allyn & Bacon, Inc., 1971), p. 8.

Occupational and Educational Information

Since its earliest inception, the school guidance movement has had a strong vocational guidance influence. It is therefore not surprising that the providing of occupational and educational information has an historical acceptance as one of the basic activities in which counselors engage. Traditionally, this activity has been viewed as one in which descriptive materials and media are accumulated, organized, and then disseminated through planned group activities, as well as utilized in individual advising and counseling. These materials, media, and activities are designed to provide school-age youth with information about occupational and educational opportunities which, in turn, will be useful in their planning and decision making. In the 1970s the concept of this basic service was broadened and a new—now more appropriate—label assigned: *career guidance*. This term seemed more compatible with the rapidly developing career education movement and also represented in the minds of many (but not all) a broadening of the school guidance program's responsibility in the career development of school-age youth. The career guidance approach is a developmental one, which suggests certain experiences and understandings at each stage of one's growth that will provide for the building of appropriate foundations for later career planning and decision making.

Placement and Follow-up

The placement and follow-up service has traditionally focused upon educational placement in courses and programs. In actual practice this has meant that many school counselors have had responsibility for student scheduling, a not unconsuming task and one that has been viewed with considerable controversy as an administrative, rather than a guidance function. Another aspect of educational placement were those activities associated with the college admissions of the college-bound. The other obvious component of the placement service—employment placement—has had much less emphasis and planning, as the authors of this text discovered in a national survey of school placement activities.[8] This type of placement seeks to match students seeking part-time or regular employment with available jobs. Follow-up activities are a means of assessing the effectiveness of the guidance program's placement activities. Placement and follow-up activities have taken on increasing importance with the increased emphasis on career education and guidance. All of these activities are discussed in Chapter 8.

[8] Robert L. Gibson et al. *The Dissemination and Implementation of Effective Concepts and Practices in Placement and Follow-up Services for School Guidance Programs,* funded by State of Indiana, 1977. See also Marianne H. Mitchell and Robert L. Gibson, "Job Placement: Fact or Fiction?" *American Vocational Journal,* **52**:39 (Oct. 1977).

PATTERNS OF GUIDANCE PROGRAM ORGANIZATION

Because it was noted earlier in this chapter that school guidance programs must reflect the differences in their populations and settings, it is appropriate to assume that these differences will also result in differing organizational structures for programs. Consequently, it must be recognized there are many successful, yet differing, patterns of program organization for all educational levels. Further, these structures differ according to the educational levels (elementary, middle, secondary, or higher education) they serve. This chapter attempts to briefly illustrate only a few of the more traditional and popular program formats.

Organizational Patterns in Elementary Schools

As has been already noted in discussions of the historical development of guidance in American education, guidance programs are just beginning to emerge in the elementary schools of this country, despite supporters of this concept for more than fifty years. Because there are no established, traditional organizational formats with which the subject of elementary guidance programs might be comfortably introduced, let us examine some possible considerations.

In determining appropriate approaches to program organization and development in the elementary school, elementary educators have considered those characteristics and goals of the elementary school, especially those that highlight the special role of the elementary school as an educational institution. These include the missions of orienting the elementary school child to the educational environment and providing the elementary school pupil with the basic educational-developmental experiences that are essential for future development of the individual. Other special characteristics of the elementary school are also important as considerations in the organization and development of their guidance programs, including the following:

1. Most elementary schools are homeroom-teacher-centered. The elementary pupil in a self-contained classroom has one teacher for most of the school day, and he is with this teacher for at least one academic year. As a result, pupil and teacher get to know each other better in the elementary school than in schools at higher levels.
2. There is an emphasis on learning through activity. Physical activity and exercises related to learning are characteristic of the elementary school.
3. The elementary school pupil is a member of a reasonably stable group. Although some school populations are relatively transient, it is common for a child to be with the same group of fellow pupils

for most of each school year and, in many elementary school situations, with many of the same pupils throughout his elementary years.

4. Elementary schools are usually smaller and less complex than secondary schools.
5. Parental interest and involvement are generally greater at the elementary level.[9]

Further reflected in the elementary school's educational approach and structure are the characteristics of the elementary school pupils. It must be noted by anyone who has ever set foot in an elementary school that there is no such thing as the "typical" elementary school pupil. And parents and teachers who interact with these children on a daily basis can further testify to the difficulties of characterizing this age group. It is therefore appropriate to suggest that the common characteristic that all elementary youth share is that no two are alike. Despite this, it is not inappropriate to briefly note some broadly recognized needs and characteristics of this youthful population, even though there have been, and will continue to be, innumerable studies made and volumes written about the needs of children.

As a basis for guidance in the elementary school, we will view these needs from two standpoints: (1) those basic needs which continuously demand satisfaction and (2) those developmental needs which must be met during different life stages.

Man's basic needs have been presented by Maslow in a hierarchy or priority ordering of needs in which the higher-order needs will emerge only when the lower-order needs have been fairly well satisfied. In his discussions, Maslow has pointed out that the best way to repress the higher motivation of man is to keep him chronically hungry, insecure, or unloved. According to Maslow's theory, as the teacher and counselor view the elementary pupil and his ability to become self-actualized and develop his potential, the teacher or counselor must be concerned with, and aware of, the degree to which the pupil's lower-order needs are being met.

The developmental needs of man, according to his life stage, have been well presented by Havighurst in his popular "developmental tasks." Counselors and teachers in the elementary school should take note of the following developmental tasks for middle childhood.

1. Learning physical skills necessary for ordinary games.
2. Building wholesome attitudes toward oneself as a growing organism.
3. Learning to get along with age mates.
4. Learning an appropriate masculine or feminine social role.
5. Developing fundamental skills in reading, writing, and calculating.
6. Developing concepts necessary for everyday living.
7. Developing conscience, morality, and a scale of values.

[9] Robert L. Gibson and Robert E. Higgins, op cit., p. 14.

8. Achieving personal independence.
9. Developing attitudes toward social groups and institutions.

The presentations of Maslow and Havighurst stress both the personal and the cultural nature of the needs of children as they grow and develop. There is also an implied "developmental task" for educational programs—the task of providing learning experiences appropriate to the needs, both basic and developmental, of the elementary school child.

In addition to the needs of children, plans for guidance in the elementary school should take into consideration the following characteristics of the pupil.

1. He/she is experiencing continuous growth, development, and change.
2. He/she is constantly integrating experiences.
3. He/she is relatively limited in the ability to verbalize.
4. His/her reasoning powers are not fully developed.
5. His/her ability to concentrate over long periods of time is limited.
6. His/her enthusiasm and interest can be easily aroused.
7. His/her decisions and goals serve immediate purposes—he/she does not yet make long-range plans.
8. He/she displays feelings more or less openly.

The implications of these characteristics and needs for programs of pupil guidance in the elementary school must be reflected in both guidance program structure and guidance counselor role and function.[10]

On the basis of these identifiable characteristics of the elementary school and of the characteristics and needs of elementary school pupils, it is evident that any program in the elementary school that focuses on the pupil, to be successful, must have not only the approval but also significant involvement of the faculty; it must be teacher-centered. Further, close and frequent contact with parents must be anticipated, especially in the primary years. It is also clear that any program that relies too heavily on "talking at" the elementary school pupil, even when supplemented with films and other media or material aids, is doomed to failure. The elementary school is activity-oriented, and the guidance program in this setting must "do as the Romans do." Finally, the elementary years are noted as developmental years. The elementary school guidance program must therefore respond accordingly with a developmental rather than a remedial emphasis, an emphasis that suggests, for example, less individual adjustment counseling and more developmental group guidance activities.

With these guidelines and limitations in mind, let us briefly examine an example of organizational structure for an elementary school guidance program, illustrated in Figure 2–1.

---

[10] Robert L. Gibson, *Career Development in the Elementary School* (Columbus, Ohio: Charles E. Merrill Publishing Company, 1972), pp. 19–20.

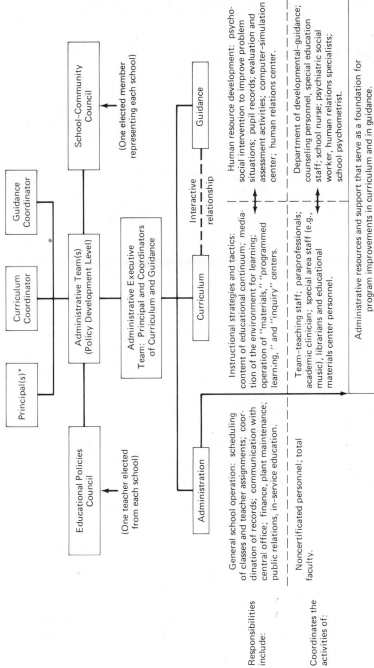

Figure 2–1.
A model of personnel relationships in the administration of an elementary school guidance program. *June G. Shane, Harold G. Shane, Robert L. Gibson, and Paul F. Munger,* Guiding Human Development *(Worthington, Ohio: Wadsworth Publishing Co., Inc., 1971), p. 346.*

Organizational Patterns in the Secondary School

Since their early, sometimes timorous, and sometimes tenuous beginnings in the twenty years after Parsons, through their experimental growth years of the 1930s and 1940s into the boom years of the 1950s and 1960s, school guidance programs have been almost the exclusive property of the American high school. Although different influences and emphases in both the secondary school and the counseling and guidance movement have often altered concepts of program structure and function, the movement has maintained its steady growth in both numbers and professionalization, and just as steadily has developed recognizable images of program structure, role, and function. These, however, may also be more readily understood if one renews acquaintance with the characteristics of the secondary school (so well eulogized in *Is There Life After High School*[11]) and with the high school student as well.

Although adolescence is identified as that period between puberty and adulthood, nothing defies standard definition or description more than the adolescent. They are as varied, unpredictable, and uncontrollable as their peer group permits. They give meaning to the expression "generation gap," of which many adolescents are proud and before it's over, many adults are thankful for. Most persons view their adolescent years as different from those of today. They probably were, for adolescents today not only exhibit wide variation in individual characteristics but the group characteristics also seem to change just as rapidly from generation to generation. As an extreme example, many may recall that some of their grandparents seemed to go directly from childhood to work and adulthood. They completed their eight to ten years of schooling and went to work as a farmer, miner, and so forth. Today, some youths stretch their adolescence into their 20s, resisting growing up, or accepting responsibility, and rejecting independence. For all who are concerned with youth during these magical years, for those who may hope to "ease their passage," it is important to recognize some of the characteristics of adolescents as follows:

1. It is a period of continuous physical growth, not the least of which is the awakening of sexual impulses. Girls discover boys, and boys discover girls who discover boys. "Puppy" love becomes a serious crush which becomes "undying love" (at least for the moment).
2. It is a period of movement towards maturity with all its implications for independence, responsibility, and self-discipline; a period often very trying to parents who want to keep little Janie tied to her mother's apron strings or Johnnie still passing the football to old "butter fingers" Dad.
3. Reveling in their newly acquired independence, many adolescents exaggerate their ability to solve "the problems of the world"—and those

---

[11] Ralph Keyes, *Is There Life After High School* (Boston: Little, Brown and Company, 1976).

that are personal for them. At the same time, many become critical of adult solutions to social problems, their life-styles, and values, but deny that adults are in a position to evaluate life among the adolescents.

4. Further, with the acquisition of the privileges of adulthood—independence, responsibility, and self-direction—there is a movement from childish to adult forms of expression, reaction, and behavior. For better or worse, adult behavior is mimicked and often exaggerated.

5. Self-selected (not adult-imposed) peer group memberships are important to the adolescent. The peer group becomes the center of most of their significant social-recreational activities and, in the eyes of many parents (and many authorities as well) their initial sex education "program." Too, while demanding their independence from parents and other adult controls, adolescents in turn may surrender much of their independence and individuality to peer group conformity.

6. It is a period when they seek direction, a set of values, and their own personal identity. The latter demands treatment as an individual—a demand that the home and the school often appear to overlook. In the quest for this new identity, the adolescent encounters, with peers, many of the common problems of this journey. Although a multitude of studies have investigated the priority concerns of youth, most of these tend to be outdated immediately following their publication. Recognizing this limitation, we would use three categories to classify a consensus of common adolescent problems from current studies, including one participated in by the authors.[12]

   a. *Developing as a social being.* This includes problems of one-to-one personal relationships, particularly dating, love, sex, and marriage. It also involves group living and acceptance and, in general, the development of human relationship skills.

   b. *Developing as a unique being.* The adolescent is concerned with the development and recognition of the uniqueness as individuals. It is a time when they are seeking to develop their own value system and often find they face value conflicts. Anxieties are often created as a result of constant demands to "measure up" made by evaluative testing and other appraisal techniques that appear to standardize them. They are also concerned when they fail to gain parental or other support for their "new self."

   c. *Developing as a productive being.* In this regard, youth are concerned with their educational adjustments and achievements, their career decisions, future educational directions, impending financial needs, and employment prospects. Many become concerned because school is not providing them a marketable skill. Others feel that staying in school is delaying earning a living.

---

[12] Robert L. Gibson and Marianne H. Mitchell, "Theirs and Ours: Educational-Vocational Problems in Britain and the United States," *Vocational Guidance Quarterly* **19**:108–112 (Dec. 1970).

Let us now briefly note some of the significant characteristics of the secondary school, because these characteristics are important considerations in the organization of all programs, including those of counseling and guidance. Although there are, of course, many exceptions to any attempt to characterize schools at any level, the following are generally appropriate for many secondary schools in the United States and Canada.

1. Secondary schools are generally large, complex institutions populated by a heterogeneous student body.

   The size and complexity of the secondary school have implications for both guidance program development and guidance program activities. Since the larger student bodies tend to be more heterogeneous in composition, often representing many cultural minority groups, the identification of these groups and response to their needs can represent a major challenge to the guidance program.

2. Secondary school faculties represent a variety of academic specialities.

   The secondary school faculty member tends to concentrate on a particular subject area. As a result, the secondary school faculty represents a variety of specializations which provide a reservoir of resources which the school guidance program may use in the career, educational, and personal-social development of the student.

3. Secondary school years are important decision-making years for the individual student.

   During a student's secondary schooling, he is usually confronted with at least two lifetime influencing decisions. The first of these decisions occurs when he must select a curriculum to follow upon entering secondary school. This curriculum may determine both his vocational and educational future. A second important decision that many youths make during this period of time is whether to complete their secondary schooling. Various dropout studies indicate that approximately one third of our high school youth make the decision to leave school prior to finishing their secondary school program. In addition, many students make important decisions regarding job or college choice during their senior year. The wide variety of course offerings and activities available in most secondary schools prompts a nearly continuous series of minor decisions for the student. They may also be confronted with significant personal decisions regarding sex and marriage, use of tobacco, alcohol, and drugs; and friends and friendship.

4. Secondary schools are subject-matter oriented.

   Schedules and classes still tend to be formal and rigidly organized in many secondary schools, with considerable emphasis on academic standards, homework, and grades (rather than personal growth). The homeroom which many students have experienced in the elementary school years ceases to exist in most high schools, except as an administrative checkpoint. As a result, at a time when the student is accelerating his development as a social being, the second-ary school structure often tends to inhibit this growth and development by placing him in a series of formal, academically oriented subject-matter class experiences. At the same time, many schools fail to provide him with an organized scheduled group (such as homeroom) where he might develop his social skills and attitudes. This suggests a challenge to the subject-matter teacher and the counselor to work cooperatively to incorporate social development experiences into the academic program.

5. School spirit, or esprit de corps, is usually more evident in secondary schools than in any other educational institution.
This school spirit is usually reflected in the quest for winning athletic teams, championship bands, and other public indications of excellence. Often the competition among students for participation in significant school events is keen. Social divisions may often arise between those who have "made it" and those who haven't in terms of these activities. On the positive side, however, school spirit in competitive activities can often be a potential factor in motivating students to remain in school, in making them seek higher academic achievements, and in promoting pride in the school.

6. The school principal is the single most influential person in the secondary school setting.
Decisions, policy development, and practices all emanate or are subject to the approval of the school principal. Unlike the elementary principal, he is frequently assisted by several assistant principals, supervisors, department heads, and specialty chairmen. In addition, probably no other individual is so significant in establishing the tone or atmosphere of the school and its inhabitants.[13]

Although the adolescent and the adolescent's school share many characteristics in common, there are also wide variations among both secondary schools and secondary school populations. Counseling and guidance programs in secondary schools seem to reflect these ambivalences as counselors engage in many of the same basic activities but within a variety of organizational structures. Figures 2–2 through 2–5 present four of the more traditional models of school guidance program organization. Figures 2–6 and 2–7 take note of one characteristic—school size—and how that factor can influence the organizational framework within which school guidance programs function. For example, larger schools in larger school systems may have resource specialists and specialized services (computer and data processing, test scoring) available in the administrative offices of the school system. These resources are available to supplement the efforts of the local building counselors. On the other hand, small schools may often have to share counseling and

---

[13] Robert L. Gibson, Marianne H. Mitchell, and Robert E. Higgins, *The Development and Management of School Guidance Programs* (Dubuque, Iowa: William C. Brown Company, Publishers, 1973), pp. 191–192.

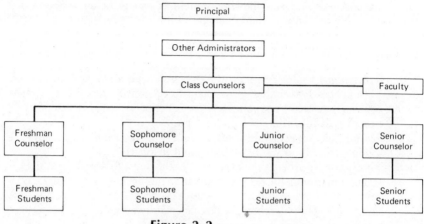

Figure 2–2.
Class counselor model.

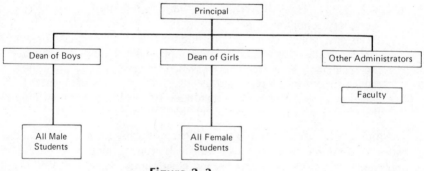

Figure 2–3.
Separate deans model.

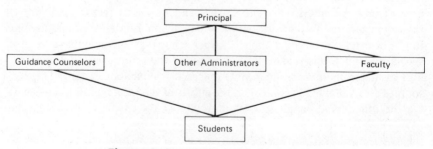

Figure 2–4.
Guidance counselor (generalist) model.

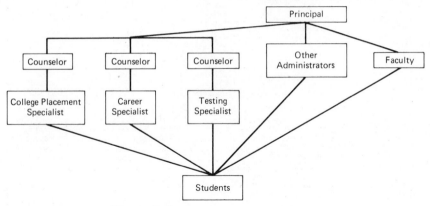

Figure 2–5.
Guidance counselor (specialist) model.

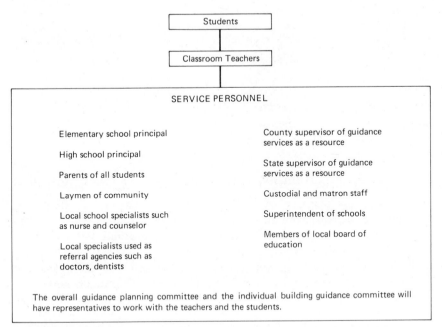

Figure 2–6.
Organization chart for the small school guidance program. *Howard L. Blanchard and Lawrence S. Flaum,* Guidance: A Longitudinal Approach *(Minneapolis: Burgess Publishing Company, 1968), p. 43.*

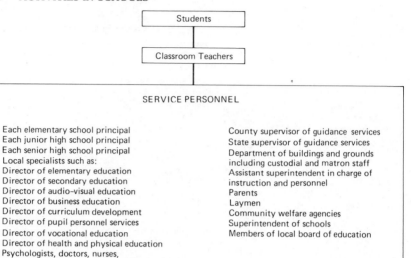

Figure 2–7.
Organization chart for the large school guidance program. *Howard L. Blanchard and Lawrence S. Flaum,* Guidance: A Longitudinal Approach *(Minneapolis: Burgess Publishing Company, 1968), p. 44.*

other specialized personnel. These personnel may operate out of the central administrative offices of the school system and be available on certain days to each school that shares their assignment.

Organizational Patterns in Institutions of Higher Education

Although the popular view of the "Ivory Tower" seems to most frequently focus on the football stadium, the pretty coeds and, sometimes, the distinguished professor, a serious look at most college and university campuses confirms the existence of counselors and attending programs of counseling and guidance. As might be anticipated, these programs are as unusual or as traditional as the institutions they represent. The burgeoning junior and community college movement appears to be developing programs that often suggest "open marriage" between elements of secondary school guidance programs and traditional university student personnel services programs. Four-year colleges and universities maintain, although often with interesting innovations, programs based on traditional student personnel services models—programs in which guidance and counseling services are frequently pro-

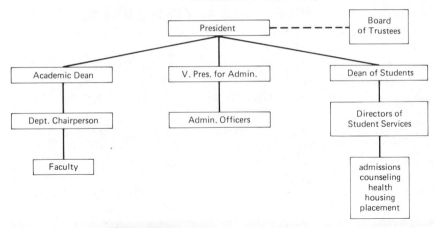

Figure 2–8.
Organization chart for a four-year college.

vided through campus counseling centers or clinics, residential counselors, and career counseling offices. Figure 2–8 illustrates an organizational chart for a four-year college, with counseling services provided as a part of the college or university's student services. Figure 2.9 displays counseling services as a unit of a large university program.

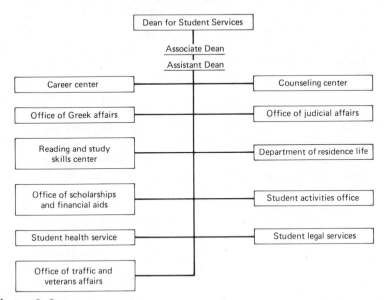

Figure 2–9.
Organization chart for student services division in a large university (Indiana University).

FUTURE DIRECTIONS FOR SCHOOL PROGRAMS OF COUNSELING AND GUIDANCE

All of us engage in predicting the future. Much of our speculation on what lies ahead is, of course, short-range; we predict that the weather will be better tomorrow, the price of coffee will go up again next month, or the football team will be a winner next fall.

While predicting the future is fun, it is also risky, especially if one is bold enough to put these speculations in print. However, despite the many uncertainties attending even the most scientific efforts—and there are highly reputable scientific institutes engaged in such studies today—no less than in the past, we read our horoscopes in the daily paper, have our palms read or our handwriting analyzed, read with interest the annual New Year's predictions of those "gifted" with visions of the future, and note that books such as Toffler's *Future Shock*[14] become international best sellers.

Although the high level of interest in knowing what the future holds in store for us and our societies does not appear to have diminished over the centuries, both the nature and the need for future insights have undergone significant change. We have noted the emergence since World War II of a "futuristic" science, with an emphasis on scientific, data-based, and computer-assisted forecasting, and the development of organizations such as The Institute for the Future (Middletown, Connecticut) and the World Future Society (formed in Washington, D.C. in 1966). The need for some form of reasonably accurate future forecasting has become increasingly evident.

One indicator that change will probably take place in any product, activity, or organization is strong and significant criticism of their present state. Even those who "see no evil, hear no evil, speak no evil" are well aware of the volume and intensity of critical charges leveled at education over the years, criticisms that have and will continue in the future to promote change. It is therefore appropriate to note, as a predictor of future change, that during the past decade, school programs of counseling and guidance have also come under frequent attack. Included have been suggestions that school programs of counseling and guidance and related counselor education programs must remodel to provide for more relevant and effective roles and functions in the decades ahead or disappear from the American educational scene. Counselors should be aware that as far back as 1971 the Gallup poll on education in that year revealed that out of sixteen proposals for economizing in education, counselor removal was ranked fourth in priority. During the same year, Cook expressed it well in his *Guidance for Education in Revolution,* when he suggested that:

> Guidance is at a crossroads as we begin the decade of the 1970s. The path travelled thus far has brought the guidance counselor out of the

---

[14] Alvin Toffler, *Future Shock* (New York: Random House, 1970).

shadows of teaching and into relatively high visibility as a professional person in his own right. But visibility creates special perils and responsibilities that are not so evident when a profession is young and seeking an identity. For the past several years school counseling has been wrapped in an identity crisis, struggling with the question, "What is our role?" Now the signs point to an increasing likelihood that more and more the question will be raised by those outside the profession of school counseling, including those who hold the tightening purse strings of education, "Is what you are doing effective, making any difference in the lives of pupils, and do you even know what you are supposed to be doing?[15]

A report of the June 1972 National Advisory Council on Vocational Education[16] called upon the field of counseling and guidance to initiate significant changes that would, in effect, increase the effectiveness of counseling youth for today's world of work.

Another critical study, *The Nationwide Study of Student Career Development,* by Prediger, Roth, and Noeth,[17] reported a sharp contrast between youths' need for career planning and the help recieved. This study confirmed that youths were seriously deficient in knowledge about the world of work and career planning and that they were unable to cope with the career development tasks posed by society during the difficult high school to post-high school transition and placement period. Prediger and colleagues recommended the reorientation of the traditional school counseling model to provide increased as well as more realistic assistance in career guidance and placement.

Other counseling professionals have expressed their concern. McQueen voiced the view in *Education Digest*[18] that "There is a growing feeling that guidance must touch the lives of many more youngsters and touch them more deeply. There is widespread acknowledgment that the guidance counselor of the seventies must move in new directions and use a variety of procedures." Pine, writing in the *Phi Delta Kappan*[19] stated that:

The volume and intensity of the criticisms are reflected in a variety of charges which appear in the professional literature: Counselors isolate themselves from other school personnel; spend a disproportionate amount of time on the errant child and the child with special needs; spend the bulk of their time in counseling activities and exclude consultation; are unwilling and unable to work as part of pupil personnel teams

---

[15] David R. Cook, *Guidance for Education in Revolution* (Boston: Allyn & Bacon, Inc., 1971), p. 517.
[16] National Advisory Council on Vocational Education, *Counseling and Guidance: A Call for Change,* 1972, 6th Report.
[17] Dale Prediger, J. D. Roth, and R. J. Noeth, *Nationwide Study of Student Career Development: Summary of Results,* Research Report No. 61, American College Testing Program, 1973.
[18] Mildred McQueen, "Trends in Guidance and Counseling," *Education Digest,* **38:**48 (Mar. 1973).
[19] Gerald J. Pine, "Quo Vadis, School Counseling?" *Phi Delta Kappan,* **56:**554 (Apr. 1975).

with specialists from other disciplines; appear uninformed of new practices and developments in the field of guidance and counseling; are not effective in dealing with student unrest; are afraid to face up to questions of accountability; meld readily into the Establishment and are perceived by students as hypocrites, ineffectuals, and maintainers of the *status quo;* have not demonstrated that their work has purpose and has yielded meaningful results; and know very little about the world of work outside of education.

These and other criticisms suggest that some future changes in the school guidance programs are inevitable. The real ability of the forecaster lies in the accurate prediction of the nature of these changes. A significant study reported by the North Central Association of Colleges and Schools[20] sought to identify "those activities that will be emphasized in school guidance programs of the future." This study sampled 1,280 administrators, teachers, and counselors representing 616 different secondary schools, hypothesizing that current users and producers of guidance services would provide professional educators' viewpoints of appropriate futures for school programs of counseling and guidance in the last decades of the twentieth century. The questionnaire phase of the study drew responses as indicated in Table 2–1.

Although the data were initially summarized by respondent categories to identify differences between administrator, counselor, and teacher viewpoints, there were surprisingly few differences among their responses with the exception of five items. These items indicated counselors anticipated much less standardized testing in the future than did either teachers or principals, whereas principals and teachers anticipated more emphasis on student job placement than did the school counselors in the sample. Counselors, however, believed that group counseling would have more emphasis in the future, although few teachers or principals agreed with them.

In the study's follow-up, twenty-four administrators, counselors, and teachers further discussed the topic "Future Directions for School Guidance Programs" individually or in groups. In general, these discussions substantiated the findings displayed in Table 2–1. Additionally, there were some suggestions that appeared frequently enough in these discussions that the North Central Association's project staff believed they merited mentioning in its report. They recommended that:

1. Counselors must get out of their offices—must become more active and visible in the school and community.
2. Counselors must function more as guidance service personnel and less as therapists.

[20] R. L. Gibson, "Future Directions for School Guidance Programs," a study by the North Central Association of Colleges and Schools, *Viewpoints,* **54,** No. 1 (Jan. 1978).

3. Counselors must become more attuned to minority groups' characteristics and needs.
4. Counselors must become more cognizant of the need to overcome sex biases in their practices.
5. Counselors must become more skillful in their public relations, including communications with school staff, pupils, and parents.
6. Counselors must become more conscious of their local environment and its resources for enrichment of all aspects of the school guidance program.
7. Counselors cannot ignore pupil behavior. Both teachers and parents expect counselors to be concerned with unacceptable behavior, its causes, and modification.
8. Counselors, as all others in the educational system, must be accountable.
9. There is a need for counseling and guidance programs at all educational levels. Currently, the biggest deficit exists at the elementary school level.
10. Counselor training programs must become more selective and conscientious in their admissions practices.
11. Counselor training programs must become more relevant and field-based, as well as conscious of the needs and new directions of schools.

A review of the data gathered from various other future studies and centers indicates some future directions for education which, in turn, may have implications for future directions for school guidance programs. As one example, it is statistically evident that the nation's birth rate has declined while, at the same time, life expectancy has increased. As a result, the Department of Agriculture's Economic Research Service[21] projects that the median age of the population will rise steeply from 28.8 in 1975 to 31.1 in 1985 to 34.8 by the year 2000. In 2000, people more than sixty-five years of age will constitute at least 12 per cent of the population and will be enjoying better health and much longer life expectancies than today's sixty-five-year-old person. Similarly, it is also statistically clear that school populations are going to decline until the mid-1980s, and then probably stabilize at the lower levels for the remainder of this century. This means that education could either stagnate or utilize other strategies to maintain vigor (as well as enrollment) in the educational establishment. The latter is predicted as the more probable course of action with the most likely activities leading to increased program offerings for all age groups, preschool through late adulthood plus programming schools on a year-round basis. Products of these changes could lead to a wider variety of course offerings, programs, and educational alternatives, and recreational opportunities for all ages of the population. Schools could then be called upon, under those circumstances,

[21] Harold G. Shane, "America's Next 25 Years: Some Implications for Education," *Phi Delta Kappan,* **58:**78–83 (Sept. 1976).

to provide recreational education, as well as more planned activities open to all age groups.

Many futurists are also predicting the steady spread of alternate family structures, including child sharing and a view of marriage as an instrument

Table 2–1.

Educators' Opinions of School Guidance Programs of the Future

	FUTURE EMPHASIS		
	Less Emphasis (%)	About Same As In Past (%)	More Emphasis (%)
1. Activities (Traditional)			
(a) Individual one-to-one counseling	34	40	26
(b) Group guidance (advising and information giving) activities	3	30	67
(c) Occupational and educational information activities	4	17	79
(d) Appraisal activities such as standardized group testing	34	58	8
(e) College placement	19	70	11
(f) Scheduling and curriculum placement	13	58	29
(g) Part-time and/or full-time job placement	8	45	47
(h) Follow-up and evaluation studies	10	38	52
2. Activities (Controversial)			
(a) Attendance	51	34	15
(b) Student discipline	61	29	10
(c) Group "therapy" counseling	29	39	32
(d) Group sensitivity activities	55	25	20
(e) "Back-up" administrator to school principal	65	31	4
(f) Student activity coordinator	59	37	4
3. Activities (Current Trends)			
(a) Career guidance	2	7	91
(b) Consultant to teachers and other educators	8	31	61
(c) Consultant to parents	—	34	66
(d) Community resource coordinator for educational development	3	68	29
(e) Human relationship specialist	3	68	29
(f) Parent sensitivity training	5	54	41
(g) Counselor as team teacher	31	38	31
(h) Counselor as local systems researcher	33	45	22
(i) Counselors in elementary schools	6	22	72

	Disagree (%)	Uncertain (%)	Agree (%)
4. Role, Function, and Training			
(a) To be certified, school counselors should have teaching experience	9	10	81
(b) Counselor education programs should be initiated at the undergraduate level	33	12	55
(c) Youth counselors should be community-based rather than school-based	38	38	24
(d) A significant work experience should be a requirement for school counselors	8	35	57
(e) Counselor training programs should be competency-based	6	28	66
(f) Counselors should be more active in counseling parents	9	21	70
(g) Counselors should be more active as education change agents	14	36	50
(h) Counselors should be more active as curriculum consultants	15	20	65
(i) Counselors should be more knowledgeable and active in areas of ecology-environment-nature conservation	29	37	34
(j) Counselors should be more active and skillful in the area of needs assessment	4	21	75
(k) Counselors should be more active and skillful in the area of accountability and evaluation	11	20	69
(l) Counselors should be more knowledgeable in the area of data processing and computer utilization	24	36	40
(m) Counselors should be agents for affective or humanistic education in schools	2	16	82
(n) Counselors should be skillful in value clarification techniques	3	17	80
(o) Counselors should be "futuristically" oriented	4	30	66

Source: **R. L. Gibson, "Future Directions for School Guidance Programs," a study by the North Central Association of Colleges and Schools, *Viewpoints, 54,* No. 1 (Jan. 1978).**

of self-fulfillment, convenience, and enjoyment rather than a lifelong contract.[22] The perfection and ready availability of birth control techniques for
both sexes will further regulate family size both within and without the traditional family structure.

As final examples, increased uses are predicted for computers, media,
and other forms of technology. Initially, educational placement as well as
career work experiences will be facilitated by national and, eventually, worldwide data processing networks that instantly identify specific career or educational opportunities. Current trends toward accountability, career education,
and placement will become accepted as established practices, and a new trend
may emerge in future studies.

The data reported in the preceding paragraphs represent only a micro-
sampling of the collected data reviewed for the North Central Association
study. These data, however, appeared to have some important implications
for the future directions of school guidance programs.

But what do such studies mean? What can they tell counselors of the
future to expect? Let us project, on the basis of the data gathered through
the North Central Association's study and a review of selected "futures"
data, that the future look for school programs of guidance and counseling
might be envisioned as follows:

1. School guidance programs will continue to play an important role in
    the educational system, including an increased emphasis on guidance
    programs in elementary schools.
2. School guidance programs will not be dramatically reshaped in the imme-
    diate decades ahead. (As can be noted in Table 2–1, school administrators,
    teachers, and counselors recommend continued emphasis on many of
    the activities traditionally associated with the school guidance program.)
3. However, the concept of guidance will continue to shift from remedial
    to developmental and preventive activities. This trend will be related to
    increased efforts to increase the attractiveness and relevance of education
    at all levels for all age groups.
4. School counselors will serve a wider age range of clientele with a wider
    and differing range of concerns. For example, client needs for sexual
    understandings, recreational guidance, and values counseling can be fore-
    seen, along with a continued emphasis on career guidance and placement.
5. The *modus operandi* for school counselors will change. They will function
    more as consultants and less in administration-related roles such as atten-
    dance and scheduling. They will also be less officebound and correspond-
    ingly more visible to students, the school staff, and the general public.
    As computer-based systems become increasingly and more economically

[22] B. Bruce-Briggs, "Futurism—What Will Life Be Like in 1985?" *The Graduate,* 10–12 Approach
193–30 Corp. (1974).

used in education, counselors will supplement the guidance process through direct use of computer data. This will be especially notable in career and educational placement, which will be facilitated by national and, eventually, worldwide data processing networks that instantly identify appropriate opportunities for students.

6. The increased financial supports for quality education will include school guidance programs. It will be anticipated that school counselors will be better prepared and will function as "elite" and fully accountable specialists.

7. Finally, school counselors will become future specialists for purposes of educational, career, and environmental placement.

SUMMARY AND CONCLUSIONS

If the colleagues of one of your authors in the Morgantown High School (West Virginia) guidance program of the early 1950s could have become literally encapsulated counselors and frozen in time capsules to emerge today, they would probably comment, upon concluding the reading of this chapter, thirty years later, "so what's new?" Most of the basic principles and traditional activities enumerated here have, as Chapter 1 suggested, an historical relationship with the development of the guidance movement in American education. Although the organization of these activities into program formats differs across the various educational levels, the mention of the importance of individual assessment, one-to-one counseling, group guidance activities, providing of information and placement, and follow-up would evoke a ringing round of applause from the West Virginia Guidance Association convention of thirty years ago and the New York Vocational Guidance Association convention of thirty years before that. Now, assuming we could all crowd into this magical space capsule for a quick trip into the future, we would apparently find, as suggested in the last section of this chapter, that the same basic activities are being seriously expounded and still thunderously applauded at the 2009 APGA convention held in Green Plateau on the planet Mars.

It may be concluded that although a relatively young profession, counseling and guidance are developing traditions, establishing their role and worth, and will cope resourcefully and imaginatively with the demands of the future. The following represent some reflections related to traditions, activities, and effective guidance program organization and functioning.

1. Traditions are the hallmarks of a profession. They are often seen as indices of the professional maturity of a discipline and are often synonomous with guiding principles for a profession. They represent guidelines for newcomers (and reminiscences for the "old timers") to the profession. They become powerful determinants of the profession's goals and actions,

and, in time, become extremely resistant to elimination or alteration. Thus, although there are those in education who have and will call from time to time for drastic change—even elimination of programs of counseling and guidance in schools—it is not the fundamental beliefs or traditional activities of the counselor that must change, but rather, how the activity is interpreted or viewed and carried out that will determine the merits of a counseling and guidance program in any setting.

2.   Relevancy is a key to the success or failure of a program's activities and services. It is doubtful that the counseling skills and understandings that we, your authors, possessed when we first entered the profession would be relevant to the demands of today's youth and it is certain that both the concept of careers and the occupational information at our disposal then would not be in any way relevant today. As C. Gilbert Wrenn stressed in his classic book *The World of the Contemporary Counselor* "the need of the counselor is to attempt to understand contemporary youth and the world in which they live."[23] That is relevancy—seeing and understanding the environment that surrounds our clients, not just the clients.

3.   There is no *one* right way or model format of program organization that can be utilized such as a successful cookbook recipe in all settings. Program organization and activities must reflect the uniqueness of both the clientele and the settings and, in addition, must not neglect the uniqueness of the counselors.

4.   Whatever the program formats and activities, counseling and guidance in schools will continue to require a great deal of guiding, listening, and informing, a considerable amount of counseling, and an abundance of caring . . . and if you care, you will perpetuate the grandest tradition of the counseling profession, you will be relevant, and you will understand the uniqueness of your clients and their environments.

[23] C. Gilbert Wrenn, *The World of the Contemporary Counselor* (Boston: Houghton Mifflin Company, 1973), p. 3.

The School Counselors' **3** Role and Function

TRAINING PROGRAMS FOR COUNSELORS

As previously noted, guidance programs in schools are an educational develop-ment of this century and they have, until recent years, been unique to the United States and Canadian educational systems; the same is true of training programs for counselors. Similarly, since the initial years of the National Defense Education Act (1958–1960), there has been a rapid growth in both the number and size of counselor training programs. The supporting facts indicate that in 1964 there were 327 institutions of higher education supporting counselor preparation programs with 706 faculty. By 1977, this number of programs had increased to 453 with 3,263 faculty. Thus, if you had entered a counselor training program in 1964, you could have anticipated a training staff of slightly more than two full-time faculty; however, if you delayed your entry until 1977, you could expect, on the average, a staff of 7.6 full-time faculty.[1]

Because many of you reading this text may already be enrolled in pro-grams of counselor education, it is quite possible that the initial discussion

[1] J. W. Hollis and R. A. Wantz, *Counselor Education Directory* (Muncie, Ind.: Accelerated Development, Ind., 1977), pp. 26–27.

of this chapter will serve only to remind you to see your advisor about the course work that lies ahead or how your own program may differ or be similar to others. We are certain, however, that you recognize the significant relationships between what you are trained to do and your role and function once you are on the job. Too, as Thomas noted in *The Schools Next Time*,[2]

> Control of the lower schools (elementary and secondary) by the colleges is again obvious when one remembers that all certified school personnel are college trained; they cannot be licensed without such training. Teachers, counselors, and administrators are all enculturated with the biases of academia.

As a means of putting into perspective who functions at what level and with what training or expertise, see Table 3–1, which indicates that individuals with appropriate *experience* and/or *training* and the *skills* to communicate, can function at the advice-giving level. In the school setting, for example, all teachers and most staff would qualify as *advisors* for many occasions and should serve in this important role in the school's program of pupil guidance. At the second level, special training to at least the master's degree level is required, and it is this training that provides the school counselor with special expertise as a counselor, an expertise that sets the counselor apart form other professionals in the school setting, which establishes his or her unique qualifications to interact with or on behalf of students in meeting their routine development, adjustment, planning, and decision-making needs. The third level represents the highest levels of professional training available and usually terminates with an earned doctorate. As practicing counselors, these professionals are most frequently used as resource personnel for referrals and consultation. Their clients are usually those with serious personality disorders, requiring intensive and long-term counseling. In addition to counseling, these higher-trained counselors may also seek careers in research or university teaching.

Table 3–1.
Levels of Training and Responsibility

Level	Training	Responsibility
First	Appropriate educational and/or experience background	Advising; information giving.
Second	Master's degree in counseling and guidance.	Developmental and normal adjustment counseling.
Third	Doctorate in counseling and guidance or counseling psychology.	Serious personality disorders.

[2] Donald R. Thomas, *The Schools Next Time* (New York: McGraw-Hill Book Company, 1973), p. 216.

Table 3–2.
Initial Employment of Graduates from Master's Level and Sixth-Year Programs

Frequency Rank	Initial Employment Settings	Number of Institutions in Each Percentage Interval.							
		0%	1–10%	11–25%	26–40%	41–60%	61–75%	76–90%	91–100%
2	Elem. or Middle School	44	136	126	49	9	0	1	0
1	Jr. or High School	24	39	106	92	65	20	16	3
4	Community or Jr. College	101	196	56	10	2	0	0	0
9	Voc. or Tech. School	195	156	14	0	0	1	0	0
5	University or College	143	167	39	11	3	1	1	0
3	Mental Health Clinics	117	161	52	21	12	0	1	1
8	Correctional Institutions	175	173	15	2	0	0	0	0
13	Diagnostic Centers	290	71	3	1	0	0	0	0
10	Employment Agencies	208	148	8	0	1	0	0	0
11	Hospitals	250	109	5	1	0	0	0	0
12	Pastoral Counseling Agencies	281	82	2	0	0	0	0	0
6	Rehabilitation Agencies	161	141	43	18	2	0	0	0
14	State Depts. of Educ.	327	35	2	1	0	0	0	0
7	Others	287	40	23	7	5	2	0	0

Source: J. W. Hollis and R. A. Wantz, op. cit., p. 30.

Table 3–3.
Initial Employment of Graduates from Doctoral-level Programs

Frequency Rank	Initial Employment Setting of Graduates	Number of Institutions in Each Percentage Interval							
		0%	1–10%	11–25%	26–40%	41–60%	61–75%	76–90%	91–100%
9	Elem. or Middle School	69	23	1	2	0	0	0	0
4	Jr. or High School	38	42	9	6	1	0	0	0
3	Community or Jr. College	33	32	24	5	2	0	0	0
11	Voc. or Tech. School	77	16	2	1	0	0	0	0
1	University or College	2	12	15	21	28	10	8	0
2	Mental Health Clinics	18	29	36	11	1	0	0	1
8	Correctional Institutions	67	23	3	2	1	0	0	0
12	Diagnostic Centers	79	14	2	1	0	0	0	0
14	Employment Agencies	88	7	1	0	0	0	0	0
5	Hospitals	53	34	5	3	1	0	0	0
13	Pastoral Counseling Agencies	84	10	2	0	0	0	0	0
6	Rehabilitation Agencies	60	25	10	1	0	0	0	0
10	State Depts. of Education	70	24	1	1	0	0	0	0
7	Others	68	16	10	2	0	0	0	0

Source: Ibid., p. 47.

Additional insights into the relationships between levels of training and the counselor's role and function as represented by initial employment may be noted by an examination of Tables 3–2 and 3–3. In comparing these tables, it is clear that the majority of master's degree graduates find their initial employment in elementary, middle/junior, or senior high schools, whereas the majority of doctoral graduates enter university and college settings and mental health clinics.

In examining the content of training programs available, one cannot help but note course content consistency among master's programs across the United States and Canada. A great deal of this conformity in the United States is undoubtedly the result of state certification patterns, which reflect, with little deviation, an expectancy of training to perform the traditional basic services. Because a number of states (fourteen) specify preparation in broad general terms (that is, a master's degree in counseling and guidance), Table 3–4 depicts the specific courses most frequently required for school counselor certification among those thirty-six states identifying specific courses.

Approximately one fourth of the counselor training institutions also offer a specialist or sixth-year degree.[3] In many states this degree qualifies one with appropriate experience for the director or supervisor of guidance or director of pupil personnel services certificates.

Approximately 125 counselor training institutions in the United States and Canada offer programs leading to an earned doctorate. These programs tend, according to the nature of the program, to prepare their candidates for positions on university counselor education faculties, in colleges and uni-

Table 3–4.
Commonly Required Courses for School Counselor Certification

Title of Course	Number of States Specifying Requirement
Counseling Practicum	33
Counseling Techniques or Counseling Theory	30
Individual Appraisal or Testing or Individual Analysis	29
Occupational-Educational Information or Career Guidance or Vocational Guidance	28
Principles of Guidance or History of Guidance or Introduction to Guidance	27
Group Guidance or Group Counseling or Group Process	14
Organization and Administration or Management and Leadership or Program Development	13

Source: **Elizabeth H. Woellner,** *Requirements for Certification,* **42nd Ed. (Chicago: The University of Chicago Press, 1977).**

[3] J. W. Hollis and R. A. Wantz, op. cit., p. 30.

versity counseling centers, for rehabilitation counseling, mental health clinics, and other agency or institutional settings. Some may also elect to enter private practice. Variations in program emphasis and preparation patterns are more commonplace than at the master's level.

CREDENTIALING OF SCHOOL COUNSELORS

Today, *counselor* seems to be used with ever-increasing frequency in a variety of settings. There are home buyer counselors, financial counselors, landscape counselors, used car counselors, and diet counselors. There are also counselors who may be distinguished from the first group on the basis of certification or legal licensure. These include legal counselors, investment counselors, psychological counselors, and school guidance counselors. The licensure or certification indicates that the holder has successfully completed and been examined on learning and experience criteria recommended by the representative professional organizations and the appropriate licensing boards or agencies. The late C. Harold McCully, in his discussion of "The School Counselor: Strategy for Professionalization,"[4] suggested eleven characteristics of a profession. These included the statement that

> A profession is an occupation in which the members of a corporate group assure minimum competence for entry into the occupation by setting and enforcing standards for selection, training, and licensure or certification.

Advantages

There are advantages to some sort of a credentialing process, including the following:

1. *It provides a measure of protection for the public against those who would masquerade as possessing certain skills and trainings.* A number of years ago, an article in the old *Look* magazine entitled, "Beware of the Psycho-Quacks," gave examples of the various guises for preying on the public under counseling and psychological titles. Many have read the book or seen the movie, "The Great Imposter," in which one individual assumed a variety of professional careers and proceeded to prosper in one after the other. Although these and other similar reports sometimes amuse and often attract sympathetic admirers of those who have "beat the system," very few individuals would knowingly like to be treated by a physician who isn't a physician, represented by a lawyer who isn't a lawyer, or counseled by a counselor who isn't a counselor. The implications of these examples are appropriate

[4] C. Harold McCully, "The School Counselor: Strategy for Professionalization," *Personnel and Guidance Journal* (Apr. 1962), p. 682.

reminders of the need for some sort of a procedure that protects the public against professional misrepresentation and fraud.

2. *It provides, at the very least, minimally accepted training and experience requirements.* Credentialing and training requirements (and experiences) are closely interrelated. This interrelationship provides for a common core of learning experiences and achievement expectancies. These are related to the profession's concept of preparatory standards for entry into the profession. This is not only helpful to candidates considering entry into training programs and protects them from misleading training schemes, but also provides some reassurances for employers as well as the general public who utilize the services.

3. *It can provide a legal base for the protection of the membership of the profession.* Because credentialing suggests standards that benefit the public, law-making bodies are prone to provide the profession and its membership with certain legal protections. For example, individuals cannot legally practice medicine without a license, and lawyers legally have the right of privileged communication with their clients. In many states, the right to enter private practice in such fields as psychology and professional counseling is limited by law.

4. *It may provide a basis for special benefits.* In addition to legal benefits, credentialed professionals may also qualify for certain financial benefits. Physicians' and lawyers' fees may qualify for insurance payments. Physicians, including psychiatrists, also qualify for national health insurance payments such as Medicaid. Psychologists may also qualify as mental health providers for insurance payments in some states. Credentialed school counselors have, on occasion, been qualified to receive special training grants to increase their qualifications. Because credentialing qualifies individuals for membership in professional organizations, they become eligible for the benefits such memberships provide. These may include special training opportunities, publications, and group insurance programs.

There are two common methods used to credential practitioners of a profession such as counseling. These are certification and licensure. Differences between certification and licensure have been described as follows:

Certification: This is a process of recognizing the competence of practitioners of a profession by officially authorizing them to use the title adopted by the profession. Certification can be awarded by voluntary associations, agencies, or by governmental bodies, some of which are recognized by state laws. In school counseling, certification is usually handled by an office within the state government's department of education or its branch for executing public instruction matters. Certification officials commonly check transcripts for evidence that the applicant has completed required courses from preparation programs that are known to be acceptable.

Licensure: This is a process authorized by state legislation that regulates the practice and the title of the profession. Because of its legislative base, licensure subjects violators to greater legal sanctions than does certification. Licensure is generally considered to be more desirable when a substantial proportion of a profession's practitioners are in private practice, because of the broader coverage and greater potential for using sanctions against violators. Licensure boards are usually established with quasi-legislative power to make rules and examine applicants who seek licenses.[5]

Another activity that has significance for the credentialing process, whether it be certification or licensure, is accreditation. *Accreditation* is a process

whereby an association or agency grants public recognition to a school, institute, college, university, or specialized program of study that has met certain established qualifications of standards as determined through initial and periodic evaluations. "Program approval" is another name for accreditation. In some professions, graduates of accredited preparation programs are considered credentialed. Sometimes a registry is used by a profession to list graduates of accredited programs.[6]

Most programs preparing school counselors are accredited by their regional accrediting associations whose evaluative criteria reflect the standards of the American School Counselors' Association (ASCA) and the Association for Counselor Education and Supervision (ACES). Counselor training programs in schools or colleges of education may also have accreditation by the National Council for Accreditation of Teacher Education (NCATE) and programs both within and outside of education may qualify for approval by ACES and the American Psychological Association (APA). In addition, many state departments of public instruction accredit higher education training programs within their jurisdictions.

Issues

During the 1970s, credentialing became one of the major issues facing the counseling profession. Although school counselor certification existed in all states prior to 1970, the issue of licensure became of greater concern as the APA moved to secure legal recognition of the more or less exclusive right of psychologists and those trained in psychological counseling programs to engage in and identify themselves in private practice as counselors. Many counselors trained in counselor education programs viewed this as limiting their options to primarily school or certain agency settings. A major focus

[5] Jerald R. Foster, "What Shall We Do About Credentialing?" *The Personnel and Guidance Journal* (June 1977), p. 573.
[6] Ibid., p. 573.

of the American Psychological Association's legislative efforts has been to establish psychology as a profession to provide health services (and as previously noted, qualifying them for insurance reimbursements). As part of the growing trend to licensure, other counseling groups such as marriage, family, drug, alcohol, and rehabilitation counselors are now licensed or certified in some states. There are a variety of training programs which, despite different orientations, can lay claim to training counselors, such as counseling psychology, school counselors, marriage counselors, rehabilitation counselors, and others. The movement towards licensure has been rightfully or wrongly viewed in many instances as an effort to limit and restrict the practice of counseling to those who come from a particular training background. Another alternative to licensure and one that has been drafted into some legislation is that of *professional disclosure*. This is a method in which

1. Disclosure is to be made to prospective clients before any counseling for which a fee may be charged. It is to be legible, on a printed form, and also posted conspicuously.
2. The fact that disclosure is required must be disclosed, including information about the particular department of state government that oversees the procedure so that a complainant would know to whom a complaint is to be made.
3. A notarized form is filed annually or whenever a change in the statement is made.
4. Additional disclosure forms are necessary for supervisors and employers.
5. Complaints are made to the department of state government that has responsibility for investigation and public hearings.
6. Provision is made for privilege of counselor records during processing of complaints.
7. Judicial review of decisions is made possible.
8. The offense covered by the statute is the willful filing of false or incomplete information.
9. Punishment includes the judgment (in several classes) of "misdemeanor" and the prohibition from practice.[7]

In general, it is the view of most of the counseling profession that the movement towards licensure is one that in the long run will protect both the public and the profession. The issues primarily center around what training for what role and function and under whose jurisdiction and/or approval.

Certification and the School Counselor

As previously mentioned, all states require certification for those who would perform as school counselors. In general, these requirements are very

[7] Stanley J. Gross, "Professional Disclosure: An Alternative to Licensing," *Personnel and Guidance Journal* **55**:588 (June 1977).

Table 3–5.

Counselor Certification Requirements in the State of Indiana

 I. Candidates will be qualified for the School Services Standard License-Counselor when they have:
   A. Three years of teaching experience.
   B. A valid Standard or Professional License in Early Childhood, Kindergarten-Primary, Elementary, Junior High/Middle School, Secondary, or All-Grade Education.
   C. A master's degree from a regionally accredited institution and have completed 24 semester hours in counseling and guidance of which at least 18 are at the graduate level.
   D. Knowledge and/or competencies in the following areas with course work directed toward counseling at the basic preparation level of the Standard or Professional teaching license held by the candidate:
     1. Principles and/or philosophy in counseling and guidance.
     2. Techniques of individual counseling theory and practice.
     3. Career development theory and information.
     4. Assessment, interpretation, and diagnosis of individual and group testing.
     5. Group and/or family counseling.
     6. Guidance program development, management, and leadership.
     7. Multicultural awareness and human relations.
   E. Completed a supervised practicum in counseling.
   F. Been recommended by the accredited institution where the approved qualifying program was completed.
 II. Coverage: The holder of the School Services License-Counselor is eligible to serve as a counselor in grades K–6 if the basic preparation level of the teaching license is Early Childhood, Kindergarten-Primary, Elementary Education, or All-Grade Education (excepting the Special Education Major).
III. Renewal: The School Services Standard License-School Counselor may be renewed for one five-year period upon the completion of six semester hours of graduate work in counselor education directed toward professionalization of this license and with the recommendation of the institution where the renewal credit was earned.
IV. Professionalization: The School Services Standard License-Counselor may be professionalized when the holder has:
   A. Completed three years' experience in accredited schools as a school counselor subsequent to the issuance of the Standard License, with at least half time in counseling.
   B. Completed 18 or more graduate hours in counselor education beyond hours required for the Standard License, including four additional areas from the following:
     1. Evaluation and Accountability.
     2. Consultation.
     3. Data processing.
     4. Statistics.
     5. Research.
     6. Strategies for developing and expanding human potential.
   C. Been recommended for the Professional License by the institution where the approved professionalization program was completed.

Source: Teacher Education and Certification Handbook (TEACH) Rules 46–47, **Indiana Department of Public Instruction, issued by Commission on Teacher Training and Licensing of the Indiana State Board of Education, 1976.**

similar across states and account for the considerable degree of reciprocity whereby candidates certified in one state may be eligible for certification in another state. For example, the vast majority of certification programs require the counselor's minimal completion of a master's degree. Too, most certification patterns require the completion of course work appropriate to the basic guidance services. That includes courses in appraisal or, sometimes, standardized testing, occupational and educational information or career guidance, individual counseling, group guidance and counseling, and a course in either principles of guidance and/or organization of school guidance programs. In addition, some sort of supervised practicum experience is typically required. The majority of states also require prior teaching experience of from one to three years. An increasing number of states have, in recent years, however, amended their certification requirements to provide for an alternative experience to teaching such as an internship. Appendix A at the end of this text presents a detailed analysis of certification requirements by states in 1977. Table 3–5 presents an example of one state's (Indiana) requirements for counselor certification.

It is probably a "chicken or egg" situation to attempt to determine whether training influences practice or vice versa, and it is not the intent of this chapter to bias that argument. We have, by choice, discussed training and resulting certification first. In the paragraphs that follow, counseling practices in various educational settings will be discussed. One may take note of the relationship between these practices and training patterns previously presented. It should be emphasized that this discussion is a brief overview only, and greater detail and specificity will be provided in later chapters.

COUNSELOR ROLE AND FUNCTION IN SCHOOL SETTINGS

An Overview

The counselor's role and function by educational levels for school settings, as described in official American School Counselor Association statements for the elementary, middle-junior high schools, secondary schools, and post-secondary institutions are presented in Appendices B through E.

Another, but not contradictory, view of the role and function of the school counselor (but also appropriate to counselor functioning in a variety of nonschool settings as well) is suggested by the cube depicted in Figure 3–1. This figure indicates with whom the counselor will work, what the purpose of the counselor's involvement will be, and the methods or techniques that will be utilized. The architects of the cube, in their discussion of the dimensions of counselor functioning, describe their model as follows:

Counseling interventions comprise all counselor functions designed to produce changes in clients, groups, or institutions. This article introduces a model that provides for the description and categorization of a very broad range of possible counseling interventions. The figure presents a model of the three dimensions to be discussed. This model permits the identification and classification of a variety of counseling programs or counseling approaches and thereby serves as a means of categorizing and describing the potential activities of the counselor in a variety of settings. The three dimensions described are the intervention target, purpose, and method.[8]

The Target of the Intervention

Interventions may be aimed at (a) the individual, (b) the individual's primary groups, (c) the individual's associational groups, or (d) the institutions or communities that influence the individual's behavior.

The Purpose of the Intervention

The purpose may be (a) remediation, (b) prevention, or (c) development.

The Method of Intervention

The method of reaching the target population may be through (a) direct service, which involves direct professional involvement with the target; (b) consultation with and training of other helping professionals or paraprofessionals; or (c) indirect interventions utilizing media, i.e., computers, programmed exercises, books, television, and other media.

Any intervention has these three dimensions: who or what the intervention is aimed at, why the intervention is attempted, and how the intervention is made.[9]

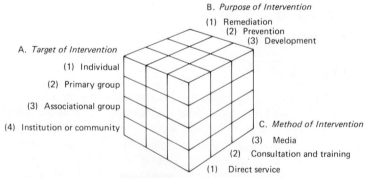

Figure 3–1.
Counseling interventions.

---

[8] Weston H. Morrill, Eugene R. Oetting, and James C. Hurst, "Dimensions of Counselor Functioning," *The Personnel and Guidance Journal,* **52**:355 (Feb. 1974).
[9] Ibid., p. 355.

The variety in school settings will, of course, account for some differences in the ways counselors may carry out their roles. There are, however, some common influences determining counselors' role and function, regardless of the setting. The first of these are what might be called professional constants or determinants that tend to indicate what is appropriate and not appropriate to the counselors' role and function. These include guidelines and policy statements of professional organizations, licensing or certification limitations, accreditation guidelines and requirements, and the expectancies of professional training programs. In addition to these professional constants, there are also those personal factors that inevitably influence role and function. These include the interest of the counselor, such as what he/she likes to do versus what he/she doesn't like to do; what he/she gets encouraged to do and is rewarded for doing by the school, community, or his/her peers; what the counselor has resources to do; what the counselor perceives as the appropriate role and function for a given setting; and finally, how life in general is going for the counselor. The counselor's attitudes, values, and experiences both on and off the job can influence how he/she views the job.

It has also been increasingly noted in recent years that counselors and other professional helpers are coming to grips with the facts that traditional roles and delivery systems in human services may have imposed real limitations on their ability to deal directly and effectively with the critical needs of clients. Thus, as we further view counselor role and function, we are seeking to integrate for you, our reader, not only those concepts that have proven themselves over the years, but also current and promising directions that seem necessary for the guidance counselor to remain a viable entity in the school setting.

The Elementary School Counselor

In Chapter 2 it was noted that the characteristics of the elementary pupil and the elementary school dictate certain characteristics in program organization that distinguish elementary school guidance programs from those in secondary schools and at other educational levels. It therefore follows that the elementary school counselor's role and function will also reflect these differences. The differences, however, are not so much in what the elementary counselor does, but how he/she does it. For example, counselors and other elementary school specialists must work closely and effectively with the classroom teacher. This provides a natural relationship for an emphasis on consultation and coordination. In addition to counseling, coordination, and consulting functions, the elementary school counselor has responsibilities for the orientation, assessment, and career development needs of pupils. A brief description of these various roles follows.

Counselor. Although one-to-one counseling in the elementary school may take correspondingly less of the counselor's time than counseling at other levels, the counselor should be available to meet individually or in groups with children referred by teachers or parents or identified by the counselor or other helping professionals as in need of counseling. The counseling process recognizes where the pupil is in his/her growth and development and the implications of this for counseling practice.

Consultant.   As a consultant, the counselor may confer directly with teachers, parents, administrators, and other helping professionals to help an identified third party such as students in the school setting. In this role, the counselor helps significant others to assist the student-client in dealing more effectively with developmental and/or adjustment needs.

Coordinator.   Elementary school counselors have a responsibility for the co-ordination of the various guidance activities in the schools. Coordinating these with ongoing classroom and school activities is also desirable. As the only building-based helping professional, the elementary school counselor may be called upon to coordinate the contributions of school psychologists, social workers, and others. Other coordination activities could include intra-school referrals and interagency referrals.

Agent of Orientation.   As a human development facilitator, the elementary school counselor recognizes the importance of the child's orientation to the goals and environment of the elementary school. It is important that the child's initial education experiences be positive ones, and it is in this regard that the counselor may plan group activities and consult with teachers to help children learn and practice the human relationship skills necessary for their adjustment in the togetherness enforced by the school setting.

Assessment.   The counselor in the elementary school can anticipate being called upon to interpret and often gather both test and nontest data. To the counselor will also fall the task of putting these data into focus to not only see but be able to interpret the child as a total being. Beyond the tradi-tional data used for pupil understanding, the counselor should also understand the impacts of culture, the sociology of the school, and other environmental influences that are determinants of pupil behavior.

Career Developer.   The importance of the elementary school years as a foun-dation for later significant decisions of the individual underscores the desirabil-ity of planned attention being given to the elementary pupil's career develop-ment. Although the responsibility for career education planning rests with the classroom teachers, the elementary school counselor can make a major contribution as a coordinator and consultant in developing a continuous, sequential, and integrated program.

Some additional insights into the role and function of the elementary

Table 3–6.
**Rank Ordering of Elementary School Counselor Activities
As Assigned by 183 Elementary School Educators
(Rank Ordered on a Scale of Zero to Ten with Ten Being the Highest
and Zero Being of No Priority)**

Rank	Activity	Mean
1	Individual Counseling	8.4
2.5	Consultation with Teachers	7.7
2.5	Group Counseling	7.7
4	Consultation with Parents	7.4
5	Behavior Modification	6.5
6	Parent Counseling	6.4
7	Values Clarification Activities	5.7
8	Assessment Activities	4.6
9	Career Guidance	3.8
10	Middle/Senior High School or Secondary School Placement and Follow-Up	3.7
11	Research and Evaluation	3.2

school counselor may also be provided by examining the results of a study conducted by the North Central Association of Schools and Colleges (1977).[10] This study, which sampled or interviewed more than 180 elementary school teachers, administrators, supervisors, and counselors, concluded that the elementary school counselor's priority activities should focus on (in descending order) individual counseling, group guidance (including counseling) activities, and consultation with teachers and parents. Other high priority activities recommended by these elementary school practitioners included parent counseling, behavior modification, values clarification activities, and career guidance.

Table 3–6 shows, in rank order, a priority of counselor activities in the elementary schools as viewed by this sample of elementary educators.

As the role and function of elementary school counselors has begun to clarify, so have the demands for counselors in elementary schools. For example, a national survey conducted in 1967 indicated that there were 3,837 elementary school counselors in forty-eight states. Less than ten years later, a 1975 study indicated approximately 10,770 counselors employed in public elementary schools in fifty states. Although the study pointed out that 15 per cent of these counselors were working in more than one elementary school, it is important to note the nearly tripling of the number of elementary school counselors in less than ten years.[11]

[10] Unpublished study, Counseling and Guidance Committee, North Central Association, 1976–1977.
[11] Robert D. Myrick and Linda Moni, "A Status Report of Elementary School Counseling," *Elementary School Guidance and Counseling,* **10:**156 (Mar. 1976).

The Middle/Junior High School Counselor

In recent years, the trend has shifted from the elementary, junior, senior high school organizational concept to the elementary, middle, senior high school concept. These changes have not been without their attending controversies, but the middle school in concept and function may not really be all that different from the more traditional junior high school. For example, many contend that the junior high school was originally conceived as an institution to meet the developmental and transitional needs of youth from puberty to adolescence, from elementary to secondary school. Early in the middle school movement it was suggested that "the rationale for the middle school concept is primarily based on the basis (or beliefs) that modern youth reaches physical, social, and intellectual maturity at a younger age than did previous generations and that the junior high school does not typically meet the developmental needs of these students."[12] Regardless of whether a school system adopts a middle school type of intermediate school or stays with the more traditional junior high school, it would appear that either institution will reflect such characteristics as providing for (1) the orientation and transitional needs of students; (2) the developmental needs of students who, as a group, are moving toward adolescence; and (3) the educational and social developmental needs of their student populations. In such a setting, middle and/or junior high school counselors will be actively involved in:

Student Orientation.   This would include the initial orientation of entering students and their parents to the programs, policies, facilities, and guidance activities of their new school and later, their pre-entry orientation to the high school they will attend upon completion of their junior high or middle school program.

Appraisal or Assessment Activities.   In addition to typical school record and standardized test data, counselors may increasingly encourage the use of observation and other techniques to identify emerging traits of individual students during this critical development period. Values clarification activities may also be increasingly used for assessment and developmental purposes during this time.

Counseling.   Both individual and group counseling should be utilized by school counselors at this level. In practice, it appears that middle and junior high school counselors tend to utilize group counseling more frequently than individual counseling.

Consultation.   Counselors will provide consultation to faculty, parents and, on occasion, school administrators regarding the developmental and adjust-

[12] Donald H. Eichborn, *New Knowledge of 10- Through 13-Year-olds,* paper presented at the Conference on "The Middle School Idea," Nov. 11, 1967, University of Toledo, Toledo, Ohio.

ment needs of individual students. Counselors will also consult with other members of the school system's pupil personnel services team.

Placement. Counselors are usually involved in course and curricular placement of individuals, not only within their own schools, but also cooperatively with their counterparts in the feeder secondary schools.

The Secondary School Counselor

Of all the educational levels in which counselors serve, the secondary school is the one in which counselors and the general educational public (teachers, pupils, parents) are most likely to have some consistent understandings of "what the school counselor does." Although the role and function of the secondary school counselor has changed and expanded over the years, it is clearly the most traditional and most readily identified, even though the secondary school counselors' role has been more frequently and seriously challenged than their elementary or collegiate counterparts. However, despite these challenges, there have not been and likely will not be any drastic or "overnight" changes. As the North Central Association's future study, presented in Chapter 2, predicts, secondary guidance programs in the future will still be built around the traditional basic services. Although the emphasis and techniques will undoubtedly change, counseling, as a professional activity in schools, will never have the opportunity to "start from scratch" again. It is anticipated that the role and function of the secondary school counselor will continue to be built around these traditional expectancies as follows:

1. Assessment of the individual's potential and other characteristics.
2. Counseling the individual.
3. Group counseling and guidance activities.
4. Career guidance, including the providing of occupational-educational information.
5. Placement, follow-up, and accountability-evaluation.
6. Consultation with teachers and other school personnel, parents, pupils in groups, and appropriate community agencies.

The roles and functions of the secondary school counselor are not dissimilar to those in the elementary and middle-junior high schools; it should be emphasized that the differences occur in how counselors in the secondary school discharge their role and function and in the different emphases appropriate to the secondary school setting. For example, the emphasis at the secondary school level shifts drastically from the preventive to the remedial in dealing with many common counseling concerns. Many of these concerns are now potentially serious life problems, such as addiction to drugs and alcohol, sexual concerns, and interpersonal relationship adjustments. Further, there is less client emphasis on preparing for decisions and more emphasis on making decisions. These include immediate or impending career and/or further education decisions; decisions relevant to relationships with the opposite sex and perhaps marriage, and decisions involved in developing personal values systems.

In addition to these different emphases contrasted with counseling needs at other educational levels, there are indications that counselors anticipate more emphasis on consultation and on a broader understanding of the environmental impact on students' behavior; a shifting emphasis towards a closer relationship with the classroom teacher in the school environment, as opposed to the traditional "medical" model (where the client in need comes to the office for a "prescription") and, finally, a change in emphasis from reactive to proactive and change agent in both the school and community.

Counselors in Vocational Schools

The image and the significance of vocational education changed markedly in the 1970s. Once regarded as a "dumping ground" for the unwilling or unable student—with facilities usually appropriate to this image, vocational education programs have made a dramatic turnaround in recent generations. Today they are attracting students at all ability levels and are preparing them for jobs that are in demand in some of the finest educational facilities in the country. School counselors need to become aware of both the nature of vocational education programs and the opportunities available to those who complete them. Additionally, counselors in preparation need to recognize some differences in emphasis in the role and function of the counselor in the vocational school.

Counselors in Higher Education

A wide variety of counseling services is available to students in programs of higher education across the United States and Canada. Some of these counselors function in specialized facilities such as career guidance services and college admissions and placement offices. The majority of counselors, however, are employed in university counseling, mental health, or psychological service centers. These centers typically offer personal, academic, and vocational counseling as the main focus, although group counseling has increased in popularity in recent years. Many of these centers are interdisciplinary in terms of staffing.

A noticeable trend in the activities of college counseling center programs is their move to assist larger numbers of students on their campuses through such activities as outreach programs, special workshops, dormitory groups, and peer counseling. On some campuses, counselors are also becoming more active in consultation with their faculty peers, campus administrators, and leaders of student organizations.

TEACHER AND ADMINISTRATOR ROLES IN THE SCHOOL GUIDANCE PROGRAM

The Role of the Classroom Teacher

Although it seems heresy to the counseling profession, it has been and could continue to be possible for schools to exist without the benefit of guidance counselors. Possibly, many pupils will not achieve their potential, solve their problems, or make appropriate decisions and plans, but nonetheless most of them will learn, will progress, and will be viewed as educated. It is also possible for schools to exist without the presence of an even more prominent member—the school principal. Although teachers would be even more over-burdened with administrative responsibilities, and their teaching effectiveness would undoubtedly suffer, pupils would still be taught, would learn, perhaps at a slower rate, would graduate, even without the principal's handshake, and would be viewed as educated. Schools without teachers, however, cease to be schools. They become, instead, detention centers, social clubs, or temporary shelters, but they are not schools, and any learning that takes place would be both incidental and accidental. It therefore becomes obvious, and has been since the beginning of schooling, that the teacher is the key and most important professional in the school setting. Teacher support and participation are crucial to any program that involves the students. The school guidance program is no exception. It is therefore important to examine the role and function of the classroom teacher in this program, recognizing, of course, that differences may be anticipated at differing educational levels and in different educational settings.

a. Role As a Listener-advisor

Most classroom teachers see their pupils every day, five days a week, for at least forty-five minutes per day on the average of 180 school days per year, often for several years, all of which represents a staggering amount of contact time exceeded by no other adult except the parent, and that exception does not always hold true. The inevitable result is that the teacher, more than any other professional in the school setting, is in the position to know the students best, to communicate with them on an almost daily basis, and to establish a relationship based on mutual trust and respect. The teacher thus becomes the first line of contact between the student and the school guidance program; a contact in which the teacher will frequently be called upon to serve in a listening-advising capacity.

b. Role As a Referral and Receiving Agent

The classroom teacher is, inevitably, the major source of student referrals to the school counselor. Because the counselor's daily, personal contacts with students are necessarily limited, the counselor's personal awareness of individuals needing counseling are similarly limited. The guidance program must, therefore, depend on the alertness of the teaching faculty to ensure that students with counseling needs will not go unnoticed and uncounseled. Of course, it may not be enough to simply identify the student to a counselor. In many instances, the teacher must orient and encourage the student to seek counselor assistance. Nor does the teacher's responsibility necessarily end when the pupil has entered a counseling relationship. The teacher may still be involved, if only in the role of supporting the student's continuation with the counseling process. Teachers may also anticipate a role as a receiving agent for not only those students he/she has referred, but others in their classes as well. In such situations, the teacher in a sense "receives" the counseled student back into the classroom environment and, it is hoped, supports and reinforces the counseling outcomes. The importance of this reinforcer role cannot be overemphasized.

c. Role As a "Human Potential Discoverer"

Each year every teacher witnesses a talent parade through his/her respective classes. Although teachers may lack training, experience, or versatility sufficient to identify the special talents of the vast majority of students, most teachers have the expertise to identify those who may have some special talents for their own particular career specialty. That expertise multiplied across the many career fields represented in most school programs represents a near-army of talent scouts that should ensure the probability that every student will have his/her talents and potentials identified and his/her development encouraged and assisted. This teacher role as a human potential discoverer is significant in fulfilling not only a mission of the school guidance program, but also in meeting education's responsibility to the individual and to society.

d. Role As a Career Educator

Closely related to the foregoing is the teacher's central role in the school's career education program. As career education is recognized as a part of the total education of the individual, it is important to also recognize the classroom teacher's responsibility to incorporate and integrate career education into subject matter teaching. Career education cannot succeed without career guidance, and vice versa. It therefore follows that the success of the career guidance program is tied to the success of the career education program, a success that rests largely with the classroom teacher.

The career education responsibilities of the teacher include the developing of positive attitudes and respect for all honest work, a challenging responsibility in view of the many adult-imposed biases with which the student is constantly confronted. Additionally, the teacher must promote the parallel development of positive student attitudes towards education and its relationship to career preparation and decision making. The pupil must also have the opportunity to examine and test concepts, skills, and roles and to develop values appropriate to his/her future career planning. The security of the classroom group provides an ideal setting for these experiences.

e. Role As a Human Relations Facilitator

The potential for success of any school guidance program depends to a considerable degree upon the climate or environment of the school, an environment that is conducive to the development and practice of positive human relations. The influence of the classroom teacher on that environment is dominant, as ably expressed by Hain Ginott:[13]

I have come to the frightening conclusion
I am the decisive element in the classroom
It is my personal approach that creates the climate
It is my daily mood that makes the weather
As a teacher I possess tremendous power to make a child's
   life miserable or joyous
I can humiliate or humor, hurt or heal
In all situations it is my response that decides whether a
   crisis will be escalated or de-escalated, and a child
   humanized or dehumanized.

Among the recent research emphasizing the importance of a favorable classroom and school environment for learning is that reported in Benjamin Bloom's book *Human Characteristics and School Learning.*[14] Bloom suggests that it is possible for 95 per cent of the students to learn all that the school has to teach at or near the same achievement level. His research indicates that most students will be very similar in both learning and their motivation to learn when they are provided the favorable conditions or environment for learning. On the other hand, his research also demonstrates that when the environment in the classroom is unfavorable, differences occur that widen the gap between high and low achievers. In this role as a human relations facilitator, the classroom teacher has the opportunity to be a model to demonstrate positive human relations. The teaching and practicing of these skills should occur as a regular procedure in the classroom as he/she plans and directs group interactions that promise positive human relationship experiences for each individual participant.

f. Role As a Guidance Program Supporter

Someone once said, "Counselors are the most human of all humans." Be that as it may, counselors, as all humans, need and respond to the encourage-

---

[13] Beatrice Gross and Ronald Gross, *Will It Grow in a Classroom* (New York: Dell Publishing Company, 1974), p. 39.

[14] Benjamin S. Bloom, *Human Characteristics and School Learning* (New York: McGraw-Hill Book Company, 1976).

ment and support of their fellow beings. Therefore, a significant contribution that the classroom teacher can make to the school guidance program is one of counselor encouragement and support, and the creation of a motivating environment. Support can be especially influential in determining how pupils view and utilize the services of the school's guidance program. Too, teachers' reactions do not go unnoticed by school administrators and supervisors. Of course, it is also to be hoped that evidences of teacher support for guidance will extend to parent contacts and out into the community as well.

Despite the importance of the classroom teacher in any program of pupil guidance at any educational level, evidence indicates that in far too many settings the classroom teacher is still only incidentally involved in the school guidance program. Many classroom teachers may feel uncertain regarding the goals of their school programs and may feel a lack of communication and involvement in the guidance programs. In such situations, the pupil is the real loser and both the counselor and the teacher must share the blame. Because the school guidance program is the responsibility of counselors, they must initiate communications and interaction with their teaching faculties, they must actively pursue teachers' involvement and assistance, and they must exemplify their claim to human relations expertise. They must also recognize that although teachers are willing to accept their role in the school guidance program, as many studies have indicated, they may lack some understanding of what that role and function is. Hutson[15] reported a study of university catalogues and state certification requirements to ascertain the extent to which teachers and school principals were prepared for their roles on the guidance team. His study indicated that some universities and certifying authorities recognize the responsibility of preparing teachers and administrators for that role and function, but that the majority do not. Hutson's survey further indicated that only about one half of the teacher education curricula at the graduate level recognizes guidance as a desirable element in their advanced preparation. He suggests that it is highly improbable to expect to realize the full potential of the team when teachers and principals have made no study of the guidance function.

The Role of the Chief School Administrator

Whether he/she is the building principal or a university president, the chief on-site administrator is potentially (and usually) the most singular important person in the development of any educational program in a respective setting. Most staff members of schools (including principals and college presidents) think of chief administrators in terms of power—what the chief administrators

---

[15] F. W. Hutson, "The Education of the Guidance TEAM," *Counselor Education and Supervision,* **9:**234 (Summer 1970).

permit them to do and not to do. Previous studies reported by the authors[16] have noted that administrative support was ranked in the highest priority category in the establishment and development of school guidance programs. Other studies[17] have noted that program development and change are far more likely to succeed if stimulated from the top than from the bottom up. These emphasize the significant role the school principal and other educational leadership can and should play in any program of guidance and counseling within their jurisdiction. This role may be appropriately expressed through leadership, consultation, advice, and resource support. Some of the characteristics of these activities follow.

a. Role As a Program Leader and Supporter

The leadership behavior of the school principal in behalf of the school guidance program is a major determinant of the program's prospects for success. Because the school administrator represents the educational leadership in both the school and the community, he/she has the responsibility of giving clear, open, and recognized support for the school guidance program. This will include responsibilities for communicating program characteristics, achievements, and needs to school boards and others within the educational system and to the tax-supporting public.

b. Role As a Program Consultant and Advisor

The chief school administrator has the best overview of all activities and planning within the institution. This position enables the chief administrator to make a valuable contribution to the school guidance program as advisor and consultant on school needs that can be served by the school guidance program, school policies that affect guidance program functioning, resolution of problems encountered by the program, and procedures or directions for program development and improvement.

c. Role As a Resource Provider

The chief school administrator is usually responsible for the institution's budget—its makeup and utilization. In this role, he/she provides advice and direction to the school guidance program regarding budget expectations, staffing possibilities, facilities, and equipment. He/she may also be aware of possible external resources such as state or federal funding, which the school guidance program may wish to explore.

---

[16] Robert L. Gibson, et al., *The Development and Management of School Guidance Programs* (Dubuque, Iowa: William C. Brown and Company, Publishers, 1973), pp. 59–61.
[17] Daniel E. Griffiths, "Administrative Theory and Change in Organizations," in *Innovations in Education,* ed. by Matthew B. Miles (New York: Teachers College Press, 1964), pp. 425–436.

THE COUNSELOR AND RELATIONSHIPS WITH OTHER HELPING PROFESSIONS

As already noted, one of the school counselor's important roles is as a team member. Unlike the gifted athlete who may have to limit membership to one team, the counselor may play on several teams. One of the most important and logical of these is the pupil personnel services or helping professions team. This team typically includes the school psychologist, social worker, speech and hearing specialists, and health personnel. To work effectively with each other, members of these teams must understand the expertise and responsibilities of their team members and how they support each other. These brief descriptions present only a superficial overview. Unfortunately, most training programs do little in the way of interdisciplinary planning or training. Therefore, it becomes the responsibility of the school counselor and other helping professionals to initiate and develop positive, cooperative working relationships consistent with the team concept.

The School Psychologist

In 1977 it was estimated that there were more than 9,000 school psychologists practicing in the United States and Canada. These were prepared in approximately 150 training programs.[18] In the 1970s, school psychologists increased as a result of state and federal laws mandating equal educational opportunity for the handicapped. Because school psychology has its historical antecedents in clinical psychology, the school psychologist is heavily trained in the use of such clinical tools as those which measure mental and personality characteristics of the individual. In the school setting, they work with individual children to assess learning and emotional problems, and they consult with teachers, administrators, and parents regarding individual pupils. Gregersen noted that ten common roles for school psychologists, as described in the literature, include the following:

1. Psychometrician.
2. Clinician/counselor/therapist.
3. Diagnostic-prescriptive consultant.
4. Mental health consultant.
5. Educational evaluator/consultant.
6. Researcher.
7. Organizational development specialist/social system analyst.
8. Administrator-supervisor.
9. Community liaison.
10. In-service trainer.

[18] Gerald D. Gregersen, "What to Expect From Your School Psychologist: Some Reasons Why You Might Not Get It," *Viewpoints,* **53**:7 (Jan. 1977).

Obviously, many of these roles or broad categorical definitions of activities are not mutually exclusive. In fact, most school psychologists in practice tend to fill more than one role and, at different times, are involved with most of these activities. Obviously, when a classroom teacher seeks consultation or assistance in dealing with a classroom problem, whether it emanates from an individual child or from some broader instructional difficulty, the adequacy of the information or assistance that he/she receives is dependent on the kind of role or nature of service which the school psychologist provides.[19]

Counselors may often find it desirable to refer students to the school psychologist for clinical diagnosis, whereas on the other hand, the school psychologist will often identify, through his diagnostic evaluations, pupils in need of counseling.

Too, "with the present movement in special education to reintegrate handicapped children into the regular classroom, the counselor's role in the school takes on an exciting, yet challenging, new meaning. Whereas traditionally counselors have been concerned with the child's psychological and emotional adjustment and the impact of the child's emotional life on his readiness to learn, the integration of handicapped children will require that the counselor be prepared to respond to a wider range of behavior problems."[20] Therefore, the school counselor will work directly with the school psychologist and special educators, as well, in offering direct counseling and psychological support services to handicapped children and the classroom teachers teaching such children. Counselors and school psychologists will also find themselves members of teams that consult with the parents of handicapped children.

The School Social Worker

Social work has been defined by Crouch[21] as "the attempt to assist those who do not command the means to human subsistence in acquiring them and in attaining the highest possible degree of independence." The school social worker provides helping services for those children who are unable to make proper use of their educational opportunities and who find it difficult to function effectively in the school environment. In this role, the social worker is a referral source for those children who appear to have emotional or social problems that are handicapping their learning and social adjustment to school. The school social worker has special interviewing and case work skills that are used within a school-child-parent context. The school social worker is also usually the pupil personnel services team member who works

---

[19] Ibid., p. 6.
[20] Therese Cristiani and Peggy Sommers, "The School Counselor's Role in Mainstreaming the Handicapped," *Viewpoints in Teaching and Learning,* **54:**20 (Jan. 1978).
[21] Robert C. Crouch, "Social Work Defined," *Social Work,* **24:**46 (Jan. 1979).

closest with community agencies and nonschool professional helpers, such as physicians, lawyers, and ministers. Meares reported a study (May 1977) that ranked the importance of tasks performed by school social workers. Four major, interrelated priority activities were identified as follows:

(1) *clarifying* the nature of the child's problem and the parameters of social work services, (2) *assessing* the child's specific problem, (3) *facilitating* better relationships among school, community, and pupils, and (4) *educational counseling* with the child and his parents. Most activities emphasize the importance of the liaison role. Thus, there has been a transition from the primarily clinical casework approach to serving children in schools to that of home-school-community liaison and educational counseling with the child and his parents.[22]

The school social worker is an important member of the school services team. Counselors and other helping professionals may depend on the social workers to provide broader and deeper understanding of the child, especially in regard to the home environment and the nature of the pupil's behavioral problems.

School Health Personnel

Most school systems employ professional health services personnel, at least on a part-time basis. Most common are the school nurse and the dental hygienist, and a number of school systems also utilize school physicians. Your personal recall of these helping professionals may consist of memories of immunization shots, opening your mouth to say ah, the taste of the tongue-depressor, and the admonition of the dental hygienist when she discovered a cavity. Such recalls are fairly characteristic of the role of these providers of basic, preventive health services for all school children. These professionals also identify children who need special medical treatments or referrals for the correction or alleviation of defects. Counselors will find these medical specialists a resource for referrals and a help in determining whether or to what extent physical ailments or defects are an obstacle to a student's anticipated development or adjustment.

Psychiatrists

Psychiatrists are physicians with specialized training in the treatment of behavioral abnormalities. As physicians, psychiatrists are permitted by law to use drugs and other physical means of treatment for mental problems. Counselors often suggest to parents that they refer their son or daughter to a

[22] Paula Allen Meares, "Analysis of Tasks in School Social Work," *Social Work*, 22:198 (May 1977).

psychiatrist if it is suspected that the child may have an emotional disturbance requiring the use of medication. Many psychiatrists perform an important consultative role to pupil personnel workers, as well.

SUMMARY AND CONCLUSIONS

An article in *Better Homes and Gardens* noted that "if you graduated from high school before 1960, chances are the only school counselors you have known are your child's."[23] This chapter assumes that most of those who graduated from high school after 1960 also knew little about how their counselors were trained or licensed and had little familiarity with their role and function. It is perhaps this very lack of understanding that has led the counseling professions in the past decade to move more energetically into the public communications arena to "tell what they're about," to upgrade their training, and to seek protection of their profession from unqualified intruders through certification and licensure. Much has been accomplished in a short period of time if one considers that at the turn of this century there were no counselors in schools. More than eighty years and 80,000 school counselors later, we can identify tremendous progress in training, certification, and practice. Today, counselor training is available at the master's, specialist, and doctoral levels, with the possibility of undergraduate and postdoctoral programs in the future. All states specify some type of counselor preparation or certification for employment in school settings, with the exception of postsecondary institutions. These requirements in general reflect role and function expectancies. Differing characteristics of various school levels, settings, and clientele, by necessity, result in variations in that role and function. The cooperation and contributions of teachers, administrators, and other helping professionals are vital to the success of any school guidance program.

[23] Margaret Daly, "How Good is Your Child's School Counselor," *Better Homes and Gardens* (Feb. 1979), p. 15.

Counselors in Other Settings 4

INTRODUCTION

Although educational institutions are by far the largest single employers of counselors, there are a variety of other settings in which counselors may and do seek employment. These include community mental health agencies, employment and rehabilitation agencies, correctional settings, crisis prevention centers, and, of course, private practice. In addition, various business and industrial settings are also increasingly employing counselors to deliver a variety of helping services.

The training of counselors for these various settings shares a great deal in common with the training of school counselors, and in many training programs there is little distinction, with the possible exceptions of practicum and internship settings and a few specialized courses. In other training programs, however, counselors may be trained in separate departments or in programs with distinctly different emphases. Greater distinctions will be noted at the doctoral level where preparation tends to focus on one's anticipated professional work setting. The similarities and dissimilarities in both training and on-the-job functioning may be noted by examining the definitions appropriate to their profession in three professional organizations, representing trainers and practitioners in the fields of counseling and guidance. These are the American Personnel and Guidance Association, the American Mental Health Counselors Association, and the American Psychological Association.

The description of professional counseling proposed by the American Personnel and Guidance Association's Licensure Committee (1978) is

> counseling procedures include but are not restricted to the use of counseling methods and psychological and psychotherapeutic techniques, both verbal and non-verbal which require the application of principles, methods, procedures of understanding, predicting and/or interpreting tests of mental abilities, aptitudes, interests, achievement, attitudes, personality characteristics, emotion or motivation; informational and community resources for career, personal or social development, group and/or placement methods and techniques which serve to further the goals of counseling; and designing, conducting and interpreting research on human subjects or any consultations on any item above.[1]

The American Mental Health Counselors Association Certification Committee in 1978 defined the professional counselor as one who is involved in

> the process of assisting individuals or groups, through a helping relationship, to achieve optimal mental health through personal and social development and adjustment to prevent the debilitating effects of certain somatic, emotional. and intra- and/or inter-personal disorders.[2]

By the American Psychological Association definition, the practice of psychology (including counseling psychology) is

> rendering to individuals, groups, organizations, or the public a psychological service involving the application of principles, methods and procedures of understanding, predicting and influencing behavior, such as the principles pertaining to learning, perception, motivation, thinking, emotions and interpersonal relationships; the methods and procedures of interviewing, counseling, and psychotherapy; of constructing, administering and interpreting tests of mental abilities, aptitudes, interests, attitudes, personality characteristics, emotions, and motivation; and of assessing public opinion. The application of said principles and methods includes but is not restricted to: diagnoses, prevention, and amelioration of individuals and groups; hypnosis; educational and vocational counseling; personnel selection and management; the evaluation and planning for effective work and learning situations; advertising and market research; and the resolution of interpersonal and social conflict.[3]

---

[1] *Licensure Committee Action Packet* (Washington, D.C.: American Personnel and Guidance Association, 1978), p. 20.

[2] American Mental Health Counselors Association, Certification Committee, unpublished report, Washington, D.C., 1978.

[3] American Psychological Association, "A Model for State Legislation Affecting the Practice of Psychology," 1967 report of APA Committee on Legislation, in *American Psychologist,* **22**:1095–1103 (1967).

It should be noted that these organizations in their definitions stress the developmental as well as the remedial activities. Whereas for many years the image of the counselor tended to be that of a remedial agent, it is clear that the present and future orientation of the counseling professions will place an increasingly significant emphasis on developmental services. This emphasis was encouraged by Kagan in his presidential address to Division 17 of the American Psychological Association in which he said

> So-called "normal" people no longer are content to seek help only when they are vocationally uncertain, depressed, grieving or unable to grieve, preorgasmic or impotent. They want prevention and enrichment. They want the wherewithal to anticipate and deal with the many major personal and interpersonal events of living—they want a tool kit along with the car, so that they themselves are able to effect maintenance and repairs when things don't run smoothly. There is a need and a demand for self-directed personal and vocational exploration programs, personal and marital enrichment programs, mental health checkups and preventive maintenance programs. There is a need for participation of counselors on health teams with workers from other professions and for the further development and dissemination of structured learning experiences in human interaction as a part of secondary school curriculum and in medical, law and nursing school programs. These too soon will be very much in demand. Also needed are family counseling and family interaction education courses as a routine part of termination of long-term hospital care or prison confinement. Another exciting area for us is the teaching of mutual counseling skills for people to become colleague counselors for each other—physicians, dentists, police. All this I see as the immediate future—the long-range possibilities are mind-boggling, but let's be conservative and stay with the immediate future for now.[4]

Lewis and Lewis also sounded a similar challenge in regard to community counseling when they suggested that

> Educational programs should be made available to the entire community being served. These programs can involve two distinct thrusts: (1) educating community members *about* mental health, and (2) providing experiences that can enhance community members' own development and prevent the occurrence of serious problems.
>   Programs dealing with mental health itself as a subject matter should help to clarify what is presently known about the positive factors that encourage health and effectiveness in everyday living. They should attempt to eliminate the lay person's assumption that mental problems always involve some kind of illness that comes from within the individ-

---

[4] Norman Kagan, Address, Division 17, *The Counseling Psychologist,* Vol. 7, No. 2 (Aug. 1977).

ual. They should, instead, encourage recognition of the notion that mental health cannot really be understood without an understanding of the relationships between individuals and their environments. This kind of program might help to erase the stigma that is all too often placed on people who have needed intensive assistance with psychological problems in the past.

Educational programs should attempt to increase understanding of the dynamics of mental health and mental illness and should also define the kind of contribution that the mental health agency is trying to make. This can help community members to set their own mental health goals and to become more actively involved in the planning and evaluation of the services that are offered.[5]

Thus, as we proceed to examine the role of the counselor in a variety of nonschool settings, we would emphasize that the nonschool counselor will and should be dealing with the developmental and growth needs of clients as well as the more traditional remedial and adjustment concerns.

COMMUNITY MENTAL HEALTH AGENCIES

Community mental health agencies provide counseling services for the general population within a specified geographical locale. Many community mental health agencies have been initiated under the provisions of the Community Mental Health Act of 1963, which provides initial funding for such centers that must be developed following the guidelines of the National Institute of Mental Health. These agencies were designed to provide preventive community mental health services. Typically, such centers offer inpatient and outpatient services, emergency services, and educational and consultation services. Many centers also provide partial hospitalization services, diagnostic services, and precare and aftercare in the community through programs of home visitations, foster home placement, and halfway houses.

Lewis and Lewis suggest that the community mental health concept has great potential

because agencies dealing with specific "catchment areas" have the opportunity to develop well-coordinated human services and, at the same time, to recognize environmental situations and assist in organizing the local population to deal with them. This can occur in a small agency dedicated to out-patient care, or in a major mental health center providing comprehensive services to meet a variety of mental health needs.[6]

---

[5] Judith A. Lewis and Michael D. Lewis, *Community Counseling* (New York: John Wiley & Sons, 1977), pp. 249–250.
[6] Ibid., pp. 248–249.

Table 4–1.

Community Counseling in Community Mental Health Agencies

	Extensive	Intensive
Experiential	Educational programs concerning the nature of mental health. Educational programs encouraging community involvement in planning and evaluating services. Educational programs to enhance effective mental health development and prevent psychological problems.	Ongoing counseling and rehabilitation programs. Walk-in assistance with problems of living. Crisis intervention.
Environmental	Assistance in organizing local community to bring about needed environmental change. Class advocacy in behalf of individuals such as former or present mental patients. Organizing and planning for alternatives to hospitalization.	Linkage with support systems and helping network. Advocacy in behalf of individual clients. Attempts to secure placements more appropriate than hospitalization. Consultation with helping network.

Source: Judith A. Lewis and Michael D. Lewis, *Community Counseling* (New York: John Wiley & Sons, 1977), p. 249.

A multifaceted approach that such agencies might attempt to implement is illustrated in Table 4–1.

The Agency Team

In most community mental health agencies, counselors are employed as team members with other helping professionals. These typically include psychiatrists, clinical psychologists, and psychiatric social workers. Psychiatrists are usually considered to be the leaders of the team, inasmuch as they have a medical background and may perform physical examinations, prescribe drugs, and admit people to hospitals in the treatment of behavior abnormalities. In addition to their basic medical training, certification as a psychiatrist typically requires three years of residency in a psychiatric institution plus two years of further practice.

Counseling or clinical psychologists are prepared in programs that require a minimum of three academic years of full-time resident graduate study. Although emphases in programs will vary somewhat from institution to institution and depend on whether one is trained in a clinical or counseling psychology program, the psychologist receives general training in basic psychology, counseling and psychotherapy, psychological assessment, and psychological research. Some report that the difference between clinical and counseling psychology has never been entirely clear, but

> there appear, however, to be some important distinctions which warrant continued separation, albeit with close cooperation. The tools which each use most typically (for example, different kinds of psychological tests) are different enough to warrant separate, although overlapping, training programs, and the problems presented by their clients are also different enough to justify different practicum and internship experiences.[7]

A tentative distinction might be that clinical psychologists tend to work with behavioral abnormalities and personality reorganization, whereas counseling psychologists emphasize increased understanding of the adjustment problem of normal persons.[8]

Psychiatric social workers are trained minimally to the master's degree level in two-year programs. One year of this program is devoted to supervised internship in a clinical or hospital setting. Social workers are trained to give assistance to people in the community who are experiencing economic or other problems. This assistance is facilitated through welfare and other programs. The psychiatric social worker, however, is more frequently found in hospital or community mental health settings. In such settings, they may gather data regarding patients and their families and often will work with the patient's family in assisting the client's adjustment. In many community mental health centers, psychiatric social workers may also conduct treatment of a nonmedical nature.

A study by Randolph presents data of interest to those counselors in training who may be interested in possible employment in community mental health and other community settings. His study identified skills that were important in providing counseling, therapy, and consultation; testing, diagnosis, and research; dealing with specialized personality and personal qualities desired. The results of his study representing 117 directors of community mental health facilities are presented in Tables 4–2, 4–3, 4–4, 4–5, and 4–6.

For example, the most important overall skill desired in the preparation of counselors (among those surveyed) can be noted in Table 4–3 as skill in individual therapy and counseling. The most important skill in the area of

[7] W. Schofield, "Clinical and Counseling Psychology, Some Perspectives," *American Psychologist*, **21**:122–131 (1966).

[8] J. P. Jordaan, R. A. Myers, W. L. Layton, and H. H. Morgan, *The Counseling Psychologist* (New York: Teachers College Press, Columbia University, 1968).

Table 4–2.

Ratings of Major, Department Title, Licensure, and Psychology Course Work Items

Item No.	Item	Mean Rating	Average Rank in 76 Items
55	Course in abnormal psychology	1.32	3
56	Course in personality theory	1.35	5
57	Course in learning theory	1.43	9
60	Course in developmental psychology	1.56	14
31	Hold degree from a psychology department	1.57	16
59	Course in behavior modification	1.60	19
58	Course in social psychology	1.60	19
34	Trained as a clinical psychologist	1.62	21
75	Licensed as a psychologist	1.63	22.5
66	Course in child development	1.69	26
35	Trained as a counseling psychologist	2.07	36
70	Course in physiological psychology	2.18	41
36	Trained as a community psychologist	2.22	43
76	Licensed as a school psychologist	2.32	47
37	Trained as a psychiatric social worker	2.44	51
74	Training in social and rehabilitation services	2.45	52.5
65	Course in vocational development theory	2.48	54
32	Hold a degree from a social-work department	2.51	56.5
39	Trained as a social worker	2.63	60
33	Hold a degree from a counseling and guidance department	2.78	63
41	Trained as a school psychologist	2.81	64
40	Trained as a community counselor	2.89	66
38	Trained as a correctional counselor	3.17	73

Source: **Daniel Lee Randolph, "The Counseling-Community Psychologist in the CMHC: Employer Perceptions," presented in** *Counselor Education and Supervision,* **17:246 (June 1973).**

testing, diagnosis, and research and, overall, the second most desirable skill for counselors to possess were skill in the diagnosis of psychopathology. The third most important item in the study, and the highest rated item in Table 4–2 is a course in abnormal psychology.

Counseling in the Agency Setting

Counselors in school settings deal with youth, encompassing the educational level at which they are employed (elementary, secondary, higher education), and usually are concerned with routine and adjustment-developmental needs of their clients, with a heavy educational emphasis. Counselors in community settings deal with widely diverse populations and a wide variety in both the type and nature of human concerns. These range from continuous developmental needs of individuals to crises requiring immediate emergency attention. Table 4–7 describes the general types of counseling situations with which community agency counselors deal.

In further examining the professional activities of counselors in community settings, Goodyear suggested three levels of psychological intervention: primary, secondary, and tertiary. These may be noted in Table 4–7a and Figure 4–1.

In addition to community mental health agencies, a variety of what might be labelled alternative and nontraditional, yet related, community counseling services have developed over the past several generations. These nontraditional service centers have had a variety of titles, but most of them can be categorized under the labels of hot lines or crisis centers, "drop in" or open-door centers, and specialized counseling centers such as those catering to drug and alcohol abusers, young adults or the aged.

Hot lines or crisis phones have been one of the most popular and older alternative services offered. They are frequently staffed by nonprofessionals or paraprofessionals with, in some settings, professional volunteers available, or a professional supervisor on call. Usually hot lines or crisis phones are designed to provide (1) sympathetic and helpful listeners and (2) reliable

Table 4–3.
Ratings of Counseling, Therapy, and Consultation Items

Item No.	Item	Mean Rating	Average Rank in 76 Items
1	Skill in individual therapy and counseling	1.15	1
22	Skill in providing therapy and counseling services for families	1.34	4
2	Skill in group therapy and counseling	1.41	6.5
9	Training in crisis intervention	1.50	11
21	Skills in providing consultative services for families	1.53	13
3	Skill in using supportive and reflective techniques	1.63	22.5
10	Training in mental health consultation for prevention	1.66	24
5	Skill in using behavioral therapy techniques	1.88	31
4	Skill in using reality therapy techniques	2.02	34
6	Skill in using Gestalt therapy techniques	2.05	35
20	Skill in providing play therapy for children	2.10	38
8	Skill in using transactional analysis techniques	2.23	46
7	Skill in using rational therapy techniques	2.45	52.5
24	Skill in providing vocational and career counseling	2.51	56.5
71	Training in biofeedback	2.59	58
72	Training in alphagenics	2.91	67

Source: **Daniel Lee Randolph, ibid., p. 247.**

Table 4–4.

Ratings of Testing, Diagnosis, and Research Statistics Items

Item No.	Item	Mean Rating	Average Rank in 76 Items
15	Skill in diagnosis of psychopathology	1.23	2
13	Skill in administering individual mental tests for clinical-diagnostic purposes	1.49	10
62	Course in the Wechsler	1.51	12
12	Skill in administering individual mental tests for educational screening	1.57	16
14	Skill in administering projective personality tests	1.57	16
63	Course in the Binet	1.68	25
64	Course in testing for learning disabilities	1.74	27
61	Course in experimental psychology	1.90	32
68	Course in statistics	2.12	39
19	Skill in administering, scoring, and interpreting group-administered tests	2.27	45
16	Skill in conducting and publishing scientific research	2.37	49
67	Course in computer programming	2.73	61
73	Experience in conducting experiments with rats	3.01	71

Source: **Ibid., p. 248.**

information for dealing with such common concerns as drug overdoses, suicide, spouse abuse, alcoholism, and mental breakdown.

It is obviously desirable that crisis situations be handled by trained, professional counselors wherever possible. These

crisis situations can be related to suicide attempts, unwanted pregnancy, death of loved one, divorce, hospitalization, job relocation, new family member, loss of job, imprisonment, infidelity, retirement, drug addiction, or financial problems. Regardless of the nature of the crisis, the counselor needs to accept the situation and maintain personal poise and self-assuredness. This type of confidence can help to reduce the anxiety on the part of the client, as the counselor models responsibility for the client at this time. Through reassurance and expression of hope to the client, the counselor can deal with this immediate situation and then, in the future, aid the client in a developmental sense.[9]

In Table 4–8 on page 91 are some suggestions made by Belkin (1975) for counselor behavior in a crisis situation.

Open-door or drop-in centers provide havens for individuals who need a place to come to and, in larger cities, to get off the streets—a place where

[9] John J. Pietrofesa, et al., op. cit., p. 22.

Table 4–5.
Ratings of Specialized Populations and Settings Items

Item No.	Item	Mean Rating	Average Rank in 76 Items
30	Specialized training in dealing with marital and sex problems	1.94	33
28	Specialized training in dealing with alcohol abuse	2.16	40
29	Specialized training in dealing with drug abuse	2.21	42
26	Experience in working with disadvantaged Blacks	2.33	48
53	Specialized training in working with institutionalized mental patients	2.43	50
54	Specialized training in working with geriatric populations	2.49	55
49	Specialized training in special education and retardation	2.60	59
52	Specialized training in working with noninstitutionalized public offenders	2.74	68.5
51	Specialized training in working with institutionalized public offenders	2.84	65
27	Experience in working with native Americans	2.92	68.5
69	Course(s) in a foreign language(s)	2.92	68.5
50	Specialized training in working with the physically disabled	2.99	70
25	Fluency in speaking Spanish	3.09	72

Source: Ibid., p. 249.

Table 4–6.
Ratings of Personality, Personal Qualities, and Miscellaneous Items

Item No.	Item	Mean Rating	Average Rank in 76 Items
11	Training in intake-interviewing techniques	1.41	6.5
44	Good oral and written communication skills	1.42	8
47	Communicate high degree of personal warmth	1.60	19
23	Knowledge of community resources for referral of clients	1.82	28
18	Skill in organization and administration of helping services	1.87	29.5
42	Neat personal appearance	1.87	29.5
46	Skill in publicizing and public relations	2.09	37
17	Skill in grant and proposal writing	2.24	44
48	Communicate coolness or aloofness in interpersonal relations	4.35	74
43	Sloppy, unkempt personal appearance	4.44	75
45	Poor oral and written communication skills	4.63	76

Source: Ibid., p. 250.

Table 4–7.
General Types of Counseling Situations

Type	Time Lines	Possible Concerns	Possible Counselor Activities
Crisis	immediate	suicidal drug anxiety rejection by lover	personal support direct intervention gather additional support individual counseling or refer to appropriate clinic or agency
Facilitative	varies (short to long term)	job placement academic problems marriage adjustment	individual counseling including: reflection of content and feelings informing interpreting confronting directing activities
Preventive	specific time span (depending on the program)	sex education self- and career awareness drug awareness	information giving referral to relevant programs individual counseling regarding program content and process
Developmental	continuous (over lifespan)	developing positive self-concept in the elementary school mid-career change acceptance of death and dying	aiding values clarification reviewing decision making individual counseling regarding: personal development in conjunction with significant others and environmental placement

Source: **John J. Pietrofesa, Alan Hoffman, Howard H. Splete, and Diana V. Pinto,** *Counseling: Theory, Research and Practice* **(Skoie, Ill.: Rand McNally & Company 1978), p. 21.**

Table 4–7a.
Counselor Activities at Each Level of Intervention

Primary	Secondary	Tertiary
Deliberate psychological education	Crisis counseling (drug & alcohol related, acute emotional upheavals, vocational choice point crisis)	Vocational rehabilitation of emotionally disturbed
Career education		Supportive therapy
Parent education	Marriage & family counseling	
Death education		
Sex education	Sex therapy	
Consultation/supervision	Brief therapy, individual & group	
Paraprofessional training	Developmental counseling	
	Long-term therapy	

Source: **Rodney K. Goodyear, "Counselors as Community Psychologists,"** *Personnel and Guidance Journal,* 54:510–511 (June 1976).

they can feel secure and receive sympathetic attention and counseling assistance. Some of these centers actually provide minimal accommodations where a person can "sleep it off." For the most part, however, they simply provide an opportunity for the individual to face emergency counseling assistance. In many of these centers, record-keeping is at a minimum and clients may not even be required to give their name or other personal data unless they wish.

In a number of more populous communities, various specialized counseling service centers appear also to be on the increase. These centers tend to focus on special clientele, defined either by the nature of the problem, such as alcohol or drug addiction, spouse abuse, marital relations, sexual information; by age classifications, such as the elderly, retired, or youth and young adults; black or special racial populations and, on occasion, by religious denominations. These speciality centers tend to be staffed by a mixture of professionals, paraprofessionals, and volunteers. Facilities are equally diverse. For example, the Norfolk, Virginia Redevelopment and Housing Authority has established a system of community-based counselors who function with aides to assist individuals and families living in eleven public housing parks in that city. These counselors and their aides give support to residents in crisis situations and provide information they need to cope with their problems, including the rules and regulations of the housing authority. Counseling activities tend to focus particularly on strengthening families.[10]

O'Brien and Lewis, in describing their community adolescent self-help

[10] Eugene W. Kelly, Jr., Vera S. Franklin, and Gertrude C. Jackson, "Counseling in Public Housing," *Personnel and Guidance Journal,* **54:**521–523 (June 1976).

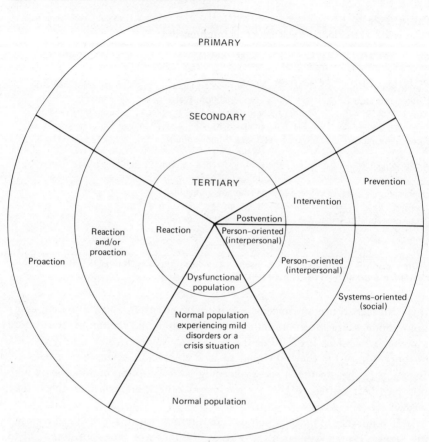

Figure 4–1.
Levels of psychological interventions. *Rodney K. Goodyear, "Counselors as Community Psychologists," Personnel and Guidance Journal, Vol. 54, No. 10 (June 1976), p. 512.*

center, point out that in this alternative to the traditional community mental health agency,

> members work on their own behalf, striving to control their futures and change those conditions that affect their lives. Members also gain a sense of prestige, self-esteem, and responsibility as positions of leadership and control within their organizations are made available to each of them. Self-help centers narrow the social distance between the care giver and the recipient by empowering members and equipping them with the tools and information necessary to meet their needs.[11]

[11] Bernard A. O'Brien and Mel Lewis, "A Community Adolescent Self-Help Center," *Personnel and Guidance Journal*, **54:**213 (Dec. 1975).

Table 4–8.
Do's and Don'ts in Crisis Intervention Counseling

Do's	Don'ts
1. Remain calm and stable. Prepare yourself psychologically for the turbulence of emotion which is soon to flow from the client.	1. Don't try to "cheer up" the client, to tell him that his problems are not as bad as they seem, to reassure him unless he specifically requests these types of interventions (which is, by the way, the exception rather than the rule).
2. Allow the client full opportunity to speak. Attempt to determine the type of crisis, its precipitating forces, and its severity. Interrupt only when it is for the client's benefit, never to relieve yourself of distressing feelings being induced by the client.	2. Don't ask the suicidal client to abandon his plans. Always make such a request a temporary delay.
3. When indicated, ask object-oriented questions. These should, if asked properly, have a calming effect upon the client. If they fail to have such an effect, the counselor should consider the possibility that he is asking ego-oriented questions.	3. Don't attempt to solve the total personality adjustment difficulty. Some counselors make the error of minimizing the crisis itself and attempting to get the client to speak about more "fundamental" things.
4. Deal with the immediate situation rather than its underlying, unconscious causes that may be left for later. "In the crisis period," Brockopp (1973) points out, "the person is open to change; the sooner we can work with him, the more likely we are able to minimize the possible deterioration of the personality and to develop an effective solution which will improve the personality functioning of the individual."	
5. Have readily available local resources to assist the counselor: community, medical, legal, etc.	

Source: **Gary S. Belkin, Practical Counseling in the Schools (Dubuque, Iowa: William C. Brown Company, Publishers, 1975), p. 336.**

In describing the functioning of this particular center, referred to as "the City," they stated that

> The City is run much of the time by student staff volunteers who manage the center; they coordinate activities, engage in crisis counseling, and handle discipline problems and referrals. They have the authority to open or close the center as they deem necessary, and they assist the senior staff in deciding what programs and activities should be initiated and funded.[12]

EMPLOYMENT COUNSELING

In 1933, the Department of Labor established the Employment Security offices that were to provide job placement and attending advising or counseling

[12] Ibid., p. 213.

functions for the unemployed. Counseling was more specifically provided for in the GI Bill of 1944, which provided job counseling for returning veterans from World War II. By the 1960s, the Department of Labor was encouraging the states to upgrade their counselors to the professional or master's degree level of training.

> In the fall of 1970, the Manpower Administration initiated a massive inservice training program for selected employment service personnel. Originally, 88 colleges and universities in 33 states participated in the training program. Approximately 2,500 employment service personnel were initially involved in the training. The training was intended to increase the overall skill level of the trainees in dispensing employability assistance to those persons comprising the client population of the U.S. Public Employment Service. It was assumed by Manpower officials and participating university faculty that training in basic counseling skills and the behavioral sciences would improve the general quality of service rendered the public by employment service workers.[13]

Within the Department of Labor, an employment counselor is defined as one who performs counseling duties and who meets the minimum standards for employment counselor classification.

The Employment service also employs a number of counselor trainees who work under the close supervision of an employment counselor or an employment counseling supervisor. To qualify as a trainee, one must have (1) completed a baccalaureate degree in one of the behavioral or social sciences, such as psychology, education, and sociology, which shall include a minimum of fifteen semester hours (graduate or undergraduate) in counseling-related courses; (2) an expressed interest in becoming an employment counselor; (3) demonstrated the ability to assist individuals in a counseling type of relationship (such as helping individuals to resolve employment or employment-related problems) in such settings as the employment service, a community action agency, vocational rehabilitation agency or schools, and (4) the ability to complete successfully the necessary in-service, on-the-job, and out-service training programs for counselors.[14]

Although the focus of employment counselors, as with other employees of the employment security offices, is appropriate job placement of its clientele, the counselors are expected in the process to counsel clients on personal problems and assist them in developing attitudes, skills, and abilities that will facilitate their employment. Counselors are also involved in data gathering from their clients and in the administration and interpretation of standardized tests. Employment counselors tend to identify with the National Employment

[13] R. J. Phelps, Gary G. Peer, and Richard M. Canada, "Training Employment Service Personnel in Basic Counseling Skills," *Journal of Employment Counseling,* **10:**173–174 (Dec. 1973).
[14] Conversation with Jerry Haner, Counseling Supervisor, Indiana Employment Security Division (Aug. 1978).

Counselors Association (a division of the American Personnel and Guidance Association) as their professional organization. In 1975, this organization issued a position paper on the "Role of the Employment Counselor." Portions of this paper are presented, as follows:

Rationale for Employment Counseling

As with counselors in other work settings, the employment counselor is a member of the counseling profession, differing from other members only in terms of the work setting and the nature of the problems presented by the clientele served. The employment counselor generally assists persons who are faced with an immediate problem related to employment, usually involving job choice, job change, or job adjustment. Since counselees come to the employment counselor's attention as a result of applying for a job, they are often referred to as "applicants." In providing the needed assistance the employment counselor considers factors both within and outside the counselee, such as psychological, physical, and socioeconomic factors that bear on the counselee's current status and that may have some effect on his or her future. Thus the employment counselor is concerned with the individual's potential and actual strengths and weaknesses, and with helping the counselee to understand the physical, mental, and emotional growth processes of individuals, but he or she must also understand these processes to use human service facilities and job opportunities for the benefit of the counselee.

The employment counselor believes that each person should have equal opportunity to develop and use individual talents for the betterment of self and the community, and that this is a developmental, lifelong process in which any number of institutions and other individuals, including the employment counselor, may play significant roles.

The employment counselor believes that work represents a meaningful expression of the individual's self-concept and values, and that individuals have the capacity to change, to grow, and to make intelligent decisions. However, the increasing complexity of the industrialized work world, constantly evolving through technological change, makes it increasingly difficult for the individual, without assistance, to make decisions regarding the choice of an occupation and preparation for it. Through the counseling process, the counselee is helped to achieve better understanding of self and of the occupational world, and to relate individual interests and talents to the demands of various occupational outlets. Thus employment counseling is an important element of the total spectrum of manpower services. For those in need of this service, it becomes an integral component of the placement process and a prerequisite to suitable job placement. Throughout the employment counseling process, the belief in freedom of choice is basic.

The employment counselor believes that there are situations in which active intervention by the counselor, or client advocacy, is an essential additional component of effective counseling. When sucessful individual adjustment is obstructed by environmental factors, and when the counselee is unable to effect needed change, the counselor has an obligation to act on the counselee's behalf within the limits of applicable law, regulation, and policy.[15]

Employment Counselor Competencies

In order to carry out employment counseling responsibilities effectively, the employment counselor must develop the following basic competencies.

Relationship skills. The ability to establish a trusting, open, and useful relationship with each counselee, accurately interpreting feelings as well as verbal and nonverbal expressions, and conveying to the applicant this understanding and whatever pertinent information and assistance is needed.

Individual and group assessment skills. The ability to provide ongoing assessment in individual and group settings involving the appraisal and measurement of the counselee's needs, characteristics, potentialities, individual differences, and self-appraisal.

Group counseling. The ability to apply basic principles of group dynamics and leadership roles in a continuous and meaningful manner to assist group members to understand their problems and take positive steps toward resolving them.

Development and use of career-related information. The ability to develop and use educational, occupational, and labor market information to assist counselees in making decisions and formulating occupational plans.

Occupational plan development and implementation. The ability to assist the counselee in developing and implementing a suitable employability plan that helps move the jobseeker from current status through any needed employability-improvement services, including training and related supportive services, into a suitable job.

Placement skills. The ability to ascertain and to communicate understanding of employers' personnel needs, to make effective job development contacts, and to assist the counselee in presentation of qualifications in relation to the employer's needs.

Community relations skills. The ability, based on extensive knowledge of the important service delivery systems in the community, to assist counselees in obtaining the services needed.

Work load management and intra-office relationships skills. The ability to coordinate the various aspects of the total counseling program in the employing agency, resulting in a continuous and meaningful sequence of services to counselees, agency staff, and the community.

---

[15] National Employment Counselors Association, "Role of the Employment Counselor," *Journal of Employment Counseling,* **12:**148–149 (Dec. 1975).

Professional development skills. The ability, based on interest in furthering professional development, to engage in activities that promote such development individually and within the profession, and to demonstrate by example the standards and performance expected of a professional employment counselor.[16]

CORRECTIONAL COUNSELING

Practitioners of correctional counseling are employed in various law enforcement settings, ranging from those involved with first-time juvenile probationary offenders to individuals incarcerated in penal institutions. Counselors in these settings usually have training backgrounds in counseling, psychology, sociology, and/or forensic studies. Their duties include counseling and interviewing, the use of various analytical techniques, including the use of standardized testing, referrals, parole recommendations, and placement. In some juvenile institutional settings, counselors may be employed as "live in advisors." Counselors working with youthful juvenile offenders work closely with police officers and other juvenile authorities. For example, Collingwood, Williams, and Douds describe two major goals of such a program in Dallas, Texas, as (1) diverting juveniles from the juvenile justice system and (2) reducing re-arrests/recidivism.[17]

In this program, police officers as well as counselors were used in helping roles, with both working in an integrative manner within the department.

The model adopted to implement the program was Carkhuff's (1971) Human Resource Development (HRD) model, which emphasizes the physical, intellectual, and emotional skills of helper and helpee. The model was applied to the selection and training of police and counseling staff and to the training-as-treatment methods employed with the juvenile offenders.[18]

Youths referred to the counseling unit were able to significantly increase their physical, intellectual, and emotional skills while in the program. Also, they appeared able to apply the skill improvement to improved functioning in certain outcome areas.[19]

Examples of counselors functioning in juvenile correctional institutions may be found in the differential treatment approach of the Kennedy Youth Center of Morgantown, West Virginia, and the Indiana Boys' School, Plainfield, Indiana. These and other similar institutions utilize the differential treat-

---

[16] Ibid., pp. 152–153.
[17] Thomas R. Collingwood, Hadley Williams, and Alex Douds, "An HRD Approach to Police Diversion for Juvenile Offenders," *Personnel and Guidance Journal,* **54:**435–436 (Apr. 1976).
[18] Ibid., p. 435.
[19] Ibid., p. 436.

ment approach, which seeks to take into account individual differences in matching inmates with counseling staff on the basis of personality or behavioral categories. In other correctional settings, counselors function as key agents in converting closed, traditional punitive systems into those that are more positive, helping, and rehabilitative. In these settings, the emphasis is on the formation of positive interpersonal climates and open lines of communication among the various members of the prison community, including inmates and correctional officers, or guards. An example of such an activity is described in Wittmer, Lanier, and Parker's article, in which prison officers (guards) in Florida participated in a race relations training program with the emphasis on communications.[20]

REHABILITATION COUNSELING

History reflects the admiration that society has always held for those who have overcome physical handicaps to achieve notable success. The man (Franklin D. Roosevelt) who was paralyzed by polio in both legs at thirty-nine, but later became the President and a wartime world leader; the girl (Helen Keller) who was deaf and blind from the age of two, but became a successful author and lecturer; or the deaf musician (Ludwig van Beethoven), and the amputee actress (Sarah Bernhardt)—to name but a few—are examples of achievement over physical adversity. Clifford Beers, mentioned in Chapter 1, is an example of individual triumph over mental illness. The achievements of these and others, despite their handicaps, were notable, but history has failed to record the tragic losses in human potential that were allowed to occur because of lack of attention, other than medical, for the disabled. Since World War II, however, the expansion of rehabilitation counseling into public agencies has provided a dramatic increase in opportunities for the handicapped to receive special counseling assistance in overcoming their disabilities.

Rehabilitation counselors work with disabled clients in overcoming deficits in their skills. Rehabilitation counselors may work with a special type of client such as the deaf, blind, the mentally ill, or the physically handicapped or, in some settings, the rehabilitation counselor may deal with all of these plus other types of handicapped and disabled as well. The rehabilitation counselor's work is often done in close cooperation with physicians and/or psychiatrists. In this regard, it is noted that although the counselor needs

to take into account what goes on in psychotherapy and how the client's illness, personality problems, and pathological family relationships affect his ability to function and his capacity to work, the rehabilitation counselor, in his interaction with a client, is committed to the *now* and *from*

---

[20] Joe Wittmer, James E. Lanier, and Max Parker, "Race Relations Training with Correctional Officers," *Personnel and Guidance Journal*, **54**:302–306 (Feb. 1976).

here on and to working to strengthen the healthy portion of the client's ego. The counselor needs to see the client as he is functioning now in his environment, and where modification can help him to get where he is or should be going vocationally.[21]

His/her role is a complex one in which he/she provides a broad range of psychological and career-oriented services and works with and often coordinates the efforts of community agencies in his/her client's behalf.

A major role which most definitely distinguishes rehabilitation counselors from workers in other helping professions is that of being a resource person. The counselor must have a wide knowledge of the occupations, including an intimate knowledge of how and under what circumstances they are practiced. Counselors must be aware of groupings of jobs so that skills which are transferable can be utilized in vocational planning. Further, the counselor develops an in-depth working knowledge of the particular personality traits that are required or contraindicated for specific jobs, so that he can help his client make an appropriate choice. The counselor must bring together the individual needs of the client and all the reasonable possibilities open to him.[22]

The rehabilitation counselor as a resource person also seeks to encourage the optimum adjustment and development of the handicapped.

In his role as resource person, the counselor must be familiar with nearby schools and training institutions and be able to evaluate their usefulness to particular clients. Further, he needs to be aware of funding sources of all kinds so that training is available to those who cannot finance it themselves.

Beyond this, a counselor must keep up with the state of the labor market in his locale so that clients are not preparing for unmarketable or outmoded occupations. He must assess clients' past work experiences to find those which are particularly marketable now. The search can be as exciting as a detective story, depending upon the attitude and creativity of the counselor.

When clients are ready for employment, the counselor becomes a teacher. He helps clients to learn the most effective way of seeking a job. He shows them how to fill out applications, how to enhance their chances of passing entry tests, how to prepare a resume, if one is necessary, and how to behave in employment interviews to maximize their chances of success with emphasis on alternate behaviors in differing circumstances.[23]

[21] H. Richard Lamb and Associates. *Rehabilitation in Community Mental Health* (San Francisco: Jossey, Bass, 1971), p. 29.
[22] Ibid., p. 41.
[23] Ibid., pp. 42–43.

Although rehabilitation counseling was originally provided by private services, since World War II the field has been largely preempted by the Veterans Administration and by state departments of vocational rehabilitation, the latter assisted by the Vocational Rehabilitation Administration in the Department of Health, Education and Welfare. Most of the rehabilitation counseling within the Veterans Administration is conducted by counseling psychologists and within the state agencies by rehabilitation counselors.[24]

MARRIAGE AND FAMILY COUNSELING

Although the marriage vows read "until death us do part," the high divorce rate in this country in recent decades indicates that thousands of couples have decided they cannot wait until their entry into eternity to part. In addition, thousands of other couples suffer through phases of their marriages or seek adjustment to marriage difficulties by means other than separation or divorce. Although not based on empirical studies, the report by the popular advice columnist Ann Landers that the top four on her readers' ten most common problems concern marriage and family is symptomatic of the need. She described these as:

1. Sexual problems between husband and wife: "I'm not getting enough" or "I'm getting too much" or "He's impotent" or "She's frigid."
2. Cheating spouses: Men used to be the cheaters nine times out of ten. Now it's almost 50–50.
3. Problems with in-laws: "They are too demanding of our time." "They interfere." "They spoil our children."
4. Teenagers complaining about parents who don't understand them: "They're living in the olden days" or "They never talk to us about anything that matters."[25]

An outgrowth of the increased recognition of the extent of marital problems has been the development of a specialty area within the field of marriage counseling. This group, represented by the American Association of Marriage Counselors, includes memberships from diverse professional preparation backgrounds, including psychiatrists, psychologists, law, and the ministry. Another representative organization of this group is the National Council on Family Relations.

Marriage counseling deals primarily with a disordered relationship between two persons. The husband and wife must not, of course, be ignored

[24] Edwin C. Lewis, *The Psychology of Counseling* (New York: Holt, Rinehart and Winston, 1970), p. 231.
[25] David Wallechinsky, Irving Wallace, and Amy Wallace, "Ann Landers' Readers' 10 Most Common Problems," in *The Book of Lists* (New York: Bantam Books, Inc., 1978), p. 296.

as individuals, but their interaction is of chief concern to the marriage counselor. If it becomes evident that the root of the difficulty lies in adjustment problems of one or both of the parties, the emphasis shifts to them as individuals, and the concern for the relationship is temporarily abandoned.

If either of the individuals appears to have deep-seated emotional problems which are contributing to the marital disruption, he will generally be advised to seek individual psychotherapy. Some marriage counselors undertake this responsibility themselves, but most prefer to refer the client elsewhere. If, at a later time, marriage counseling for the couple seems warranted, it can be resumed. By the same token, the marriage counselor should feel free to refer to other professionals, such as a lawyer or physician, when their specialized knowledge may be of value to his clients.[26]

The goal of marriage counseling is not, as many persons would suppose, the preservation of the marriage. As with any counseling, the client must be free to make his own decisions; it is the counselor's responsibility to help him think things through rationally and thoroughly, so that he can live with the decision he makes.[27]

In states that have enacted laws regulating the practice of marriage and family counseling, a doctorate plus appropriate experience is most frequently required for licensure in this area.

PASTORAL COUNSELING

From the standpoint of sheer numbers and geographic coverage, pastoral counseling provides a significant mental health resource. Not only are the clergy generally available to listen to the concerns and personal problems of their parishioners, but it appears that they are frequently the first source to which people in trouble turn. For example, the study illustrated in Table 4–9 indicates that as many as 42 per cent of the population may consider their clergyman as their first choice for mental health assistance. In recognition of the mental health function of the clergy, many theological training programs include courses in pastoral counseling, related psychology, and general counseling subjects. Special programs have also been developed in clinical pastoral education for theology students and clergymen desirous of further training. Although many of these specialized programs are comparatively short-term, others provide intensive training in clinical settings. Additionally, clergymen are increasingly enrolling in regular preparation programs in counselor education.

---

[26] Lewis, op. cit., p. 234.
[27] Ibid., p. 235.

Table 4–9.
Where People Go for Help

Of the 2,460 people interviewed in a national survey, 345 had sought professional help for a personal problem. Following are the sources of help and the percentage of time each source was sought. Because some respondents gave more than one reply, the total comes to more than 100 per cent.

Source of Help	Per Cent
Clergyman	42
Doctor	29
Psychiatrist (or psychologist): private practitioner or not ascertained whether private or institutional	12
Psychiatrist (or psychologist) in clinic, hospital, other agency; mental hospital	6
Marriage counselor; marriage clinic	3
Other private practitioners or social agencies for handling psychological problems	10
Social service agencies for handling nonpsychological problems (e.g., financial problems)	3
Lawyer	6
Other	11

Source: G. Gurin, J. Veroff, and S. Feld, *Americans View Their Mental Health* (New York: Basic Books, Inc., Publishers, 1960), p. 307.

ARMED SERVICES COUNSELORS

The armed services provide counseling for both the mental health and career development concerns of its members. These services are provided by trained counselors who are usually, but not always, members of the armed services. The counselor's functions are often to organize and interpret the military and civilian experience-education backgrounds of service personnel and relate them to service career opportunities. The counselor also seeks to help service personnel clearly understand the steps necessary to achieve their maximum career potential. Service counselors also aid in the transition and placement of service personnel from military to civilian careers.

PRIVATE PRACTICE

Increasing numbers of counselors, in recent years, have entered private practice. The private practitioner is often associated with teams or centers, but in many instances they may decide to "go it alone." Kilgore notes that

In thinking about establishing and maintaining a private practice, one should consider the kind of person who might do well in such an endeavor. Since the term *private practice* implies a kind of independence, the person who goes into this field must be willing to some extent to work alone and to accept the successes or failures of his own efforts. Undoubtedly, he/she will be helped by sufficient aggressiveness and organizational compulsiveness to enable him/her to stay with the difficult tasks of the early days of establishing a practice. Just as the private practitioner must be willing and able to work alone, he/she must be able to recognize his/her limitations and be willing to make referrals whenever he/she is unable to handle a case.

A private practitioner also must have a degree of accessibility to the community at large. Any counselor, and the private practitioner in particular, must recognize that the style of his/her practice reflects his/her own concepts of family living and significant relationships to the community. How he/she relates to people in the organization in which he/she participates, and the community leadership that he/she provides will model the openness and freedom that he/she helps others find in therapy. The therapist who is secure in personal as well as in counseling settings will be likely to help other people discover security.[28]

He also points out that "Private practice is a business. This fact should be understood by the practitioner and clearly communicated to consumers of his/her services. Efficient, businesslike, and professional procedures should be used in dealing with persons who seek one's services."[29]

Although most private practitioners deal with individual clients, some may also utilize counseling groups. Another area of private practice to which increasing numbers of counselors are being attracted is the private consulting firm. These firms have more of a "business world" orientation, usually specializing in the analysis and/or solution of company personnel problems and needs. These private consulting firms often conduct training programs as well, dealing with such topics as communications and human relationship skills, supervision techniques, and career planning.

SUMMARY

So you have a problem, and you need to see a counselor, but you're no longer in school and besides, your old school counselor is too busy with the current student body. So what are your options? This chapter has suggested a number of these opportunities both for employment as counselors and assistance for clients in nonschool settings.

Community mental health agencies are perhaps the most versatile in terms of their readiness to deal with a wide range of developmental as well as remedial needs. Too, the staffing of these agencies is usually more diverse,

[28] James E. Kilgore, "Establishing and Maintaining a Private Practice,' *Journal of Marriage and Family Counseling,* **1**:147 (Apr. 1975).
[29] Ibid., p. 146.

often including professionals trained in medicine as well as psychology. If one is seeking less conventional settings, many communities have crisis centers, "hot line" counseling, open-door agencies, and other nontraditional approaches to providing mental health services.

If your problem is one of career decision making or job placement, you might want to seek the assistance of a government employment office counselor (unlike private employment agencies, they charge no fees and are more likely to employ trained counselors).

Of course, if you are confined to a correctional institution, your only option may be your institutional counselor. Unfortunately, in many such institutions counseling personnel may not be employed.

For assistance in overcoming a physical or mental handicap, rehabilitation counselors can be a valuable resource because they have received special training to work with the developmental needs of the handicapped. Veterans can seek such assistance through the Veterans Administration, of course, and other "rehab" counselors may be found in community and other governmental agencies, hospitals, and a small number in private practice.

If your problem is marriage- or family-related, there can be help for you too. Marriage and family counseling is a growing area of specialization. Like many of your friends and neighbors, you may turn to your family clergyman. The likelihood is increasing that your minister, priest, or rabbi will have received some counseling preparation in his/her ministerial studies, or will have some assistant specially trained to provide counseling services. Another source of counseling assistance, if you are by chance a member of the armed services, would be your service counselor. A final option, one that would probably cost you more dollars, is to seek out a counselor in private practice. Large population centers, university-oriented communities, and upper socioeconomic suburbs are the more likely habitats of the private practitioner. Obviously, evidence of appropriate training, such as licensure, is important.

Nonstandardized Techniques for Human Assessment 5

INTRODUCTION

On occasion, one is called upon to explain, sometimes even justify, why one of our close friends "behaves or acts the way he or she does." The reply may, at least subconsciously, draw upon one's knowledge of our friend's home and family background, the environment in which he or she grew up and/or now lives, the cultural background, the physical and psychological characteristics, as we perceive them, or the experiences of the friend. In these instances, a wealth of background information provides insights into the behavior of those we know well. Nor is this knowledge limited by our own particular occupation or discipline. Some of what we know might be classified as cultural or anthropological, some as environmental or sociological, other as psychological.

In a similar vein, most of us feel more confident with our family physician who has looked after our ailments for years—who knows us from a broader standpoint than what we are as a physical specimen—who understands us totally. Something that an equally competent, but "newcomer" physician could not duplicate.

In the world of sporting competitions there are frequent references to "psyching out the opponent." This "psyching out" of the opposition is an indication of intent to go beyond understanding the athletic skills of the opponent appropriate to the contest, a suggestion that "the better we know the competition, the better we can play them."

These examples suggest the theme of this chapter, namely, that by increasing and broadening our understanding of our client population, we increase the probability of providing effective counseling and guidance services to meet their needs. In the paragraphs that immediately follow, interdisciplinary concepts of human assessment are presented, followed by some suggested guidelines or principles of human assessment. This chapter then focuses on nonstandardized techniques commonly employed for individual analysis by counselors in various settings. It should be noted that standardized techniques, such as psychological testing, are those with a precise and fixed format, set of procedures, and method of scoring that enable the instrument to be utilized for the same purpose in a variety of settings and times. Standardization suggests uniformity and objectivity. Nonstandardization suggests a broader, variable, and more subjective approach to data gathering and interpretation for human assessment.

CONCEPTS OF HUMAN ASSESSMENT

The most intelligent, yet most complicated and difficult to understand living organism known to civilization today is the human being. When we place these complicated and often changing human beings in their environment, a rapidly changing and complex society, we cannot help but recognize the enormity of the task of those who seek to understand, predict, and assist the development of human behavior. In undertaking this responsibility, we are quick to recognize that no one discipline or area of expertise alone possesses the theoretical or technical basis for an understanding of "modern people in modern society." To this end, then, those who study human behavior—whether from an individual or societal viewpoint, whether from the viewpoint of an anthropologist, sociologist, or psychologist, whether from the viewpoint of an American, Japanese or German—must be willing to both learn and share with those who have this common interest. It is in this context that we suggest that counselors, regardless of the setting in which they may function, can better understand the behavior of their clients through insights that may be gained through the study of behavior in the context of other disciplines and cultures. The following is not intended to substitute for such study, but only to briefly examine these other perspectives and their implications for counselors.

Sociology

Sociology is a social science and a behavioral science that focuses on the study of individuals and groups in society and how they behave and interact with one another. The science of sociology contributes to an understanding of the social networks and their impact on individuals, individual roles, and relationships within those networks. Further, sociology is concerned with the study of socialization agents or institutions. These institutions, such as the family, church, school, and government, assume the responsibility of teaching individuals within that environment what constitutes normal and abnormal behavior for the society. These patterns of normal and abnormal behavior are further shaped by customs, folkways, mores, and laws. Sociology also helps understanding of behavior that deviates from the norms of a group or society. The study of social deviance helps in understanding behaviors, including alcoholism and crime, that are defined as social problems. Such study also helps us to recognize that what is considered "normal" behavior in one group may be defined as deviant behavior in another group. Further, study in this area can help the counselor recognize the influence of social controls or pressures on the behavior of clients, students, and others. For counselors, it is also important to keep in mind that human beings are social beings, affected by the society of which they are members and, at the same time, expected to contribute to that society.

Counselors will find sociological understandings contribute to their understanding of the groups and structures within the society of which they are a part. It is particularly important to understand the significance of groupings and roles of clients, the influences on client behavior of the various groups of which he/she is a member, the role and relationships that are most significant to the client, and the restriction on client's behavior and behavior change of the social systems of which he/she is a part. For the counselor, it is important to understand the various roles of individuals and the behavior that occurs or is anticipated as a result of these roles. That also includes an understanding of the significance of status, already noted in many psychological studies. Some suggest that perhaps there has never been a more status-conscious society than our own. Sociologists help us understand status and its implications through the study of social stratification. Such study helps us understand social classes, social mobilities, social structures and, in general, the ranking of social positions within society.

The sociologist, like the psychologist, is also concerned with the study of the development of the individual's self-concept. Sociological study focuses upon self-concept development through the socialization process and its influence by others. It is especially important for counselors to recognize the impact of "significant others" and reference groups (both within the domain of sociological study) on the development of an individual's self-concept.

Who are the individuals whose judgments, imagined or otherwise, are significant to one's self-concept, and what are the groups that one uses to develop and test attitudes, beliefs, and so forth.

Anthropology

Anthropology is the study of the culture of a society and the characteristics of its social behavior. It involves the recording, describing, and analyzing of the cultures of humankind throughout the world and throughout history. In these studies, anthropology identifies the traditions, norms, patterns of learning, coping styles, and other behaviors, both from a current and an historical perspective. Among the understandings that the study of anthropology can provide for counselors are (1) recognizing that different cultures have different concepts; (2) the importance of the cultural background of the client; (3) the importance of the cultural background of the counselor; and (4) the significance of recognizing subcultures within the larger societal or cultural context. The application aspects of anthropology are suggested by James Clifton when he notes that "a description of culture is a statement of what one has to know in order to understand events in a community as its members understand them and to conduct oneself in a way that they will accept as meeting their standards for themselves."[1]

In this context, culture is viewed as the beliefs and practices of people within a society, including guidelines for their behavior in given situations (such as religious ceremonies, funerals, weddings, the reaching of puberty, maturity, and so forth). Human development is dependent upon environmental characteristics. The characteristics of the environment that have been developed by the past inhabitants of the environment comprise the culture with which the individual interacts. That culture provides the individual with his/her initial values, behavioral guidelines, and expectancies for the future. As just noted, the self-concept is central to the study of personality and behavior by psychologists and sociologists, and the study of anthropology contributes through an understanding of the nature of self as culturally defined. We also view ourselves as influenced by the perspective we have of self in relation to culture. The study of anthropology alerts us to the fact that personality, as it develops, seeks to prepare the individual for living in his or her culture and, by the same token, that a culture only functions through the personalities of those who comprise it, thus enabling predictions regarding overt behavior on the basis of a knowledge or a culture and its traditions.

Today, we are aware that different subcultures often have different values and life-styles, facts of which counselors must be aware. For example, coun-

[1] James A. Clifton, Ed. *Applied Anthropology: Readings into the Uses of the Science of Man* (Boston: Houghton Mifflin Company, 1970), p. 221.

selors should be able to understand the life-styles and values of such populations as Blacks, Indians, Orientals, Hispanics, Jewish, Polish, and others. It is not only helpful to be able to function free of ignorance in helping relationships with clients from various backgrounds, but also to interact without prejudice and bias.

Economics

Economics is a science that studies human production, consumption, and distribution. Its significance in the creation of status, influence, and economic influences on our wants shapes many of our behaviors.

Economics is another social science concerned with individual behavior and human relationships. The economist's concern is with people living in various types of economic systems. Because the economic environment in which people live is so closely interwoven with nearly every activity in which counselors engage, we cannot be uninvolved in this area.

C. Gilbert Wrenn noted the importance of economic learnings by counselors when he commented that "the school counselor cannot afford to be a graduate student in psychology and a second-grader in economics."[2] For the counselor, understandings of the influences on career choices of economic systems and theories can be meaningful. In addition, the impact of economic systems on human behavior should not go unnoticed by counselors who propose to assess human behavior. The influence of the socioeconomic level of the home on the self-concept of the developing child is also of concern to the counselor.

Political Science

Political science is a discipline that is more frequently examined by accident than by deliberate attempt in seeking to broaden our understandings of individual behavior. However, as Wasky noted,

> the focus of the behavioral approach on the individual is not sufficient; how individual decisions are aggregated is also vital, because individual preferences cannot themselves explain collective decisions. In explaining the individual we must turn to the social setting in which he is found; perhaps it is more accurate to talk of a focus on "the individual in his social environment," as when social psychologists talk of "personality in culture," not personality and culture.[3]

[2] C. Gilbert Wrenn, *The Counselor in a Changing World* (Washington, D.C.: American Personnel and Guidance Association, 1962), p. 42.
[3] Stephen L. Wasky, *Political Science—the Discipline and Its Dimensions* (New York: Charles Scribner's Sons, 1970), p. 45.

Interdisciplinary Implications for Counselors

The preceding sections present a brief overview of perspectives from other disciplines. From these perspectives, implications can be drawn that have relevance to counselors and their functioning in a variety of settings, as follows:

1. Counselors must reflect a greater awareness of the various cultures that may be represented within the client population they are hoping to serve.
2. To be effective and relevant, counselors must increase their understandings of the language that is vital in communicating with different cultures, which results from living in one culture and living or learning in another; role expectancies of cultures; cultural biases in schools and other basic institutions, which create tensions, hostilities, and distrust among many subcultures.
3. Counselors must have an understanding of the social structures of the communities and institutions within which they function. They must also recognize the impacts of these and other social structures on how the individual views himself/herself, his/her work, education, and other experiences.
4. Counselors should acquire a deeper understanding of the various societal influences on behavior, growth, and development of the individual, based on an interdisciplinary approach.
5. In schools, counselors must function more effectively as consultants to faculty, staff, and parents. In this capacity, the counselor has the opportunity to interpret the social and cultural characteristics of students and their implications for the educational program.

Guidelines for Human Assessment

As we move toward an examination of specific tools and techniques available to counselors for assessing human characteristics, it is important next to recognize some basic principles or guidelines. These guidelines provide a framework for effectively and professionally functioning in the sometimes delicate task of individual assessment.

1. Each individual human being is unique and this uniqueness is to be valued. Although the principle of individual differences has been eulogized throughout educational and societal circles the better part of this century, in practice, constant pressures encourage conformity and standardization. Counselors will not enlarge this gap between principle and practice but will stress the principle that assessment is a means of increasing understanding of the uniqueness of the individual, a uniqueness that sets one apart from all other individuals, that provides each person with the basis for his/her own personal worth. That uniqueness is to be valued, not standardized.

2. Variations exist within individuals. Each individual is unique as well as distinct from others. This principle notes that individual assessment seeks to identify, for example, the special talents, skills, and interests of the individual and, at the same time, forestall tendencies to generalize from a single or several characteristics of the individual, such as, "anyone who excels in math can excel in anything," or "you give me an 'all-American' in one sport and I'll make them 'all-American' in another." Nor do we overlook the shortcomings. Although the emphasis on assessment is on the strengths and positive attributes of the individual, all of us have our weaknesses—shortcomings which we must recognize if we are to overcome, bypass, or compensate for them.

3. Human assessment presumes the direct participation of the individual in his/her own assessment. For human assessment to be as meaningful and accurate as possible, the individual must be willingly and directly involved. This involvement includes input by the client, feedback, clarification, and interpretation, as appropriate, by both the client and counselor, and evaluation by the client. This principle presumes more than the client's one-way feeding in of data, such as taking a standardized test or completing a questionnaire. It assumes his/her right to interpretation and response to that interpretation. It presumes the client's right to clarify and expand his/her response and, as others come to know the client better, to gain better understandings of himself/herself as well.

4. Accurate human assessment is limited by instruments and personnel. The effective utilization of assessment techniques is dependent upon a recognition of the limitations of instruments and personnel as well as acceptance of their potential. These limitations begin with the human element—ourselves—our knowledge and skill in the techniques we would utilize. Counselors should not under any circumstances utilize assessment techniques, including standardized tests, in which they have not been thoroughly trained. Additionally, the limitations of clients in responding to individual items as well as instruments must be taken into consideration. These limitations may include unwillingness as well as inability to respond. In addition to these human elements, there are the limitations of the instruments themselves to consider. These include an awareness of the particular shortcomings unique to a given instrument or technique and the general recognition that any of these provide at best only a "sample," only clues, not absolutes, and results that may vary among similar instruments and techniques.

5. Human assessment accepts the positive. A goal of human resource assessment is the identification of the potential of each individual. It is a positive process which, as noted earlier, seeks to identify the unique worth of each individual. Assessment can lead to the identification of worthwhile goals and positive planning. It should be a process clothed in optimism rather than, as so often is the case, fear of outcomes and predictions of doom. The counselor's own attitude becomes important in the establishment of the positive environment for assessment and in utilization of results for the best interests of clients.

6. *Human assessment follows established professional guidelines.* It is important for counselors, and all other helping professionals who utilize human assessment techniques, to be aware of the relevant ethical guidelines established by their professional organizations. These guidelines are aimed at protecting both the client and the professional practitioner. Ethical standards for counselors, which address assessment as well as other aspects of practice, are presented in Appendix F.

DOING WHAT COMES NATURALLY—OBSERVATION

On any given day most of us are the subjects of informal analysis by others, and vice versa. These "analysts" are not among the handful of psychiatrists, psychologists, or counselors with whom we may be acquainted, but are amateurs doing what comes naturally—observing their fellow human beings, both friend and stranger, and drawing some conclusions about the kind of persons they are, based on what they observe. Depending on what we see and how we interpret it, we may variously categorize individuals as executive types, models, drifters, untrustworthy, fun-loving, and so on. Further, we are often prone to defend or "validate" our observations by noting, "I knew there was something that just didn't look right about him," or "You could tell he was a real athlete by the way he walked," and, on other occasions, calling upon old clichés (many of which are sexist) as backup evidence, such as, "just another dumb blonde" or "watch out for those fiery redheads."

When we make observations "au naturel," we are, in effect, studying behavior as it is occurring in "real life." Although we must recognize—and we will help you to do this—the weaknesses of the uncontrolled observation method, we must at the same time recognize that many important questions about an individual's natural social behavior cannot be determined through a controlled or clinical approach, much less be measured by standardized instruments. Ecological psychologists, such as Barker, have encouraged the study of behavior "intact" within the natural setting of the individual being observed.

It is therefore appropriate as we begin an examination of the various techniques counselors use for gaining a better understanding of their clients that we begin with the most natural and popular of all these techniques—observation. As previously noted, we all employ this technique to varying degrees in drawing conclusions about others, but this is not to suggest that all observations are equally useful for human assessment. As a basis for recognizing the differing levels at which observation may take place, we suggest the following:

Levels of Observation

First Level: Casual Information Observation.   The daily, unstructured and usually unplanned observations that provide casual impressions; engaged in daily by nearly everyone. No training or instrumentation expected or required.

Second Level: Guided Observation.   Planned, directed observations for a purpose. Observation at this level is usually facilitated by simple instruments such as checklists and rating scales. The highest level used in most school counseling and guidance programs. Some training desired.

Third Level: Clinical Level.   Observations, often prolonged, and frequently with controlled conditions. Sophisticated techniques and instruments utilized with training, usually at a doctoral level.

Common Weaknesses of Observation

Because observation is a technique we all use and use frequently, it is only natural that we assume we are pretty accurate in our observations. However, that is a misleading assumption. Observation can be one of the most abused techniques in human assessment. Let us therefore proceed to examine some of these abuses or common weaknesses, followed by suggestions for increasing the effectiveness of this valuable assessment technique.

One of the popular questions on the written examinations for drivers' licenses in many states is to ask the applicant to identify, by shape only, the meaning of the various traffic signs. Perhaps you would like to pause and test your recall of these signs, which all of us see each day in our driving:

Now compare your responses to the following answers: stop, yield, warning, information, railroad. How did you do? For many at least, this points up one of the glaring weaknesses in undirected observation as follows:

1. Casual observations do not lend themselves to consistent accurate recall.

Envision yourself on the witness stand in the classical courtroom scene where you are matching wits with the prosecuting attorney. In his/her best "you are guilty" voice, the prosecutor asks, "who were the first three people you observed on the morning of October 13th a year ago?" Some witnesses might have their recall saved by habit (the wife and kids) or a special event (the minister, my best man, or my future father-in-law), but most would have difficulty recalling with accuracy and certainty the first three people they observed on "that fateful day" and even more difficulty in accurately describing what they were wearing. Although most of us have confidence in our ability to accurately recall what we have observed in the past, courtroom testimony, witnesses to accidents, observers of historical or sensational events, and even news reporters are so frequently found to be in error as to definitely suggest that we are not so accurate in our recall of the past, especially the details, as we often assume. Another weakness of undirected observations, then, would be stated as follows:

> 2. Complete and accurate recall of undirected or casual observations tends to decrease with the passage of time.

Now let us involve you in another situation. Assume that you are a devout sports fan and supporter of a favorite team. Your team is involved in a close game in the closing minutes when an official calls a penalty that could conceivably cost your team the game. Regardless of how flagrant the offense or the call, it would be highly predictable that you, and those supporting your team, would have "observed" the call differently than did the officials and the supporters of the other team. It would be clear to an impartial witness that different observers were viewing the same situation differently. Similar illustrations may occur when two different observers describe the same western desert scene as "a beautiful blending by nature of sand, greenery, and beautiful hills" and "a wasteland of sand and drab plants running into bleak mountains." All of us have experienced the discrepancies that often occur as someone describes a boyfriend or girlfriend and as that same individual appears to us. The point is that individuals differ in how they view the same event, person, or place, and also in the details they observe. We would note this as another weakness in casual and informal observations for assessment purposes:

> 3. Similar observations will be viewed differently as each individual has his/her own unique frame of reference for interpreting what he/she sees.

These and other shortcomings suggest that undirected and casual observations of our clients may result in incomplete, misleading, or erroneous assessments. The values and opportunities of observation in client analysis are recognized, but it is apparent that some guidelines and instruments must be developed for increasing the accuracy and effectiveness of this technique. Here are some guiding principles for client analysis through observation, followed by a discussion of some useful instruments for reporting and recording our observations of others.

Guidelines for Client Analysis Through Observation

1. Observe one client at a time.

Observation for individual analysis is just that; it focuses on the individual. We are intent on noticing every observable detail of client behavior that may be meaningful in the counseling context. This is just as desirable an objective for observations of individuals in external group settings as in the more restricted setting of the counseling office.

2. Have specific criteria for making observations.

We observe our clients for a purpose. We are observing for characteristics of the individual appropriate to this purpose. These provide a basis for the identification of specific criteria which in effect tell us "what to look for." For example, if we are observing a young person for the purpose of determining his/her relationship with adults, we might decide that two criteria or characteristics of this relationship that we would specifically observe would be interactions with teachers and interactions with parents. Of course, it is important that the criteria we utilize are appropriate to our observational objectives.

3. Observations should be made over a period of time.

Although there is no specific time span formula for conducting observations, they should take place over a long enough period of time with sufficient frequencies to establish the reliability of our observation. A single sample of behavior is seldom enough for us to say with certainty that this is characteristic of the individual. An illustration of this principle is to recall how your later impressions of the individuals often differ from your first impressions, once you have had the opportunity to observe them over a period of time. Too, although concentrated periods of observation may be appropriate, the amount of observational time should not be confused with the span of time over which observations take place.

4. The client should be observed in differing and natural situations.

Natural behavior is most likely to occur in natural situations. Although these situations vary somewhat among individuals, for most youth, the school, home, neighborhood, and favorite recreational locales will be natural; with adults, the place one works will replace the school. Even within these natural settings, individuals will behave differently but naturally in different locales. For example, a pupil may behave differently within the school in the classroom, the cafeteria, the gym, the hallways, and on the playground.

If possible, therefore, the client should be observed in those settings and situations that are typical for him/her. Furthermore, this means a reasonable variety of those settings. For example, the school-aged youth may exhibit different behavior in one class at school than in others, and exhibit completely different behavior in social-recreational settings. An adult may behave differently on the job than at home and differently again in other social settings. Observing in these different settings may help us determine if some behaviors are limited to or conditioned by specific environments or situations.

5. Observe the client in the context of the total situation.

In observation for human analysis, it is important to avoid a "tunnel vision" approach, or one in which we are so visually intent on observing just the client that we may miss noting those interactions and other factors in the setting that cause the individual to behave the way he/she does. An example might be a classroom situation in which we observe that at the conclusion of nearly every math class, Nancy always leaves in tears, but we fail to observe that her classroom "neighbors" Joe and Jay appear to tease her throughout the class every day. We have observed the results but not the cause.

6. Data from observations should be integrated with other data.

In individual analysis it is important to bring together all that we know about our client. Because we are seeking to see the individual as a whole person, we would combine the impressions we gained from our observations with all other pertinent information available to us. The case study technique, utilized by most helping professionals, illustrates this point of integrating and relating data prior to interpretation.

7. Observations should be made under favorable conditions.

Anyone who has tried to witness a parade three rows back or watch a key play at a game when the crowd jumps up in front can bear witness to the importance of favorable conditions for making observations. In planned observation it is desirable that we are in a position to clearly view what we are planning to report. Ideally, we should be able to conduct our observation for a sufficient period of time without either obstructions or distractions. There are also attitudinal considerations in creating favorable conditions for observation. These include an approach that is free from bias towards the client, any projections of expected behavior, or the permitting of one trait to predict another. It is just as important to have a clear psychological viewing point as a physical viewing point for observation for individual analysis. We should also be alert to another form of bias which may occur when the individual being observed modifies his/her behavior as a result of being aware that he/she is under observation.

It has been said, "Anticipation is a wonderful thing. It often ensures that we will see what we want to see whether it is there or not."

OBSERVATION INSTRUMENTS

A variety of instruments are available to counselors for use in recording their observations. Most are designed to eliminate one or more of the common weaknesses of undirected or casual observation. They provide a means of recording and preserving an impression of what was observed—an impression that is as accurate a year later as when it was initially recorded. Additionally, many instruments for reporting observations (checklists, rating scales, observation guides) provide specific directions or traits to guide the observer. Some instruments such as rating scales also provide for some degree of discrimination among the traits observed. Because many of these instruments also provide definitions or descriptions of their items that users are to accept and follow, they can also form a "mutual frame of reference" that can promote some consistency among observers viewing the same subject. The most popular of these instruments are rating scales, checklists, observation and anecdotal reports.

Rating Scales

Rating scales, as the name implies, are scales for rating each of the characteristics or activities one is seeking to observe or assess. They enable an observer to systematically and objectively observe an individual and record those observations. Although such scales are not limited to the recording and evaluating of observation, those are the common and popular uses of the instrument.

Rating scales have long been valued as an observation instrument available to counselors. They are useful as a means of focusing on specific characteristics, increasing the objectivity of the rater, and providing for comparability of observations among observers and are easy to employ.

Designing a Rating Scale

Although there are commercially designed rating scales available, counselors may find it more desirable under most circumstances to design their own. A good self-designed scale will be more appropriate for both the situation and rater(s), can be revised if needed, and, of course, is economical to use. The potential of any rating scale, however, is first determined by its design and five steps are suggested in the order presented.

Determine the Purpose(s). An obvious initial step is to determine the potential population and the purpose of the observations and/or ratings. Usually, the purposes or objectives of such an instrument should be limited in both number and scope. This tends to prohibit the development of scales that are too lengthy and overlapping and that discourage user completion. Scales that are clear and concise and directed towards limited and precise objectives also increase the likelihood of accurate responses.

Identify the Items.   Once the purposes or objectives of the scale have been established, the developer next identifies appropriate criteria or items to be rated. These items should be clearly and directly related to the objectives of the observation. Too, they should be clearly understood, easily observed, and assessed.

Identifying the Descriptors.   Although there is often a subtle difference between items and descriptors, it is important to honor this difference. Items may not be ratable, so descriptors are used to effect a transition between an "identifying item or statement" and an "objective description."

Example 5–1.   Developing the Rating Scale

The Beatty-Tingley Secondary School has a history of high incidence of pupil dropout prior to graduation. The problem has become particularly severe in the past three years and various remedial efforts have had little effect. It has therefore been determined by the school board that a concerted effort will be made to identify potential early school leavers and then design possible preventive measures. The counseling staff has been requested to design an instrument that may lead to the identification of these potential early leavers through the observation of certain behavioral traits. They proceeded to develop a rating scale by first stating the purpose as follows:

The Purpose: to identify potential dropouts

Following a review of relevant research, the counselors agreed upon four criteria of potential school leavers as follows:

Possible Criteria: 1. Interest in school.
2. Relations with peers.
3. Relations with teachers.
4. Coping styles.

Having identified criteria, the next step was to agree upon descriptors appropriate for the designing of items on the rating scale. These were determined to be:

Descriptors for: 1. *Interest*
Attention in class.
Participation in class activities.
Preparation for class.
2. *Relations with peers*
Frequency of interaction with peers.
Nature of interaction with peers.
Attitude of peers.
Friendships with peers.
3. *Relations with teachers*
Frequency.
Nature.

Attitudes towards teachers.
Attitudes of teachers.
4. *Coping styles*
Problem-solving skills.
Dealing with frustration and failure.
Work habits.

They then began the designing of the rating scale. The first items were designed to assess the interest of students in their classes, as follows:

Rating Scale Items
Interest in School. (Check most appropriate category)

Class attention:

Never | Rarely | Sometimes | Usually | Always

Consistent and general alertness to ongoing activities in the subject matter class

Comments:

Class participation:

Poor | Below Average | Average | Excellent | Superior

Quality of participation; knowledgeable and appropriate contributions and interactions

Comments:

Frequency of participation:

never | seldom | occasionally | often | at every opportunity

Comments:

Preparation for class:

never | seldom | occassionally | usually | always prepared

Readiness in terms of reading and other assignments for meaningful participation in class

Comments:

Identifying Evaluators. As the label implies, evaluations or ratings on some kind of a scale are an anticipated characteristic of this particular technique for making and reporting observations. There are a variety of options for this purpose, such as the number of intervals or points on the scale, the defining of the evaluators, and deciding whether or not to provide space for comments.

Determining the Format. A part of the format will be determined by the identification of evaluators, as described in the previous step. Additionally, the organization usually relates items together; the length—not too long; and the directions for completion will all be items to attend to in determining the final format for the instrument.

Limitations of the Rating Scale

Limitations in using rating scales are basically those to which all instruments administered and developed by humans are subject—the limitations of the instrument and the limitations imposed by the user. The most common instrument limitations are (1) the result of poor and unclear directions for the scales' use, (2) a failure to adequately define terms, (3) limited scales for rating, (4) items that tend to prejudice how one responds, (5) overlapping items, and (6) excessive length.

The limitations that raters impose are equally prevalent and can be even more serious, because they can distort or misrepresent the characteristics of an individual. The following are common examples.

Ratings made without sufficient observations. Many raters have an apparent need to complete all the items on a scale and, as a result, will "take a stab" at items with which they are unfamiliar. Others, in their haste to complete the scale, will make a rating on the basis of limited observation.

Overrating. There is a growing conviction among those who frequently utilize rating scales that overrating is a common practice among raters. For example, a recent review of rating scales used in conjunction with admissions to graduate work in a Big Ten university setting revealed that *all* 324 candidates were rated "considerably above average" or higher in three categories: appearance, social skills, and leadership.

Middle rating. Another group of raters appear to play it safe by using only the average or middle categories on a scale, thus avoiding either extremes of high or low assessments. Such ratings tend to misrepresent everyone as being just about average in everything.

Biased ratings. In addition to personal bias, bias may occur in ratings when raters permit one item that they particularly value or emphasize to set a pattern for the rating of other items. Although the focus of this discussion has centered on the utilization of rating scales in reporting observations, it should also be noted that this instrument is not limited in use to only the reporting of observations. Rating scales are also used extensively by counselors and others for performance ratings, evaluations—both personal and institutional, and as measures of attitudes, aspirations, and experiences.

Checklists

Another instrument that may be utilized for recording observations is the observer checklist. This instrument is typically designed to direct the observer's attention to specific, observable personality traits and characteristics. It is relatively easy to utilize inasmuch as it not only directs the observer's attention to certain specific traits, but provides him/her with a simple means of indicating whether those traits are characteristic to the individual being observed. Unlike the rating scale, the observer checklist does not require the observer to indicate the degree or extent to which a characteristic is present. Figure 5–1 shows an example of a simple form of a checklist.

Observation Checklist

Personal characteristics of _____
(name of student)

Observed by (name or code) _____

Periods (dates of observation: from _____ to _____

Conditions under which student was observed: _____

Instructions: Place a check mark in the blanks to the left of any of the following traits you believe to be characteristic of the student.

Positive Traits	Negative Traits
_____ 1. Neat in appearance	_____ 16. Unreliable
_____ 2. Enjoys good health	_____ 17. Uncooperative
_____ 3. Regular in attendance	_____ 18. Domineering
_____ 4. Courteous	_____ 19. Self-centered
_____ 5. Concerned for others	_____ 20. Rude
_____ 6. Popular with other students	_____ 21. Sarcastic
_____ 7. Displays leadership ability	_____ 22. Boastful
_____ 8. Has a good sense of humor	_____ 23. Dishonest
_____ 9. Shows initiative	_____ 24. Resents authority
_____ 10. Industrious	_____ 25. A bully
_____ 11. Has a pleasant disposition	_____ 26. Overly aggressive
_____ 12. Mature	_____ 27. Shy and withdrawn
_____ 13. Respects property of others	_____ 28. Cries easily
_____ 14. Nearly always does his/her best	_____ 29. Deceitful
_____ 15. Adjusts easily to different situations	_____ 30. Oversolicitous

Comments: _____

_____

_____

Figure 5–1.
Observation checklist. *R. L. Gibson and R. E. Higgins,* Techniques of Guidance: An Approach to Pupil Analysis *(Chicago: Science Research Associates Inc., 1966), p. 130.*

Anecdotal Reports

Anecdotal reports, as the label implies, are descriptions of a client's behavior in a given situation or event. Such reports are subjective and descriptive in nature and are recorded in a narrative form. Often a counselor will collect several of these reports, which then become an anecdotal record of a client's behavior over a period of time and/or situations.

Design of Anecdotal Reports

The format for anecdotal reports usually consists of three parts. They are (1) recording identifying data; (2) reporting of the observation; and (3) comments of the observer. There are several variations of this format, as may be noted by examining three different designs for anecdotal records. Figure 5–2 presents a format that follows in sequence the three parts previously identified. Figure 5–3 alters this format to provide space for comments alongside that are appropriate to particular statements of the anecdotal description. Figure 5–4 provides space for comments of additional observers, if desired.

Using the Anecdotal Reporting Method

The first consideration in anecdotal reporting is the selection of incidents that may be significant to report. These may be incidents that are typical of a client's behavior and are relevant for the counselor and/or client's better understanding of the client. They may also be incidents so atypical of the

```
┌─────────────────────────────────────────────────────────────────────┐
│                                                                       │
│  Anecdotal Report Form                                                │
│  Henry H. Higgins High School                                         │
│                                                                       │
│  Name _____     Observed by _____    │
│                                                                       │
│  Where observed _____   When:  Date _____     │
│                                                                       │
│                                           Time _____ to _____    │
│  ─────────────────────────────────────────────────────────────────    │
│                                                                       │
│  Description:                                                         │
│                                                                       │
│                                                                       │
│                                                                       │
│  Comments:                                                            │
│                                                                       │
│                                                                       │
│                                                                       │
└─────────────────────────────────────────────────────────────────────┘
```

Figure 5–2.
Anecdotal record: Form A.

Anecdote		Return to: Guidance Offices Nelson Elementary School
Student's name		
Description of incident observed	Comments:	
Observed by _____		
Time _____	Place _____	

Figure 5–3.
Anecdotal record: Form B.

client's behavior that their reporting and understanding may be advisable. In some situations, a series of anecdotes reporting similar behaviors over a period of time would increasingly suggest that the observed characteristics are typical of the client's behavior. Different observers making similar observations of a client's behavior on a specific occasion, or over a period of time, would have similar implications. Too, anecdotal reporting covering a period of time may identify trends or changes in client behaviors.

In school settings, teachers may be encouraged to use anecdotal reports in calling counselor attention to students who may need their assistance, or in contributing to case studies, or just a better understanding of individual students. The following examples illustrate uses of anecdotal reporting in school settings, as well as the counselor's interpretations of these reports.

Anecdotal report for		
Name	Date	
Situation		
Description		
Comments:		
Observor:		
Comments:		
Observor:		

Figure 5–4.
Anecdotal record: Form C.

Example 5–2.   Uses of Anecdotal Reporting in School

Student's Name: Therese
Incident One
Reported by: Mr. Michael
                      History Teacher

Date: January 16 (Monday)

Therese was not herself in class today. She usually is very active in the class discussions and always responds to questions when no one else seems to have the answer. However, today she sat quietly in her seat. At one point, when the discussion was bogging down, I called on Therese as always, asking her, "what were some of the factors that kept the United States from joining the League of Nations after World War I?" I could barely hear her response, but I thought she said "who cares?" and then in a louder voice which almost bordered on breaking into tears, "I'm sorry, I don't know the answer."

Teacher's
Comments: Therese is one of my more mature and capable students. Something is upsetting her and it would be helpful if a counselor could talk with her.

Student's Name: Therese
Incident Two
Reported by: Ms. Haggerty
                      Chemistry Teacher

Date: January 18 (Wednesday)

For the first time in the two years I have known Therese as a student, she has fallen behind in her work in my class. Further, her behavior has been almost disruptive. For example, today, when one of her best friends, Ann, asked her if she could borrow a test tube from her, Therese snapped back at her, saying, "Don't you ever have enough stuff to do your own assignments? No, I'm not lending you anything any more!" The exchange obviously was unexpected to Ann, who didn't exchange another word with Therese for the rest of the period, while Therese seemed to spend most of the period simply staring at her lab book.

Comment: Something is clearly wrong with this girl. This behavior is not typical at all. She needs to see a counselor.

Student's Name: Therese
Incident Three
Reported by: Ms. Findley
                  Physical Education Teacher

Date: January 19 (Thursday)

Today, Therese approached me before my fifth period in which she is enrolled and said, "Ms. Findley, I am quitting the gymnastics team and I don't want to talk about it." When I put my arm around her and said, "That's O.K., Therese, I hope you're all right," she broke into tears and said, "I'll never be all right again!" and then ran into the locker room. I decided to leave her alone and didn't follow up on our conversation at this time.

Teacher's
Comments: I have noted for the past couple of weeks that Therese hasn't seemed to be herself, but today things seemed to explode. I don't know what the difficulty is, but I do intend to follow up on her problem, whatever it may be, when I see her next week. Do you have any suggestions?

In this situation it is obvious that the school counselor, by the end of the week, is able to put together a picture of a young lady who is clearly upset. Although there are no indications of cause in the incidents described, there is sufficient reason for the counselor to either call in Therese or, through consultation with Ms. Findley, attempt to provide her with appropriate help.

The previous is an example of how a series of anecdotes can lead to the identification of a student in need of counseling assistance. In some situations, however, even a single anecdote is enough to alert the counselor to an individual in need of assistance.

Student's Name: Barry

Reported by: Mr. Franzen
                  English Teacher

Date: April 8

Barry's behavior in class today was most unusual. For example, every time a door slammed or there was any unexpected noise, he would jump as though suddenly startled. On one occasion, Sue accidently knocked her textbook on the floor, and Barry grabbed his desk tightly and exclaimed, "My God!" Most of the period he was continuously looking around the room as if expecting to be hit from all sides, and I noticed that he was in a cold sweat when he left the classroom at the end of the period. When I asked him, as he was leaving, "Barry, are you feeling O.K.?" he replied, "We are all going to get it . . . you just wait and see."

Teacher's
Comments:

Barry is usually so unobtrusive in class that he attracts little attention to himself. Today, however, everyone noticed his unusual behavior.

Advantages versus Disadvantages

Because anecdotal reports are designed to subjectively describe what has been observed, they become more lifelike than more objective measures. They present a broader, more complete viewpoint of a situation, which at the same time avoids the bleakness of the more quantitative or objective methods of reporting.

The major limitations of anecdotal reporting are those imposed by the observer-reporter. Most common of these are the reporting of "feelings about" rather than actual "behavior of" the individual observed. The tendency to "read in" biases or expectancies can result in misleading reports. Overinterpretation or misinterpretation by inexperienced observers are not uncommon. The reporting of insignificant, rather than meaningful, behavior can also limit the usefulness of anecdotal reporting.

Instrument Selection

The preceding paragraphs have discussed a variety of observation techniques and instruments. In many situations, counselors and other observers will make a decision as to which instrument or instruments are most appropriate for the observation task at hand. They may be aided in determining which type or types of instruments to use by considering the following:

1. Is some direction for recording observation(s) for individual analysis desired? (The answer to this is usually yes—or should be)
2. Is a descriptive or objective report more appropriate?
3. Will more than one observer be reporting observations of the client (or potential client)?
4. Are assessments or evaluations of what has been observed desired?
5. Are comparisons among different clients or between client and other populations likely to be made?
6. Are opinions or impressions—not necessarily facts or factually based information—desired?

7. Does the instrument avoid complex observations and recording methods?
8. Will the instrument make it relatively easy to complete a report in a short period of time, even if some accuracy or depth of observation may be sacrificed?
9. Will instruments be used by counselors or others who are experienced and/or trained in their use?

SELF-REPORTING: THE AUTOBIOGRAPHY AND OTHER TECHNIQUES

Up to this point we have been discussing observation and observation techniques for client assessment. In such techniques clients may be aware of their being observed, but rarely are they direct participants in the process.

Some of the most valuable techniques for human assessment for counseling purposes are those that call for the active involvement of the client. These techniques not only provide special insights for the counselor, but can be valuable to the clients as they engage in a process of guided self-assessment. The use of such techniques as the autobiography, self-expression essays, structured interviews, and questionnaires can facilitate both counselor and client understanding of the client's strengths, weaknesses, and uniqueness.

The Autobiography: A Popular Technique

The autobiography has been one of the most popular forms of literature throughout the ages. Humankind has consistently been interested in the personal view their fellow humans had of their own life's experiences. Additionally, almost everyone, famous or obscure, has at one time jotted down his/her personal view of his/her life's experiences. Some hope for publication, whereas others write for their own personal satisfaction only. It is probably appropriate to say that there is a time or times in nearly everyone's life when he/she feels compelled to examine and set down in writing his/her life's experiences. For the majority of those so inclined, it is unlikely that desire will coincide with a need for counseling. Nonetheless, the autobiography, even when it represents a nonvoluntary effort, can be a useful source of information to the skilled counselor. Let us therefore briefly examine its use as a nonstandardized technique in human assessment.

Autobiography: A Different Technique

At this point it is probably appropriate to indicate that counselors should avoid the use of overlapping or similar techniques. For example, there is little to be gained in using both rating scales and observation checklists to report observations of the same type of behavior, or to use three different achievement tests to measure the same area of achievement. A feature of the autobiography is that it is different from any other technique available to the counselor, for the autobiography provides the client (or student) the opportunity to describe his/her own life as he/she has experienced it and views it. The autobiography lets one express what has been important in one's life, to emphasize likes and dislikes, identify values, describe interests and aspirations, acknowledge successes and failures, and recall meaningful personal relationships. Such an experience, especially for the mature client, can be thought-provoking, insightful, and a stimulus for action. On occasion, the experience can also be a tension reliever.

The Autobiography As an Assignment

As previously indicated, there are times in most individuals' lives when they reach a state of psychological readiness for writing one's own life story. However, because this is unlikely to occur at the time such information may be needed for counselor use, some attention should be paid to the autobiography as a client and/or student assignment. If the autobiography is to be requested and used solely by the counselor, the suggestion should be presented as naturally and straightforwardly as possible, with an indication of how it will be helpful to both the counselor and the client in the counseling process. It should also be emphasized that the contents of the autobiography will at all times (within legal limits) be treated as confidential information. The counselor should also indicate possible content and approaches for preparing this assignment. Written guidelines may also be prepared for use in such a situation. An example of one such set of guidelines provides the client three possible options for preparing his autobiography.

Example 5–3   Guidelines for Preparing an Autobiography

Purpose: 1. To provide you the opportunity to experience the planning, organizing, and writing of your autobiography.
2. To provide you, the writer, and me, the reader, opportunities for increased understandings, insights, and appreciations of you, the writer.

Each writer may develop and work to an outline which suits his/her own style. The emphasis and detail that you give any period, event, or person will be whatever you determine as appropriate. The following are *examples only* of outlines and topics that might be appropriate for inclusion in an autobiography. (Note: I will be the only reader of your autobiography and will, of course, regard its contents as confidential.)

Example A.

Part I. My preschool years.
         My family, where I lived, early memories, friends, likes and dislikes.
Part II. My school years.
         Elementary, junior, senior high school, college, teachers, friends, subjects liked and disliked, activities, significant events, experiences, travels, concerns, and decisions.
Part III. My adult years.
         Where I lived, work experiences, friends and family, travels, hobbies, continued education, concerns, and decisions.
Part IV. The current me.
Part V. My future plans.

Example B.

1. Significant people in my life.
2. Significant events and experiences in my life.
3. Significant places in my life.

Example C.

Start your autobiography as far back as you can remember—your earliest childhood memories. Tell about those things that really made an impression on you, that stood out in your memory, whether happy or sad. Try to include those events that you believe have affected your life, such as moving to another city or entering junior high school.

As you write about the event, try to show how the event affected you, what people have truly influenced your life the most, and how they affected the way you feel and act today. Mention your hopes and plans for the future—what you hope to be doing ten years from now, for example.

When a counselor desires that a client emphasize a certain aspect of his/her life's experiences, that should be indicated to the writer.

In the school setting, the autobiography is often collected through a subject matter classroom. It is most frequently a written assignment in an English class at the secondary school level and in the elementary school, as a language assignment or an assignment related to the study of famous historical figures. As a classroom assignment, the autobiography should be treated in such a way that the student will regard it as a worthwhile educational experience. This suggests that it is treated as a regular assignment for a grade, although, if grades are assigned, the teacher must emphasize that one is not receiving an A or F for their life thus far, but rather for the technical manner in which he/she described it in relation to the assignment.

Limitations

There are a number of potential limitations of the autobiography that counselors and other users must take into consideration. One obvious limitation is that many individuals may find the writing of an autobiography a chore; thus, it will become a brief, bleak, and usually boring document that contributes little to a better understanding of the writer. The writing ability of the author as well as the conditions under which it is written will influence the potential usefulness of this technique. Too, as with any recall-based instrument, the ability of the writer to recall past experiences accurately and in considerable detail is important. Self-insight is another important factor. The reader must also be aware of distortions that overemphasize insignificant happenings or ignore those that are important, or inject falsehoods or fantasies, which very often are descriptive of the ideal or hoped-for life experiences of a writer. Current values may also influence how an author views past experiences and associations, and these may not be consistent with how they are viewed at the time.

Interpretation

With both the possible advantages and limitations of the autobiography in mind, let us note possible analyses by the counselor. The counselor/reader

I	Significant incidents

II	Organization—length, language (choice of vocabulary, depth of expression)

III	Omissions, glossing over, inaccuracies

IV	Points to check further

V	Summary comments

Figure 5–5.
Analyzing an autobiography. M. A. Kiley, Personal and Interpersonal Appraisal Techniques *(Springfield, Ill.: Charles C Thomas, Publisher, 1975), p. 66.*

may first of all prepare a checklist or summary form for those items that would be particularly relevant to the counseling needs of the client. In other situations, the counselor may simply summarize at the conclusion of the reading what he/she believes are the most relevant aspects or, assuming that the copy will be for the counselor's viewing only, may underline or make appropriate notes in the margins. In a general reading one might utilize the following format (Figure 5–5) for analyzing an autobiography.

Autobiographical Excerpts

Two brief excerpts are presented as examples of significant statements that are often found in student autobiographies.

> When I moved from East Park High School to Newry High School I guess I had assumed that things would go on as usual. I had been a big wheel at East Park—you know what I mean—member of the Student Council, president of the "Jokers"—most popular boys' club in school; king of the Sophomore Stomp, member of about half a dozen other clubs, invites to all the parties and social activities that were of any importance. But at Newry, many of the clubs I had belonged to before didn't exist. There were no boys' social clubs and, try as I might, I couldn't seem to make friends that moved in the "popular" circles. A lot of the kids spoke to me and were pleasant enough, but they never thought of me at party time. I found as time went on I missed East Park more and more, and I even began cutting school so I could drive back and visit East Park while school was in session. I had been a "B" student before at East Park, but my grades really took a beating at Newry. In fact, I think some of the kids at Newry began thinking of me as "dum-dum" and I know many of the teachers did.

The counselor in this instance found a significant clue in this portion of the client's autobiography to explain his poor grades and the subsequent difficulty he was having in securing college admission.

> I guess I felt like a nobody as far back as I can remember. I think maybe my mother resented me because I wasn't a girl, because when I was born she already had five boys. I know as a kid I could never seem to do anything right, and my mother used to say I couldn't do anything right because I was a nobody. I remember that she and my Dad both began calling me "ole nobody." Then my oldest brother, the one with the sense of humor, started calling me "N.B." (for nobody). The rest of the family thought that was real "cute" and so when I started to school, and all through school, I have been called "N.B." Actually, my name is James Lucifer Laswich. But I often have to stop to think what my real name is, I'm so used to N.B. I guess one reason I am so used to it is that I just seem to fit the name "Ole Nobody"

so well. I sometimes don't think there is a single teacher in this school who remembers me once I leave the class, and I know most of the kids don't. I must be the only kid in school who doesn't have a "best friend."

The case of "Ole Nobody" is another example of a significant statement in an individual's autobiography that provides the counselor with clues to his client's seemingly withdrawn behavior and poor self-concept.

Autobiographical Tapes

In recent years, an innovative deviation from the usual written autobiography—the autobiographical tape—has been found useful by counselors with some clients. The autobiographical tape presents the client an opportunity to orally describe and discuss one's life. In utilizing this technique, the counselor may first determine whether it is likely to be more useful than the written autobiography. Once the counselor has determined that the verbal approach is more appropriate, the counselor may then decide whether to provide the client with a structured outline to respond to or simply to describe the client's life as it comes to him/her. There may be some advantages to the autobiographical tape that will determine the circumstances under which it will be used. For example, some individuals can express themselves better orally than in writing. Further, because this method requires less preparation and effort on the part of the client, he/she may more freely present details that would otherwise be omitted. In addition, some clients may feel that there is less likelihood that the contents of a tape "give away one's secrets" than in a written document. Voice tone on a taped autobiography may also reveal feelings and emotions of the client and, because of the nature of recording, the autobiography by tape is less likely to client editing or censoring. Finally, it should be noted it is also evident that the taping of an autobiography for some clients is a more fascinating or innovative approach than the traditional writing experience.

There are, of course, disadvantages as well, to the taping of one's autobiography. The usual shortcomings of the written autobiography, such as lack of recall, exaggeration, and fantasy, are every bit as probable in this approach. In addition, there are some clients who lack the ability to express themselves clearly orally. Too, for some, the "unnaturalness" of this approach will be an inhibitor. Nonetheless, the taped autobiography is a tool that the counselor may wish to consider for certain clients under certain circumstances.

Self-Expression Essays

In addition to the autobiography, another useful technique that counselors may want to employ on occasion is the self-expression essay. This technique seeks to solicit the client's response, usually in a short, written essay form, to a particular question or concern. The objective of this technique is to elicit spontaneous, uncensored responses to a topic or topics relevant to the counseling needs of the client. Examples of appropriate topics would include the following:

My biggest concern is . . .
I'll bet you don't know that . . .
I value . . .
My future plans are . . .
My job is . . .

It should be emphasized that such documents can elicit positive responses as well as descriptions of possible problems or concerns. An example, which incidentally illustrates a positive response, is the following brief essay.

Example 5–4. "My School Problem"

My school problem is that I have no problem! Look at us! We have a beautiful school and, just my luck, a great faculty. We can't seem to lose more than once or twice a year in any sport. The greatest gang of kids go here and the crowning blow—even the food in the cafeteria is edible. So I have a problem because I'm a natural born griper—I'm at my best when I can complain—I have a feeling of accomplishment when I can point out the weaknesses of others. I used to have a field day before I came to Lee Street High. Now I'm dejected because I'm not rejected.

To help solve my problem I suggest that:

1. The students get busy and deface the school, mark up the restrooms, pull out the shrubbery, and all the other things that make a school more homelike.
2. The faculty get busy telling us how stupid we are; that they quit treating us like humans (I actually feel superior to my dog now), and that they get back in the ole game of teacher versus student to the bitter end.
3. That our teams lose a few more games, and that our coaches get rid of their coats and ties and wear baggy sweatshirts and swear loudly at the officials so they won't be mistaken for ladies and gentlemen, and that our student body do something pronto to get rid of that disgraceful "good sportsmanship" trophy.
4. That the students start forming cliques, avoid welcoming newcomers, and in general act more like adolescents than young adults. Oh, yes, we need a few more "kookie" dressers also.
5. Finally, that the school cafeteria manager go copy the menus and recipes from some other schools (mashed potatoes should always be served cold, and lumpy gravy should taste like glue, and fried chicken served stringy and dried out).

The Self-Description

The self-description is another client-participation tool that enables the counselor to see the client as he sees himself. The client is requested to "paint a picture" of himself in words, in one page, if desired. Such a "portrait" may share whatever aspects the client wishes to have the reader know. It is usually desirable to do this in the early stages of counseling to give the counselor an additional means of getting to know the client. This differs from the self-expression essay, because the self-description is one's view of one's self, whereas the essay may describe one's attitudes toward activities, events, and beliefs.

Example 5–5. Excerpts from Self-Description Essays

Sample 1

I would describe myself as a pleasant and amiable person. Others remark about my easygoing manner and happy-go-lucky personality. Honesty is a virtue I hold very dearly, and I perhaps trust others equally, thinking that they have my virtues.

My mother had always taught me that I should be conscious of others' feelings and do my best to please them. I went for many years applying this philosophy, yet found that others were not as conscious of my feelings. This led me to be hurt and used by others emotionally and mentally. I had to almost retrain myself to believe that thinking of myself was not altogether selfish and at times is the only way to think in order to lead a happy life.

Counselor's Notations: The counselor would no doubt notice the section of this self-description that indicates the client has been hurt and used by others emotionally and mentally. Also of interest to the counselor is the client's statement, "I had to almost retrain myself to believe that thinking of myself was not altogether selfish."

Sample 2

I believe that a person should not be too overtly predictable, but should possess a consistency of covert thought and feeling. I do not mean to say that I delight in the misconceptions of those who wish to categorize or predict the responses of others. I am not one to purposely masquerade, or, for some reason, to mislead those I work with or come in contact. But oftentimes an unpredictable action, comment, or response will reveal or trigger a surprising reaction on the part of an eager conversationalist. I do not become close to many, and am not always patient enough to seek out the best points of my peers or colleagues. My point of view has been said to be too sensitive at times, but I like to think that my increased sensitivity allows me to take a deeper breath of life and enjoy what beauty I may sense.

I am idealistic, serious, extremely concerned about those who need help, and a good listener.

Counselor's Notations: The counselor reading this self-description might note the fact that the client keeps his/her distance from colleagues and is considered at times to be overly sensitive. This self-description is of interest, too, for the writer's description of interactions with his/her peers.

Daily Schedules and Diaries

As with the autobiography, many of us have kept a diary from time to time. We may recall how we "bared our soul" in those secret pages, often protected with a little tin lock, that if reread today might help us better understand some of our present behavior and attitudes. Probably today's clients are no more willing than their predecessors to share such recordings, but when a client willingly maintains and shares diary entries with the counselor, they can provide valuable insights into understanding the client and his/her problem. Some clients will find it easier to present some aspects of their behavior and experiences in writing than in oral communication and, should this be the case, the counselor may decide to suggest the keeping of a diary for a period of time.

Another technique for systematically recording the client's daily activities is the daily schedule. This is a simple listing, usually an hour-by-hour account-

Diary for _____	Week of _____	
Morning	Afternoon	Evening
Monday: 6:45 Get up 8:00 Leave for school 8:15–12:15 School	12:15–1:00 Lunch in school cafeteria 1:00–3:30 More school 4:00 Get home 4:00–5:00 Loaf around with gang 5:00–5:30 Go to store for Mom 5:30–6:00 Read evening paper, mostly sports	6:00–7:00 Dinner 7:00–8:00 Watch TV 8:00–9:30 Study English and history 9:30–9:45 Take dog for walk 9:45–10:15 Study French 10:45 Bed
Tuesday: Same as Monday	12:15–12:45 Lunch in school cafeteria 12:45–1:00 Talk to Mr. Leonard 1:00–3:30 Classes 3:30–4:30 Work on chemistry experiment 4:45–6:00 Get home, read paper, listen to records	6:00–7:00 Dinner 7:00–8:00 Watch TV 8:00–8:30 Study English and chemistry 8:30–9:00 Watch favorite TV program 9:00–9:30 Study English and chemistry 9:30–9:45 Phone call 9:45–10:15 Study French 10:15 Bed
Wednesday: Same as Monday	12:15–1:00 Bring lunch; eat in Mr. Leonard's class and watch experiment 1:00–3:30 Classes 4:00 Get home 4:00–4:45 Study trig 4:45–5:30 Loaf around with guys who come by	6:00–6:30 Dinner 6:30–8:00 Study for history test 8:00–8:30 Watch TV 8:30–9:45 Study for history test 9:45–10:00 Walk dog 10:00–10:30 Study French 10:50 Bed

Figure 5–6.
Daily schedule. *R. L. Gibson and R. E. Higgins,* Techniques of Guidance: An Approach to Pupil Analysis *(Chicago: Science Research Associates Inc., 1966), p. 238.*

ing of a client's daily activities. This technique can be useful in helping the counselor and client understand how the latter is organizing and using his/ her time. Whereas the diary is usually a summary of the day's activities, often with feelings and interpretations, the daily schedule is a more objective presentation or listing of the day's activities.

Figure 5–6 presents an example of the less familiar of these two instruments, the daily schedule.

QUESTIONNAIRE

An extremely popular nonstandardized instrument with which all of us have had many encounters is the questionnaire. Questionnaires today appear to be a part of the American way of life as they are constantly used to inventory public reactions, solicit opinions, predict needs, and evaluate a wide range of commodities, services, and activities. This popularity does not, however, belittle their importance as an instrument for the economical collection of data from individual clients or groups of clients.

The questionnaire has a variety of uses for the counselor. In a broad, general way, it obviously provides an opportunity to easily collect a great deal of information that may be useful in further understanding the client. Too, the questionnaire is a client-participation technique that promises opportunities to advance the self-understanding, at least under some circumstances, of those completing it. More specifically, questionnaires may be designed in such a way as to collect specific types of information related to specific needs of the counseling clientele. Questionnaires may also seek information for the purpose of validating other data already available to the counselor. Additionally, questionnaires can be useful in identifying problems of individuals or groups, as well as their opinions, attitudes, or values. The questionnaires can also be valuable in collecting needs assessment data as a basis for establishing program objectives and evaluation data as a basis for program improvement.

The usefulness of the instrument, however, will be determined, at least in part, by the kind of information it seeks to collect, the appropriateness of the questionnaire's design, and the skill of the person who administers it.

In questionnaire design there are certain basic considerations to keep in mind. These are briefly as follows:

1. *Directions:* Indicate the purpose of the instrument and give clear, concise directions for its completion.
2. *Item Design:* Design items that are clear, concise, and uncomplicated. Items should solicit only one response and should be stated in such a

way that the responder will not be biased or influenced in how he/ she responds. Questionnaire items should also reflect the language level of the anticipated respondents.

3. *Item Content:* Questions should be designed to collect the kinds of information appropriate to the assessment purpose of the instrument. However, caution must be taken in eliciting socially sensitive, culturally restricted, or other personal-private information. Even a few such items (such as, Would you engage in sexual activity outside of marriage? Have you ever thought of committing a crime?) can arouse resentment and/or suspicions of some respondents that will affect their response to the total questionnaire as well. Although unsigned questionnaires may secure reasonably accurate group responses to a sensitive topic, the counselor will find such unidentified responses of considerably less value in individual counseling.

4. *Length:* A final consideration, obvious but important, is the length of the questionnaire. Often, we receive questionnaires of such length that we are discouraged from even beginning them. Clients and student populations are no exceptions in their reactions to lengthy questionnaires. Such instruments must be of short to reasonable length if they are to facilitate the data collection for which they are designed.

STRUCTURED INTERVIEW

Another basic and popular technique for increasing a counselor's understanding of the client is the structured interview. This technique not only provides opportunities for client observation under certain controlled conditions, but, equally important, enables the counselor to obtain specific information and to explore in-depth behavior or responses. Interviews that are structured are usually planned to serve a particular purpose. Once the purpose has been clearly specified, questions are designed that are suitable to achieve the goal or purpose of the interview. These questions are usually arranged in some sort of a logical sequence, although the interviewer must be flexible to alter both the nature and sequence of the questions as circumstances suggest.

Although the basic principles of counseling are appropriate for the one-to-one interview—and these will be discussed in some detail in Chapter 9—it is appropriate at this point to note that the interviewing process and setting, to be successful, should be as natural as possible, not anxiety producing. Because the interviewing setting and process may be natural and comfortable to counselors, they may, on occasion, forget that for the interviewee, unfamiliar with either, it can be a frightening experience. Perhaps if one recalls his/her own experiences when called in for an income tax audit by the Internal Revenue Service or when interviewed for a first job, he/she can appreciate a client's wariness. One must also recognize the possible existence of such human qualities as client forgetfulness, exaggeration, or trying too hard to give the "right" answer as limitations in some structured interviews.

For an example of a structured interview, let us go again to the Beatty-Tingley High School and its high school dropout problem. Once potential dropouts had been identified through combining of the rating scale with other data, the counseling staff decided to conduct structured interviews with those students who were willing to do so. The purpose of these interviews was to further explore each individual student's views and attitudes about school in relation to their educational and career planning. They then proceeded to structure the interview as follows:

STRUCTURED INTERVIEW

1. Introduction and explanation of the purpose of the interview, how we will proceed, and the answering of any questions.
2. First, tell me how it has been going for you in school this year.
3. What have been the best things about school this year?
4. What have you disliked the most about school?
5. How do you spend your time when you're not in school?
6. Have you ever thought of dropping out? If so, what would you plan to do then?
7. How could school be made more enjoyable for you?
8. Let's talk a little about your future—what are your job or career plans? (Follow up with questions regarding reasons for choice; long-range goals and further education.)
9. Are there any questions you'd like to ask me? Anything else you'd like to say?
10. Conclude.

You will note that an initial explanation is made of the purpose and procedures of the interview. Also, the questions are structured in such a way as to elicit discussion rather than a "yes" or "no" response. Finally, the interviewee is given the opportunity to ask questions or make additional comments before the interview is terminated.

GROUP ASSESSMENT TECHNIQUES

Group guidance and counseling techniques will be discussed in greater detail in Chapter 10, but it is appropriate in this chapter dealing with nonstandardized assessment techniques to review briefly techniques for assessing roles and relationships of individuals in groups. The understanding of our clients as total beings is heavily dependent on our understanding their group associations. Groups are a natural form of human association. In today's world, the hermit is an almost extinct species, and the individual no longer is the rugged individualist, going it alone. Group associations are natural and all of us belong to many different and diverse groups. For example, some of us may, within the brief period of twenty-four hours, associate with our family group, our work group, our social recreational group, a civic group, political group, and church group. In each of these several different roles and different relations, the roles and relationships are significant in the shaping of our behavior, both within and without the group. Too, in many of these groups, an outsider would find it difficult to accurately assess roles and relationships by only a casual observation of the group. Probably you have experienced going to a party, a class, or some activity where there were in-group jokes, a history of previous group activities that precluded you, and apparent roles and relationships that you didn't understand.

Even experienced group observers such as teachers and counselors find it helpful to utilize structured assessment instruments on occasion to facilitate accurate understandings of individuals in the group setting as well as group interactions themselves. The more popular of these techniques include sociograms, "Guess Who," communigrams, and social distance scales.

Sociometric Techniques

Sociometric techniques are basic approaches for the study of social relationships, such as degrees of acceptance, roles, and interactions within groups. Sociometric instruments provide a means for assessing and displaying such information as interpersonal choices made by group members.

Although sociometric devices appear to be relatively easy to devise, administer, and interpret, these impressions are deceiving. In fact, extreme caution and careful planning and analysis should be prerequisites to the utilization of these methods. In determining the appropriateness of conditions for utilizing sociometric analyses, the following must be considered.

1. *The length of time the group has been together.* The longer the group has existed, the more likely that the data collected will be meaningful.
2. *The age level of the group.* A general rule of thumb is that the older the participants, the more likely that the information provided will be reliable.
3. *The size of the group.* Groups that are too large, or too small will provide less valid information. It is important to also remember that all members of a group must be included in any sociometric studies.
4. *The activity provides a natural opportunity to secure responses.* In order for group members to participate willingly and honestly in sociometric analysis, the group activities for this purpose should appear logical and meaningful to the members.
5. *The group chosen for study should be appropriate to the informational needs of the counselor.* For example, if it is a school counselor seeking

to identify the causes of behavior problems in a given classroom, the observation of the same identical group of students in, for example, a recreational setting outside the classroom would not be as appropriate.

Cautions in Interpretation

As previously noted, sociometric data must be interpreted with a great deal of caution. It is perhaps most appropriate to say that sociometric techniques do not analyze or provide interpretations in themselves, but, rather, they initiate or contribute to assessment or understanding of individuals. It is also important to remember that in many group settings the choices of group members may say more about the chooser than the chosen. Finally, we should recognize that some students may not want to be chosen; they may prefer to be alone or with a few friends in certain group settings.

Perhaps the easiest of the different kinds of sociograms to make is that shown in Figure 5–7. This sociogram uses concentric circles in a targetlike pattern, with each student represented by a number.

Only mutual positive choices are shown, and preferential rank is not considered. The highly chosen individuals, or sociometric stars, are placed in the small center circle; the sociometric isolates, students not chosen and who chose no one, are placed in the large outer circle;

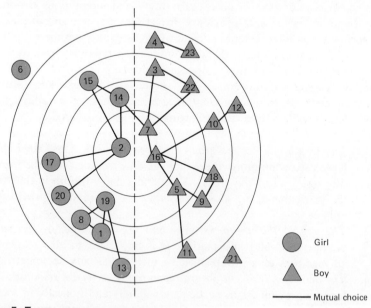

Figure 5–7.
Sociogram depicting mutual choices. *Robert L. Gibson and Robert E. Higgins,* Techniques of Guidance: An Approach to Pupil Analysis *(Chicago: Science Research Associates Inc., 1966), p. 140.*

and all other students are placed in the area between the inner and outer circles, those more frequently chosen being placed closer to the inner circle. Sex is indicated by different geometric designs: the boys' numbers are placed within a triangle; the girls' numbers are encircled. For even clearer differentiation, boys are confined to one side of the figure, girls to the other.[4]

The "Guess Who" Technique

Another useful sociometric technique is the "Guess Who?" questionnaire. This technique is best used with relatively well-established groups in which members have had the opportunity to become reasonably well acquainted. It is also most effective when the questions are positive in nature rather than negative. For example, "who is most friendly?" is a better "Guess Who?" than "who is the least friendly?" The "Guess Who?" questionnaire provides for the association of characteristics or activities with individuals. It can help us understand why some members of a group receive attention, behave in certain ways, or function in certain roles. We may also be able to identify those who are "popular" with group members and those who receive little, if any, recognition. The "Guess Who?" instrument is usually designed to collect specific information that counselors, teachers, or other group observers believe would be helpful in working with the group and its individual members. Figure 5–8 presents an example of a short "Guess Who?" instrument.

The directions for this technique may be altered to permit individuals to list all group members they believe are, for example, funny, friendly, helpful,

---

Group _____ Date _____

Directions: Write the name of at least one but no more than two persons whom you would identify as most outstanding in your group for the trait or activity listed. Your teacher (counselor, group leader) will use the results from your responses for planning group activities. If you cannot identify a group member for an item, you may leave it blank. It is not necessary to sign your name.

1. Tells the funniest jokes or stories. _____
2. Enjoys funny jokes and stories the most. _____
3. Is the most friendly. _____
4. Is the most helpful. _____
5. Is the most sincere. _____
6. Can always be depended on. _____
7. Has the best imagination. _____
8. Is a good organizer. _____
9. Is optimistic. _____
10. Is a good leader. _____
11. Has special talents. _____
12. Is generous. _____

Figure 5–8.
"Guess Who" example.

[4] Robert L. Gibson and Robert E. Higgins, *Techniques of Guidance: An Approach to Pupil Analysis.* (Chicago: Science Research Associates, Inc., 1966), p. 140.

and so on. Teachers or other group observers may use a simple tally system that notes the total number of times each group member was mentioned for each item. A popular variation in school settings is one in which pupils are asked to assume that the class is going to put on a play. They are provided a list of characters and asked to nominate classmates that could best portray the roles described. Examples of such characters might be as follows:

This person is known as "the arbitrator." They are always ready to try and prevent arguments from growing serious by suggesting compromises. They usually can see both sides of an argument and as a result rarely take sides.

This person is known as "the good humor person." They are always pleasant and good-natured. They smile a lot and laugh easily. They rarely show anger.

One other variation is to tell a story or describe a situation, real or fictional, in which group members are asked to assign to their peers the different characters. For example:

Example 5–6.   The "Guess Who" Technique

Ron Bakersfield is a new student who has just enrolled in Snow Deep High School. In his previous school, Ron was an outstanding and all-round athlete, a good student, and popular with his fellow students. He is a handsome young man who dresses neatly and cleanly, but on this day he is a bit unsure of himself. He wonders if his new schoolmates will accept him, how long it will take him to get acquainted, who his new friends will be, what his new teachers will be like, and if he will make the teams. The school counselor, recognizing Ron as a new student, has called in two of the more popular students in the school to meet Ron and show him around. The first one to arrive is Marie Shafer, an attractive, personable girl, who greets Ron with a handshake and a big smile. The counselor suggests to Ron that Marie is known as the sunshine girl in the school because she is always smiling and has a friendly word for everyone. The next arrival is Craig Brewer whom the counselor introduces as one of the more popular students in the school and whose hobby is photography. Craig appears also to be pleasant, but a bit more reserved than Marie. With an assurance that "we'll see that Ron gets around," Craig and Marie usher him out of the counselor's office. On the way to his first class, Ron is introduced in quick succession to Darlene, whom they refer to as "Miss Energy"; Tom, a serious student who is taking pilot lessons; Rex, who was introduced as the most interesting storyteller in the school; and Dave, to whom they gave the label "Mr. Reliable."

At this point, Ron is beginning to feel more at home and more welcome in his new school and already sees the prospect of making some good friends with fine qualities.

After reading this brief scenario, to whom would you assign the roles of Ron, Marie, Craig, Darlene, Rex, Dave, Tom?

Communigrams

Another aspect of observation of individuals in a group setting and of the group process is an assessment of the verbal participation of its members. This is perhaps the easiest communication pattern to observe and record because, in its simplest form, we are recording who talks and how often they talk over a given period of time. Figure 5–9 shows a chart in which the number of participations of each member of the group is noted with a check mark. Each check mark represents one communication, usually defined as an uninterrupted statement.

Figure 5–10 illustrates an alternative that uses the same form, but to indicate positions of members within the group to each other and to the group leader. Such reportings not only will identify those who frequently participate versus those who don't, but may also, for example, indicate the amount of discussion

Susan Armstrong ꜹꜹ ꜱꜱꜱ   Mary Smith   ꜹꜹ

Billy Bell   ꜱꜱ   Tommy Talbot   ꜱꜱꜱ

Amy Christoph   ꜱ

Figure 5–9.

Figure 5–10.
Gail E. Myers and Michele Tolela Myers, The Dynamics of Human Communication *(New York: McGraw-Hill Book Company, 1973), p. 135.*

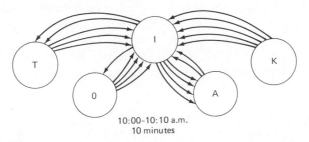

Figure 5–11.
Gail E. Myers and Michele Tolela Myers, The Dynamics of Human Communication *(New York: McGraw-Hill Book Company, 1973), p. 137.*

generated by certain topics and how members individually react to one topic and not another; enable comparisons between groups in terms of their frequency of communication, and, if carried one step further as noted in Figure 5–11, will also indicate the direction of communication among members.

Social Distance Scales

Another client participation technique that counselors may find useful are social distance scales. Social distance is usually defined by social psychologists as that distance the individual indicates exists between other persons and himself/herself. This distance is usually identified through the reaction to statements that measure and compare attitudes of acceptance or rejection of other individuals. An example of a social distance item might be the following:

Tommy Rott					
	I would like him as a close friend	I would like him as a friend	I would like him as an acquaintance	I am indifferent toward him as a friend or acquaintance	I would prefer not to have him as a friend or acquaintance

Other social distance items may be built around such choices as whom one would like to be with in different types of groups; take trips with; study together; or go to a dance with. The results from social distance scales may indicate a self-social distance and group social distance. The degree of acceptance of the group by an individual may be an index of "self-score" and the degree of acceptance of the individual by the group would be the "group score." Many studies of social distance scales in classrooms have tended to lead to the conclusion that the greatest contribution of social distance scales is in revealing the wide range of acceptance and rejection of any one student in a group. Again, as with many other client participation techniques, there is frequently a tendency to overuse and/or misinterpret because of their simplicity of administration. Counselors and other users should be aware that such information does not reveal the "why" of an individual's accepting or rejecting of others. Further, the users of this instrument must determine how they can use negative data such as indicated group rejection to the client's advantage. (Obviously, calling the client's attention to his rejection by the group will create more problems than it would solve.)

RECORDS

It has often been suggested that the first slabs of stone that our prehistoric ancestors carved out of the mountains were for the purpose of setting up personnel files. It appears that systems of recording are as old as civilization and that the primary object of much that has been recorded over the ages has been the individual. Record keeping is a reflection of the historical curiosity of humans to understand to the fullest extent possible their fellow humans (and just so we won't forget what we have already learned, we record it). Records are of importance to counselors and other helping professionals in understanding and working effectively and efficiently with their clients. It is in this context that records are discussed in the following paragraphs.

Basic Considerations

If records or a record system are to serve their potential for client understanding and assistance, certain basic considerations need to be examined prior to determining the nature and characteristics of the record and its attending system. These include the following:

The Extent of Record Keeping

The ever-increasing and seemingly never-ending preoccupation with record keeping may give all of us cause to wonder how many records we actually have in our name, where they're located, for what purpose, and so on. Extensive records have been maintained by the educational institutions which we attended, for even as students we become aware of the extensive and varied record data that the school maintains "to understand us better." Figure 5–12 rather accurately (but not too seriously) depicts the varying views to which the many records or types of data might, on occasion, seem to lend themselves. For recent students, the advent of the computer and other technological advances have, if anything, seemed to stimulate a challenge to gather and record data in a manner befitting these new developments in data storage, manipulation, and retrieval. Nor can school counselors belittle the importance of the decisions made on the basis of such recorded data—decisions that most frequently influence career directions and educational opportunities. Counselors working with school-age clients through community agencies and other nonschool settings must also be aware of the extent and impact of school-maintained records.

Who Will Use the Client's Record?

The answer to that question varies across the many places in which counselors function. For example, counselors in private practice may, subject to legal limitations, have exclusive access to a client's record, whereas, at the other extreme of the continuum, many school counselors may be expected to share client record data with school administrative and supervisory personnel, teachers, parents, and, of course, the client. Counselors, ever concerned with client confidentiality, must at the onset determine who legally and ethically will have access to any data recorded in a systematic or institutional manner.

Figure 5–12.
"Harry High School" as seen through a multirecord system.

The use of student and client records also raises the question of record security. Although students and parents may exercise the right to examine their records, that does not lessen the counselor's responsibility in the school, or any setting, to provide proper security for those records that are the responsibility of the counseling program. These responsibilities include provisions for the "lock and key" security of client records at all times, instructions and policies for nonprofessional (clerical) handling of records, and stated policies including ethical and legal guidelines for access to and review of records by clients, parents, and others. In determining "access" to school records, it must be noted that certain records of students are at least quasi-public in nature. The questions that arise are who may inspect such records for what purposes, and when?

Public records that are required to be kept and maintained by public officials are open to public inspection during reasonable office hours. Inspection of quasi-public records has been restricted mainly because of the sensitivity and confidentiality of the data contained in them. A general rule laid down by the courts may thus be stated: a person may inspect quasi-public records if the person can establish, to the satisfaction of the court, a justifiable interest in the records.[5]

What Are Other Legal and Ethical Considerations?

Practicing counselors, as well as those in preparation, may be confused somewhat by the apparent proliferation of statements by professional organizations providing ethical guidelines for the maintenance and use of client records. However, an examination of statements by the American Personnel and Guidance Association and the American Psychological Association, to mention a few, would indicate little that is in conflict and much general agreement. These standards are presented in Appendices F and G.

In addition, your attention is directed to the American Bar Association's suggestions in regard to school policies for pupil records.

To minimize the risk of improper disclosures, academic records should be kept separate from disciplinary records. The conditions of access to each should be set forth in an explicit policy statement. Transcripts of academic records should contain only information about academic status. Information from disciplinary or counseling files should not be available to unauthorized persons within the institution or to any person outside the institution without the express consent of the student involved, except under legal compulsion or in cases where the safety of persons or property is involved. No records should be kept which reflect political activities or beliefs of students. Special provision should be made to prevent misuse of old disciplinary records of former students. A student should have access to his records under reasonable circumstances. Administrative staff and faculty members should respect confidential information about students which they acquire in the course of their work. Students are likewise bound to respect the confidentiality of the files and records of faculty and administrators.[6]

The primary legal concerns of counselors insofar as records and recording are concerned continue to focus upon the confidentiality of the counseling records and the right of privileged communications. Although attorneys have

[5] Henry E. Butler, Jr., K. D. Moran, and Floyd A. Vonderpool, Jr., *Legal Aspects of Student Records,* Nolpe Monograph Series, No. 5, 1972, p. 26. (Commissioned by ERIC Clearinghouse on Educational Management; Published by National Organization on Legal Problems of Education, 825 Western Avenue, Topeka, Kansas 66606.)

[6] A Legal Memorandum, "The Confidentiality of Pupil School Records" (Washington, D.C.: National Association of American School Principals, Sept. 1, 1971).

possessed this right by common law over the centuries, and statutory law has extended this privilege to physicians, clergy, and, sometimes, psychologists, counselors have limited legal guarantee in terms of statutory provisions.

School counselors must be particularly aware of the provisions of the Family Educational Rights and Privacy Act of 1974. Key statements from this act point out the following:

A student (or his parents) must be given access to his records within forty-five days from the time a request is made.

A student (or his parents) must be granted a hearing by the institution upon request to determine the validity of any document in the student's file.

Confidential letters or statements placed in the file prior to January 1, 1975, need not be disclosed under the law.

A student may waive his right of access to confidential letters regarding admissions, honors, or employment.

An educational institution cannot, with certain exceptions, release personally identifiable information about students.

Educational institutions must notify students and parents of their rights under the law.[7]

The detailed provisions of this act are presented in Appendix H.

Further, counselors must be aware of the implications of Title IX of the Education Amendments of 1972, effective July 1975, which provided that:

no person . . . shall on the basis of sex be excluded from participation in, be denied the benefits of, or be subjected to discrimination under any education program receiving federal financial assistance.[8]

The implications for record keeping are clear; sexual discrimination must not be maintained. That includes standardized test results based on male/female norms, and career exploration activities and counseling that reflect sex-role stereotyping.

School counselors should also be aware of other kinds of unacceptable statements often found in student records. Wilhelm and Case[9] noted these frequent examples:

1. Libelous, unverified statements regarding the student.
2. Unverified statements regarding parents, family, or home.
3. Ambiguous, opinionated, subjective descriptions of the student, "glop" statements.

[7] Thomas Flygare, *The Legal Rights of Students* (Bloomington, Ind.: Phi Delta Kappa Educational Foundation, 1975), p. 15.

[8] Charles D. Wilhelm and Madelyn Case, "Telling It Like It Is—Improving School Records," *School Counselor*, **23**:85 (Nov. 1975).

[9] Ibid., p. 85.

4. Factual but biased statements with negative implications.
5. Factual but inconsequential statements that add nothing to understanding the student.
6. Inferential statements with negative implications that may or may not be verifiable.

What Purposes Will the Client's Record Serve?

The use of the client's records will, of course, be determined to a large extent by the answer to the question previously raised—who are the users? There are certain traditional uses appropriate for almost all types of personnel records, such as:

They provide an available pool of basic information about the individual. They provide a means for recording and preserving meaningful information about the individual for later use.
They assist the users of the information in gaining a better understanding of the individual with whom they will be interacting.
They assist the individual on whom the record is maintained to gain new insights and perspectives on himself/herself.

In addition, counselors use records in:

Preparation for the counseling interview.
The development of case studies.
Client placement or referral.

Consultation with other therapists, medical personnel, parents.
Follow-up and research studies.

School counselors also use records for the following purposes:

Identifying students who may be in need of counseling assistance.
Identifying students who possess special talents or interests.
Identifying students who may have special needs because of physical handicaps, for example.
Assisting faculty and parents in gaining a better understanding of the individual student, which, it is hoped, may contribute to positive student-parent and student-teacher relationships.
Assisting the individual student to gain self-understanding.
Contributing to school and community needs assessments of school-aged populations.
Facilitating the orientation of new pupils.

These listings are meant to be illustrative only and not exclusive, as any practicing counselor could readily expand on it.

Record Interpretation

The interpretation of any kind of counseling or personnel record will obviously be limited by the data recorded and the skill and understanding of the user. Some guidelines or safeguards include the following:

Records provide only clues to behavior—no more, and some clues will be relevant whereas others are not.

Does the present—the time at which you are examining the record data—compare to the past—the time when the data were originally recorded?

Look for trends or significant changes, but beware of the fact that many individuals have unique patterns of growth and development.

Feelings, attitudes, and intensity of emotions seldom show in recorded information.

Distinguish between symptoms and causes.

Determine if record data are based on substantiated facts or merely represent opinions.

Remember that records present only a small sample of the client's behavior. School records, especially, can also provide opportunities to examine certain habitual performance measures, such as attendance, grades, and health.

SUMMARY

This chapter has presented an overview of nonstandardized techniques that may be used in human assessment. Although many nonstandardized techniques cannot lay claim to either the validity or reliability of standardized instruments, they nonetheless provide the counselor with a wide range of data collection options from which one can choose, according to the dictates of the counseling situation and the assessment needs of one's clients.

Observation was noted as the most popular of the techniques usually used to assess others; however, in order that it be as accurate and meaningful as possible, it was suggested that some forms for recording observations such as anecdotal records and further directing observations towards specific characteristics such as rating scales and checklists might be used. Questionnaires and autobiographies were suggested as techniques in which useful information can be collected. Assessing behavior and roles in groups by such techniques as sociograms, communigrams, social distance scales, and role playing were suggested. There followed an examination of the role of records in human assessment and some of the legal and ethical considerations in record keeping.

Standardized Testing and **6**
Human Assessment

INTRODUCTION

Few activities in American education have remained as consistent an issue
over the past fifty years or been subject to the controversy and debate that
has accompanied the standardized testing movement in schools. From statements in Cubberly, *Public Education in the United States*[1] (1934) through
Gross, *The Brainwatchers*[2] (1963) to the more current "Use and Misuse of
Tests in Education: Legal Implications," (Nolte, 1975)[3] "IQ Tests and Culture
Issue,"[4] (Ornstein, 1976), and "Standardized Tests: Are They Worth the
Cost?"[5] (Herndon, 1976), the pros and cons of standardized test usage have
been presented not only to the education profession, but to the American
public as well.

[1] Ellwood Patterson Cubberly, *Public Education in the United States* (Boston: Houghton Mifflin
Company, 1934).
[2] Martin L. Gross, *The Brainwatchers* (New York: Signet Books, 1963).
[3] Mervin Chester Nolte, "Use and Misuse of Tests in Education: Legal Implications," *Educational
Horizons,* **54**:10–16 (Fall 1975).
[4] Allan C. Ornstein, "IQ Tests and the Culture Issue," *Phi Delta Kappan,* **57**:403–404 (Feb.
1976).
[5] Terry Herndon, "Standardized Tests: Are They Worth the Cost?" *Education Digest,* **42**:13–
16 (Sept. 1976).

Nor have the discussions shown signs of abating. Confrontations have frequently occurred, as in the 1976 discussion between representatives of such professional organizations as the American Personnel and Guidance Association and the major testing producers (American College Testing, College Entrance Examination Board, Educational Testing Service, and others). Further evidence of this continuing concern was reflected in the results of a 1977–1978 survey sponsored by the North Central Regional Accreditation Association of Colleges and Schools. In this survey, schools were asked to check problems or concerns. The responses indicated the highest single area of concern for more than 40 per cent of the respondents involved problems and issues related to standardized testing.[6]

Prominent educators have also expressed concern over the continued uses and abuses of standardized testing. For example, Lee J. Cronbach, an internationally recognized expert on psychological and educational testing, noted, "There is a considerable risk that many students will draw inappropriate conclusions from test results."[7] Ralph Tyler stated that standardized tests get "small answers to small questions."[8] Richard McKenna, speaking for the National Education Association's instruction and professional development offices, noted that

Test content does not reflect local instructional objectives or specific curriculums.

Much of the content is unimportant or irrelevant to anything students need to know or understand.

Test content measures mainly recall-type learning, neglecting the higher thought processes—analyzing, synthesizing, and drawing generalizations, and applying them to new phenomena.

The tests give an incomplete picture of student learning progress, because items that all or almost all students have learned are removed from the tests in order to keep the norming procedure statistically sound.

The test maker uses a language that is not commonly used in other activities in the real world.

Test items are unduly complex and require too many different manipulations; sometimes instructions for the items are unclear.

Test vocabularies and illustrations are often unfamiliar to those who are not of white middle-class cultures or for whom English is a second language; that is, the tests are culturally and linguistically biased.[9]

[6] "Standardized Testing in Schools Today," North Central Association of Colleges and Schools, unpublished project report, 1979.

[7] *Guidepost* (an American Personnel and Guidance Association publication), Feb. 16, 1978.

[8] Bernard McKenna, "What's Wrong with Standardized Testing?" *Today's Education,* **66:**35–38 (March–April 1977).

[9] Ibid., pp. 35–38.

Jerrold Zacharias, prominent physicist and professor emeritus at Massachusetts Institute of Technology, pointed out that

> it is not sufficient to "retreat" to catch phrases like "I know these tests are not very good, but they are all we have." There are many other ways to assess a child's general competence. They may not look numerical or scientific, but they are known to every teacher and every school principal who reads this journal.[10]

Speaking to the other side of the issue, Herbert Rudman concluded that

> I believe that some of the critics and their criticisms are responsible but that others—and all too many, for a subject this important—are poorly qualified to speak with wisdom, knowledge of the facts, and insight. And unfortunately, too many of them are speaking in the name of groups that they do not faithfully represent. What started as an opportunity to stimulate discussion has developed into increasingly non-factual rhetoric and hysteria.[11]

In addition, these controversies have been further complicated by the increasing popularity and attending discussions of the merits of competency-based/criterion-referenced testing and the suggestions by many educators that this is a more appropriate approach for measuring a pupil's educational progress. Although the critics of standardized testing abound and criticisms continue to be directed toward standardized measurement, much of the criticism may be as appropriately directed at the misuse and misinterpretation of the instruments as at the tests themselves. The misuse of tests in schools, especially, appears to stem from test users who are inadequately prepared in the administering and interpretation of standardized tests. At the same time, however, in many schools and school systems, as well as in a wide variety of agency settings, tests are used with prudence and caution by counselors and psychologists who are adequately trained in their utilization. In most institutional or agency settings where counseling takes place, including schools, standardized tests have been the counselor's basic instrument for objective assessment of academic achievement, aptitude, interests, and other characteristics of the individual. It therefore is most appropriate to introduce potential counselors to this important area of counselor understanding and skill, recognizing the continuing debates and issues, but assuming that a knowledge of these plus a basic understanding of these areas of testing will enable you to more effectively discriminate between usages and abuses and to retain in the counselor's repertoire a useful analytical tool.

[10] Jerrold R. Zacharias, "Trouble with IQ Tests," *National Elementary Principal,* **54:**23–29 (Mar., 1975).
[11] Herbert C. Rudman, "Standardized Test Flap," *Phi Delta Kappan,* **59:**179–185 (Nov., 1977).

STANDARDIZED TEST SCORES—WHAT DO THEY MEAN?

Whenever we evaluate someone, we do it in terms of some kind of comparison or point of reference. For instance, we may refer to Paul as the handsomest one in the group, Kathy as the best student in the class, and Nancy as the hardest worker in the bookstore. Here, we are comparing Paul to all others in the group; Kathy to the other students in her class, and Nancy's point of reference will be the other workers in the bookstore. Although we might attempt to make some predictions or deduct some other traits for Paul, Kathy, and Nancy from our observation, these would amount to nothing more than speculations, and we could justifiably be accused of unreliable procedures and data. If Kathy, Paul, and Nancy were to seek counseling, their counselor would want more objective and valid data before attempting to describe their traits and performances against the average traits and performances of others with comparable characteristics and experiences. An elementary understanding of statistics and statistically based tests, however, would enable the counselor to do this.

These basic understandings of educational and psychological statistics enable the counselor (1) to describe the characteristics of an individual or group in comparison with a specific group or population, (2) to predict the probability of future success or failure in a given area on the basis of present or past behavior, and (3) to infer the characteristics of a population from a sample of that population. It therefore follows that a good working knowledge of elementary statistical concepts is important for anyone who uses the various techniques of individual analysis and is mandatory for all who use tests and other tools of measurement. This section offers a brief overview of descriptive statistics, the basic statistical terms, and essential computational procedures, beginning with perhaps the most common—and most commonly misunderstood—of all statistical terms, *average*.

Averages

When Linda reports to her parents that she scored "70" on her history test, should they be pleased, satisfied, disappointed, or what? Until they have more information, they cannot be sure how to react, because 70 could represent 70 per cent of the questions answered correctly, 70 answered correctly out of 75 asked, a formula score of 70 (i.e., rights minus wrongs), or 70th in a class of 120 taking the exam. In this example, you may note that a *score* in and of itself is of little value. A score only becomes meaningful when it provides an index of how well or how poorly one performed in comparison with others taking the same test and, knowing that, what other significance can be interpreted from the results. Linda's parents are asking what is an *average* performance on this test and how does she *differ from* the average. Also, one asks to what does her score relate—what does it mean? Let us begin then by reviewing what is meant by *averages*.

Most educational and psychological evaluation is based on an individual's position in a group compared with others who comprise the group. The average position in a group becomes an important point of mathematical reference in standardized testing for human assessment. It is important to note that there are three distinct statistical types of averages. These averages are known as *measures of central tendency*. These three measures are the *mean,* the *median,* and the *mode*. For most nonstatisticians, the definition of the *mean* is commonly associated with the term *average,* for the mean is defined as the mathematical average of a group of scores. The *median* is the midpoint of a set of scores with 50 per cent of the scores being distributed above and below that point. The *mode* represents the most frequent score in a set of scores. Of these three averages, the mean is the most useful and popular, and the mode, having little statistical value, is the least popular.

Variations from the Average

Once we have determined what is average, we must utilize a statistical methodology whereby we can measure the degree to which each individual varies from this established average, or point of central tendency. Such statistical measures are called *measures of variability.* Two common measures of variability are the *range* and the *standard deviation*. The *range* may be defined as the spread from the lowest score to the highest score in a distribution. The actual statistical formula is the highest score in a group, minus the lowest score plus one. (The *plus one* in this formula extends the range to its real limits, which are one half of a score unit below the lowest.) The range is a relatively simple measurement device with limited descriptive value.

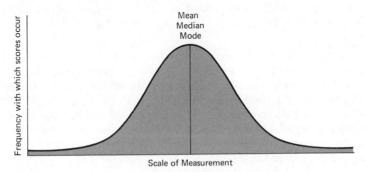

Figure 6–1.
The normal curve. (Note: *It rarely occurs that the mean, median, and mode are the same.*)

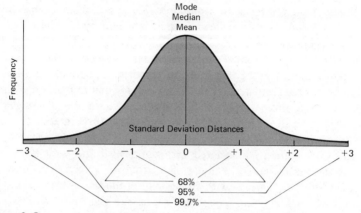

Figure 6–2.
Scores in a normal distribution. *Robert L. Gibson and Robert E. Higgins,* Techniques of Guidance: An Approach to Pupil Analysis *(Chicago: Science Research Associates Inc., 1966), p. 195.*

The *standard deviation,* on the other hand, is a statistical process that enables one to make an exact determination of distances of scores from the mean.

The mean and the standard deviation, when computed for a specific set of test scores, enable a counselor to determine how well an individual performed in relation to the group. This interpretation is made possible by the fact one can specify standard deviation distance from the mean and determine the proportion of the population that will be beyond or deviate from it, assuming that the scores are normally distributed. This normally distributed population is most popularly viewed as a *normal curve,* as shown in Figure 6–1.

In Figure 6–2, the normal curve is, in effect, sliced into bands, one standard deviation wide, with a fixed percentage of cases always falling in each band. Figure 6–2 then illustrates a significant fact:

> The mean plus and minus one standard deviation encompasses approximately 68 per cent of a normally distributed population; the mean plus and minus two standard deviations encompasses approximately 95 per cent of that population; and the mean plus and minus three standard deviations encompasses 99.74 per cent of that population. This information, which remains constant for *any* normally distributed set of scores or values, enables one to make a meaningful interpretation of any score in a group.[12]

[12] Robert L. Gibson and Robert E. Higgins, *Techniques of Guidance: An Approach to Pupil Analysis* (Chicago: Science Research Associates, 1966), p. 194.

As you view the normal curve and its segmentation into standard deviations, note that these facts are handy for interpreting standard scores. Further, whenever you can assume a normal distribution, you can convert standard scores to percentile scores, and vice versa. Thus, three basic facts for deriving a statistical evaluation of an individual's performance on a psychological test are the individual's raw score, mean, and standard deviation for the group with which the individual is being compared.

Relationships

Once you have determined the meaning of an individual's score in relation to others who have been administered the same measure, you must ask what are the other relationships or meanings of this score. The score and its comparative standing will take on meaning when it can be related to some meaningful purpose. For example, if students who score high on a college entrance examination actually perform at a high academic level in college, then one can assume that there is a relationship between scores on the examination and performance in college. The test score then becomes meaningful in terms of its prediction of college success, a meaningful purpose.

When you look for a statistical method to express relationships between two variables such as test scores and academic performance, you can compute a correlation coefficient. *Correlation coefficients* range from plus one through zero to minus one. A plus one indicates a perfect positive correlation; that is, the rank order of those taking the college entrance exam and their academic rank order in the college program are identical. On the other hand, a correlation of minus one means that the scores go in exactly the reverse direction. Thus, a correlation of minus one would indicate that individuals who score highest on the entrance exam achieve the lowest in college. A zero correlation would represent a complete lack of relationship between two sets of data. A frequently computed coefficient of correlation is the Pearson product-moment coefficient.

Statistical Symbols

It is important for the counselor, teacher, or others who read test manuals, interpret test data, or in other ways seek to interpret simple statistical data to have a familiarity with basic statistical symbols. Although there is no "universal statistical language," the following are some of the more commonly recognized symbols and their meanings.

M	mean
Σ	the sum of
SD (or S)	standard deviation for a particular set of scores

X	actual or "raw" scores obtained
MD	median
x	distance (or score difference) of a score from the mean
N	number of cases
i	size of a class interval in scale units
M'	assumed mean
r	a coefficient of correlation
z	scale value of the standard normal distribution;. the standard deviation of distance of a given score from the mean
f	frequency; the number of times a particular score occurs
p	percentage of persons getting a test item correct
q	percentage of persons getting a test item wrong ($p + q = 100$)

Presenting Test Scores

Inasmuch as raw test scores are in themselves meaningless, they have little value for the reporting of individual test results. As previously indicated, a raw score becomes meaningful only when it can be converted into some type of comparative score—one that enables an individual to be compared against others of a group. Most standardized tests, therefore, utilize one or more of the following methods of converting raw scores into a more meaningful method of presenting an individual's test results.

Percentiles

A *percentile score* represents the percentage of persons in the standardized sample for a given test who fall below a given raw score. An individual's percentile ranking indicates his or her relative position in a normative sample. For example, if 60 per cent of the students answer fewer than thirty problems correctly on an English usage test, then a raw score of thirty corresponds to the sixtieth percentile. Percentiles are probably the most common method of presenting scores and are relatively easy to interpret. Because of their relative ease of interpretation, however, several cautions should be noted. In working with nontest-sophisticated populations, such as parents, students, and most general populations, it is important to emphasize that percentiles do *not* represent percentages. Because percentiles represent comparison scores, it is also important to note the population with which an individual is being compared and the valid purposes for which comparisons can be made. It should also be noted that there are inequalities in percentile units.

The reason such distortion occurs is quite simple. When a raw-score distribution approximates the normal curve, there are many more moderate scores, which fall in the middle of the distribution, than either high or low scores, which occur at the ends. Since percentiles are based on the raw-score distance encompassed by a specified percentage of the total group, percentile distances near the median with its high concentration of cases will encompass a much smaller raw-score difference than the same percentile distance farther from the median. Hence the 15 points of raw-score difference between the 5th and 10th percentiles may shrink to 5 points of difference between the 40th and 45th.

These distortions make it difficult to use percentiles for profiling and other comparisons of a student's performance on two or more tests. To overcome the limitations in test interpretation resulting from the inequality of percentiles, more and more test publishers are turning to some type of standard score for norming.[13]

Standard Scores

Standard scores have become increasingly popular with standardized test developers. A *standard score* expresses the individual's distance from the mean in terms of the standardized deviation of the distribution. For example, let us return to Kathy, Paul, and Nancy and their scores on a test.

Mean of the test takers	75
Standard deviation	15
Kathy's score	90
Paul's score	65
Nancy's score	45

Using the formula $\dfrac{X\,(\text{raw score}) - M\,(\text{mean})}{SD\,(\text{standard deviation})}$ the following standard scores are obtained:

Kathy:	$\dfrac{90 - 75}{15}$	$= +1.0$
Paul:	$\dfrac{65 - 75}{15}$	$= -0.7$
Nancy:	$\dfrac{45 - 75}{15}$	$= -2.0$

Because both decimal points and plus and minus signs may be confusing or easily misplaced, they can be transformed into a more convenient form by multiplying each standard score with some constant. For example, if we multiply these scores by 10, we have $+10$, -7, and -20. We can then eliminate the plus and minuses by adding a constant of 100. Thus, Kathy's score becomes 110, Paul's 93, and Nancy's 80. An example of this practice may be noted on the Scholastic Aptitude Test (SAT) of the College Entrance Examination Board, which adjusts standard scores to a mean of 500 and a SD of 100. Thus, a standard score of -2 on this test would be $(500 - 200) = 300$.

[13] Ibid., p. 216.

Stanines

Another variation for normalizing standard scores was developed by the United States Air Force in World War II. The name *stanine* is a contraction of standard nine, a nine-point scale having a mean of five and a standard deviation of two. The percentages of a normal distribution that fall within each of the nine stanines are as follows:

Stanine	1	2	3	4	5	6	7	8	9
Percentage	4	7	12	17	20	17	12	7	4

Relationships among various types of test scores and the normal curve may be noted in Figure 6–3.

Norms

Armies over the centuries have had a favorite expression of the soldiers in the ranks—*snafu* (situation normal—all fouled up). We label individuals as normal or abnormal if they deviate from our concept of normalcy, and we use such expressions as "he would normally do this," or "under normal conditions you can expect that . . ." The term *norm* or *normal* is a popular one that most persons use frequently to denote the expected, or that which can be reasonably anticipated. The concept of normal or norm as utilized in standardized testing terminology also implies normal or average performance on a given test. Norms are derived during the process of standardizing a test. As a basis for determining the norms, a test is administered to a sample (usually large) that is representative of the population for whom the test is designed. This group then comprises the standardization sample to establish the norms for the test. These norms reflect not only the average performances, but also the relative frequency of the varying degrees of deviation below and above the average.

Age Norms

The use of *age norms* or standards is a fairly popular one in the nonscientific sense. We often suggest that Joey is as big as a ten-year-old or Janie has the vocabulary of a six-year-old. The use of this concept in reporting standardized testing results became popular when the term *mental age* was used during the translations and adaptations of the original Binet scales. From this initial usage, age norms were frequently used to measure any trait that showed progressive change with age. For example, in physical development, it would be relatively simple to prepare norms for the height or weight of growing children by years. In testing, age norms represent the test performance of individuals grouped and normed according to their chronological age. This type of score is more likely to be noted in the reporting of achievement tests, especially in the elementary school grades. There are two shortcomings to this concept of scoring and reporting results. First, there is a lack of

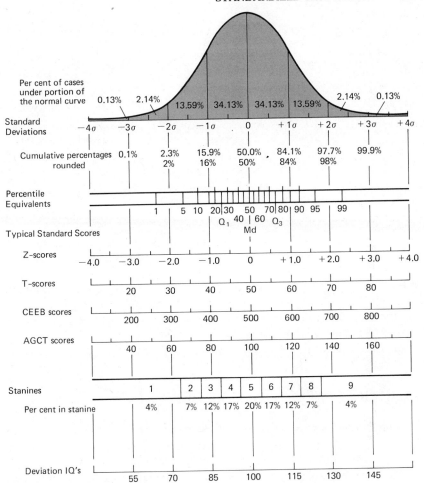

Figure 6–3.
Relationships among different types of test scores in a normal distribution.
Robert L. Thorndike and Elizabeth Hagen, Measurement and Evaluation in Psychology and Education, *2nd ed. (New York: John Wiley & Sons, Inc., 1964), p. 140.*

agreement regarding when children should be introduced to certain basic academic subjects and at what rates, and what comprehension level should normally be expected in these subjects. Also, age norms assume uniform growth from year to year, an assumption of questionable validity.

Grade Norms

Grade norms are similar to age norms inasmuch as they are based on the average score earned by students at a specific grade level. Again, grade norms

Table 6–1.

Main Types of Norms for Educational and Psychological Tests

Type of Norm	Type of Comparison	Type of Group
Age norms	Individual matched to group he equals.	Successive age groups.
Grade norms	Same as above.	Successive grade groups.
Percentile norms	Per cent of group surpassed by individual.	Single age or grade group to which individual belongs.
Standard score norms	Number of standard deviations individual falls above or below average of group.	Same as above.

Source: **Robert L. Thorndike and Elizabeth Hagen,** *Measurement and Evaluation in Psychology and Education,* **2nd ed. (New York: John Wiley & Sons, Inc., 1964), p. 127.**

are popular for reporting achievement test results in terms of grade equivalents. This method of reporting standardized test results, however, suffers from the same shortcomings as do age norms and are more readily viewed as suggesting standards to which teachers should aspire. Table 6–1 contrasts the main type of norms for educational and psychological tests.

SELECTING A TEST—WHAT CRITERIA?

The numbers and variety of standardized tests available to counselors and other users today require a recognition and application of appropriate criteria in test selection. Further, much of the criticism of standardized testing over the years has focused on poorly designed instruments and poorly prepared users, implying the need of criteria for both. Minimally, the criteria for tests would respond to the following questions: Is this a valid instrument? Is it reliable, and is it practical? (The latter item also suggests user preparation.)

Validity

Validity is traditionally defined as the degree to which an instrument measures what it claims to measure or is used to measure. For example, does the Whiffinpoof Mechanical Aptitude test really measure one's aptitude for mechanical activities, as claimed, or does it simply reflect one's previous experiences in the areas being tested? Or to raise a question of traditional controversy, do I.Q. tests really measure basic or native intelligence, or do they more appropriately reflect one's cultural and educational experiences? In establishing validity, one must note the importance of the appropriateness of test or interview questions and of situational samples to the evaluation objectives. Since it is impossible to include all possible questions or situations in an evaluation tool, those selected for inclusion must be representative of the content areas or behavioral patterns being assessed and must be appropriate for the individual under study and for the given circumstances. When an instrument meets these conditions, it is said to have *content* validity.

There are occasions when it is impractical to use a desired instrument; for example, its use may take longer than the time available for evaluation. But another instrument may be available that yields similar information about the individual and requires less time. The degree to which the second instrument obtains the same data as the first when they are administered at very nearly the same time is the second instrument's *concurrent* validity.

When the foregoing types of validity do not or cannot provide sufficient evidence of a test's validity, its *construct* validity may be cited. Construct validity pertains to the adequacy of the theory or concept underlying a specific instrument. In other words, it involves logically ascertaining the psychological attributes that account for variations in the test scores or other derived data. Construct validity is reported in terms of the kinds of responses the test should elicit, and the ways in which those responses should be interpreted on the basis of logical inferences about the behavior the test is designed to appraise.[14]

Reliability

The second major criterion to be applied in standardized test selection is *reliability*. Reliability represents the consistency with which a test will obtain the same results from the same population but on different occasions. An instruments's reliability enables a counselor or other user to determine the degrees to which predictions based on the established consistency of the test can be made. Two techniques are popularly used to establish reliability. One is the test-re-test method. When this method is used, timing between the tests is of crucial importance because growth or decline in performance could occur if the interval is too long, whereas recall of original test items might occur if the interval is too short. A second approach for determining reliability is by establishing an instrument's internal consistency. This consistency is established by comparing an individual's responses to the odd-numbered questions with the consistency of his/her responses to the even-numbered questions.

Practicality

A third important, but often overlooked, criterion in the selection of a standardized instrument is that of *practicality*. First and foremost of the practical

---

[14] Robert L. Gibson and Robert E. Higgins, op. cit., p. 52.

considerations is whether or not trained personnel are available to administer, score, if necessary, and interpret the particular standardized test under consideration. The importance of users' understanding the fine points of interpretation cannot be overemphasized. A second and not unimportant practical consideration is the cost of the instrument and accompanying materials. The expense of scoring is included in this consideration. Additionally, many standardized tests can only be used for one testing, so replacement costs may become another factor. Time required for administration is also a practical consideration, especially, but not exclusively, in school settings. Many school administrators prefer, even insist, that any group standardized test be one that may be administered within a normal class period in order to keep disruptions at a minimum. This may be carrying practicality a bit too far, although time is a practical consideration in test selection. While a recent publication date is frequently a validity criterion, it may be a practical consideration as well, when familiarity of content is important.

TYPES OF STANDARDIZED TESTS

Having briefly examined statistical concepts, methods of scoring, and criteria for the selection of standardized tests, let us now proceed to examine the specific areas for which standardized tests are available. These include aptitude, achievement, interest, and personality testing. There is admittedly some overlap in these categories, especially in interest and personality, but let us examine them as discrete, though not exclusive, areas for the classification of standardized tests. This discussion will focus on group standardized tests. Although recognizing the value of individual tests and that counselors and psychologists in a variety of nonschool settings frequently use individual tests, beginning counselors, especially in educational settings, work almost exclusively with group tests.

Intelligence or Aptitude?

The terms *aptitude* and *intelligence* are often used synonymously. However, in the discussion of standardized tests, one should examine the subtle differences that distinguish measures of intelligence from measures of aptitude. One distinction is that intelligence tests tend to provide a broad measure of overall or general ability, primarily related to one's potential for learning, whereas aptitude measures tend to focus more narrowly on specific factors. Mehrens and Lehmann note the following:

> One distinction that has been made is whether the measure we obtain is considered a *general* measure. If so, the test frequently is called an intelligence test. If the test measures *multiple* or *specific* factors, then

it is termed an aptitude test. Thus, we might conceptualize different measures of intelligence (aptitude) as lying on a continuum, with global measures falling at one end and specific measures at the other. At some point along the continuum we could arbitrarily change the label of the construct we are measuring, from intelligence to aptitude. Although this scheme has been suggested by some, it certainly is not universally followed. It does present some difficulties because there are some tests, such as the Wechsler Adult Intelligence Test, that are considered measures of a general factor, yet report subscores.

Another distinction between the meaning of the two terms has a historical basis. During the time intelligence tests were first being developed, psychologists thought of intelligence as being an innate characteristic not subject to change. This assumption is invalid. However, the term *intelligence* unfortunately still carries to some the connotation of complete innateness. To avoid the implications of innateness, many test makers prefer to use the term *aptitude*. Because these aptitude tests are most useful in predicting future school success, some persons have suggested that the phrase *scholastic aptitude* is the most honest and descriptive. Other people prefer to refer to all such tests as measures of learning ability.[15]

Intelligence Testing

The most popular area of aptitude or ability testing is the category that includes tests purporting to evaluate general academic ability, mental ability, and intelligence. Of these subsets, intelligence or I.Q. testing is the oldest and most controversial. This controversy has in recent generations led to their renaming with more popularly accepted labels such as academic ability, scholastic ability, or academic aptitude tests. Initially, the administrative usefulness of intelligence tests

> made them attractive to a great many institutions in our society, and to schools particularly. Their practical success reinforced the public's misperception of them. Most intelligence tests, after all, have been validated on school performance. They have therefore been good predictors of academic success in our school systems. They were hailed as a major advance over the much more subjective teacher's rating, which was more susceptible to bias and error. They also provided a tool for identifying children who would probably suffer failure in the regular system of instruction but who, once identified, could undertake school programs better tailored to their educational needs.[16]

[15] William A. Mehrens and Irvin J. Lehmann, *Measurement and Evaluation in Education and Psychology,* 2nd ed. (New York: Holt, Rinehart and Winston, 1975), p. 412.
[16] A. E. Brown, "Intelligence Tests and the Politics of School Psychology," *Interchange,* 7:29 (1976–1977).

On the other hand,

> the most fundamental problem of general intelligence judgments is that
> they lead us to overlook important differences in *types* of intellectual
> ability and hence important distinctions between individuals who differ
> in the extent to which they have various intellectual abilities.[17]

Other shortcomings of general intelligence assessment are that different
people arrive at the same end by different intellectual means, the importance
of intellectual abilities in living life well has probably been exaggerated; there
has been a tendency to link judgments about intelligence with judgments
about human worth, and, finally, there has been a strong tendency to overlook
the cultural and value relativity of intelligence judgments.[18]

Two popular group intelligence tests are the Lorge-Thorndike and the
Henmon-Nelson Tests of Mental Ability. The Lorge-Thorndike intelligence
test is available in two forms for grades three to thirteen. It provides both
verbal and nonverbal batteries for those grades in a single reusable booklet.
The verbal battery is made up of five subtests, using only verbal items: vocabulary, verbal classification, sentence completion, arithmetic reasoning, and verbal analogy. The nonverbal battery uses items that are either pictorial or
numerical. The three subtests involved are pictorial classification, pictorial
analogy, and numerical relationships. The tests in this battery yield an estimate
of scholastic aptitude that is not dependent upon an ability to read. The
working times are verbal battery, thirty-five minutes; nonverbal battery,
twenty-seven minutes.

The Henmon-Nelson Test of Mental Ability is available in two editions:
Form 1 for grades three through twelve, and a primary battery for kindergarten through grade two. The primary battery is normatively integrated with
Form 1, permitting school systems to use the Henmon-Nelson tests throughout the entire kindergarten through twelve grade range.

Form 1 for grades three through twelve has three levels (three to six,
six to nine, and nine to twelve), consisting of ninety items presented in order
of increasing difficulty. Form 1 of the Henmon-Nelson Tests of Mental Ability
was standardized in the fall of 1972 on a national sample of 35,000 subjects
in grades three through twelve.

The primary battery for kindergarten through grade two consists of
three separate subtests: a listening test (general information, thirty items);
a picture vocabulary test (thirty-three items); and a size and number test
(twenty-three items). These short subtests measure simple verbal and quantitative skills considered important in assessing readiness for schoolwork.

Standardization in grade two was carried out concurrently with the

---

[17] Clive Beck, "Why General Intelligence Assessment Should be Abandoned," *Interchange,* 7:29
(1976–1977).
[18] Ibid., p. 30.

norming of the Henmon-Nelson in grades three through twelve during the fall of 1972. For grades kindergarten and one, standardization was done in early 1973 on a sample of approximately 5,000 pupils drawn from the same schools that participated in the grade two through twelve norming program.

It should also be noted that many I.Q. tests have for years been suspect of cultural bias—a bias that would discriminate against minorities and populations in special environments. It would therefore appear appropriate to approach the use of intelligence tests with extreme caution, *if, in fact, they are to be used at all.*

Aptitude Tests

Aptitude may be defined as a trait that characterizes an individual's ability to perform in a given area or to acquire the learning necessary for performance in a given area. It presumes an inherent or native ability that can be developed to its maximum through learning or other experiences. However, it cannot be expanded beyond this certain point, even by learning. Although that may be a debatable concept, it is stated here as a basis on which aptitude tests are developed. In theory, then, an aptitude test measures the potential of one to achieve in a given activity or to learn to achieve in that activity.

Aptitude tests may potentially be used by counselors and others because (1) they may identify potential abilities of which the individual is not aware; (2) they may encourage the development of special or potential abilities of a given individual; (3) they may provide information to assist an individual in making educational and career decisions or other choices between competing alternatives; (4) they may serve as an aid in predicting the level of academic or vocational success an individual might anticipate; and (5) they may be useful in grouping individuals with similar aptitudes for developmental and other educational purposes. It should be emphasized that these are *potential* advantages only and will accrue only under optimal conditions, which include appropriate and proper instruments relevant to the client's needs.

Special Aptitude Tests

Special aptitude tests usually refer to those that seek to measure an individual's potential ability to perform, or to acquire proficiency in a specific occupation or other type of activity. Tests that measure special aptitudes are sometimes referred to as single aptitude tests, because they only secure a measure for one specific aptitude. Tests of special aptitude have generally declined in popularity as aptitude batteries have increased in popularity. Counselors most frequently use standardized tests to measure a single aptitude in areas of mechanical, clerical, or artistic abilities. Single aptitude tests have also been developed for use in various graduate and professional schools. Aptitude tests are also available for particular school subjects, especially in the areas of mathematics and foreign languages.

Vocational Aptitude Batteries

Multiple aptitude tests are an outgrowth of factorial studies of intelligence. The principal objective of factor analysis

> is to simplify the description of data by reducing the number of necessary variables, or dimensions. Thus, if we find that five factors are sufficient to account for all the common variance in a battery of 20 tests, we can for most purposes substitute five scores for the original 20 without sacrificing any essential information. The usual practice is to retain from among the original tests those providing the best measures of each of the factors.[19]

These batteries typically consist of a series of subtests that relate in varying combinations to a series of occupations or occupationally related activities. The major advantages of batteries over single aptitude tests are (1) convenience in administration as a result of having in one package a test that can be used to measure potential in a variety of activities; (2) the norming of all of the battery's subtests on the same population, thus yielding comparable subtest norms; and (3) the opportunity to compare potential in a wide variety of areas with one test. The most popular and widely used of these multiple aptitude batteries are the General Aptitude Test Battery (GATB), used by the United States Employment Services; the Differential Aptitude Battery (DAT); the Flanigan Aptitude Classification Test (FACT); and the Academic Promise Test (APT). A brief examination of the characteristics of these tests may help you further understand the nature of aptitude batteries.

General Aptitude Test Battery. The General Aptitude Test Battery, known by its initials as the G.A.T.B. is administered through the United States Employment Service. However, it is available to nonprofit institutions such as schools for counseling purposes. As may be noted in Figure 6–4, this battery has twelve subtests, which yield nine scores. It should also be noted that these aptitudes are not all independent as some of the subtests are used in determining more than one aptitude score. As might be anticipated, this battery is primarily used in counseling for job placement.

Differential Aptitude Test. The Differential Aptitude Test consists of a battery of eight subtests. This is designed primarily for students in grades eight through twelve and consists of eight subtests as follows: verbal reasoning, numerical ability, abstract reasoning, clerical speed and accuracy, mechanical

---

[19] Anne Anastasi, *Psychological Testing,* 4th ed. (New York: Macmillan Publishing Co., Inc., 1976), p. 362.

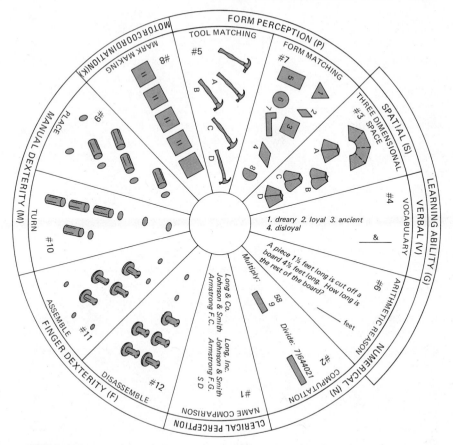

Figure 6–4.
Nine aptitudes measured by twelve tests in the general aptitude test battery B1002 (Indiana State Employment Service).

reasoning, space relations, language usage-spelling, and language usage-grammar. This battery has for many years been one of the most popular in common use in schools as a means of assisting counseling for vocational and educational decision making.

Flanigan Aptitude Classification Test. The Flanigan Aptitude Classification Test is one of the more time-consuming multiple aptitude tests, requiring approximately eight hours to administer. This comprehensive aptitude test battery was based on the job elements approach basic to performance in a wide range of job classifications. The battery consists of nineteen subtests, as follows:

1.	Inspection.	11.	Arithmetic.
2.	Mechanics.	12.	Ingenuity.
3.	Tables.	13.	Scales.
4.	Reasoning.	14.	Expression.
5.	Vocabulary.	15.	Precision.
6.	Assembly.	16.	Alertness.
7.	Judgment and comprehension.	17.	Coordination.
8.	Components.	18.	Patterns.
9.	Planning.	19.	Coding.
10.	Memory.		

The results of these tests are profiled for various occupational areas. Counselors may use these results as an aid in job placement or career and educational planning.

Scholastic Aptitude Tests

Scholastic or academic aptitude tests propose to measure one's potential for performing in academic situations. Such tests as those that comprise the SAT and PSAT batteries have much merit insofar as predicting academic performance at higher educational levels. However, a more appropriate label would be academic achievement, because they tend to predict future academic achievement on the basis of past learning, rather than on the basis of native ability.

Achievement Tests

Achievement measurement is an area of standardized testing to which most students have been subject, not on just a single occasion or two, but probably numerous times during their educational programs. Of all of the areas of standardized testing, achievement tests are the most popular in terms of numbers administered to numbers of different individuals. For example, a study recently reported through the North Central Association of Colleges and Schools[20] indicated, on the average, that students graduating from secondary schools in that association would have taken standardized achievement tests twelve times during their twelve years of schooling. This study also reported that nearly 100 per cent of the school systems within the association's nineteen state region administered achievement tests at some point or points during their pupils' educational programs. Despite the widespread popularity of achievement tests, they are not infrequently confused with other measures, especially aptitude tests. It is therefore appropriate to note that *achievement tests* may be defined as those designed to measure the degree of student

[20] "Standardized Testing in Schools Today," North Central Association, unpublished project report, 1979.

learning in specific curriculum areas common to most schools, such as mathematics, English usage, and reading.[21]

Achievement tests are used to provide measures of (1) the amount of learning, (2) the rate of learning, (3) comparisons with others or with achievement of self in other areas, (4) level of learning in subareas, and (5) strengths and weaknesses in a subject-matter area. Because of their extensive use and the relatively easy task of identifying appropriate content measures, achievement tests are among the best-designed standardized measures available to counselors. There are, however, certain considerations that users of achievement tests must keep in mind if such instruments are to be utilized appropriately by counselors and others.

First, it is important that the content of the test is relevant to the subject-matter content the student has experienced. In other words, the test should measure what the student has had the opportunity to learn.

Further, it is important that the emphasis within the test, in terms of topical areas covered, is appropriate for the emphasis the student has experienced in the subject-matter class.

Additionally, the level of difficulty of the test items must be appropriate for the age-grade level being tested.

A final consideration, one that bears repeating, is the norming sample on which the test has been standardized.

If this sample is representative of the general population appropriate to the age-grade level being tested, comparisons with this general population may be appropriate. If the population of the sample is similar to the population being tested, that would usually be desirable. On the other hand, if the norming population is considerably dissimilar, it may not be an appropriate group against which to compare the group being tested.

One of the popular achievement test batteries is the Iowa Test of Basic Skills. This series is available in two forms for grades three through eight. Depending on which level and form are used, testing time is sixty to eighty minutes. The five major areas tested by this battery are vocabulary, reading comprehension, language skills, work-study skills, and mathematical skills. The test developers point out that this battery measures pupils' abilities to use and acquire skills, for no test or subtest is concerned with only the repetition or identification of facts.

Related to the Iowa Tests of Basic Skills are the Tests of Academic Progress. These tests are normed for grades nine through twelve and consist of six subtests of forty-five minutes each. The subtests are social studies, composition, science, reading, mathematics, and literature.

---

[21] Gilbert Sax, *Principles of Educational Measurement and Evaluation* (New York: Wadsworth Publishing Co., Inc., 1974), p. 361.

Standard score norms, grade percentile norms for individual students, and grade percentile norms for school averages are provided; the grade percentile norms for individual students and for school averages are provided for the beginning, middle, and end of the school year.

The Student Profile Chart, a cumulative record sheet for plotting a student's scores for five testings, can be used to record standard scores.

A Student Report Folder, "Your Record on TAP," is also available for reporting test results in grade percentiles to students and parents.[22]

These tests may be obtained through the Houghton Mifflin Company in Boston.

The Metropolitan Achievement Test consists of eight battery levels for measuring performance from the beginning of kindergarten through grade twelve. This battery consists of single tests for reading comprehension, mathematics, language, social studies, and science. The basic battery consists of the first three tests. The complete battery utilizes all five tests. This battery is available from the Psychological Corporation, a subsidiary of Harcourt Brace Jovanovich, Inc., New York.

Interest Tests

In a student discussion on career planning, one might hear such statements as

"I've always been interested in nursing."
"The thought of teaching really turns me off."
"I know I'd enjoy selling cars."
"Being a flight attendant would be the most exciting career I could imagine!"

Such pronouncements of career interests are common among adolescents and young adults. Equally common are statements of uncertainty and frustration regarding career choices, such as:

"I wish somebody would just tell me what career I should enter."
"I can't make up my mind between engineering or coaching."
"I'm really upset because I can't think of any job I'm interested in."

Discussions and other explorations of interests are valuable aids for career planning and related career counseling and guidance; even a simple listing in hierarchical order of possible careers may be as valid in some instances as standardized, inventoried interests. Super and Crites suggest "four approaches that can be used to ascertain individual's interests: (1) direct ques-

[22] *1976 Catalogue: Measurement and Guidance* (Boston: Houghton Mifflin Company), p. 46.

tioning; (2) direct observation; (3) tested interests; and (4) interest inventories."[23]

However, there are certain values that may result from the use of standardized interest inventories, of which counselors, teachers, and others who assist youth and adults in career and related decision making should be aware. These potential values include the following:

1. A comparative and contrasting inventory of an individual's interests.
2. Verification of an individual's claimed interest or tentative choice.
3. Identification of previously unrecognized interests.
4. Identification of the possible level of interests for various (usually career) activities.
5. Contrast of interests with abilities and achievements.
6. Identification of problems associated with career decision making (no areas of adequate interest; high stated interest versus low inventoried interest in a career field).
7. A stimulus for career exploration and/or career counseling.

If, however, these values are to be realized, interest tests or inventories should, according to Holland, ideally have many positive characteristics, such as:

1. Provide occupational forecasts of satisfaction and achievement. Although any information about a person or a vocation may be helpful, information with high predictive validity is especially helpful.
2. Provide the full range of vocational options by both type and level. All inventories fail to suggest all possible vocational options, even for the most favored persons in our culture (tall, white, college-educated, Protestant males, without physical or psychological difficulties).
3. Provide information or influences that are stable or reliable from one time to the next.
4. Provide an experience that is effective. Interest inventories should stimulate vocational exploration, reassure people about wise choices, upset people about unwise choices, provide long-range perspectives, provide new information (new to the person), such as more vocational alternatives, support people resisting destructive cultural forces, and promote self-reliance and understanding.
5. Provide information that is in accord with a person's life history, current circumstances, and personal potential, rather than factors such as age, race, sex, and social status.
6. Be based on a useful theory of vocational behavior, including a classification system to organize all possible alternatives. Theoreti-

[23] William A. Mehrens and Irvin J. Lehmann, *Measurement and Evaluation in Education and Psychology,* 2nd ed. (New York: Holt, Rinehart and Winston, 1978).

cally based as opposed to empirical inventories provide a more explicit rationale that is more amenable to public examination and revision.

7.   Include auxiliary materials to increase positive influence and avoid negative side effects. For example, brochures that summarize information about an inventory's strengths and weaknesses should be included with every test booklet.

8.   Be oriented toward the most common occupations and to some degree toward the spectrum of the future world of work.

9.   Be adaptable to new educational and occupational information. To some extent, the easier an inventory is to revise, the more likely it is that revisions will occur.

10. Be relatively resistant to client or counselor abuse and distortion. The more complete and explicit an inventory is and the more independent of the vagaries of counselors and clients, the less likely it is that its positive effects can be twisted by human hands and minds. Likewise, an inventory that lends itself to simplicity of interpretation and scoring should be less vulnerable to abuse than one that does not.[24]

The popular development of interest tests evolved from studies indicating that people in a given occupation seemed to be characterized by a cluster of common interests that distinguish them from individuals in other occupations. It was also noted that these differences in interests extended beyond those associated with job performance and that individuals in a given occupation also had different nonvocational interests—hobbies and recreational activities that could distinguish them from those in other occupations. Thus, interest inventories could be designed to assess one's interests and relate them to those of various occupational areas. Two of the earlier and more popular of these inventories, still extensively used today, were the Kuder Preference Records and the Strong Vocational Interest Blanks, currently designated as the Strong-Campbell Interest Inventories.

The Kuder Preference Record is the original and most popular of the various Kuder interest inventories. It provides a series of interest items arranged in triads, from which the respondents choose the one they would like most and the one they would like least. The results are scored and profiled for the occupational areas of outdoor activities, mechanical, computational, scientific, persuasive, artistic, literary, music, social service, and clerical. Revision of the original preference record, the Kuder General Interest Survey, extends the use downward to the sixth grade by employing a simpler vocabulary that requires only a sixth-grade reading ability (the original version was usually considered appropriate for use in grades nine through twelve).

[24] John L. Holland, "The Use and Evaluation of Interest Inventories and Simulations," in *Issues of Sex Bias and Sex Fairness in Career Interest Measurement,* ed. by Esther E. Diamond. (Washington, D.C.: Department of Health, Education and Welfare, National Institute of Education, Career Education Program, Spring 1975).

The Kuder Occupational Interest Survey is still another version that provides scores showing similarities with occupational and college-level areas. The various Kuder inventories may be obtained from Science Research Associates, Inc., Chicago.

The Strong-Campbell Interest Inventory is a revision of the earlier forms of the Strong Vocational Interest Blank. The various interest inventories have been suggested as usable with older adolescents and adults who may be considering higher-level professional or skilled occupations. The Strong-Campbell Interest Inventory (SCII) can only be scored by computer. This later version contains 325 items grouped according to occupations, school subjects, activities, amusements, types of people, preference between activities, and personal characteristics. Results are displayed on a variety of scales. For example, the six general occupational theme scales provide scores for realistic, investigative, artistic, social, enterprising, and conventional categories. The major and most popular scales for the Strong Vocational interest series are the occupational scales, which, for SCII, profile scores for 124 occupations. The Strong-Campbell Interest Inventory may be obtained through the Stanford University Press, Stanford, California.

The Ohio Vocational Interest Survey (OVIS) is one of a number of newer interest inventories developed for use with high school students. This inventory was developed after the model on which the Dictionary of Occupational Titles is based (a cubistic model of data, people, and things). The OVIS is separated into three parts: (1) a student questionnaire, (2) a local information survey, and (3) the interest inventory. The OVIS reports its results on twenty-four scales. The Ohio Vocational Interest Survey is available through Harcourt Brace Jovanovich, Inc., New York.

The Career Maturity Inventory, although not precisely an interest inventory, has been designed to measure the maturity of attitudes and competencies that are involved in career decision making. The attitude scale surveys five attitudinal clusters: (1) involvement in the career choice process, (2) orientation toward work, (3) independence in decision making, (4) preference for career choice factors, and (5) conceptions of the career choice process. In contrast, the competency test measures the more cognitive variables involved in choosing an occupation. The five parts of the competency test are (1) self-appraisal, (2) occupational information, (3) goal selection, (4) planning, and (5) problem solving. The Career Maturity Inventory is available from McGraw-Hill Book Company, New York.

Personality Tests

Of all the areas of standardized testing, none is more intriguing to the general public, and perhaps to the counseling profession as well, as personality assessment. From the do-it-yourself personality test in the daily newspaper to sophisticated, projective techniques requiring highly specialized psychological training, personality testing represents a universal quest of the individual to understand what makes him/her and fellow human beings "tick." But personality testing is as complex as what it seeks to measure. Let us examine some of the questions or concerns that must be taken into consideration.

What Is Personality?

Personality has been variously defined as follows:

> the visible aspects of one's character as it impresses others; a person as an embodiment of a collection of qualities[25];

> as the individual's unique pattern of traits; the pattern that distinguishes him as an individual and accounts for his unique and relatively consistent way of interacting with his environment."[26]

Thorpe suggests that definitions of personality may be classified into the following categories:

1. The *biosocial,* which points up the "social stimulus value" concept.
2. The *biophysical,* which emphasizes organic traits.
3. The *omnibus,* which endeavors to include everything of importance about the individual.
4. The *integrative,* which defines patterns and suggests personality as that which organizes various types of behavior into a congruent whole.
5. The *adjustment* concept, which assumes personality to be a reflection of the struggle to adjust.
6. The *uniqueness* view, which sees personality as the quality which sets each individual apart from all others.
7. The *core* or *essence* theory, in which personality to a degree is equated with the "what-a-man-really-is" concept, that is, what facets of personality are "most typical and deeply characteristic of the person."[27]

Let us submit a definition of personality as the sum total of the characteristics of an individual. You can readily discern the wide variations in viewpoints regarding this topic by asking in almost any group the question, "what is personality?" and noting the wide range of responses. It may be concluded that the concept of personality is a difficult one to treat with the precision

[25] *The Random House Dictionary of the English Language, College Edition,* ed. by Laurence Urdang (New York: Random House, Inc., 1968), p. 990.
[26] James C. Coleman, *Personality Dynamics and Effective Behavior* (Glenview, Ill.: Scott, Foresman and Company, 1960), p. 75.
[27] Louis P. Thorpe, *The Psychology of Mental Health,* 2nd ed. (New York: The Ronald Press Company, 1960), p. 287.

usually associated with standardized tests. Thus, constructors of personality tests face the challenge of determining what workable definition of personality they will use and what aspect or aspects of that definition they will measure.

What Is "Normal" Personality?

This question will probably elicit a wide range of responses from the public. Most persons tend to view "normal" in terms of their own behavioral-personality traits and values. Thus, an extremely extroverted individual, viewed as normal by one group, may be viewed as "abnormal" by another group. Even if able to objectively identify norms for specific behavioral responses, one still must determine at what point the deviations from those norms become "abnormal."

Can Personality Be Measured?

This question has objectively been answered affirmatively by many authors of standardized personality measures and has further been affirmed by many practicing counselors, psychologists, and psychiatrists utilizing observation and other nonstandardized techniques. Some of the difficulties involved in obtaining accurate assessments are client-based and must be the concern of the test interpreter. They are as follows:

1. The capability of the individual to accurately analyze many aspects of his or her personality is questionable. In some instances, the client may not possess the insight to respond accurately. Although the client's view of self is important, it may not be appropriate to the intent of the measuring instrument. In other instances, one must recognize that the individual's view of self can be distorted, can differ from the perceptions of others, and can be misleading to the test interpreter.

2. Some individuals may deliberately falsify their responses. Sax notes that

> when an individual responds to a statement regarding some personality trait, his response is usually assumed to be either candid or deliberately deceptive.[28]

Most often, deception occurs when an individual responds in a manner that he or she views as more socially acceptable than perhaps his or her true response might be. For example, little children almost inevitably respond that they love their parents, even when they don't know them or when they actively dislike them. Too, one can anticipate that some respondents will project an ideal self rather than the real self in their answers. An individual

[28] Gilbert Sax, op. cit., p. 447.

may respond as the friendly and popular person he/she wishes he/she was, rather than the withdrawn individual with few friends that he/she recognizes himself/herself to be. The intimate nature of a question may dissuade the respondent from answering accurately. Most notable examples in this category are questions dealing with an individual's sexual activities, beliefs, and values.

Several of the more popular personality inventories or standardized personality assessment instruments are the Mooney Problem Checklist, the Edwards Personal Preference Schedule, and the Minnesota Multiphasic Inventory. The latter two instruments require special training and supervised experience prior to their use in school or clinical settings.

The Mooney Problem Checklist consists of a series of problems to which the client reacts by underlining the problems that are of some concern, circling the problems that are of the most concern, and then writing a summary in his/her own words. The Mooney Problem Checklist is useful for group surveys and for identifying individuals who want or need counseling assistance with personal problems.

The Edwards Personal Preference Schedule is designed to show the relative importance for the individual of fifteen key needs or motives. These are as follows:

Achievement	Affiliation	Nurturance
Deference	Intraception	Change
Order	Succorance	Endurance
Exhibition	Dominance	Heterosexuality
Autonomy	Abasement	Aggression

Another clinically oriented instrument is the Minnesota Multiphasic Personality Inventory (MMPI). This instrument is constructed entirely on the basis of clinical criteria and contains 566 statements covering a wide range of subject matters related to the instrument's ten scales. These scales are as follows:

Hypochondriasis	Paranoia
Depression	Psychasthenia
Hysteria	Schizophrenia
Psychopathic Deviate	Hypomania
Masculinity-Femininity	Social Introversion

Four other scores are obtained: the Question score, the Lie score, the Validity score, and the K score (a suppressor variable refining the discrimination of five of the clinical variables). As mentioned earlier, the Minnesota Multiphasic Inventory requires special training and supervised experience prior to its utilization. This test is rarely used in high school settings.

CRITERION-REFERENCED TESTING

In the 1978–1979 study of standardized testing sponsored by the North Central Association of Colleges and Schools,[29] one of the most frequently raised issues was that of criterion-referenced testing versus norm-referenced testing. Many educators will suggest that it is not a case of either/or, that, in fact, criterion-referenced testing complements normed reference testing and vice versa, but the inference cannot be ignored when, in many school systems as criterion-referenced testing has increased, norm-referenced testing has decreased. One cannot deny the rapid gains in popularity that criterion-referenced testing, aided by the accountability movement, has made in recent years.

Criterion-referenced tests have been defined by Robert Glaser and A. J. Nitko as ones "that are deliberately constructed to yield measurements that are directly interpretable in terms of specific performance standards."[30] A criterion-referenced test measures whether or not an individual has attained the desired or maximum goal in a learning experience. If we were to contrast criterion-referenced testing with norm-referenced testing by using a practical example, we might note that a sixth-grade class could achieve an average score ahead of 52 per cent of other sixth-grade classes in a representative nationwide sample. This information, however, might not tell those interested, such as teachers, parents, and students, more specifically, how well this sixth-grade class reads, or what they have learned to read. On the other hand, a typical criterion-referenced test result would indicate how many pupils in this sixth-grade class can read at a certain rate of reading, can comprehend at a certain level of comprehension, and can recall with reasonable accuracy what they have read after passage of a specific period of time. In the first instance, a class is competing against other classes to demonstrate to what degree pupils have learned or not learned to read. In the latter case, however, pupils are competing against a locally established standard, a learning objective, a criterion.

Writing in the November 1972 issue of *Today's Education,* William F. Brazziel noted that the advantages of criterion-referenced tests seemed to outweigh the disadvantages. Six advantages were listed as follows for criterion-referenced testing:

1. They permit direct interpretation of progress in terms of specific behavioral objectives.
2. They facilitate individualized instruction.

---

[29] Robert L. Gibson, "A Study of Standardized Testing in Secondary Schools of the North Central Association" unpublished report, Indiana University, 1979.

[30] R. Glaser and A. J. Nitko, "Measurement in Learning and Instruction," in *Educational Measurement,* ed. Robert L. Thorndike. (Washington, D.C.: American Council on Education, 1971), pp. 625–670.

3. They eliminate a situation where half of American schoolchildren must always be below the median.
4. They enable teachers to check on student progress at regular intervals.
5. They eliminate pressures on teachers to "teach to the test" in order to have children make a good showing.
6. They enable teachers to compile a comprehensive record of the child's development and peg further instruction on clearly identified points.[31]

Brazziel cited four disadvantages of criterion-referenced testing, as follows:

1. Reporting systems will vary and must be interpreted for children moving into new districts.
2. Further work must be done on constant validation on whether the given test items are measuring progress accurately.
3. Comparisons of performance of school districts are not yet readily available.
4. Materials for teaching towards specific objectives must always be available if tests are to be valid.[32]

Perhaps Hawes expressed it best in noting the popularity of criterion-referenced testing when he entitled his article, "Criterion-Referenced Testing—No More Losers, No more Norms, No More Parents Raising Storms."[33]

SUMMARY

Standardized testing is an important tool in the counselor's array of techniques for understanding the client. Despite the historical and extensive use of standardized tests, counselors and other users must be aware of the many criticisms and concerns that have been voiced regarding their use for diagnostic purposes. Understanding of these criticisms and concerns and the degree to which they are valid will enable the careful counselor and other users to effectively, but safely, utilize standardized tests in their practices.

The importance of understanding basic statistical processes should not be underestimated. An understanding of averages and variations from the average, as expressed in statistical terminology, and of relationships, as computed mathematically, are basic to the interpretation of standardized tests. It is also important that the user of standardized tests be aware of and be able to apply the criteria for test selection. These basic criteria are the validity,

[31] William F. Brazziel, "Criterion Referenced Tests," *Today's Education.* **61:** (Nov., 1972), pp. 52–53.

[32] Ibid, p. 53.

[33] Gene R. Hawes, "Criterion-Referenced Testing—No More Losers, No More Norms, No More Parents Raising Storms." *Nation's Schools.* **91:**35–41 (Feb., 1973).

reliability, and practical characteristics of the test under consideration. Strengths and weaknesses of the common areas of standardized testing should be understood. It is also important that the user recognize the limitations as well as the strengths of a given instrument if it is to be intelligently utilized in practice. Counselors and others may also want to consider criterion-referenced tests as a substitute or supplement to their programs of standardized testing.

Values Clarification Techniques for Human Assessment

7

INTRODUCTION

When we state that we believe in free speech, freedom of the press, equal rights for women, and access to education for all, we are, in effect, expressing values. Those values might appropriately reflect the consensual values of our society. Each society is characterized by well-defined, articulated values that are passed on to and practiced by the members of the society. On the other hand, when we extoll the pleasures of travel abroad, the virtues of exercise and careful diets, and the inspiration of a specific religious faith, we may, in effect, be expressing our personal values. Thus, values also represent what a person considers important in life, and these ideas as to what is good or worthwhile are acquired through the modeling of the society and the personal experiences of the individual.

A discussion of values is basically a discussion of what people believe in, what they stand for, and what is important in life. They are the reasons people behave and even think the way they do. They motivate one to plan and act and serve as a standard for judging the worth of activities, achievements, things, and places. In short, it has been claimed that values give direction to one's life and, hence, one's behavior. On the other hand, individuals who do not know what they value often engage in meaningless, nonproductive, and usually frustrating behavior. In counseling, then, an understanding of the client's values can facilitate the counselor's understanding of the client's behavior, goals, or lack of goals, and what is or has been of significance in the client's life.

VALUES DEFINED

The proliferation of values clarification techniques and the increasing emphasis on values education in the school curriculum, as with any popular movements, have clouded traditional definitions and brought forth complex explanations of what is meant by values. We do not propose to add to this confusion, but rather, to present several of the more popular definitions as appropriate to those engaging in counseling. First, the *Random House Dictionary of English Language* defines values as "ideals, customs, institutions, etc., that arouse an emotional response, for or against them in a given society or a given person,"[1] a simple, straightforward, and, we think, acceptable definition. Another equally clear definition is that suggested by Smith and Peterson that values "are those elements that show how a person has decided to use his or her life."[2] Other relatively simplistic definitions of values have been presented by Ziegler,[3] who describes values as "symbolic categories—ideas, notions, articulated feelings, if you will—which enable us to rank behaviors and events and discover which we prefer and which we don't."

A popular and more complex definition of values in the behavioral sciences is that of the Harvard Study Group which suggested, "A value is a conception, explicit or implicit, distinctive of an individual or characteristics of a group, of the desirable which influences the selection from available modes, means, and ends of action."[4] Counselors will be interested in Smith's definition in which he refers to the value system in more psychological terms, as follows:

> The *value system* of the individual is best described as a multifactor spiral or behavioral bias which molds and dominates the decision-making power of the particular person.[5]

[1] *The Random House Dictionary of English Language,* College Edition, ed. by Laurence Urdang (New York: Random House, Inc., 1968), p. 1453.

[2] Darrell Smith and James Peterson, "Values: A Challenge to the Profession," *Personnel and Guidance Journal,* **55:**228 (Jan. 1977).

[3] Warren L. Ziegler, "If We Do Not Speak Out on Behalf of Mankind, Who Will?" *Penney's Forum* (Spring/Summer 1972), p. 18.

[4] Clyde Kluckhohn, et al. "Values and Value-Orientations in the Theory of Action," in Talcott Parsons and Edward Shils (eds.), *Toward A General Theory of Action* (New York: Harper & Row, Publishers, 1962) p. 395.

[5] David W. Smith, "Value Systems and the Therapeutic Interview," in *Counseling: Selected Readings,* Herman J. Peters, et al. (eds.) (Columbus, Ohio: Charles E. Merrill Publishing Company, 1962), p. 372.

Values seem to depend for stability or instability on beliefs. Individual beliefs are of two origins: in reference to what is or was; and to what ought to be or ought to have been. The first of these is usually referred to as *facts;* the second as valuations, judgments, or opinions.[6]

For further clarification of what is meant by values, it may be helpful to note what a value is not. Peterson in *Counseling and Values*[7] made the following contrasts:

1. Value is NOT the same as need.

In support of his contention, Peterson sights statements from Kluckhohn and Patterson, as follows:

> Since a value is a complex proposition involving a cognition, approval, selection and affect, then the relationship between a value system and a need or goal system is necessarily complex. Values BOTH rise from and create needs. A value serves several needs partially, inhibits others partially, half meets and half blocks still others.[8]
>
> Values are thus not simply derived from needs, appetites or interests, which include valuation but are not values, but come into play when a choice must be made which is NOT decided simply on the basis of a need, but is influenced by the ego ideal. . . . Values reflect needs and interests but are neither of these.[9]

2. Values are NOT the same as goals.

"Values appear as the *criteria* against which goals are chosen, and as the *implications* which these goals have in the situation."[10]

3. Value is NOT the same as a belief.

> Value involves beliefs concerning one's self and the context in which he lives but is not deducible to belief alone. Value involves more than mere belief alone and necessitates some degree of commitment to the belief. A person may have numerous beliefs that do not really involve him actively. Belief, then, as defined here, is a mere affirmation of possibility, whereas value involves commitment to action.[11]

4. Value is NOT the same as an attitude.

> Attitude is an organizing and directing influence upon behavior, but value is more than mere attitude, for attitude lacks primarily the imputation of the desirable and is exclusively referable to the individual.[12]

---

[6] Ibid., p. 373.

[7] James A. Peterson, *Counseling and Values* (Scranton, Pa.: Intext, Inc., 1970).

[8] Clyde Kluckhohn, et al., op. cit. p. 428.

[9] C. H. Patterson, *Counseling & Psychotherapy: Theory & Practice.* (New York: Harper & Row, Publishers, 1959), p. 55.

[10] Clyde Kluckhohn, et al., op. cit., p. 429.

[11] James A. Peterson, op. cit., p. 49.

[12] Ibid., p. 50.

5.   Value is NOT the same as a mere preference.

Value is more than preference; it is limited to those types of preferential behavior based upon conceptions of the desirable.[13]
   A value is not just a preference but is a preference which is felt and/or considered to be justified—"morally" or by reasoning or by aesthetic judgments, usually by two or all three of these.[14]

Peterson then concludes that some common principles can be generally agreed upon regarding values:

1.   Values are hypothetical constructs.
2.   Values represent the desirable in the sense of what one "ought" to do or what he perceives is the "right" thing to do in any given circumstance.
3.   Values are motivational forces.[15]

Another contrast of concepts that may be useful is one suggested by Mace[16] who contrasted values with standards and behavior. He noted that

values are the ultimate ideals and goals of mankind, which do not undergo basic change. The standards represent the attempts of human communities and groups to make rules which will ensure that the values are preserved and expressed. Behavior represents the manner in which individual men and women interact with each other, normally by conforming to the standards in order to preserve the values.[17]

VALUES THEORY AND PROCESS

It is appropriate to begin this section with a statement on values clarification theory by Kirschenbaum, Harmin, Howe, and Simon (1975), underlining a major hypothesis of values clarification. This hypothesis states that "if a person skillfully and consistently uses the 'valuing process' (explained later), this increases the likelihood that the confusion, conflict, etc., will turn into decisions and living that are both personally satisfying and socially constructive."[18]
   Raths, Harmin, and Simon have translated this theory into a process consisting of seven subprocesses grouped under three categories. They then suggest that a value in one's life must meet the following criteria:

[13] Clyde Kluckhohn, et al., op. cit., p. 422.
[14] Ibid., p. 396.
[15] James A. Peterson, op. cit., pp. 51–52.
[16] David R. Mace, "Values as a Constant," *Penney's Forum* (Spring/Summer 1972), p. 17.
[17] Ibid., p. 17.
[18] H. Kirschenbaum, et al., "In Defense of Values Clarification: A Position Paper" (Saratoga Springs, N.Y.: National Humanistic Education Center, 1975).

Choosing: (1) freely
                (2) from alternatives
                (3) after thoughtful consideration of each alternative

Prizing: (4) cherishing, being happy with the choice
                (5) willing to affirm the choice publicly

Acting: (6) doing something with the choice
                (7) repeatedly, in some pattern of life.[19]

One of the authors of this process, Simon, with deSherbinin, noted that

> the process of values clarification involves knowing what one prizes, choosing those things which one cares for most and weaving those things into the fabric of daily living. This process is sometimes taught by working on real-life situations, at other times by dealing with made-up stories, but always by grappling with issues that are of real concern in people's lives.[20]

Howe and Howe[21] suggested a process that seemed particularly adaptable to counseling strategies. This process consisted of the following steps:

1. Developing a climate of acceptance, trust, and open communication.
2. Building self-concepts.
3. Creating awareness of prizing and publicly affirming values.
4. Helping individuals choose freely from alternatives after weighing the consequences.
5. Helping individuals learn to set goals and take actions on their values.

Having broadly viewed values and their impact on behavior, noted a basis for values theory, and similarities between valuing and counseling processes, let us examine further some of the relationships between values and counseling.

VALUES AND COUNSELING

Historical Concerns

From the very beginning of the guidance movement in American education, leaders in this movement have expressed concern

---

[19] L. Raths, E. M. Harmin, and S. B. Simon, *Values and Teaching: Working with Values in the Classroom* (Columbus, Ohio: Charles E. Merrill Publishing Company, 1966).

[20] Sidney B. Simon, and Polly de Sherbinin, "Values Clarification: It Can Start Gently and Grow Deep," *Phi Delta Kappan,* **56:**679 (June 1975).

[21] Leland W. Howe, and Mary Martha Howe, *Personalizing Education: Values Clarification and Beyond* (New York: Hart Publishing Co., Inc., 1975).

both in their actions and writing, with values. The "father" of this movement, Frank Parsons, has been described as a "utopian social reformer," believing in the perfectibility of mankind. He viewed guidance as a means to a mutualistic society and the counselor's role as one leading to social goals by offering prescriptive advice. Davis preached the moral values of hard work, ambition, honesty, and the development of good character as assets in the business world.[22]

Much later, Carl Rogers stated his beliefs in the goodness and worthwhileness of man and man's abilities to chart his own destiny. C. Gilbert Wrenn in *The Counselor in a Changing World*[23] and *The World of the Contemporary Counselor*[24] discussed the values of the counselor and his clients. In the former book he stated

It has become increasingly clear that the counselor cannot and does not remain neutral in the face of the student's value conflicts. Even the counselors who believe most strongly in letting the student work out his own solutions have firm values of their own and cannot help communicating them. They communicate their values in what they do and don't do even if they never mention their beliefs verbally. Furthermore, we expect more and more of the counselor with reference to the needs of society. Just to accept the need for the full development of abilities in the interest of a stronger nation as well as the interest of the individual is a manifest expression of a social value. Because the counselor cannot escape dealing with values and expressing values in his own behavior, he must be clear about the nature of his own values and how they influence his relationships with other people.

A second developing conviction about values is that they are now seen by some psychologists as the central difficulty for many troubled people. Fifty years ago values were clearly defined, and acute maladjustment seemed to result from a willful violation of them. Psychological treatment consisted primarily of freeing the individual from an overwhelming sense of guilt over his transgression against his parents and other representatives of society. But today the picture seems almost the reverse of what it was. The maladjusted person feels himself more lost than guilty. Social expectations have become more diverse, less well defined, less insistent. The social processes of inculcating strong values are less effective today, in part because family and community are less cohesive.

As a consequence the individual feels a lack of purpose and direction. He feels less estranged from others and even from himself; he

[22] Perry J. Rockwell, Jr. and John W. Rothney, "Some Social Ideas of Pioneers in the Guidance Movement," *Personnel and Guidance Journal*, **40**:349–354 (Dec. 1961).
[23] C. Gilbert Wrenn, *The Counselor in a Changing World* (Washington, D.C.: American Personnel and Guidance Association, 1962).
[24] C. Gilbert Wrenn, *The World of the Contemporary Counselor* (Boston: Houghton Mifflin Company, 1973).

feels worthless and unsure of his identity. He must discover character in himself for himself. Values strongly felt are the foundation upon which he can build an increasingly satisfying personal existence. Thus, clarifying values and perhaps acquiring new values becomes a major task for the individual in counseling, as in education generally.[25]

In the later publication, *The World of the Contemporary Counselor,* he discussed the counselor's and client's values as follows:

The Counselor's Values

A first concern is that the counselor examine his own hierarchy of values and check it against the contemporary scene. I do not suggest that the counselor must change his values to meet changing assumptions, but rather that he attempt to increase his openness to the intrusions of change. A feeling of great certainty that what he now thinks is right and is right for all time can become a simple rigidity. It is too easy to retreat into a secure castle of one's own construction and close the gates to all that might disturb. It is healthy to be disturbed, for this means that one is required to think, to test assumptions, to question thoughtfully the bases for conduct. It is more realistic to confess confusion than to parade conviction.

On the other hand, admitting confusion could be interpreted as justifying having no convictions, no assurances of vital values. I must anticipate at this point what I want to discuss more carefully later, that one can be *committed* to values and goals even though they are tentative. In fact, one must be committed to be real, but the commitment may be to values which are seen as subject to modification, as changing with experience. "Tentativeness and commitment" paralleling each other are powerful principles.[26]

The Client's Values

The second area of concern is the acceptance of the client's right to be *different* in his values. This difference between the values of the client and those of the counselor is often a difference between generations or between cultures. Always, of course, the values of the client are the product of his life experience, unique to him and often markedly different from the experience of the counselor. The 30-year-old, middle-class, socially accepted, college-educated counselor cannot be expected to understand in all cases the values of a 16-year-old, ghetto-reared, socially-rejected boy or girl or those of an affluent, socially amoral, parentally rejected youth. In fact, experiential understanding of another is rare. What is most important, however, is that the counselor accept the client's values as being as real and as "right" for him as the counselor's values are for the counselor. There is too frequently a tendency

---

[25] C. Gilbert Wrenn, op cit., 1962, pp. 62–63.
[26] C. Gilbert Wrenn, op. cit., 1973, pp. 34–35.

to protest inwardly, "He can't really *mean* that," when the value expressed by the client is in sharp contrast to a related value held by the counselor. The point is that the client does mean that; his value assumption is as justifiable to him as yours is to you.

So far I have said nothing about the counselor's responsibility for helping the client to examine a given value assumption, particularly if the value is likely to result in behavior harmful to another or to society. He has such a responsibility, I am sure, differing widely from client to client and varying often with the client's psychological readiness to examine values. Basic to the success of any such confrontation, however, is the counselor's acceptance of the "right" of the client to have different values. If a counselor enters into a discussion of another's point of view with the implicit assumption that he is "right" and the other is "wrong," failure is assured.[27]

Relationship to Counseling Theory

As we proceed to examine values clarification and its relationship and potential usefulness for counselors and other helping professionals, let us examine its relationship to some of the traditional, theoretical approaches to counseling. For example, Simon and deSherbinin[28] noted that values clarification skills were natural companions of other skills that help people to develop their potential and live life more fully. Values clarification skills, it was suggested, go hand in hand with the work of Carl R. Rogers, emphasizing warmth and genuineness among people. Simon and deSherbinin went on to state that

> Values clarification can borrow something from Harvey Jackin's reevaluation counseling model, in which people make commitments to help each other grow. Generally, people divide the time they have for each other into two equal segments during which each works as both client and counselor. This reciprocity generates power that penetrates deeply into people's lives; values clarification techniques can be used in exactly the same way.
>
> More and more, people working in T-groups are also coming to see that values clarification exercises rapidly advance their aims of getting people close to others' thought and feelings.
>
> It has also found its way into the training of Gestalt therapists. Gestalt teachers have sensed that its various strategies are useful in clarifying the way people respond to each other's problems.
>
> Other counselors simply fit a values clarification exercise into a transactional analysis technique. One way that transactional analysis workers have used values clarification is to ask a client to respond to

[27] Ibid., p. 35.
[28] Sidney B. Simon and Polly deSherbinin, op. cit., p. 683.

a values question as if the child inside of him or her is speaking, then the parent inside, and then the adult.[29]

Smith and Peterson noted the relationship between counseling theory and values as the common ground for "teaching human beings how to live meaningfully with self and with one another."[30] It is then pointed out that a number of theoretical approaches to counseling and psychotherapy have long advocated this. For example, "All counseling and psychotherapy teaches values either directly (knowingly) or indirectly (unknowingly) . . ."[31]

Smith and Peterson conclude that the actualization of consensual values in human affairs is an enormous task that requires the involvement of all persons who render guidance services.[32]

The Counselor and Values Clarification Techniques

Values clarification theory and practice has much in common with counseling theory and practice. In theory, both are seeking to assist individuals in realizing their fullest potential. Both are clearly aligned with the humanistic and human potential movements in society. In practice, both values clarification and counseling seek to assist the individual in developing better self-understandings and a positive self-concept, in making appropriate decisions and meaningful choices, and in satisfactorily adjusting to the demands of everyday living. Let us, therefore, examine these relationships further in the context of such traditional counselor activities as individual appraisal, career counseling, individual and group counseling.

Values Clarification Techniques and Appraisal

Values clarification techniques are becoming increasingly popular with counselors as their potential for client appraisal is recognized. As noted in Chapter 6, the primary assessment technique utilized by practicing counselors today is the standardized test. Counselors in school settings tend to rely heavily on school records, which also include standardized test results. Although observation reporting techniques have some popularity, only minimal use is made of techniques in which the client is a more direct participant in his/her own self-analysis. Values clarification techniques provide such an opportunity, for, as one participates, one is continually called upon to look at himself/herself and his/her behaviors in various senses and settings, to examine his/her relations with others, to make and examine decisions. Not only do values clarification techniques provide such opportunities, but the values approach is considerably less threatening than such traditional methods as standardized

[29] Ibid., p. 683.
[30] Darrell Smith and James Peterson, op. cit., p. 230.
[31] Ibid., p. 230.
[32] Ibid., p. 230.

Table 7–1.
Contrasting Approaches to Human Assessment

Directive		Nondirective
Nonhumanistic - - - - - - - -	approach - - - - - - - - - -	Humanistic
Standardized tests- - - - - -	client assessment	- - - - Values clarification
and records	process	techniques
Threatening - - - - - - - - -	client viewpoint of - - -	Nonthreatening
	process	
Results are - - - - - - - - - -	client feedback- - - - - -	Client involved
interpreted to		at all stages in
client by counselor		learning about self

testing. Our experiences indicate, as a result, that the client also responds and participates more *willingly* in values clarification assessment techniques. Thus, the values clarification approach not only provides the client with more feedback and opportunity to learn about self, but also provides the counselor with the potential for a greater in-depth understanding of his/ her client's behavior. Utilizing the traditional directive versus nondirective theoretical categories, Table 7–1 contrasts the extremes of approaches to client assessment with and without values clarification techniques.

Values Clarification Techniques and Individual Counseling

The process of counseling and the processes of values clarification share much in common. As contrasted in Table 7–2, both have a heavy dependence on relationship establishment and maintenance; both seek to identify and explore the consequences of appropriate options; both emphasize that choices or decisions are made by the student or client; and both processes recognize the importance of carrying out decisions through action.

At this point it may have been noted that most values clarification techniques appear to emphasize group participation—and although this is true, it does not necessarily limit their utilization or inclusion in the process of individual counseling. Many of the techniques can be completed by an individual client and then shared and examined within the framework of the counseling process. Such exercises (some of which will be described in more detail later in this chapter) as drawing a hobby plaque, listing twenty things one likes to do, selecting from alternatives, and discussing situational anecdotes are examples of those that can be satisfactorily completed by the client, discussed and examined with the counselor, with a potential for leading to the confirming and practicing of more appropriate and satisfying behavior.

Values Clarification and Group Counseling and Guidance

Because values clarification techniques are popularly practiced in groups, their potential for group counseling and guidance is considerable. For example, numerous values clarification techniques designed to promote individuals

Table 7–2.

Similarities Between Values Clarification and Counseling Processes

Stage	Values Clarification	Counseling
1	Getting acquainted Develops a climate of: trust acceptance open communication.	1. Relationship establishment Developing a helping relationship which facilitates the client's communication of his/her reasons for seeking counseling assistance.
2	Builds an individual's self-concept.	2. Identification and exploration of client's concern.
3	Helps an individual become aware of his/her values.	3. Awareness and examination of options available to client.
4	Helps individuals choose and affirm their values freely from alternatives after weighing the consequences.	4. Client makes decisions after weighing consequences of each option.
5	Helps individuals set goals and take action on their values.	5. Implementation of decision. Goals are set and client takes action.

getting acquainted and developing interpersonal relationship and communication skills would have their appropriate moments in group counseling and guidance. Group values exercises designed to facilitate self-assessment, self-concept clarification, and reinforcement for change would have their usefulness for the group counselor. Exercises that give the individual the opportunity to compare, examine, and defend his/her behavior, values, and interests against the norms of others can also be useful in group counseling.

Values Clarification and Career Guidance

Values play an important role in career exploration and decision making. They will also influence how one may eventually function on the job. An integrated theory of career choice and values clarification might hypothesize that careers are most productive and stable when

1. They are freely selected.
2. They are selected from alternatives.
3. They are selected from high priority possibilities.
4. They are planned for.
5. They are consistent with the abilities, interests, and values of the individual.
6. They are reinforced by significant others in the individual's life.

We can examine this further by noting that career education views a career as a way of life, not just a job description (thus, there are implications for and implementation of self-concept, values, satisfaction). Although career education and career guidance have been mentioned as inseparable allies, each supplementing the other, we would add values education as well and would suggest that they (career education, career guidance, and values education) complement, implement, and are essentially inseparably interwoven in any program of human potential development.

Values Clarification Techniques

The utilization of values clarification techniques presumes certain responsibilities on the part of the counselor. For example, it is important for counselors and others who would use such techniques to understand their own values and how they may contrast with those of colleagues and clients. If counselors are to directly help clients examine and develop their values, they must accept the client's right to values that may differ from their own. The counselor should, therefore, eliminate any tendency to moralize or engage in any actions that would discourage the client's examining and thinking through his/her own values. Being nonjudgmental also helps create a climate that is open and accepting and that facilitates the use of values clarification techniques. It is also important to recognize that even subconsciously counselors will be modeling values for many of their clients. This is not to suggest that counselors must present themselves as neutral or "nothing" personalities, but, rather, must be aware of the impact that value modeling may have on others and also recognize that their own value system may in some instances even be inappropriate for others to model or aspire to.

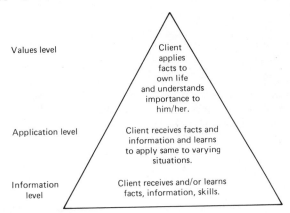

Figure 7–1.
Values pyramid. *Adapted from Merrill Harmin, Howard Kirschenbaum, and Sidney B. Simon,* Clarifying Values Through Subject Matter *(Minneapolis: Winston Press, 1973), p. 8.*

The remaining section of this chapter is devoted to some examples of values clarification techniques that counselors may find useful. These techniques have been organized under the five categories or stages previously identified in Table 7–2. In the utilization of these and other values clarification techniques, the counselor is seeking counseling outcomes, which, as may be noted in Figure 7–1, represent the highest or values level on the counseling pyramid.

Of course, many of the exercises can be appropriately considered under several of the categories and the counselor and other users of values clarification techniques should feel free to utilize that technique which applies most appropriately in a given time and situation.

Stage 1: Getting Acquainted

The initial step which both the counseling and values clarification process share in common is that of getting acquainted. In getting acquainted, the obvious initial activities should focus on learning one another's name and learning some basic characterizations of each other. These values exercises are easy starters for getting acquainted and require only minimal verbal interaction initially.

Exercise 7–1. Name Tag

Materials Needed:

Large pieces of cardboard or art paper for each participant (or newsprint).
Colored felt tip markers.
Masking tape or straight pins.

Procedures:

Materials are described to each individual, who proceeds to draw a name tag, with perhaps only a first name or nickname in the center (they may use colors that they believe symbolize them as a person). Next, they are requested to use the different corners of the name tag to draw symbols to represent different personal characteristics as indicated by the counselor or facilitator. For example, see Table 7–3, which represents one possibility.

Table 7–3.
Name Tag Example.

Your favorite place:		Something you like to do:
	NAME:	
Prized material possessions:		A recent success:

Following the completion of the name tag, the individual may display his/her name tag by taping it to a table, a chair, or a wall for others to see and speculate about the symbols he/she has drawn. An alternative is for the individual to pin on or string the name tag around his/her neck and walk around the room sharing information. After every participant has had the opportunity to examine the name tags of others, the originator of the name tag then makes a brief explanation of the symbols.

Variation:

Another version of this exercise is known as "hobby plaques" in which an individual places his or her name at the top of a plaque and lists his/her special hobbies or favorite recreational activities. Group members then get together in clusters with others who have the same or similar hobbies for introductions or discussions of their hobby.

Exercise 7–2. Name Game*

Procedures:

An individual, usually a volunteer, initiates the procedures by saying his/her name and telling the group in a few words something he/she likes to do, such as, "My name is Linda and I like to cook." Moving in a clockwise direction, each person repeats the preceding names and what each person likes to do. The speaker then gives his/her name and what he/she likes to do. It would go something like this: "Her name is Linda and she likes to cook. My name is Herb and I like to play golf." The process is repeated until the original starter repeats all the names and the descriptors. When a group member cannot recall a person's name or what he/she likes to do, it is appropriate for the rest of the group to help that individual, because the emphasis is on getting acquainted and not in testing or comparing one's memory.

Exercise 7–3. Paper Collage

Materials Needed:

Newspapers and magazines.
Glue.
Scissors.
Poster paper or newsprint.
Masking tape.

---

* Idea for name game from Leland W. Howe and Mary Martha Howe, *Personalizing Education: Values Clarification and Beyond* (New York: Hart Publishing Co., 1975), pp. 41–42.

Procedures:

Each participant cuts out and places on the newsprint sheet pictures, statements, advertisements, or articles that in some way are representative or reflective of the individual participant. Individuals display their posters, and, following examination by other members of the group, explain their descriptors to the group as a whole.

Developing a Climate of Acceptance, Trust, and Open Communication

At this stage, it is important to move from getting acquainted to open communications. Such communications require a climate of acceptance and trust.

Jack Gibb, a social psychologist and originator of the Trust, Openness, Responsibility, Interdependence method of interpersonal development (TORI), has identified several types of "noise" which produce defensive reactions in receivers and diminish the effectiveness of a communication. He sees communication as a "people process" rather than a "language process"; accordingly, to increase the effectiveness of communication, one must make changes in interpersonal relationships so that the receiver does not feel threatened by the communication. Threat closes the windows of perception and turns the eye inward upon the self, away from the message and sender.[33]

Gibb has identified six categories of behavior which tend to raise defensiveness in communication and six contrasting behaviors which lead to open, supportive communication. Hawley and Hawley have modified Gibb's categories to produce a series of six continuua along which a communication can be rated, from highly defense-producing to highly open and supportive. These continuua are as follows:

Defense-producing	*Supportive*
Evaluative	Descriptive
Controlling	Cooperative
Hidden	Open
Neutral	Empathetic
Superior	Equal
Certain	Provisional[34]

Hawley and Hawley then proceed to identify three pointers to understanding better communications as "(1) recognizing that almost every question has a statement underlying it; (2) identifying introjectors, those questions and statements that try to force a value position on another person; and (3) being aware of put-down or killer statements."[35]

---

[33] Robert C. Hawley and Isabel L. Hawley, *Human Values in the Classroom: A Handbook for Teachers* (New York: Hart Publishing Co., 1975), p. 103.
[34] Ibid., p. 104.
[35] Ibid., p. 109.

To initiate more open communications in a revealing but nonthreatening way, such exercises as the following can serve as starters.

Exercise 7–4. Three-ses

Materials Needed: None

Procedures:

Members of the group are asked to identify three people that are currently living and/or three historical personages from the past they would like to meet. They then share their choices with the group and briefly explain in two or three sentences for each personage why they would like to meet them.

Variation:

For a variation on this particular activity, individuals might specify three current or historically significant events they would like to witness.

Exercise 7–5. Solve a Problem

Materials Needed:

Paper and pencil.

Procedures:

This exercise involves members of the group in working on solutions to each other's problems. Each individual writes down a problem or concern for which he/she would appreciate some suggestions for possible solutions. These are then rotated clockwise around the group with each individual contributing a one- or two-line suggestion. (Note: Individuals whose suggestions have already been used or who have no suggestions may be passed.)

Exercise 7–6. Conflict Resolution

Materials:

Descriptions of conflict situations such as the following:

Conflict Situations:

A. Kathy and Tom are a young married couple, both working, who have each saved $500 over the past year for their first vacation together. Kathy wants to go to the beach and argues that the choice should be hers because once she begins raising a family she may not always be able to go away on a vacation. Also, because

Tom will be the sole provider then, he would have more say on vacation choices. Tom wants to go to the mountains. His argument is that because he will be the long-range provider for the family, it is important that he get off to a good start in his career. He says he feels he needs a good vacation away from the crowds and the heat if he is to keep up the pace of his initial successful year. The costs of the two possible vacations would be nearly indentical.

B. Mrs. Blanch, a high school English teacher, in discussing her grading practices with one of her five high school senior English classes, announced that she has always (in twenty-four years of teaching) graded on a skewed curve with approximately 20 per cent of the class receiving A's; 30 per cent, B's; 40 per cent C's; and 10 per cent D's and F's. She feels this has been time-tested and almost always gives some of the weaker students a break and lets her classes know what to expect.

The students in her fifth-period class are nearly all (80 per cent) members of the school's scholastic honorary society. They believe it is unfair for their particular class and they elect Nancy Lee as their spokesperson to argue against this ''arbitrary standard'' instead of some form of evaluating each person only on the basis of what that individual has learned.

Having examined these situations, now proceed to apply the five steps which are suggested in the procedures which follow. (This exercise may be completed individually or in small groups).

Procedures:

A part of the process of developing a climate of acceptance, trust, and open communication is the development of processes for the no-lose resolution of conflicts. No-lose conflict resolution helps to create a climate in which all involved feel respected and in control of their lives. It does away with a power struggle that appears to be characteristic of so many classroom and other group settings.

Howe and Howe suggest the following five-step process for resolving interpersonal conflicts, which may be adapted to conflict situations, actual or contrived.

Step 1. Formulating a Statement of the Problem. The statement should take the form of an ''I message.'' Each person takes a turn making (or reading) his or her statement, while the other person uses active listening.

Step 2. Clarifying the Dimensions of the Conflict. After each person has made his or her statement, the pair try to define the dimensions of the conflict, noting the specific areas of agreement and disagreement. Questions are allowed during this step, but they should be of a clarifying nature.

Step 3. Brainstorming All the Possible Solutions to the Conflict. When the dimensions of the conflict have been defined, the two individuals are then to brainstorm—shoot out ideas as fast as they can think of them—as many possible solutions to the conflict as they can think of in the time limit set by the leader.

Step 4. Identifying the Consequences. Once the brainstorm of alternative solutions is completed, the pair turns its attention to identifying the consequences of each of the most viable solutions. Both the pros and the cons of each alternative should be listed.

Step 5. Choosing a Mutually Acceptable Solution. Finally, the two evaluate each of the alternative solutions and attempt to select one with which they can each be satisfied. If the individuals cannot find a solution that is mutually acceptable, they are to return to Steps 2 and 3 and repeat the process until they can arrive at a mutually acceptable solution.[36]

Exercise 7–7. Brainstorming or Buzz Sessions

Materials Needed: None

Procedures:

In this exercise, a topic, situation, or idea that may be controversial is introduced to the group by the counselor or facilitator. Each individual is encouraged to speak out as long as he/she doesn't interrupt another speaker. When someone is speaking, everyone else must listen. Reactions to other speakers cannot be negative, argumentative, or confrontive. Disruptive or destructive behavior is not accepted. Members of the group encourage each other until all possible suggestions or comments have been exhausted or the established time limit has expired.

Stage 2: Building Self-Concept

The individual's self-concept is a significant characteristic in determining the extent to which one fulfills his/her potential. Developing a positive self-concept becomes a significant outcome for much personal adjustment and/or developmental counseling. These value clarification strategies may be useful to clients and others in recognizing and developing their self-worth.

Exercise 7–8. The IALAC Sign*

Materials Needed:

Uniform-size pieces of art paper. Masking tape or string.

Procedures:

Ask group members to make a big IALAC sign proclaiming that "I AM LOVABLE AND CAPABLE." As the individual goes through the day (or time period for which the sign is appropriate), the individual's sign gets bigger or smaller, depending on how others greet the individual. When someone or something makes the individual feel good, he/she adds a piece of paper to his/her sign. If, on the other hand, something makes the individual feel less loved or less capable, a piece of the sign gets ripped off. At the end of the day (or the time period), individuals may get together and discuss their experiences.

[36] Leland W. Howe, and Mary Martha Howe, op. cit., pp. 77–78.

* This technique is suggested in *I Am Lovable and Capable*, by Sidney B. Simon (Niles, Ill.: Argus Communications, 1973).

Exercise 7–9. Plea for Me

Materials Needed:

Paper and pencil.

Procedures:

The purpose of this exercise is to examine and acknowledge our positive traits. This exercise can also be used as a basis for making improvement by repeating it again at a later date. Those participating in this exercise are asked to imagine their survival will depend on how valuable they are to society as determined by some external panel of unknown judges. They are therefore to write in three pages or less, a "plea for me" statement, which stresses their strengths and potential as a basis for their being approved for survival. An oral variation of this exercise may be to have an individual present his/her case orally to a panel of "judges" or to "hire" some member of the group to represent the individual before a panel of judges. The group is divided into subgroups, and each individual presents his/her case. Other members of the group react only supportively and make any additional positive suggestions that come to mind.

Exercise 7–10. Strength Bombardment

Materials Needed:

Newsprint.
Felt tip markers.
Masking tape.

Procedures:

For this exercise to be effective, the group members should know each other reasonably well. Each individual places his or her name at the top of his/her sheet of paper. Papers are then passed clockwise around the group, and each member of the group writes a positive statement that reflects a strength or likeable characteristic of the individual. After each individual has his or her sheet returned, each then stands before the group and shares the comments. The group applauds each presenter.

Exercise 7–11. Buildup Game

Materials: None

Procedures:

For this exercise, groups are organized into three's and members may be rotated. Each group has two contestants and a referee. Member A starts by telling Member

B something positive or something that he/she likes about Member B. Member B reciprocates. The exercise continues until one of the members can no longer respond tit for tat. The role of the referee is to ensure that statements are meaningful and honest. After the exercise is completed, members of the group are given five minutes to reflect on their feelings as a result and then share these with others members of the total group.

Exercise 7–12. Ad Game

Materials Needed:

Newsprint.
Masking tape.
Felt tip markers of varying colors.
3 x 5-in. index cards.
Rosters of group members (with sufficient copies to distribute to each participant)

Procedures:

The facilitator distributes a single file card to each small subgroup that consists of three or four people each. Each file card contains a single word that is characteristic of a positive attribute, such as smile, politeness, honesty, hard work, helpful, dependable. Subgroups then proceed to lay out an ad for the word on the newsprint; for example, "SMILE—it makes you feel better and helps others too! Ask those smilers." Or, "Politeness pays. Polite people you like are _____." Ads are then posted. Members of the group rotate among the posters, placing names of individuals on them that they believe represent the trait. Every member in the group must be placed on at least one poster. (Individuals may check off each name from the roster as they place it on a poster.) At the conclusion of this phase, group members then go around the posters and identify where they have been most frequently listed. They then discuss in their small groups what they have found out about themselves.

Exercise 7–13. Matching Games

Materials Needed:

Newsprint with lists of famous people. Roster of group members (with sufficient numbers to distribute to each person).

Procedures:

The facilitator or counselor prepares a roster that includes at least as many names of famous people as there are individuals in the group. The names should be of people who are generally viewed positively, such as well-known and popular movie and TV stars, outstanding sports figures, well-known scientists and scholars, popular government officials and politicians. When provided with the names, group members are told they are to match each member of the group with one of the famous personages listed. They may list several group members for the same personality. Upon the conclusion of the exercise, the matching sheets are then passed counter-clockwise, and each group member tabulates the number of times he or she was matched with a given personality. These results are then discussed in small groups.

Stage 3: Becoming Aware of Individual Values

Once a climate of acceptance, trust, and open communication has been developed and the individual's self-concept has been reinforced or strengthened, it is appropriate to move toward assisting each person in creating an awareness of what he/she values and how relatively important each of his/her values is.

Exercise 7–14. Listing/Ordering

Materials Needed:

Paper and pencil

Procedures:

In this exercise, each person in the group is requested to list a specific number (ten, fifteen, or twenty) things he/she loves to do. On completion of the list, group members are then asked to rank items in order of importance, with one being the most important. This same exercise may be repeated with material possessions. For example, they may be asked to list their ten or fifteen most prized material possessions and then to rank them in order of importance. Individuals may also be given prepared lists and asked to rank items in order of importance as noted in the following exercise.

Exercise 7–15. Rank Order Exercise

Materials Needed:

Paper and pencil.

Procedures:

Participants rank the following in order of their importance to them, with the number one being the most important activity and number fifteen being the least.

—— 1. Travel.
—— 2. Participation in a sport (sports).
—— 3. Being out of debt.
—— 4. Alcohol.

—— 5. Watching sports.
—— 6. Music (performance or listening).
—— 7. Sex.
—— 8. Being politically active.
—— 9. Being loved.
——10. Home ownership.
——11. Many friends.
——12. Good books.
——13. Driving a nice car.
——14. Good eating.
——15. Smoking.

Exercise 7–16.　Wishing Makes It True

Materials Needed:

Handout with directions and list of items (note the following example).

Procedures:

Rank in order of importance to you the following items if your wish could come true.

—— 1. Receive a million (tax free) dollars.
—— 2. Live a happy, healthy life until at least the age of eighty-five.
—— 3. A world free of wars for the next fifty years.
—— 4. Gradual reduction in crime, leading to its virtual elimination by 2050.
—— 5. A life with the friends and lovers of your choice.
—— 6. Become increasingly recognized as very successful in your professional field.
—— 7. A worldwide pollution-free environment now.
—— 8. Change to a new occupation of your choice and become instantly successful and famous.
—— 9. Discovery of cures for all forms of cancer, heart disease, and addiction.
——10. Rapid elimination of starvation and poverty, as we know it, by the year 2010.
——11. Indefinite continuation of our life just as it is.
——12. Your secret wish.

Exercise 7–17.　Rating Scale

Materials Needed:

Ditto sheets with items and rating scale.

Procedures:

Another exercise very similar to the listing/ordering exercises is one in which items are listed with a rating scale affixed and in which the individual rates the importance of the item, for example, on a five-point scale. This procedure is slightly less discriminating than those in which absolute rank orders must be established, but it does enable the individual to cluster those items that are most important and next most important. A brief illustration follows.

Place a check in the appropriate space on the scale indicating the importance of each of the following to you. The ranking scale is as follows:

4 = very important to me.
3 = of some importance to me.
2 = of slight importance to me.
1 = of little importance to me.
0 = not important at all to me.

Item		Rating				
		4	3	2	1	0
1. Having good friends.						
2. Having a job that pays well.						
3. Having a job I enjoy.						
4. Enjoying good health.						
5. Taking the kind of vacations I want.						
6. Being known as an individualist.						
7. Being physically attractive to the opposite sex.						
8. Being good in some sport.						

Exercise 7–18. Learning Exercises

Materials Needed: None

Procedures:

Learning exercises are designed to help the individual learn more about himself/herself and his/her values. These can take several forms. One can be a "What I learned about me today" diary in which the individual seeks to learn something new about himself/herself each day for a specified period of time. In this endeavor, the individual is free to try experimental activities, to inquire of others, or to plan activities, which may provide the individual with new self-insights. Other learning activities are a "what makes me feel good" exercise in which the client lists things that make him/her feel good a specified period of time, an "I would like to learn list," and a "yearn to" list in which an individual thinks about what he/she would like to have, again over a specified period of time.

Stage 4: Choosing Values Freely from Alternatives After Examining Consequences

Most of us have made decisions that we later regretted. Often these have been decisions, perhaps, made in haste, in which we failed to examine the possible consequences of our action. In counseling, clients are encouraged to examine the possible outcomes of each decision available to them. Various values exercises are helpful in alerting individuals to examine the consequences of their actions prior to their commitment. Hawley and Hawley[37] have divided this process into six elements, four dealing with choosing and two with acting, as follows:

Choosing

1. *Preferences:* What do I really like?
2. *Influences:* What influences have led me to this decision? How freely am I making my choice?
3. *Alternatives:* What are the possible alternatives to this choice? Have I given sufficient consideration to such alternatives?
4. *Consequences:* What are the probable and possible consequences for my choice? Am I willing to risk the consequences? Are the consequences socially beneficial or socially harmful?

Acting

5. *Acting:* Am I able to act on this choice? Do my actions reflect the choice I have made?"
6. *Patterning:* Does this choice represent a continuing commitment through action? How can I change the pattern of my life so that this choice is continually reflected in my actions?[38]

Exercise 7–19.   Either/Or Activities

Materials Needed: None

Procedures:

Either/or activities provide individuals an opportunity to choose from competing alternatives and then discuss the consequences of their choice with others making the same choice. The facilitator announces the alternatives, gives members the opportunity to briefly think about their decision, and then to move to the group representing their choice. Examples of some choices for either/or games are as follows:

Active/Subdued
Grouper/Loner

[37] Robert C. Hawley and Isabel L. Hawley, op. cit., p. 146.
[38] Ibid., p. 147.

Serious/Silly
Saver/Spender
Talker/Listener

Exercise 7–20. I Choose

Materials Needed:

Paper and pencil.

Procedures:

A variation on the either/or game is for the participants to list ten or any designated number of choices that they would make in preference to an alternative that they would specify. Some examples might be of individuals saying, "I choose fried chicken to steak; I choose crossing the ocean by ship rather than by flying. I choose working early in the mornings, rather than late at night. I choose tennis over golf." Following completion of the "I Choose" list, subgroups are formed and individuals discuss their choices and the consequences of their decisions IF they had to stick by their choices under all circumstances in the future.

Exercise 7–21. Futures

Materials Needed: None

Procedures:

"Futures" is an exercise in which an individual identifies as many future decisions he/she is going to make over the next five-year period. The counselor or facilitator will usually establish a ten- or fifteen-minute time limitation for the listing of such decisions. The counselor or facilitator then directs the participants to list plausible alternatives for each decision and then to project the consequences of each of these. Subgroups discuss the outcomes of the exercise.

Exercise 7–22. Heart Machine Exercise

Materials Needed:

List of candidates for heart machine (with sufficient number of copies for each person in the group to receive the list).

Procedures:

Individuals must become aware that often the choices from competing alternatives are difficult to make. This exercise illustrates that point. Participants are given a sheet that presents the situation as follows: A heart-mending machine has been perfected that without surgery enables the complete restructuring of the most serious heart defects. The machine is capable of treating one patient at a time for a three-month period required for complete recovery. There is currently only one such machine in existence and, because of the rare resources required, it will be two years before another is available for use. You are on a panel to select the first three patients from among ten people suffering severe heart damage. A consensus of heart specialists has agreed that none of these candidates will survive longer than ten or twelve months without this treatment. Indicate your three choices of those to receive treatment on this machine. The ten candidates are not identified by name and you will be provided only the following minimal information as a basis for selecting the three persons who will be given the heart machine treatment.

1. Black male, age twenty-eight. Married, no children.
   Occupation: famous athlete (pro football player).
2. White female, age sixty-four. Widowed, three grown children, all married.
   Occupation: state governor.
3. Twelve-year-old female from a low-income family.
   Occupation: student (average grades).
4. Thirty-five-year-old white male. Married, two children.
   Occupation: bricklayer (unemployed past three months and record of habitual unemployment).
5. Fifty-five-year-old white male. Married, two children, one of college age and one married and employed.
   Occupation: United States ambassador to a South American country (known for his skills in projecting a positive image of American foreign policy).
6. White female, age twenty-five. Honor college graduate in biological sciences. Single.
   Occupation: TV personality (famous female comedienne).
7. Black female, thirty-four. Married. Husband is a school teacher. Two children: girl, age nine; boy, age twelve.
   Her occupation: school teacher.
8. Thirty-six-year-old male. Married, two children: daughters, ten and six. Wife currently pregnant.
   Occupation: sergeant, United States Army. Much decorated hero of Vietnam war.
9. Sixty-year-old white female. Married (husband retired). Children grown and married.
   Occupation: minister (one of few female ministers in a major religious denomination in the country).
10. White male, age forty-eight. Mexican-American. Divorced, three children, two married and one in college (his custody).
    Occupation: corporation president. Millionaire who has for each of the past five years donated more than one million dollars per year to various charities.

Following the decisions made by the panel, members should be prepared to discuss, defend, and compare decisions with others in the class or group.

Exercise 7–23. Selecting Six to Survive

Materials Needed:

Paper and pencil.

Procedures:

Facilitator or counselor organizes small groups. This is similar to the previous exercise except participants are to assume that creatures from another planet have demonstrated an ability to instantaneously destroy all life on earth. They have indicated they are going to do so within the next twenty-four hours, but will allow a committee of which you are a member to identify from the world's population six individuals by name who will be permitted to survive and will be placed back on earth following the destruction of all remaining life. You cannot select friends, relatives, or acquaintances. You have one half hour to make your choices, and you must be prepared to defend these choices to outer-space representatives. Who would you select and why?

Exercise 7–24. This is Your Life

Materials Needed:

Paper and pencil.

Procedures:

One of the most significant decisions made in life is the choice of one's career. However, the impact that one's choice of career might have on one's desired lifestyle is not always realized by the inexperienced. The following exercise, therefore, is designed to present certain career options and to permit individuals to examine what impact these decisions might have on one's life. In this exercise, the participants are first asked to list in order of preference six careers they would be willing to consider if they had to make a choice at this time. Participants are then asked to list in order of preference what they perceive as their ten highest values in life. Following the completion of these two listings, participants are asked to discuss with a partner the relationship of their priority values to their career choices. (In this exercise, participants should be encouraged to discuss the kind of life they would visualize for themselves in each of the careers listed.)

Exercise 7–25. Would you be willing to _____?

Materials Needed:

List of "Would you be willing to" cases, with sufficient copies for each participant.

Procedures:

Because many life decisions are based upon a choice between a present situation and a new alternative, this exercise is designed to provide participants opportunities to examine such possibilities. For groups, it is probably helpful to have the situations duplicated, and following distribution, to give participants sufficient time for each individual to arrive at his/her own decision. Then organize participants into small groups for discussion. In individual counseling, of course, the situation could be presented verbally. The following are examples of "Would you be willing to" exercises.

1. Drop all of your activities and leave your friends and family behind for a year for an around-the-world, all expenses paid trip by ship and air?

2. Live on a deserted island for six months without any contact with human beings. You would have a radio for emergency medical purposes. You could stock the island with whatever you wished in the way of food and drink, reading and entertainment materials. No pets or animals would be allowed, however. At the end of the six months you would have your choice of either starring in a movie about your experience or writing a book that would promise to be a best seller about your experience.

3. Quit school to take an apprentice's job in a furniture factory owned by a heretofore unknown relative of yours. This relative has indicated to you that within three years he will advance you to a top-level management position of your choice, such as advertising, sales, or personnel, and that within ten years he will retire and you will take over the presidency of the company. He estimates that your annual earnings at that point would be more than $80,000 per year with fringe benefits. The company is located in a small, rural midwestern community.

4. Be part of an experimental group that would agree to being "frozen" in time, to be brought back to life 300 years later. The process has been perfected and you would be given one year to prepare. The scientist talking to you about this project has pointed out the probability that disease would have been virtually eliminated from the earth by that time and you would undoubtedly be a celebrity of that century. Would you give this project more favorable consideration if two of your best friends would agree to join?

5. Give up television, radio, stereo, and movies for a year to avoid wearing glasses the rest of your life?

6. Rob a bank of one million dollars if you knew you would be caught and sentenced to three years in prison, but if you also knew that before you were caught, you would be able to hide the money in a place where you could retrieve it and spend it without retribution over your lifetime. You also know that the bank is well insured so that the depositors will not lose their savings.

7. Live in a country that severely restricts freedom of speech, press, religion, and personal movement for a period of a year in order to study the lives of the people of that country and report your findings to your government. This would not be viewed as a spy mission, but, rather, as an important mission to study the way of life of people who are denied freedoms.

8. Move to another community that had better schools and a healthier environment

in which you would have better personal living conditions, but in which in
the five years you would be living there you would be unpopular and have
few friends because you would be viewed as an "outsider."

Exercise 7–26. Would you prefer . . .

Materials Needed:

List of competing alternatives.

Procedures:

This exercise is a variation of the either-or exercise previously described that gives
individuals the opportunity to make a selection between two competing alternatives
and then examine it through explanation and discussion of their choice in small
subgroups. Some of the options might be as follows:

Would you prefer to:
1. Live in Cleveland, Ohio, or Salt Lake City, Utah.
2. Listen to music or play in a band or an orchestra.
3. Cross the ocean to Europe by ocean liner or plane.
4. Take courses at a university or a vocational school.
5. Ride a bicycle or jog.

Variation:

A different version of the "Would you prefer" exercise is one in which a single
choice is made from among several competing alternatives. For example, in this
exercise, the question might be, "How would you prefer to spend an evening?"

1. Reading a good book at home.
2. Going to a topflight play with name actors and actresses.
3. Eating a gourmet meal in a five-star restaurant.
4. Attending a championship-level sporting event.
5. Attending a musical event by outstanding musicians.

Stage 5: Helping Clients Set Goals and Take Action on Their Values

Although becoming aware of values, learning to choose from alternatives,
and making decisions are important, they become relatively meaningless if
value goals are not set and actions taken to achieve these goals. Whereas
we may verbalize our belief in our values, it is not uncommon for us to
fail to act upon them. Experienced counselors know, too, that clients will
often verbalize their intentions to change, to behave differently, and to make
or implement a decision, but then fail to follow through or act on their
stated intentions. The following values activities are designed to encourage
individuals to translate their decisions into actions.

Exercise 7–27. My Five-Year Plan

Materials Needed:

Worksheets as indicated, with copies for each participant.

Procedures:

Participants are asked to identify and list goals they would like to achieve over the next five-year period. The facilitator may suggest that categories for organizing their goals might be educational, career, social, personal, physical well-being, recreational and leisure, and other or miscellaneous category. Once goals are listed, participants are asked to identify activities in which they should engage over the next year to initiate progress toward achieving their five-year plan. Once these have been identified, it is then suggested that they indicate the immediate steps they will take to get them started toward achieving each of their five-year goals. Worksheets may be provided to organize this task for them as follows:

Five-Year Goals

	First year's activities for progression toward goals	Getting started: First steps toward goals
1.		
2.		
3.		

Exercise 7–28. Diary Exercises

Materials Needed:

Paper and pencil.

Procedures:

Diary exercises are designed to make participants conscious on a daily basis of the degree to which they are or are not taking action on their values. Diaries may follow a variety of formats. For example, a self-improvement diary would be one in which the individual indicates what his/her self-improvement goals are over a period of time. These are listed in the front of his/her diary. The diary keeper then records on a daily basis the activities undertaken to achieve these values. He/she also may note handicaps to values practicing and changes in goals or values. Diary writings may be shared in small subgroups or with the counselor or other facilitator. A values diary is similar to the self-improvement diary with the exception that it may focus on the implementation of a single significant value. Value anecdotes are also similar to the values diary except that they tend to provide a more detailed and descriptive explanation of efforts at values implementation.

Exercise 7–29. Promissory Note

Materials Needed:

Paper and pencil.

Procedures:

Promissory note is an exercise in which the participant writes in legal terminology his or her intent or promise to achieve a certain values objective by a specified date, or pay a penalty. Promissory notes are usually negotiated between an individual participant and either another participant or the counselor or values facilitator. An example of such a promissory note might be as follows:

> I, Dudley Dudworth, do hereby promise that I will, without fail, complete all of my school assignments on time for the remainder of the semester. If I fail to do so, I will forfeit my rights to watch TV, movies, or listen to the radio for a period of thirty days.
>
> Signed _____
> Dudley Dudworth
>
> Witnessed:
>
> _____
> Jonathan Smedly Horn, Counselor

SUMMARY

In recent years much attention has been given in the press and other media to the values of youth, the shifting values of the adult world, and the significance of personal values for satisfaction in the world of work. Values, it would appear, have suddenly become everyone's concern, an endless source for studies, and an inspiration for numerous publications. Values have also become increasingly important to professional educators and professional counselors. Values clarification techniques have been developed, and numerous publications have appeared that are appropriate to the needs of teachers, counselors, and others who work in helping and/or teaching capacities.

For counselors, values clarification techniques are being gradually recognized as a helpful and nonthreatening approach to individual human appraisal and one that involves the individual actively and continuously in his/her own self-assessment and understanding. In a planned program of values clarification and development, the individual initially engages in exercises designed to identify his/her values, then shares them, next, examines them, confirms them, and, finally, practices values. Varied exercises, a small sampling of which have been presented in this chapter, are available from numerous publications. If you have resisted the temptation up to this point to try some of them, you are now encouraged to do so as an appropriate finale to this chapter.

Career Guidance 8
and Placement

INTRODUCTION

As noted in Chapter 1, the guidance and counseling movement in America has had a long and traditional association with and concern for career development and decision making. During its early years, organized guidance in American education consisted primarily of vocational guidance. This early interest, originating with Parsons, was an outgrowth of a concern for the complexity of the world of work and the resultant difficulty in career planning, a concept that is still viable today. As originally practiced by Parsons and his associates, the concept of matching youth with jobs, based on the characteristics of both, has also had a long and traditional association with the guidance movement. As the guidance concept was broadened and other basic activities added in the 1920s and 1930s, vocational guidance became a service activity most frequently identified as the providing of occupational and educational information. In the late 1950s and 1960s with the original impetus from the National Defense Education Act of 1958, placement and follow-up also became significant activities of the vocational or career guidance phase of the school guidance program. Thus, for nearly sixty years the guidance movement had been the caretaker for student career planning in American education.

In 1971, however, the United States Office of Education, through the then Commissioner of Education, Sidney P. Marland, Jr., committed more than $9 million of discretionary funds for research and development projects focusing on the establishment of comprehensive career education models. With this act, the concept of career education as an all-school responsibility was launched, and the school counselor was no longer the sole designate for the career education and guidance of the individual pupil.

THE CAREER EDUCATION MOVEMENT

Origins

Since Dr. Marland made his plea for "career education now" in a speech to the National Association of Secondary School Principals at its convention in Houston in 1971, the concept has swept the educational establishment in the United States. Educators from every field and discipline have been involved in the movement. Additionally, many state legislatures have passed career education legislation, and career education became a mandate of the Congress of the United States when Public Law 93–380 was signed by former President Ford in August 1974. In less than a decade, more than ten major national associations endorsed career education, hundreds of publications on career education were published and distributed, and an astounding array of proponents and interpreters of the career education concept emerged. However, even with the rapid development of career education and the many and varied publications and spokespeople, certain basic concepts can be noted that may assist counselors and potential counselors in understanding the background, basic principles, and relationships of this movement to counseling.

As a rationale for the movement, Dr. Kenneth B. Hoyt, director of the Office of Career Education of the United States Office of Education, stated in his paper "An Introduction to Career Education," that career education was a response to the call for educational reform. He then proceeded to identify eleven primary criticisms of American education that career education seeks to correct as follows:

1. Too many persons leaving our educational system are deficient in the basic academic skills required for adaptability in today's rapidly changing society.
2. Too many students fail to see meaningful relationships between what they are being asked to learn in school and what they will do when they leave the educational system. This is true of both those who remain to graduate and those who drop out of the educational system.
3. American education, as currently structured, best meets the educa-

tional needs of that minority of persons who will someday become college graduates. It has not given equal emphasis to meeting the educational needs of that vast majority of students who will never be college graduates.

4. American education has not kept pace with the rapidity of change in the post-industrial occupational society. As a result, when worker qualifications are compared with job requirements, we find over-educated and under-educated workers are present in large numbers. Both the boredom of the over-educated worker and the frustration of the under-educated worker have contributed to the growing presence of worker alienation in the total occupational society.

5. Too many persons leave our educational system at both the secondary and collegiate levels unequipped with the vocational skills, the self-understanding and career decision-making skills, or the work attitudes that are essential for making a successful transition from school to work.

6. The growing need for and presence of women in the work force has been adequately reflected in neither the educational nor the career options typically pictured for girls enrolled in our educational system.

7. The growing needs for continuing and recurrent education on the part of adults are not being adequately met by our current systems of public education.

8. Insufficient attention has been given to learning opportunities outside the structure of formal education which exist and are increasingly needed by both youth and adults in our society.

9. The general public, including parents and the business-industry-labor community, has not been given an adequate role in formulation of educational policy.

10. American education, as currently structured, does not adequately meet the needs of minority, nor of economically disadvantaged persons in our society.

11. Post high school education has given insufficient emphasis to educational programs at the sub-baccalaureate degree level.[1]

In addition to the needs for educational reform that prompted the career education movement, there have also been significant changes in the concepts of careers and work. Symptomatic of these changes are the following:

No longer one world—one career.

Whereas our ancestors, perhaps even our parents, could, upon identifying their life's work, enter into their own little world and career for life, there are increasing probabilities that most individuals entering the work forces in the 1980s will have, at the very least, several significant careers over the span of their life's work. From a career standpoint, we are now living in

---

[1] Kenneth B. Hoyt, *An Introduction to Career Education,* policy paper of the U.S. Office of Education, Department of Health, Education and Welfare, Washington, D.C., 1974.

an age in which the rapidity of technological developments can affect what we do and how we do it almost literally overnight. Counselors are being more frequently reminded that such changes can result in increasing numbers of adults who, either by choice or necessity, will be making mid-life career decisions.

> Evidence is mounting that the single career norm within the American workforce may soon become a phenomenon of the past. In the early 1970s, publications such as Striner's *Continuing Education as a National Capital Investment,*[2] Sheppard and Herrick's *Where Have All the Robots Gone?*[3] and the U.S. Department of Health, Education and Welfare's report *Work in America*[4] began arguing for more flexible work and educational opportunities for employed adults. Career change, in particular, began to be perceived as a necessary option for many adults seeking further growth and self-renewal.[5]

No longer is the concept "Men only—Women only" appropriate for career planning.

Recent generations have witnessed the elimination of many barriers to career entry, which in the past limited certain professions and occupations exclusively to certain populations or sexes. Career exclusiveness, for example, excluded females from such traditional male professions and occupations as engineering, airline piloting, taxicab and truck driving, to mention but a few. These once "safe" career havens for males, and some such as nursing for females, have been effectively challenged not only in the courts, but, more importantly, in the world of work. Additionally, the antipoverty and antidiscrimination movements have further challenged the exclusiveness of certain careers that were once limited to only racial majority members of upper socioeconomic income populations.

No longer the old college try and tie.

Much has also been written in recent years regarding the decline of demand in the job market for the college graduate. Although this is not necessarily, as some claim, a rationale for declining college enrollments, it indicates that career opportunities are no longer tied directly to the level and locale of educational preparation, but may be more appropriately tied to the career relevancy of one's educational preparation.

No longer can the future be predicted by the present.

[2] Herbert E. Striner, *Continuing Education as a National Capital Investment* (New York: Upjohn Institute, 1971).

[3] Harold L. Sheppard and Neal Q. Herrick, *Where Have All the Robots Gone: Workers' Dissatisfaction in the 70s* (New York: Macmillan Publishing Co., Inc., 1972).

[4] *Work in America: Report of a Special Task Force to the Secretary of Health, Education and Welfare,* (Cambridge, Mass.: MIT Press, 1973).

[5] Paul Ferrini and L. Allen Parker, *Career Change* (Cambridge, Mass.: Technical Education Research Centers, 1978), p. 3.

In other times it was possible for those interested in charting their future to make many appropriate preparations and predictions based on their knowledge of the present. However, changing technology plus national resource development and depletion have made it increasingly difficult, if not almost impossible, in recent years to adequately judge the future. This, coupled with the accelerated rate of change in modern society, prevents one from assuming, as he/she might have in the past, that the future will be similar to the present.

No longer is one in charge of one's own destiny.

It is clear that the day of the rugged individualist—one who would achieve one's own destiny—is but a memory of the past. In today's complicated society with its many interacting forces, there are many variables affecting one's destiny over which he/she has little or no control and of which he/she may be unaware. Although individuals can plan and chart their futures, they must also consider alternatives and adjustments.

Definitions and Clarifications

An outgrowth of the career education movement has been a proliferation of definitions, with attending confusion, seeking to differentiate between such terms as career education, career development, career guidance, vocational education, and human development. In this chapter and elsewhere in this text, the following definitions apply:

Career: "The totality of work one experiences in a lifetime."[6] A more limited definition would view a career as the sum total of one's work experiences in a general occupational category such as teaching, accounting, medicine, sales.

Occupation: A specific job or work activity.

Career Development: That aspect of one's total devleopment which emphasizes learning about, preparation for, entry into, and progression in the world of work.

Career Education: Those planned-for educational experiences that facilitate the individual's career development and preparation for the world of work. The totality of experiences through which one learns about and prepares for engaging in work as part of a way of living. A primary responsibility of the school with an emphasis on learning about, planning for, and preparing to enter a career.

Career Guidance: Those activities which are carried out by guidance counselors in a variety of settings for the purpose of stimulating and facilitating career development in individuals over their working lifetimes. These activities include assistance in career planning, decision making, and adjustment. In

[6] Kenneth B. Hoyt, op. cit, p. 6.

the school setting, specifically, career guidance may be viewed as a continuous developmental process that assists individuals with life career preparation through active curricular interventions that provide career planning, decision making, coping skills development, career information, and self-understanding.

Occupational Information: Data concerning training and related educational programs, careers, career patterns, and employment trends and opportunities.

Vocation: Trade or occupation.

Vocational Education: Education which is preparatory for a career in a vocational or technical field.

It should be noted that these rather limited definitions are perhaps at one end of the continuum. For example, a career is sometimes defined as the sum total of an individual's life experiences and life-styles, whereas career education is frequently viewed as consisting of all activities and experiences, planned or otherwise, that prepare the individual for work. However, straightforward and concise, though limited, definitions are most practical in specific planning for programs of career education and career guidance.

Basic Assumptions

Obviously, career development, career education, and career guidance are interwoven and interrelated. One without the other is ineffective and meaningless. As career education stimulates career development, career guidance provides direction for career education and development. Further, clarification of the career education movement and the related role and function of the guidance counselor may result from noting the basic concept assumptions suggested in the United States Office of Education (USOE) policy paper of 1974, as follows:

1. Since both one's career and one's education extend from the preschool through the retirement years, career education must also span almost the entire life cycle.
2. The concept of productivity is central to the definition of work and so to the entire concept of career education.
3. Since "work" includes unpaid activities as well as paid employment, career education's concerns, in addition to its prime emphasis on paid employment, extend to the work of the student as a learner, to the growing numbers of volunteer workers in our society, to the work of the full-time homemaker, and to work activities in which one engages as part of leisure and/or recreational time.
4. The cosmopolitan nature of today's society demands that career education embrace a multiplicity of work values, rather than a single work ethic, as a means of helping each individual answer the question, "Why should I work?"

5. Both one's career and one's education are best viewed in a developmental, rather than in a fragmented, sense.

6. Career education is for all persons—the young and the old—the mentally handicapped and the intellectually gifted—the poor and the wealthy—males and females—students in elementary schools and in the graduate colleges.

7. The societal objectives of career education are to help all individuals: (a) want to work; (b) acquire the skills necessary for work in these times; and (c) engage in work that is satisfying to the individual and beneficial to society.

8. The individualistic goals of career education are to make work: (a) possible; (b) meaningful; and (c) satisfying for each individual throughout his or her lifetime.

9. Protection of the individual's freedom to choose and assistance in making and implementing career decisions are of central concern to career education.

10. The expertise required for implementing career education is to be found in many parts of society and is not limited to those employed in formal education.[7]

Programmatic assumptions of career education (also indicated in the same policy paper) were stated as follows:

1. If students can see clear relationships between what they are being asked to learn in school and the world of work, they will be motivated to learn more in school.

2. There exists no single learning strategy that can be said to be best for all students. Some students will learn best by reading out of books, for example, and others will learn best by combining reading with other kinds of learning activities. A comprehensive educational program should provide a series of alternative learning strategies and learning environments for students.

3. Basic academic skills, a personally meaningful set of work values, and good work habits represent adaptability tools needed by all persons who choose to work in today's rapidly changing occupational society.

4. Increasingly, entry into today's occupational society demands the possession of a specific set of vocational skills on the part of those who seek employment. Unskilled labor is less and less in demand.

5. Career development, as part of human development, begins in the pre-school years and continues into the retirement years. Its maturational patterns differ from individual to individual.

6. Work values, a part of one's personal value system, are developed, to a significant degree, during the elementary school years and are modifiable during those years.

7. Specific occupational choices represent only one of a number of kinds of choices involved in career development. They can be

[7] Ibid p. 7–8.

expected to increase in realism as one moves from childhood into adulthood and, in some degree, to be modifiable during those years.

8. Occupational decision making is accomplished through the dynamic interaction of limiting and enhancing factors both within the individual and in his present and proposed environment. It is not, in any sense, something that can be viewed as a simple matching of individuals with jobs.

9. Occupational stereotyping currently acts to hinder full freedom of occupational choice for both females and for minority persons. These restrictions can be reduced, to some extent, through programmatic intervention strategies begun in the early childhood years.

10. Parent socioeconomic status acts as a limitation on occupational choices considered by children. This limitation can be reduced, to a degree, by program intervention strategies begun in the early years.

11. A positive relationship exists between education and occupational competence, but the optimum amount and kind of education required as preparation for work varies greatly from occupation to occupation.

12. The same general strategies utilized in reducing worker alienation in industry can be used to reduce worker alienation among pupils and teachers in the classroom.

13. While some persons will find themselves able to meet their human needs for accomplishment through work in their place of paid employment, others will find it necessary to meet this need through work in which they engage during their leisure time.

14. Career decision-making skills, job hunting skills, and job getting skills can be taught to and learned by almost all persons. Such skills, once learned, can be effectively used by individuals in enhancing their career development.

15. Excessive deprivation in any given aspect of human growth and development can lead to retardation of career development. Such deprivation will require special variations in career development programs for persons suffering such deprivation.

16. An effective means of helping individuals discover who they are (in a self-concept sense) is through helping them discover their accomplishments that can come from the work that they do.

17. Parental attitudes toward work and toward education act as powerful influences on the career development of their children. Such parental attitudes are modifiable through programmatic intervention strategies.

18. The processes of occupational decision making and occupational preparation can be expected to be repeated more than once for most adults in today's society.

19. One's style of living is significantly influenced by occupations he or she engages in at various times in life.

20. Relationships between education and work can be made more

meaningful to students through infusion into subject matter than if taught as a separate body of knowledge.

21. Education and work can increasingly be expected to be interwoven at various times in the lives of most individuals, rather than occurring in a single sequential pattern.

22. Decisions individuals make about the work that they do are considerably broader and more encompassing in nature than are decisions made regarding the occupations in which they are employed.

23. Good work habits and positive attitudes toward work can be effectively taught to most individuals. Assimilation of such knowledge is most effective if begun in the early childhood years.

24. The basis on which work can become a personally meaningful part of one's life will vary greatly from individual to individual. No single approach can be expected to meet with universal success.

25. While economic return can almost always be expected to be a significant factor in decisions individuals make about occupations, it may not be a significant factor in many decisions individuals make about their total pattern of work.[8]

Within this framework, the USOE position paper specified that counseling and guidance personnel would

1. Help classroom teachers implement career education in the classroom.

2. Serve, usually with other educational personnel, as liaison contacts between the school and the business-industry-labor community.[9]

Career Development (and Education) As a Part of Human Development

All aspects of human development, whether they be social, physical, emotional, or educational, are but parts of one's total development—parts that are usually interwoven and often difficult to separate and distinguish from the other aspects of human development. Career development is, of course, no exception. A recognition of these relationships and the application of certain basic principles of human development are significant in the design and implementation of programs for career development. The 1973 National Vocational Guidance Association-American Vocational Association position paper on career development highlighted seven of these developmental dimensions, as follows:

1. Development occurs during the lifetime of an individual. It can be described in maturational terms denoting progression through life stages and the mastery of developmental tasks at each stage.

[8] Ibid, pp. 9–11.
[9] Ibid, p. 13.

Although research evidence is lacking, it seems unlikely that intervention can substantially shorten this maturational process.

2. Individual development is influenced by both heredity and environment. Psychological, sociological, educational, political, economic, and physical factors affect development. Appropriate intervention strategies which focus upon these factors can influence the quality of individual development.

3. Development is a continuous process. Individual development can best be facilitated by intervention strategies that begin in the early years and continue throughout the life of the person. Programs which focus only at certain points or at certain stages in the individual's life will have limited effectiveness.

4. Although development is continuous, certain aspects are dominant at various periods of the life span. Programs designed to facilitate career development should account for the dominant aspects at given stages.

5. Individual development involves a progressive differentiation and integration of the person's self and his perceived world. Intervention strategies need to be designed to assist individuals during normal maturational stages of career development rather than to provide remedial assistance to individuals whose development has been damaged or retarded.

6. While common developmental stages can be observed and described during childhood and adult life, individual differences in progressing through these stages can be expected. Intervention programs should provide for these differences, making no assumption that something is "wrong" with those who progress at atypical rates.

7. Excessive deprivation with respect to any single aspect of human development can retard optimal development in other areas. Optimal human development programs are comprehensive in nature, not limited to any single facet. It is recognized that those who suffer from deprivation may require special and intensive assistance. Where deprivation is long term, short term intervention is not likely to be sufficient.[10]

Models for Career Education

Recognizing that career education is a developmental process and is not limited to a particular age or school group, the Bureau of Occupational and Adult Education, the Office of Career Education, and the National Institute of Educational engaged in research and developmental efforts, which led to the development of four operational models for career education, as follows:

[10] 1973 National Vocational Guidance Association-American Vocational Association Position Paper on Career Development, published by the National Vocational Guidance Association of the American Personnel Guidance Association, Washington, D.C.

1. The Employer-Based Model seeks primarily to serve teenage students through an optional out-of-school program of personalized educational experiences in an employer-based setting. The model stresses community participation, particularly by businesses and organizations, in cooperation with the schools, to offer an alternative educational program relevant to the individual's interests and needs.

2. The Home-Based Model is designed to introduce a variety of experiences using the home as a center for learning, especially for persons 18 to 25 years of age who have left shcool. The objectives are to develop educational delivery systems for the home and the community; to provide new career education programs for adults; to establish a guidance and career placement system to assist individuals in occupational and related life-roles; and to develop more competent workers. A Career Education Extension service will be established to coordinate the use of mass media and career education resources.

3. The Rural/Residential-Based Model is a research and demonstration project which will test the hypothesis that entire disadvantaged rural families can experience lasting improvement in their economic and social conditions through an intensive program at a residential center. Families are drawn from a six-state area to the project site in Glasgow, Montana. Programs will provide services to the entire family, including day care, health care, educational programs from kindergarten through adult, welfare, counseling, cultural and recreational opportunities. The objective is to provide rural families with employment capabilities suitable to the area, so that students will be able and ready to find employment in the area after completing the program.

4. The School-Based Model is, by far, the most common of the four models, and is the one of greatest interest to us. USOE sponsored the development of six demonstration projects through the Center for Vocational and Technical Education of the Ohio State University. The elements and outcomes presented earlier in this section are a result of this work. The development and validation effort which was undertaken is quite extensive, and includes several school districts . . . In all, about 115 schools, 4,200 teachers and administrators, and 85,000 students are involved. A single model is being developed for ALL the sites, so that the result will be a model that has been tested for applicability in a variety of settings. Local educational agencies are cooperating in the development of curricular and instructional materials to achieve specific objectives. These "treatments," along with materials located in an ongoing national search, will be classified and catalogued for dissemination to other educational agencies. Extensive in-service teacher education is part of the development program.[11]

[11] *Career Education: An Introduction* (Tallahassee, Fla.: Florida Department of Education, Division of Vocational Technical and Adult Education, 1974), p. 62.

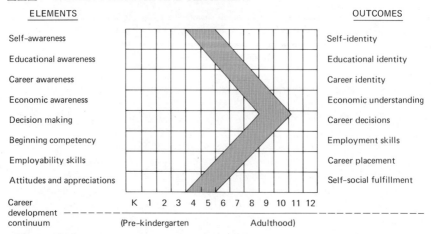

Figure 8–1.
The comprehensive career education models (CCEM) matrix. Career Education: An Introduction *(Tallahassee: Florida Department of Education, Division of Vocational, Technical, and Adult Education, 1974), p. 61.*

The school-based comprehensive education model provides a theoretical base for linkages between career guidance and career education. As Ryan noted,

> The School-Based Comprehensive Education Model (CCEM) has greater overall potential to make an impact on all students in grades K to 12 and was selected as the focus for linking career guidance to career education. The research and field testing related to CCEM have exerted a powerful influence on curriculum design and career guidance from 1971 to 1977. The CCEM illustrates a sequential program of career awareness in grades K–6, career exploration in 7–9, and career preparation in grades 10–12. The basic model presented in Figure 8–1 identifies the eight basic elements of career education.[12] Underlying CCEM is the premise that intensive career guidance permeates the curriculum throughout grades K–12. Counseling and guidance are viewed as essential elements that assist the student with developing self-awareness and career awareness and with improving decision-making skills. Each element of CCEM requires a programmatic effort across all grades and strongly suggests a career guidance curriculum to assist youth in achieving the intended outcome. Each of the eight elements is defined as follows:
>
> *Self-Awareness.* The student becomes aware of himself, his needs, strengths, and personal likes and dislikes so that he or she may develop

[12] Charles W. Ryan, "Practical Linkages Between Career Guidance and Career Education," *Viewpoints in Teaching and Learning,* **54:**12–14 (Jan. 1978).

self-knowledge and a positive self-identity that will aid in making effective life career decisions.

Educational Awareness. The student recognizes the significance of basic skill development and the mastery of content knowledge as a means of achieving career goals.

Career Awareness. The student realizes that career development includes progression through stages of education and occupational experiences, and understands that there are a variety of occupations found in the world of work and that there is a relationship between career and life-style.

Economic Awareness. The student understands the relationship between personal economics, life-styles, and occupations.

Decision making. The student understands that decision making includes responsible action in identifying alternatives, selecting the alternative most consistent with personal goals, and taking steps to implement the course of action. Students are proficient in using resource information to make career decisions.

Beginning Competencies. The student develops basic cognitive skills that are required to identify the objectives of a task, outline procedures, perform required operations, and evaluate the results.

Appreciations and Attitudes. The student develops an internalized value system that includes a valuing of personal career roles and the roles assumed by others. Appreciation of one's personal career role should lead to an active, satisfying participation in the work of society.[13]

Miller (1972) described the basic tenets of a comprehensive career education, school-based model as follows:

1. Career education is a comprehensive educational program focused on careers. It begins with the entry of the child into a formal school program and continues into the adult years.
2. Career education involves all students, regardless of their postsecondary plans.
3. Career education involves the entire school program and the resources of the community.
4. Career education infuses the total school curriculum, rather than providing discrete, high-profile "career education" blocks forced into the curriculum.
5. Career education unites the student, his parents, the schools, the community, and employers in a cooperative education venture.
6. Career education provides the student with information and experiences representing the entire world of work.
7. Career education supports the student from initial career awareness, through career exploration, careers direction-setting, career

[13] Ibid., p. 14.

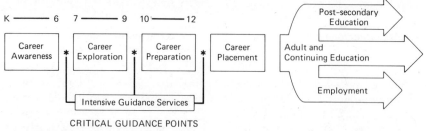

CRITICAL GUIDANCE POINTS

Figure 8–2.

A **comprehensive career education system.** Career Education: An Introduction *(Tallahassee: Florida Department of Education, Division of Vocational, Technical, and Adult Education, 1974), p. 65.*

preparation and career placement, and provides for follow-through and reeducation if desired.

8. Career education is not a synonym for vocational education; but vocational preparation is an integral and important part of a total career education system.[14]

This model may be viewed as a comprehensive career education system, providing a logical sequence of experiences that move the student from career awareness to career exploration to career preparation and, finally, to career placement. Although the counseling function is of great import throughout the learner's career development, some suggest that it becomes critically important during the transition between the phases, as indicated in Figure 8–2.

The Counselor's Role in Career Education

As has been noted, the career movement in schools has been viewed as primarily a developmental and educational process. This process provides an opportunity for the school counselor to at last function in a developmental and, in a sense, a preventive capacity. Although the teacher is clearly the key person on the career education team, the school counselor, by virture of special understandings and skills, can make a valuable contribution. These contributions may be categorized under the following activities.

Career Counseling

Programs of career education are designed to prepare individuals for the eventual selection of a career, but many adolescents and young adults will be unable to adequately cope with this critical decision making without the

---

[14] A. J. Miller, *The Emerging School-Based Comprehensive Education Model* (Columbus, Ohio: The Center for Vocational and Technical Education, Ohio State University, Apr. 1972).

assistance of a professional counselor. Parental counseling, group counseling, and group guidance activities represent contributions of the counselor to the career development of the individual and the school's career education program.

Career Assessment

An important aspect of the career education program provides students the opportunities to assess their personal characteristics in relation to career planning and decision making. The counselor can make a significant contribution to the development of appropriate self-understandings of youth through the employment of both standardized and nonstandardized assessment techniques.

Resource Person and Consultant

The school counselor has been traditionally active in the acquisition of informational materials appropriate to career decision making and planning. The counselor is also aware of such media aids as films, filmstrips, audio and video tapes. Although it cannot be anticipated that the counselor will collect any and all materials, it is reasonable to expect that the counselor will be aware of the sources from which such materials may be obtained. In this capacity, the counselor serves as a resource person to the individual teachers involved in the career education program. The counselor also serves in a consulting capacity, utilizing his or her understandings of the pupil population and his or her understandings of career development, resources, and opportunities to complement the career education program.

Linkage Agent

Increasingly, the counselor will be active in collaborative efforts, not only with teachers and others in the school setting, but with community agencies and employers.

The counselor has an important role to play in implementing and strengthening career education programs. This role does not diminish the importance of the career guidance function, however. The next section of this chapter discusses the need and nature of career guidance.

THE CAREER GUIDANCE FUNCTION

The counselor's significant role in the success of the educational system's career education program warrants a closer examination of the nature of career guidance and the counselor's attending special responsibilities. An excellent statement of the nature of career guidance is the following from the 1973 National Vocational Guidance Association-American Vocational Association's position paper:

A. The Need for Career Guidance

Today there are many social factors which converge to stimulate an interest in the career development needs of persons of all ages:

1. Growing complexity in the occupational and organizational structure of society, which makes it difficult for a person to assimilate and organize the data necessary to formulate a career.
2. Evermore rapid technological change, demanding human adaptability and responsiveness.
3. Increasing national concern with the need to develop all human talent, including the talents of women and minorities.
4. An ardent search for values which will give meaning to life.
5. The need for specialized training to obtain entry jobs.
6. The apparent disenchantment expressed by students who have difficulty relating their education to their lives.

Each one of these factors impinges on the individual in ways that make achieving self-fulfillment more difficult.

In the past, some managerial personnel in business and industry have held a "non-careerism" attitude, which viewed the typical job as an isolated event in a person's life. Whether this attitude is tenable in the post-industrial period is seriously questioned today. The evolving view is that a job should be considered as a stage in an integrated, lifelong career—a step on a career lattice which involves both horizontal and vertical dimensions. On the horizontal level it involves patterns of choice at one point in time, such as: "Should I combine employment with study? Or should I engage in volunteer work along with my employment?" Vertically, it involves choices along a time line, such as: "How do my options or behavior at this point relate to options or behavior in the near, intermediate or distant future?" As new questions are raised about the opportunities work provides for learning and self-development, the need for expanded programs of career guidance becomes apparent.

B. The Nature of Career Guidance

The nature of guidance for career development cannot be viewed as a static, tradition-based set of related services that assist individuals in making single occupational choices. The content of any career guidance program must be developed from initial assessment of the present and future career development needs of the individual; it must also account for impinging environmental factors that could affect the development and fulfillment of career expectations. Career guidance content can be organized in many ways to facilitate the individual's development. Whatever its form, the program should encourage the individual to assume responsibility for his own career development.

A career guidance program assists the individual to assimilate and integrate knowledge, experience, and appreciations related to:

1. Self-understanding, which includes a person's relationship to his own characteristics and perceptions, and his relationship to others and the environment.
2. Understanding of the work society and those factors that affect its constant change, including worker attitudes and discipline.
3. Awareness of the part leisure time may play in a person's life.
4. Understanding of the necessity for and the multitude of factors to be considered in career planning.
5. Understanding of the information and skills necessary to achieve self-fulfillment in work and leisure.

An illumination of these content areas may include career guidance experiences to insure that each individual:

Gathers the kinds of data necessary to make rational career decisions.

Understands the necessary considerations for making choices and accepts responsibility for the decisions made.

Explores the possible rewards and satisfactions associated with each career choice considered.

Develops through work the attitude that he is a contributor to life and the community.

Determines success and failure probabilities in any occupational area considered.

Explores the possible work conditions associated with occupational options.

Shows an understanding of the varied attitudes toward work and workers held by himself and by others.

Recognizes how workers can bring dignity to their work.

Considers the possible and even predictable value changes in society which could affect a person's life.

Understands the important role of interpersonal and basic employment skills in occupational success.

Clarifies the different values and attitudes individuals may hold and the possible effects these may have on decisions and choices.

Understands that career development is lifelong, based upon a sequential series of educational and occupational choices.

Determines the possible personal risk, cost, and other related consequences of each career decision and is willing to assume responsibility for each consequence.

Systematically analyzes school and nonschool experiences as he plans and makes career-related decisions.

Explores the worker characteristics and work skills necessary to achieve success in occupational areas under consideration.

Identifies and uses a wide variety of resources in the school and community to maximize career development potential.

Knows and understands the entrance, transition, and decision points in education and the problems of adjustment that might occur in relation to these points.

Obtains necessary employability skills and uses available placement services to gain satisfactory entry into employment in line with occupational aspirations and beginning competencies.[15]

As has been noted, the need for career guidance is increasingly evident in the mass of data pointing to difficulties in career decision making, the underutilization of human resources, dissatisfaction with chosen careers, and such perennial problems as hard-core unemployed. Career guidance programs are designed, in cooperation with programs of career education, to cope with such needs. To satisfactorily plan such programs, which will increase the planning and decision-making skills of students, counselors must understand how career decisions are made and the possible consequences of certain kinds of decisions. This implies an understanding of theories and related research in career decision making.

THEORIES OF OCCUPATIONAL CHOICE

One of the more fascinating aspects of the study of careers, both formally and informally, are the never-ending attempts to identify why people end up in certain careers. In history, we may read about the factors that resulted in a lifetime in politics for a Franklin D. Roosevelt, the multicareer talents of a Benjamin Franklin or a Thomas Jefferson, or the cowboy who became O. Henry, the famous author. At one time or another we have probably been curious about the career decisions of friends and acquaintances. But to become more personal, why are you in your present career? What influenced your career planning and decision making? You probably have been asked this question before, and as you reflected and responded, you probably analyzed a set of facts and/or reasons that appeared relevant to your decisions. You presented some plausible explanation. Many also offer career advice to others, based on one's own personal career experiences or personal theory of career development. Even so, one must recognize the biases and limitations of one's own experiences. To develop a theory to a usable state, it is necessary to gather data that is relevant, to study the relationships between the data, and, finally, to speculate on what these mean. One's speculations are stated as hypotheses, explanations, or predictions, which can be tested. If a theory proves to have some validity, it will be built on and developed further through research and application activities.

Guidance counselors and others who work as helping professionals with

---

[15] National Vocational Guidance Association-American Vocational Association, Position Paper, 1973, pp. 9–11.

youth and adults for their career development and planning must have some understanding of the better recognized and researched theories of career development that have emerged in the last half of this century. An understanding of such theories gives the practicing counselor the knowledge of the studies of others, usually specialists in the field. They provide a rationale for counselor action that goes beyond personal experience and intuition. Because many disciplines (education, economics, psychology, sociology) are interested and actively engaged in investigating various career questions, a multitude of theories have emerged. Both the numbers of theories and the extensiveness of investigation of some preclude any attempt here to analyze the various major theories in detail. Let us explore several of the more popular categories for illustrative purposes only and without any intent to suggest or recommend a particular theoretical approach.

The Process Theories

The process theories state, in effect, that occupational choice and eventual entry is a process consisting of stages or steps that the individual will go through. For example, Ginzberg, Ginsburg, Axelrod, and Herma[16] analyzed the process of occupational decision making in terms of three periods—fantasy, tentative, and realistic choices. This theory suggests a process that moves increasingly toward realism in career decision making as one becomes older.

In 1972, Ginzberg[17] modified the original theory to suggest that the process of vocational choice and development is lifelong and open-ended. In the process, achieving the optimum is more appropriate to describe the ongoing efforts of individuals as they seek to find the most suitable job. Originally, Ginzberg and colleagues suggested that the crystallization of occupational choice inevitably had the quality of compromise. Ginzberg's revised theory also places considerable weight on constraints such as family income and situation, parental attitudes and values, opportunities in the world of work, and value orientations. Both the early theory and Ginzberg's later revision suggest the importance of the early school years in influencing later career planning.

Blau, Gustad, Jessor, Parnes, and Wilcock[18] conceived of occupational choice as a process of compromise, continually modified, between preferences for and expectations of being able to get into various occupations. They identified eight factors determining entry into an occupation. Four of these characterize the occupation: demand, technical (functional) qualifications,

---

[16] E. Ginzberg, S. W. Ginsburg, S. Axelrod, and J. L. Herma, *Occupational Choice: An Approach to a General Theory* (New York: Columbia University Press, 1951).

[17] Eli Ginzberg, "Toward a Theory of Occupational Choice: A Restatement," *Vocational Guidance Quarterly,* **20:**169–176 (Mar. 1972).

[18] P. M. Blau, J. W. Gustad, R. Jessor, H. S. Parnes, and R. G. Wilcock, "Occupational Choice: A Conception Framework," *Industrial and Labor Relations Review,* (July 1956), p. 531.

personal (nonfunctional) qualifications, and rewards. Those characterizing individuals were information about an occupation, technical skills, social characteristics, and value orientations.

The Development Theories

The developmental theories relevant to career guidance view vocational development as one aspect of the individual's total development. A leading researcher in vocational development theory, Donald Super, formulated a theory of vocational development in 1953 that became a basis for later research and theory.

Super's original propositions were as follows:

1. People differ in their abilities, interests, and personalities.
2. They are qualified, by virtue of these circumstances, each for a number of occupations.
3. Each of these occupations requires a characteristic pattern of abilities, interests, and personality traits, with tolerances wide enough, however, to allow both some variety of occupations for each individual and some variety of individuals in each occupation.
4. Vocational preferences and competencies, and situations in which people live and work, and hence their self-concepts, change with time and experience (although self-concepts are generally fairly stable from late adolescence until later maturity), making choice and adjustment a continuous process.
5. This process may be summed up in a series of life stages, characterized as those of growth, exploration, establishment, maintenance, and decline, and these stages may in turn be subdivided into (a) fantasy, tentative, and realistic phases of the exploratory stage, and (b) the trial and stable phases of the establishment stage.
6. The nature of the career pattern (that is, the occupational level attained and the sequence, frequency, and duration of trial and stable jobs) is determined by the individual's parental socioeconomic level, mental ability, and personality characteristics, and by the opportunities to which he is exposed.
7. Development through the life stages can be guided partly by facilitating the process of maturation of abilities and interests and partly by aiding in reality testing and in the development of the self-concept.
8. The process of vocational development is essentially that of developing and implementing a self-concept; it is a compromise process in which the self-concept is a product of the interaction of inherited aptitudes, neural and endocrine make-up, opportunity to play various roles, and evaluation of the extent to which the results of role playing meet with the approval of superiors and fellows.
9. The process of compromise between individual and social factors, between self-concept and reality, is one of role playing, whether

the role is played in fantasy, in the counseling interview, or in real life activities such as school classes, clubs, part-time work, and entry jobs.

10. Work satisfaction and life satisfaction depend upon the extent to which the individual finds adequate outlets for his abilities, interests, personality traits, and values; they depend upon his establishment in a type of work, a work situation, and a way of life in which he can play the kind of role which his growth and exploratory experiences have led him to consider congenial and appropriate.[19]

As may be noted, Super[20] pointed out that like other aspects of development, vocational development may be conceived of as beginning early in life and proceeding along a continuum until late in life, passing through the stages of growth, exploration establishment, maintenance, and decline. At each of these stages the individual must master increasingly difficult tasks. Such a concept of vocational development leads logically, according to Super, to that of vocational maturity as denoting the degree of development reached on such a continuum. Super and his associates also pointed out that one's occupation makes possible the playing of a role appropriate to the self-concept of the individual.[21] This does not suggest, however, that an individual's characteristics or traits are so unique that only a specific "type" of individual would qualify. To the contrary, Super suggests that the range of individual abilities and the latitude within occupational areas result in a multipotential of appropriate opportunities for most individuals.

Zaccaria has reported that those who formulate developmental tasks generally agree on the following statements:

1. Individual growth and development is continuous.
2. Individual growth can be divided into periods or life stages for descriptive purposes.
3. Individuals in each life stage can be characterized by certain general characteristics that they have in common.
4. Most individuals in a given culture pass through similar developmental stages.
5. The society makes certain demands upon individuals.
6. These demands are relatively uniform for all members of the society.
7. The demands differ from stage to stage as the individual goes through the developmental process.
8. Developmental crises occur when the individual perceives the demand to alter his present behavior and to master new learnings.

[19] Donald E. Super, "A Theory of Vocational Development," *American Psychologist,* 8:189–190 (American Psychological Association, 1953).
[20] Donald E. Super, *The Psychology of Careers,* (New York: Harper & Row, Publishers, 1975).
[21] Donald E. Super, et al., *Career Development: Self-Concept Theory* (New York: College Entrance Examination Board, 1963).

9. In meeting and mastering developmental crises, the individual moves from one developmental stage of maturity to another developmental stage of maturity.
10. The task appears in its purest form at one stage.
11. Preparation for meeting the developmental crises or developmental tasks occurs in the life stage prior to the stage in which it must be mastered.
12. The developmental task or crisis may arise again during a later phase in somewhat different form.
13. The crisis or task must be mastered before the individual can successfully move on to a subsequent developmental stage.
14. Meeting the crisis successfully by learning the required task leads to societal approval, happiness, and success with later crises and their correlative tasks.
15. Failing in meeting a task or crisis leads to disapproval by society.[22]

Havighurst discussed vocational development as a lifelong process consisting of six stages from childhood to old age. Each age period has characteristic tasks that must be successfully achieved if the individual is to attain happiness and success with tasks appropriate to the vocational stages that follow.

Havighurst outlined the developmental stages as indicated in Table 8–1, which follows.

Personality Theories

Personality theories view vocational preferences as expressions of personality. They suggest that much career-seeking behavior is an outgrowth of efforts to, in effect, match one's individual characteristics with those of a specific occupational field. As one example, you may note Holland's theory of personality types and environmental models. This theory is based on major assumptions regarding personality types, their determination and relation to various outcomes and vocational choice. The concepts and assumptions that underlie the theory are as follows:

1. The choice of a vocation is an expression of personality.
2. Interest inventories are personality inventories.
3. Vocational stereotypes have reliable and important psychological and sociological meanings.
4. The members of a vocation have similar personalities and similar histories of personal development.
5. Because people in a vocational group have similar personalities, they will respond to many situations and problems in similar ways, and they will create characteristic interpersonal environments.

[22] J. S. Zaccaria, "Developmental Tasks: Implications for the Goals of Guidance," *Personnel and Guidance Journal,* **44**:373 (1965).

Table 8–1.
Vocational Development: A Lifelong Process

Stages of Vocational Development	Age
I. Identification with a Worker Father, Mother, other significant persons. The concept of Working becomes an essential part of the ego-ideal.	5–10
II. Acquiring the Basic Habits of Industry Learning to organize one's time and energy to get a piece of work done. School work, chores. Learning to put work ahead of play in appropriate situations.	10–15
III. Acquiring Identity as a Worker in the Occupational Structure Choosing and preparing for an occupation. Getting work experience as a basis for occupational choice and for assurance of economic independence.	15–25
IV. Becoming a Productive Person Mastering the skills of one's occupation. Moving up the ladder with one's occupation.	25–40
V. Maintaining a Productive Society Emphasis shifts toward the societal and away from the individual aspect of the worker's role. The individual sees himself as a responsible citizen in a productive society. He pays attention to the civic responsibility attached to his job. The individual is at the peak of his occupational career and has time and energy to adorn it with broader types of activity. He pays attention to inducting younger people into stages III and IV.	40–70
IV. Contemplating a Productive and Responsible Life This person is retired from work or is in the process of withdrawing from the worker's role. He looks back over his work life with satisfaction, sees that a personal social contribution has been made, and is pleased with it. While he may not have achieved all of his ambitions, he accepts life and believes in himself as a productive person.	70–+

Source: **R. J. Havighurst, "Youth in Exploration and Man Emergent," in *Man in A World At Work*, ed. by Henry Borow (Boston: Houghton Mifflin Company, 1964).**

6. Vocational satisfaction, stability, and achievement depend on the congruence between one's personality and environment (composed largely of other people) in which one works.

The following statements summarize the major assumptions of Holland's theory.

1. In our culture, most persons can be categorized as one of six types: realistic, intellectual, social, conventional, enterprising, and artistic.
2. There are six kinds of environments: realistic, intellectual, social, conventional, enterprising, and artistic.
3. People search for environments and vocations that will permit them to exercise their skills and abilities, to express their attitudes and values, to take on agreeable problems and roles, and to avoid disagreeable ones.

4. A person's behavior can be explained by the interaction of his personality and his environment.[23]

A summary of Holland's theory may be noted in Table 8–2, which describes the personality characteristics of the six categories and the work environments related to each.

"Chance" Theories

There are also theories of occupational choice that suggest individuals arrive at a particular occupation destiny more by chance than through deliberate planning or steady progress toward an earlier defined goal. Newspapers and television reports constantly remind us of individuals who seem to be "at the right place at the right time" and for no other reason end up in an unanticipated career. Another chance factor may result in occupational choice by an impulse or sudden emotional reaction in which unconscious forces appear to determine an individual's behavior and occupation choice, such as the individual who, on apparent impulse, "walks out of a good office job and is next heard from as a missionary in the African jungle." These and similar evidence, as described by Caplow,[24] indicate that occupational choice may result from an accidental or unforeseen factor(s). Accident theory, then, contends that because individuals may make decisions or be influenced by unforeseen or accidental circumstances, it is not possible to evaluate the decisive factors in their choices.

Herr and Cramer[25] note, however, that

the factors bearing on choice or development are not restricted to chance or intervening variables. The narrowness or the breadth of the individual's culture or social class boundaries has much to do with the choices which can be considered, made, and implemented.

A Composite Theory for Counselors

Hoppock,[26] drawing from two prominent theories of occupational choice, presents a suggested "composite theory for school counselors." The ten major points of his theory are as follows:

---

[23] John L. Holland, *The Psychology of Vocational Choice* (Lexington, Mass.: Blaisdell-Ginn and Company, 1966), pp. 8–12.
Also: *Making Vocational Choices: A Theory of Careers* (Englewood Cliffs, N.J.: Prentice-Hall, Inc., 1973).
[24] T. Caplow, *The Sociology of Work* (Minneapolis: University of Minnesota Press, 1954).
[25] Edwin L. Herr and Stanley H. Cramer, *Career Guidance Through the Life Span: Systematic Approaches* (Boston: Little, Brown and Company, 1979), p. 82.
[26] Robert Hoppock, *Occupational Information,* 4th ed. (New York: McGraw-Hill Book Company, 1976).

1. Occupations are chosen to meet needs.
2. The occupation that we choose is the one we believe will best meet the needs that most concern us.
3. Needs may be intellectually perceived, or they may be only vaguely felt as attractions which draw us in certain directions. In either case, they may influence choices.

Table 8–2.

A Summary of Holland's (1959, 1966) Personality Types and Environmental Models

	Description	
Type	Personality Types (Modal Personal Orientation)	Environmental Models (Occupational Environments)
Realistic (Motoric)	Enjoys activities requiring physical strength; aggressive; good motor organization; lacks verbal and interpersonal skills; prefers concrete to abstract problems; unsociable.	Laborers, machine operators, aviators, farmers, truck drivers, carpenters.
Intellectual (Investigative)	Task-oriented, thinks through problems; attempts to organize and understand the world; enjoys ambiguous work tasks and intraceptive activities; abstract orientation.	Physicist, anthropologist, chemist, mathematician, biologist.
Social (Supportive)	Prefers teaching or therapeutic roles; likes a safe setting; possesses verbal and interpersonal skills; socially oriented; accepting of feminine impulses.	Clinical psychologist, counselor, foreign missionary, teacher.
Conventional (Conforming)	Performs structured verbal and numerical activities and subordinate roles; achieves goals through conformity.	Cashier, statistician, bookkeeper, administrative assistant, post office clerk.
Enterprising (Persuasive)	Prefers verbal skills in situations which provide opportunities for dominating, selling, or leading others.	Car salesman, auctioneer, politician, master of ceremonies, buyer.
Artistic (Esthetic)	Prefers indirect personal relationships, prefers dealing with environmental problems through self-expression in artistic media.	Poet, novelist, musician, sculptor, playwright, composer, stage director.

Source: J. Zaccaria, *Theories of Occupational Choice and Vocational Development* (Boston: Houghton Mifflin Company, 1970), p. 44.

4. Occupational choice begins when we first become aware that an occupation can help to meet our needs.
5. Occupational choice improves as we become better able to anticipate how well a prospective occupation will meet our needs. Our capacity thus to anticipate depends upon our knowledge of ourselves, our knowledge of occupations, and our ability to think clearly.
6. Information about ourselves affects occupational choice by helping us to discover the occupations that may meet our needs and to anticipate how well satisfied we may hope to be in one occupation as compared with another.
7. Information about occupations affects occupational choice by helping us to discover the occupations that may meet our needs, and by helping us to anticipate how well satisfied we may hope to be in one occupation as compared with another.
8. Job satisfaction depends upon the extent to which the job that we hold meets the needs that we feel it should meet. The degree of satisfaction is determined by the ratio between what we have and what we want.
9. Satisfaction can result from a job which meets our needs today, or from a job which promises to meet them in the future.
10. Occupational choice is always subject to change when we believe that a change will better meet our needs.

Implications of Career Theories for Counselors

A review of the various theories can lead to the conclusions that career development is a process that leads to a decision, there are stages through which one passes enroute to vocational maturity and decision making, there are tasks one must accomplish at each stage, and personality traits are related to career decision making. Further, there are environmental constraints on the careers one may recognize or aspire to, and the best laid career plans may be altered by chance or accident factors.

The characteristics of these theories have certain implications for the counseling of clients with career development and/or adjustment needs. Counselors must understand the process and characteristics of human development, including readiness to learn and successfully complete particular tasks at certain developmental stages. Counselors must understand the basic human needs as well as the special needs of individuals and their relationship to career development and decision making. Counselors must be able to assess and interpret individual traits and characteristics and to apply these assessments to a variety of counselee career-related needs. Counselors must recognize the constraints imposed by environmental and cultural factors on the career planning and decision making of clients. Counselors must recognize and assist clients to recognize that unforeseen or chance factors may, on occasion, alter career planning.

In addition to individual counseling in the school setting, career guidance involves a variety of activities. Planning for these activities ensures that they will not be left to chance. Principles to guide this planning are next suggested.

GUIDING PRINCIPLES FOR CAREER GUIDANCE IN SCHOOLS

In order to emphasize the opportunities for the student's career development, certain guiding principles are suggested as appropriate objectives for the school guidance program in general and the career guidance phase in particular. The following principles are stated within a developmental framework.

1. All students should be provided the opportunity to develop an unbiased base from which they can make their career decisions. The shrinking of the pupil's occupational choice field as one proceeds through the school years is an educational tragedy. The first-grader seems to regard most occupations he/she is familiar with in a positive light. By the time he/she has reached the seventh or eighth grade and has begun to make decisions based on at least some general occupational considerations, he/she has developed or been educated toward biases which automatically eliminate many possibilities from further consideration. The large percentage of students who enter college preparatory courses at the ninth-grade level and never enter college, or even fail to complete their secondary schooling is but one evidence of this fact. In this regard, then, the school guidance program seeks, in effective cooperation with the classroom teacher, to develop in each pupil positive attitudes and respect for all honest work. This is a formidable task, for many students are almost constantly bombarded with the biases of the adult world surrounding them. It is apparent that if they are to benefit from a true freedom of choice, the career guidance program has a vital mission in the schools.

2. The early and continuous development of positive pupil attitudes toward education is critical. The deterioration of the elementary pupil's occupational choice field is unfortunate, but the failure to maintain the pupil's continuing interest in his/her optimum educational development is disastrous. For objective evidence, one need only turn to the various dropout studies and the equally countless studies concerning the lack of pupil motivation and achievement commensurate with ability. In short, career development has limited meaning without parallel educational development. Any program of pupil career guidance must have as a major objective the stimulation of the student's educational development.

3. As a corollary to these previous points, the student must be taught to view a career as a *way* of life and an education as a *preparation* for

life. Frequently pupils arrive at the educational decision-making stage of life viewing careers only in terms of job descriptions. At all educational levels the opportunity exists to develop—not only widen—occupational horizons. This broader approach to the eventual career choice is based on the realization that one's way of work is one's way of life. Similarly, there must be education in the concept of education itself, keeping in mind the idea of education for life rather than education only for one's eventual career. This approach—one of education for the fuller life— also has obvious implications for education's continuing efforts to reduce the percentage of school dropouts.

4. Students must be assisted in developing adequate understanding of themselves and must be prepared to relate this understanding to both social-personal development and career-educational planning. These understandings are significant in the fulfillment of the individual's need for self-actualization. In this context, both career guidance and pupil appraisal seek to further enrich their meaning and value to the student by preparing him/her to look at himself/herself realistically in terms of continuing educational opportunities, career requirements, and the demands and relationships of society.

5. Students at all levels must be provided an understanding of the relationships between education and careers. If pupils are to develop an attitude and belief that education is relevant, they must understand how it is relevant. Pupils need an awareness of the relationships between levels of education and related career possibilities. They should also be made aware of both the vocations and avocations that stem directly from certain subjects.

6. Pupils need an understanding of both *where* and *why* they are at a given point on the educational continuum at a given time. It is not enough for the pupil to know he/she is in the third grade this year and will be in the fourth grade next year if all goes well. If he/she is to gain an increased appreciation of his/her current educational program as well as his/her future educational possibilities, the pupil must be provided specific opportunities to gain insights into the educational process, its sequence, and its integrating of knowledge.

7. Every pupil at every stage of his/her educational program should have career-oriented experiences that are appropriate for his/her levels of readiness and that are simultaneously meaningful and realistic. This means that opportunities for participation and observation will frequently take precedence over discussions and teacher or counselor lectures.

8. Students must have opportunities to test concepts, skills, and roles to develop values that may have future career application. The school career guidance program takes advantage of natural school groupings in providing "secure" opportunities for the individual to experience

and develop human relationships and other skills, a variety of roles, and a system of values and concepts that are related to everyday living.

9.   The school career guidance program is centered in the classroom, with coordination and consultation by the school counselor, participation by parents, and resource contributions from the community. The pupil's career guidance team needs the involvement of all those concerned with his/her development, with the teacher, counselor, and parent playing key roles.

10.   The school's program of career guidance is integrated into the functioning guidance and total educational programs of the institution. The complete development of the individual is vital, and therefore the career aspects should not be separated from the whole. In fact, it is only within the total educational program framework that each segment can be strengthened by and in turn strengthen every other segment.

PLACEMENT AND FOLLOW-UP

Placement and follow-up services in comprehensive systems of guidance are significant for the success of career education in career guidance activities. Ohlsen[27] has noted that without adequate placement services young people have little direction in their job-seeking activities, have difficulty in obtaining employment, and, all too frequently, drift into unproductive or undesirable activities. Further, after consistent early failures, many youths begin to believe that they are unworthy of employment not only now, but in the future. Tolbert[28] has noted that planned placement should be an invaluable part of the guidance process for school youth, for it not only helps the young job-seeker evaluate and resolve many immediate problems in his/her initial job-seeking efforts, but also serves as a learning experience in developing skills to deal with future problems and efforts.

The *Nationwide Study of Student Career Development* by Prediger, Roth, and Noeth[29] reported a sharp contrast between youth's need for career planning and the help received. This study confirmed that youths were seriously deficient in knowledge about the world of work and career planning and they were unable to cope with the career development tasks posed by society during the difficult high school to post-high school transition and placement period. The study recommended the reorientation of the traditional school counseling model to provide increased and more realistic assistance in career

[27] Merle M. Ohlsen, *Guidance Services in the Modern School,* 2nd ed. (New York: Harcourt Brace Jovanovich, Inc., 1974).

[28] E. L. Tolbert, *Counseling for Career Development* (Boston: Houghton Mifflin Company, 1974).

[29] D. J. Prediger, J. D. Roth, and R. J. Noeth, *Nationwide Study of Student Career Development: Summary of Results,* The American College Testing Program, Research and Development Division, No. 61 (Nov. 1973).

guidance and placement and to initiate significant changes, which would, in effect, increase the effectiveness of counseling youth for today's world of work.

In a USOE study, "A Comparison of Common Educational-Vocational Problems of Secondary School Youth in the USA and the British Isles,"[30] it was noted that a high priority problem with youths in both countries was their concern for appropriate occupational placement upon leaving school. However, American youth, in contrast to their British counterparts, anticipated little assistance from their secondary schools in dealing with this concern.

Although these and others have testified about the importance of placement in human resources and career development, this is an often neglected and underdeveloped activity in many school guidance programs.

As Buckingham reported in her study *Placement and Follow-Up in Career Education,*[31] "experience in placing students in employment and following students after they leave an institution is still largely undeveloped."[32]

> [Since] career education has as its purpose the preparation of students for careers, and the successful placement of each student on the next rung of a career ladder is the only way of knowing that the preparation at one stage has been completed, placement can hardly be considered in any other way than as an integral part of the career education process, regardless of the level of education involved.[33]

In a similar vein, placement and follow-up are inseparably linked with career guidance. Further, students should never be placed and forgotten.

Educational Placement

The renewed emphasis on career placement is not limited to school settings but, in its broader context, involves institutions and agencies that are also concerned with placing their clients in the world of work. Placement has for years in secondary schools traditionally emphasized placement in institutions of higher education. This emphasis does not appear to be neglected even during the current movement towards career placement. A 1976 study indicated that in a sample of 180 secondary schools, more than 90 per cent provided for some form of college or post-secondary educational placement,

---

[30] Robert L. Gibson and Marianne H. Mitchell, "Theirs and Ours: Educational-Vocational Problems in Britain and the United States," *Vocational Guidance Quarterly* (Dec. 1970).

[31] L. Buckingham and A. Lee, *Placement and Follow-Up in Career Education* (Raleigh, N.C.: Career Education Monograph No. 7, Center for Occupational Education, North Carolina State University, 1973).

[32] Ibid., p. 1.

[33] Ibid., p. 3.

whereas only 57 per cent had specialized provisions for career placement.[34]

In general, educational placement differs little from other forms of placement inasmuch as it represents an organized effort to match the qualifications of individuals plus personal interests and resources with the requirements of institutions and programs. Typically, school counselors, with responsibilities for college and other post-secondary educational placement, provide information to students regarding institutional entrance requirements, expenses, characteristics of the institution, and program content. They frequently will also assist students in completing the necessary application forms. An example of a form that counselors may use with high school students interested in college placement is the college checklist (see Figure 8–3).

Many school counselors are also involved in educational placement within their schools. In this capacity they are concerned with placing students in appropriate curricula and specific courses. However, scheduling activities that consist largely of a mechanical process designed to get all pupils into all slots at a given time, with a total disregard of individual differences, is not considered a guidance responsibility, even though counselors report that they spend many hours in such mechanical processes.

Placement for Personal Development

In the literature, at least, if not always in practice, placement has been viewed as more than just career, college, and educational placement. In its broadest sense, placement is an activity that places or facilitates the self-placement of individuals in situations or settings that will enable them to benefit from needed experiences, make satisfactory adjustments, gain useful information, and, in general, contribute to their total development. As an example of this broader concept of placement, let us briefly examine placement that focuses on giving the individual experiences in different roles and environments.

Role placement assumes that the experiencing of different and significant roles is important for all developing pupils. Although many will experience some of these roles naturally and without planning, for the majority these developmental opportunities would be missed unless specific provisions are made. This is another opportunity for the school counselor and classroom teacher to work cooperatively in planning meaningful experiences that enhance both the instructional program and the individual's personal development. Significant role experiences would include opportunities to function periodically as a leader, a team member, an individual (isolated) worker, a teacher of others, an achiever, a responsible person, a social being, a person

---

[34] Robert L. Gibson and Marianne H. Mitchell, "Identification of Effective Concepts in Placement and Follow-up," A Technical Report, State of Indiana and Indiana University (Feb. 1976).

		Name of College		Name of College		Name of College	

I. *Entrance Requirements and General Information*

		Yes	No	Yes	No	Yes	No
1.	Does this college offer major preparation in the field of _____ (student's planned major)?	___	___	___	___	___	___
2.	Will I be eligible for admission upon completion of my currently planned program for high school graduation?						
3.	Are entrance examinations required?	___	___	___	___	___	___
4.	Must I take a physical examination?	___	___	___	___	___	___
5.	Are there other entrance requirements? (If so, list in Section VII, under Notes and Comments.)	___	___	___	___	___	___
6.	Is this a coeducational college?	___	___	___	___	___	___
7.	Is this a state- or city-supported college?	___	___	___	___	___	___
8.	Are the offerings of this college accredited by the accrediting association?	___	___	___	___	___	___
9.	Does this college have an ROTC program?	___	___	___	___	___	___
10.	What is the average enrollment?	___	___	___	___	___	___

II. *Expenses (per school year)*

11.	Room	___	___	___	___	___	___
12.	Board	___	___	___	___	___	___
13.	Tuition	___	___	___	___	___	___
14.	Activity fees	___	___	___	___	___	___
15.	Any other special expenses: (item) _____ (item) _____	___	___	___	___	___	___
16.	Total basic cost per year	$___	___	$___	___	$___	___

III. *Room and Board*

17.	Are dormitory facilities available for boys/girls?	___	___	___	___	___	___
18.	Are noncommuting freshmen required to live in the dormitory?	___	___	___	___	___	___
19.	May you select your own roommate if you desire?	___	___	___	___	___	___
20.	Are dining facilities available (three meals per day) for students?	___	___	___	___	___	___

IV. *Student Services and Aids*

21.	Are scholarships available?	___	___	___	___	___	___
22.	Are part-time jobs available?	___	___	___	___	___	___
23.	Are guidance services provided?	___	___	___	___	___	___
24.	Is there a freshman orientation program?	___	___	___	___	___	___
25.	Are placement services available for: (a) graduating seniors? (b) summertime jobs?	___	___	___	___	___	___
26.	Are health services provided? (a) dispensary care? (b) dental care? (c) hospitalization plan?	___	___	___	___	___	___
27.	Can I get special scholastic help (such as tutoring) if I need it?	___	___	___	___	___	___

V. *Student Activities*

28.	Fraternities and sororities?	___	___	___	___	___	___
29.	Honorary organizations?	___	___	___	___	___	___
30.	Social dancing permitted?	___	___	___	___	___	___
31.	Are campus recreational facilities available?	___	___	___	___	___	___
32.	Is there an intramural program?	___	___	___	___	___	___
33.	Major varsity sports?	___	___	___	___	___	___
34.	A convocation series?	___	___	___	___	___	___
35.	Dramatic opportunities?	___	___	___	___	___	___
36.	Music (band and glee club)?	___	___	___	___	___	___
37.	Any others you are particularly interested in: (item) _____	___	___	___	___	___	___

VI. Any special questions you want to ask? _____

VII. Notes and comments _____

_____   (Student's name) _____

_____ Grade   Class of _____ Period _____ to _____

B. D. Lewis Elementary School

Role Assignments	leader	team member	individual worker	achiever	responsibility	social leader	decision maker	server
Pupils' Names								
1. Marie Adams								
2. Rebecca Best								
3. Billy Collins								
4. Chester Dent								
5. Charles James								
6. Eleanor James								
7. Nancy Lee								
8. Archie Leedy								
9. Paul Lewis								
10. Katherine Louise								
11. Edith Miller								
12. Robert Nuzrem								
13. Jack Smith								
14. Billy Wagner								
15. Betty Watson								

* Dates are entered where role is assigned.
√ Indicates student has assumed or experienced this role and further assignment is not needed at this time.

Figure 8–4.
Role assignments. _Robert L. Gibson,_ Career Development in the Elementary School _(Columbus, Ohio: Charles E. Merrill Publishing Company, 1972), p. 60._

of authority and decision making, or one who serves others. A role assignment sheet, as illustrated in Figure 8–4, is a method of recording these experiences.

Environmental Placement

Environmental placement can be another developmental activity. The major focus of this type of placement is to provide students the opportunities to experience other significant, yet distinctly different, environments from their own. An example is giving city youth opportunities to spend time in rural areas as part of farm days or "country cousins" programs. City youth may exchange places with farm youth for several days or weeks. Another example

Figure 8–3.
College checklist. _Robert L. Gibson, "The College Check List,"_ Vocational Guidance Quarterly, _Vol. 9, No. 2 (Winter 1960–1961), pp. 121–123._

is a blend of educational preparation and environmental placement in which students spend some time in diverse collegiate settings, small and large.

Career Placement

Of all the guidance placement activities, none is more important or has the potential for assisting more youth in the school setting than the job placement service. Such a service can be designed to assist both in-school and out-of-school youth, both school dropouts and school graduates. Such programs are typically involved in:

1. Assessing the needs of students regarding part-time and full-time employment, training, employability skills, and further educational desires.
2. Establishing a working relationship with business, industry, and labor representatives in order to facilitate effective cooperation and communication between these groups and educators.
3. Providing avenues and assistance to students seeking part-time or full-time employment that are compatible with their abilities and interests.
4. Establishing an efficient, participatory communication-feedback network among all involved—students, business, industry, and labor personnel, community leaders, parents, media, and school personnel.

Step 1	Communicate proposed idea to superintendent, administrators, board of education.
Step 2	Establish steering committee.
Step 3	Assess available resources.
Step 4	Assess educational and business community needs.
Step 5	Develop program structure.
Step 6	Establish advisory committee.
Step 7	Submit written plan to board of education.
Step 8	Make operational decisions.
Step 9	Enact plan.
Step 10	Evaluation.

Figure 8–5.
Procedural steps for program enactment. *Marie Shafe, Darlene Gerster, and Barbara Moore,* School-Based Placement Program *(State of Indiana and Indiana University, 1976).*

With many school guidance programs currently in the process of developing or expanding the placement function, it might be helpful to note the procedural steps developed in the Indiana Model Career Placement Project for developing or expanding this phase of the school guidance program (see Figure 8–5). In considering placement program development, the existence in many communities of well-established local governmental employment programs that often give speical attention to the needs of local youth should be recognized. In such settings, the school guidance program seeks to work cooperatively and in a complementary manner with local government employment personnel to provide the best possible assistance for youthful job seekers. Even under such ideal conditions, however, it must be remembered that the important developmental aspects of school placement programs are not the responsibility of other agencies or institutions. School placement programs therefore must include activities that develop or enhance the individual's skills, attitudes, and knowledge needed for job acquisition and retention.

Placement program activities may be viewed as three-dimensional. The primary activity, of course, is student development; however, student development will obviously be handicapped if job development is not also a planned program activity, and both of these activities will be less than effective without plans for program maintenance and operation. The Indiana Model Career Placement Project suggested the following as appropriate activities:

Student Development Activities

1. Assessment of student readiness for employment—what skills, attitudes, or stereotypes does the student presently possess?
2. Preparation of student for finding and retaining a job—what skills are needed to obtain a job and, once obtained, how must one function to retain the job?
3. Individual and group career counseling—how does one develop or become competent in decision making, problem solving, and clarification of personal and career values and goals?
4. Employability skills and competencies—how does one proceed in clarifying competition for jobs? Suggested review: resumé writing, interview appearance and preparation, personal hygiene, letter of application, interpretation of job notices and terminology through job hunting clinics, employability skills and competency-building class, and/or pre-employment job hunting materials.
5. Resources for job possibilities—where does one begin? Suggested review: yellow pages, want ads, local placement office, employment office, school counselor, relatives, and friends.
6. Post-employment adjustment counseling—what does one do if one has problems related to the job or placement situation?
7. Employer-employee relationships—what is involved in employment interactions? Suggested review: respect for authority or how

to react/interact with authority, personal and social relationships, expressing criticism, work efficiency, supervision versus nonsupervision, economics of market trends, and how each affects company or business.

Job Development Activities

1. Employer lists—who are the potential employers in the general vicinity?
2. Receiving and developing job opportunities inside and outside community—what possibilities are within a particular region or district?
3. Survey employers for needs and positions available—how can the placement program be most helpful to employers?
4. Facilitation of business and industry contacts—what are the best methods for corresponding with or keeping in touch with employers or prospective employers?
5. Screening interviews—who are the seemingly best qualified applicants for employer consideration regarding a specific available position?
6. Educational referrals for another level of training (skills) or education—in light of the needs of the student, what other "next steps" are available besides immediate employment?
7. Apprenticeships—what on-the-job training opportunities are available or could be developed for students?
8. Supervision of employed students—if work experience credit is available, how can the student interrelate his/her work experience and course offerings?
9. Summer placement program—what about equivalent services for students during the summer vacation?
10. Job data bank information—what about a system that provides the job-related information readily and easily?

Maintenance-Operational Activities

1. Gathering student data—how are student needs identified? Who needs part-time or full-time employment? What student information is needed for record keeping?
2. Gathering employer data—what is available and from whom? What are the qualifications needed and job descriptions?
3. Record keeping—what type of centralized record keeping system and/or location can best serve the student and employer needs?
4. Maintenance plan whereby employers and students are contacted after placement—what is the level of satisfaction of the student placed and of the employer?
5. Ongoing reassessment of students' and employers' needs and market trends—what can be done to modify the activities of the placement program to better serve the participating populations?[35]

---

[35] Ibid., pp. 18–21.

Follow-up

Programs of placement activities, regardless of setting, must provide evidence of the effectiveness of their practices for both accountability and program improvement purposes. A large measure of supporting evidence for these purposes may be secured through carefully planned follow-up activities. As a complement to the guidance placement program, follow-up activities focus upon effectiveness in placing individuals for a variety of purposes and settings, as viewed by not only the clients, but also those to whom the client is responsible in such settings as job placement. Follow-up data may be obtained through questionnaires, checklists, interviews, and phone calls. Placement follow-up with those placed usually focuses upon how satisfied the individuals are with their placement; how satisfied they are with the process; progress they believe they are making in their situation; adequacy of their previous preparation experience; was the placement setting as anticipated or described; future plans and recommendations. Employers may be asked to respond concerning the adequacy of preparation and experience of the employee; adaptation to work; ability to work with others; progress anticipated by employee; recommendations for improvement of placement process.

In college placement, follow-up may seek to identify adequacy of high school preparation for the particular collegiate institution and program areas of strength and weakness in entering student's preparation; degree to which the student appears to be adjusting to the collegiate environment; and recommendations for improving the placement process. As follow-up data are collected, it is equally important to anticipate and plan for systematic utilization of the data.

CAREER GUIDANCE AND PLACEMENT IN NONSCHOOL SETTINGS

The initial out-of-school career contacts of many youth will be made through the assistance of their state employment services. In these offices, career guidance activities may be based on a review and discussion of the applicant's qualifications and interests in relation to available employment opportunities. Appraisal instruments, such as the General Aptitude Classification Battery, may be utilized to further assist the client and his/her counselor in his/her career planning. Counselors in these settings are usually especially well-versed in their knowledge of local job opportunities and characteristics and often have access to computerized job bank systems. These employment office counselors often work closely with high school counselors in facilitating the career planning and transitions of youth from school to work.

However, career guidance and placement can no longer be considered an activity that focuses on youth alone. A variety of factors have resulted in significant changes in the career "habitats" of adult populations. Those changes, in turn, have influenced the career guidance and placement efforts in governmental and business settings. Contributing factors to change include the impact of technological and social change, shifts in societal values, a population that is growing older and is capable of working longer, and economic necessity.

Probably the most general cause of the career change phenomenon is the impact of technological change on American life. Technological innovations have sparked continued economic development which, in turn, has perpetuated the rise in this nation's standard of living. For an increasing number of Americans, this has meant greater material security and satisfaction of basic needs. As Abraham Maslow and other psychologists have suggested, "higher" needs such as the need for self-esteem or self-actualization are awakened when basic needs have been reasonably fulfilled. In the workplace, many Americans are no longer just asking for more salary and benefits; they are also asking for more meaningful careers which will enable them to better express their unique talents and abilities.[36]

Moreover, technological change has resulted in related societal changes such as population shifts, altered consumer demands, and major new government policies regarding health, education, and welfare. These changes have had an impact on other occupations not directly affected by changing technologies. Human service occupations are a good example. Thousands of young adults entered educational programs in these fields. When they graduated several years later, they frequently found the labor market quite different from what it was when they began their schooling. Many of these individuals could not find jobs in their career areas; others took jobs for which they were overqualified and underpaid.

Americans preparing for jobs in many other occupations have encountered similar difficulties. As technological and social changes become more rapid, the difficulty of work force forecasting increases. A 1975 study by the Rand Corporation, entitled *An Evaluation of Policy-Related Research on Programs for Mid-Life Career Redirection,* concluded that: "Manpower forecasts will not give much guidance to appropriate training in a mid-life career program. They cannot give reliable estimates of the probability of being employed once training has been completed, except in very special cases. Neither can the forecasts give much information on the longevity of a career."[37]

Given this difficulty, many career changers and younger people entering the work force are becoming more cautious about investing

---

[36] Ferrini and Parker, op. cit., p. 4.

[37] Anthony H. Pascal et al., *An Evaluation of Policy-Related Research on Programs for Mid-Life Career Redirection,* 2 volumes (Santa Monica, Calif.: Rand Corporation, report prepared for the National Science Foundation R 1582/2NSF, Feb. 1975).

large amounts of time and money in preparing for occupations in which their future employment is questionable. Instead, many of these individuals are enrolling in short-term training programs or pursuing careers in which they can utilize their transferable skills.[38]

During recent generations, social and cultural change have also resulted in the alteration of traditional concepts and expectations that resulted in sex role stereotyping in the world of work. This has not only resulted in more female engineers, construction workers, airplane pilots, and more male nurses and elementary school teachers, but has also led to increasing numbers of women who, in the process of combining careers and marriage, interrupt their careers for child rearing before returning to the labor force. Vriend noted that

a woman is more likely to be in the labor force at age 45 to 54 than at age 20 to 24. This means that the average woman will have 30 to 35 active years of life starting from a mid-career point. Technological advances, more opportunities for paid employment, and social conditions such as the general movements toward human liberation and the development of individual potential, as well as the sharp rise in divorce rates, have freed women to choose employment as an alternative. Women constitute a large percentage of the mid-career crisis. Too many women don't like what they're doing, don't know what they want to do, and think they can't do anything. They need assistance to make early plans for a potentially long career outside the home, to reenter the labor market, and to find sources of continued guidance at crucial points in the career development process.[39]

Other value changes affecting the world of work are pointed out by Yankelovich who noted that some of the consequences of the old value system for the world of work were

If women could afford to stay home and not work at a paid job, they did so.

As long as a job provided a man with a decent living and some degree of economic security, he would put up with all its drawbacks, because it meant that he could fulfill his economic obligations to his family and confirm his own self-esteem as breadwinner and good provider. The incentive system—mainly money and status rewards—was successful in motivating most people.

People were tied to their jobs not only by bonds of commitment to their family, but also by loyalty to their organizations.

[38] Ferrini and Parker, op. cit., pp. 5–6.
[39] Thelma Jones Vriend, "The Case for Women," *The Vocational Guidance Quarterly,* 25:329–330 (June 1977).

Most people defined their identity through their work roles, subordinating and suppressing most conflicting personal desires.

For all practical purposes, a job was defined as a paid activity that provided steady full-time work to the male breadwinner with compensation adequate to provide at least the necessities, and, with luck, some luxuries, for an intact nuclear family.[40]

It was noted, however, that under

the onslaught of a new value system, all these consequences of the old value system have already changed or are in the process of changing. The New Breed values are expressed in the world of work in some ways that are obvious and others that are quite subtle. Three of the more striking manifestations of New Breed work-related values are (1) the increasing importance of leisure, (2) the symbolic significance of the paid job, and (3) the insistence that jobs become less depersonalized.[41]

The "aging of America" is another phenomenon increasingly challenging those responsible for providing career guidance in institutional and agency settings. As people marvel at the artistic accomplishments of a Grandma Moses at 100 or a Pablo Picasso at 90; George Burns' Academy Award-winning performance in *The Sunshine Boys* at the "youthful" age of 80; or the political activities of Konrad Adenaur, the Chancellor of West Germany, at 88; one must be aware that age is not an inevitable barrier to career accomplishments. We are also aware that life expectancy is increasing at the same time that human physical well-being and vigor are steadily improving for all age groups. It can be anticipated that increasing numbers of older and healthier citizens will be capable and desirous of work. Two projects noted that

exploring work and activity options in the postretirement period have uncovered the need for a mix of paid employment, volunteer activities, and leisure-oriented activities to fill the "young-old years."[42] The Miami-Dade Project report concluded that among older persons there appears to be a need for "education for living" as well as "education for earning."[43] The report underscored the need for leisure, volunteer, and paid employment counseling to develop appropriate total activity programs for older persons.[44]

[40] Daniel Yankelovich, "The New Psychological Contracts at Work," *Psychology Today* (May 1978), p. 47.

[41] Ibid., p. 47.

[42] A. M. Katz, *Employment Opportunities for Older Adults,* first-year report submitted to the Edna McConnell Clark Foundation, New York, 1976.

[43] *Project elderly,* an interim report from Miami-Dade Community College, Miami, Fla., 1976.

[44] Alan D. Entine, "Counseling for Mid-Life and Beyond," *The Vocational Guidance Quarterly,* **25:**332–333 (June 1977).

Entine suggested "a model for effective mid-career counseling techniques that integrated concern for both the personal and economic changes that can affect the mid-life period."[45]

In view of the projected growth of the postretirement life-stage and of the different relationship of personal and economic factors in this period, a second model was proposed to relate specifically to potential counseling needs in this life-stage. The models are described as follows:

In Model I, the mid-career model, appropriate counseling responses involve personal and career counseling. Personal counseling includes the processes that attempt to provide support and assistance so that individuals can understand the nature of the economic or personal changes that they are experiencing. Techniques utilized in personal counseling may include one-to-one counseling, self-awareness sessions, and crisis intervention workshops. Personal counseling can lead to referrals to mental health agencies for therapy and for other forms of psychological support.

Career counseling includes the processes that identify appropriate career and work options for individuals, based upon a knowledge of their aptitudes, skills, experiences, interests, and limitations. Techniques used in this process may include individual or group workshops, aptitude testing, and the identification of appropriate educational and training programs. Career counseling can lead to referrals to employment services that specialize in job placement or job creation.

Model II, postretirement, retains personal counseling but substitutes activity for career counseling. Activity counseling includes individual and group sessions that can identify appropriate full-time or part-time work, include training sessions, and may lead to referrals to voluntary employment agencies, senior citizen recreation centers, and retirement communities.

In both models the causes of potential change in each life-stage are presented in a four-quadrant matrix. Examples of change agents in the mid-life period are presented in Figure 8–6; change agent examples for the postretirement years are illustrated in Figure 8–7. In both Figure 8–6 and Figure 8–7, the vertical division separates the factors leading to possible change into internally and externally based causes. Internally based causes are related to changes that take place within the individual or within his or her immediate family. Externally based causes are related to changes that affect the individual as a result of changes that take place in the economy of the community.[46]

Counseling processes for the mid-career model, Figure 8–8, are likely to require both personal and career counseling responses. It is suggested that this combination is best determined by the type of change

[45] A. D. Entine, "The Mid-career Counseling Process," *Industrial Gerontology*, **3**:(2), (1976), pp. 106–110.
[46] Ibid., pp. 332–333.

	Internal	External

U N A N T I C I P A T E D	Examples:
	
	Serious
	  illness
	Divorce
	Death of
	  spouse
	
	1
		Examples:
		
		Unemployment
		Work dissatisfaction
		Job obsolescence
		Rapid inflation
		
		2

A N T I C I P A T E D	Examples:
	
	Empty nest
	Labor force
	  re-entry
	Voluntary
	  career
	  change
	
	3
		Examples:
		
		Planned re-
		  tirement
		Promotion
		  and advancement
		
		4

Figure 8–6.
Causes of mid-career change. *A. D. Entine, "The Mid-career Counseling Process," Industrial Gerontology,* **3** *(1976), p. 334.*

	Internal	External

U N A N T I C I P A T E D	Examples:
	
	Serious
	  illness
	Divorce
	Death of
	  children
	Social losses
	  (friends,
	  status)
	Loneliness
	1
		Examples:
		
		Inadequate
		  income
		Needed work
		  role
		Rapid inflation
		
		2

A N T I C I P A T E D	Examples:
	
	Physical
	  decline
	Death of
	  spouse
	
	3
		Examples:
		
		Desired re-
		  tirement
		Lifestyle
		  A) Work
		  B) Volunteer
		    activities
		  C) Leisure
		    activities
		4

Figure 8–7.
Causes of postretirement change. *A. D. Entine, "The Mid-career Counseling Process," Industrial Gerontology,* **3** *(1976), p. 334.*

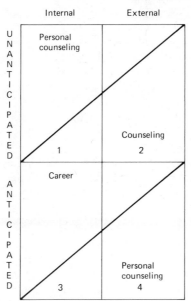

Figure 8–8.
Mid-career counseling responses. *A. D. Entine, "The Mid-career Counseling Process,"* Industrial Gerontology, **3** *(1976), p. 334.*

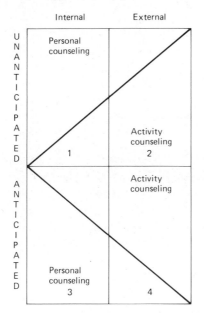

Figure 8–9.
Postretirement counseling responses. *A. D. Entine, "The Mid-career Counseling Process,"* Industrial Gerontology, **3** *(1976), p. 334.*

agent that encourages the individual to seek or require counseling assistance.[47]

Appropriate counseling responses in the postretirement period form a different pattern than those at mid-life, (Figure 8–9). Activity counseling replaces career counseling since full-time paid employment is likely to be replaced by a combination of paid work, unpaid work and leisure-oriented pursuits. Greater proportions of personal counseling to activity counseling are likely to be required to meet both unanticipated and anticipated personal changes.[48]

A final, not to be overlooked, cause in stimulating career guidance and placement activities for post-school adults is economic necessity. In a broad sense, this includes such traditional factors as job layoffs, phasing out or terminating of occupations, job shifts to increase income potential, and other not so traditional factors such as "moonlighting" on a second job to either keep up with increased costs and/or increase one's standard of living, all adults in the family working either through necessity or as a means of securing a higher standard of living, and retirees who find they cannot live adequately on their benefits. These and other factors are reminders of the opportunities to provide career guidance and placement for the post-school population. The following paragraphs examine career guidance and placement in some institutional and agency settings.

A 1978 study revealed that more than 59 per cent of semiskilled, unskilled, and clerical workers, 50 per cent of sales people, 38 per cent of the skilled workers, 30 per cent of the managers and executives, and 25 per cent of the professions believed it was likely that they would change their career in the next five years.[49] It is probable that many of those seeking new careers will again seek the assistance of counselors in the Employment Security Division of the U.S. Department of Labor. A career change model (Figure 8–10) appropriate to government and other employment agencies indicates activities that counselors may find appropriate in such settings. A variety of career opportunities are provided under the provisions of the Comprehensive Employment and Training Act (CETA) of 1973, as amended and extended in subsequent acts of 1974 and 1976. This program focuses largely on providing training employment and other related services to economically disadvantaged who are either unemployed or underemployed. Other government programs include provisions for school-to-work transition programs, senior community service employment, job corps and work incentive programs.

Career development opportunities are provided for the nation's physically

---

[47] Ibid., p. 335.
[48] Ibid., p. 335.
[49] Patricia A. Renwick, Edward E. Lawler, et al., "What You Really Want from Your Job," *Psychology Today* (May 1978), pp. 53–65.

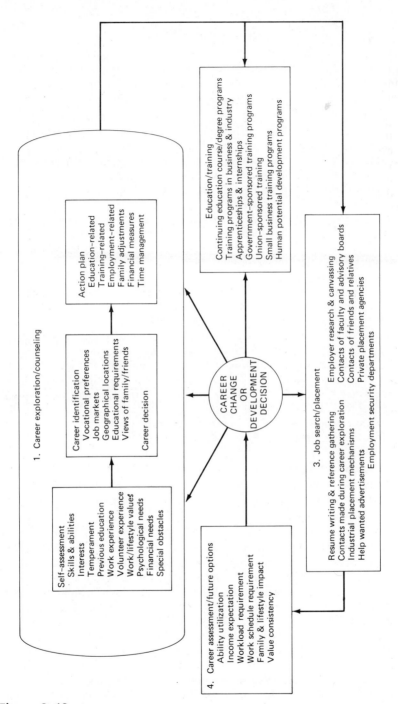

Figure 8–10.
Career change model. *Paul Ferrini and L. Allen Parker,* Career Change *(Cambridge, Mass.: Technical Education Research Centers, 1978), p. 10.*

and mentally handicapped through state-federal programs of vocational rehabilitation. Programs of these agencies are designed to enable individuals to
prepare for and engage in meaningful occupations. As Norris notes,

> Eligibility is based on a finding of a certain physical or mental problem,
> the existence of a substantial obstacle to employment, and a reasonable
> expectation that vocational rehabilitation services may enable the indi-
> vidual to engage in a gainful occupation. If necessary in making a
> decision on probable outcome, rehabilitation services can be provided
> during a period of extended evaluation to determine the individual's
> ability to benefit from them.
>
> The key to the rehabilitation process is the counselor, who through
> his or her own professional skills enables the handicapped person to
> analyze problems and needs, engage in self-exploration and self-under-
> standing, and develop a suitable plan that will lead to a productive,
> satisfying occupation.
>
> The state vocational rehabilitation programs across the nation reach
> an impressive number of handicapped people. Some are receiving and
> may be nearing completion of a sequence of services from other social
> institutions, or they may be individuals from the community at large
> who are blocked from vocational objectives by their problems.
>
> Special efforts of the state vocational rehabilitation programs reach
> target areas of highly concentrated social and economic need. These
> areas may be in rural America, or they may be in the severely depressed
> areas of cities. Such special efforts may include participation in Neigh-
> borhood Service Projects, Concentrated Employment Programs, and
> Model Cities Programs.[50]

Career development and change programs that provide supporting counseling services are also beginning to emerge in business and industry. Ferrini
and Parker in a survey of some 200 business and industrial firms (1978)
noted that some firms

> had developed information resources to assist employees involved in
> career planning activities. For example, some firms had developed job
> descriptions (including skill requirements) for their jobs. These were
> especially valuable to employees who did not know which company
> jobs would best meet their needs. Career information libraries, including
> career change relevant publications and information about internal ca-
> reer opportunities, had also been established by some firms.
>
> Extensive education and training opportunities had been developed
> by some firms. However, those firms which had outstanding counseling-
> information services usually did not have outstanding education and
> training components, and vice versa. Most firms had some sort of tuition

---

[50] Willa Norris, et al., *The Career Information Service,* 4th ed. (Chicago: Rand McNally &
Company, 1979), p. 312.

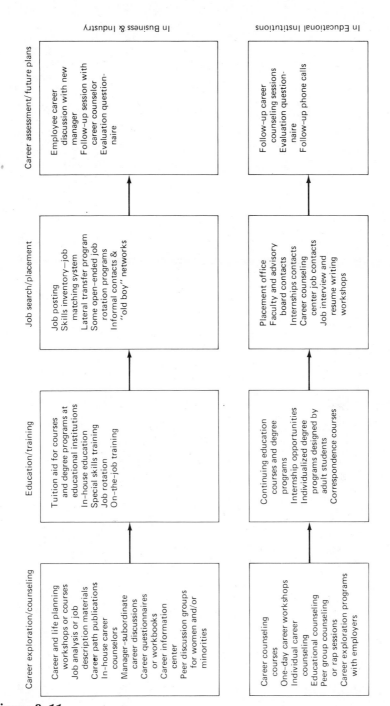

In Business & Industry

Career assessment/future plans

Employee career discussion with new manager
Follow-up session with career counselor
Evaluation questionnaire

Job search/placement

Job posting
Skills inventory—job matching system
Lateral transfer program
Some open-ended job rotation programs
Informal contacts & "old boy" networks

Education/training

Tuition aid for courses and degree programs at educational institutions
In-house education
Special skills training
Job rotation
On-the-job training

Career exploration/counseling

Career and life planning workshops or courses
Job analysis or job description materials
Career path publications
In-house career counselors
Manager–subordinate career discussions
Career questionnaires or workbooks
Career information center
Peer discussion groups for women and/or minorities

In Educational Institutions

Follow-up career counseling sessions
Evaluation questionnaire
Follow-up phone calls

Placement office
Faculty and advisory board contacts
Internships contacts
Career counseling center job contacts
Job interview and resume writing workshops

Continuing education courses and degree programs
Internship opportunities
Individualized degree programs designed by adult students
Correspondence courses

Career counseling courses
One-day career workshops
Individual career counseling
Educational counseling
Peer group counseling or rap sessions
Career exploration programs with employers

Figure 8–11.
Support services available. *Paul Ferrini and L. Allen Parker,* Career Change *(Cambridge, Mass.: Technical Education Research Centers, 1978), p. 14.*

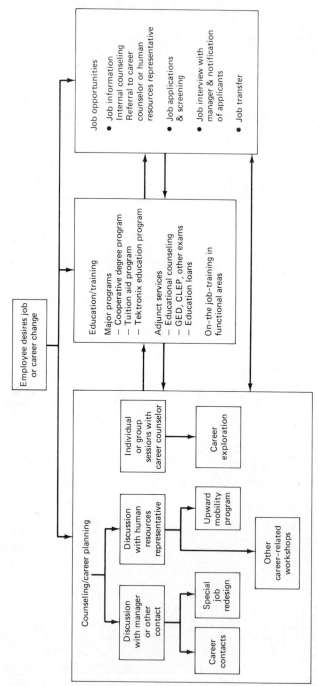

Figure 8–12.
Major career change mechanisms. *Paul Ferrini and L. Allen Parker,* Career
Change *(Cambridge, Mass.: Technical Education Research Centers, 1978), p.
42.*

aid or reimbursement program enabling employees to take job-relevant courses or degree sequences at educational institutions in the community. A few firms had extended their tuition aid benefits to include courses relevant to future company jobs. Other education opportunities in firms included on-the-job training options, ongoing in-house education courses, short-term training programs for specific jobs, and management traning programs.

A variety of placement mechanisms had also been developed in business and industry. Most firms offered some kind of job posting system for their employees. However, in many cases, employees not currently qualifying for posted jobs had difficulty using these systems. Moreover, coordination between career planning, education, and training, and job posting mechanisms appeared to be scant in most companies. Some firms had solved this problem by initiating special cross-training or lateral transfer programs which increased their participants' chances of securing career change placements. However, these programs appeared to be available only to a small number of employees.[51]

A comparison of support services available in business and industry and in educational institutions is presented in Figure 8–11. The second chart (Figure 8–12) depicts major career change mechanisms for employees in business and industrial settings.

SUMMARY

Career guidance and placement have been given a new impetus in both school and agency settings since the 1970s as a result of the national career education movement. In the past, career guidance was a recognized activity of most school guidance programs, but it received little curricular emphasis and, as a result, in many settings was less than effective. Now, however, schools recognize the inseparability of career education and career guidance. Further, agencies and other noneducational institutions which, in the past, were primarily concerned with career placement of first-time job seekers are now recognizing the probability and importance of mid-life career changes, the possibility of employment in a new field after retirement, and the elimination of many traditional barriers to the employment of women, minorities, and older adults. These and other factors have led to a renewed interest in and examination of influences on career planning and decision making. Although a number of the traditional theories were reviewed in this chapter, it should be recognized that some are challenging these theories as inappropriate for today's populations and careers. Increased attention has also been given to placement and follow-up as a planned guidance activity. This emphasis has been prompted by legislative funding and recognition that career development without placement is an incomplete process.

[51] Ferrini and Parker, op. cit., pp. 20–21.

Individual Counseling $\mathbf{9}$

INTRODUCTION

Counseling is, of course, the single most important activity in which counselors engage. They are called counselors not because they give tests, provide occupational information, or consult with teachers and parents, but because they counsel. Counseling is a skill and process distinguished from advising, directing, perhaps listening sympathetically and appearing to be interested in many of the same concerns as professional counselors.

Individual counseling has, since the early days of the school guidance movement, been identified as the heart of the guidance program. All other professional activities of the counselor lead to this most important function. Test results, career information, and autobiographies are all relatively meaningless if they do not provide information that enhances the effectiveness of the counseling process.

A popular definition identifies individual counseling as a

> personal, face-to-face relationship between two people, in which the counselor, by means of the relationship and his special competencies, provides a learning situation in which the counselee, a normal sort of person, is helped to know himself and his present and possible future

situations so that he can make use of characteristics and potentialities in a way that is both satisfying to himself and beneficial to society, and further, can learn how to solve future problems and meet future needs.[1]

Blackham suggests that "counseling is a unique helping relationship in which the client is provided the opportunity to learn, feel, think, experience, and change in ways that he or she thinks is desirable."[2]

Shertzer and Stone define counseling as "an interaction process which facilitates meaningful understanding of self and environment and results in the establishment and/or clarification of goals and values for future behavior."[3]

Cottle and Downie define counseling as "the process by which a counselor assists a client to face, understand, and accept information about himself and his interaction with others, so that he can make effective decisions about various life choices."[4]

Stefflre and Grant indicate that

counseling denotes a professional relationship between a trained counselor and a client. This relationship is usually person-to-person, although it may sometimes involve more than two people, and it is designed to help the client understand and clarify his view of his life space so that he may make meaningful and informed choices consonant with his essential nature in those areas where choices are available to him. This definition indicates that counseling is a process, that it is a relationship, that it is designed to help people make choices, that underlying better choice-making are such matters as learning, personality development, and self-knowledge which can be translated into better role perception and more effective role behavior.[5]

These are but a few of the many definitions available to students of counseling. There are semantic differences, of course, but most definitions begin by suggesting that individual counseling is a one-to-one relationship involving a trained counselor and focuses on some aspects of a client's adjustment, developmental, or decision-making needs. This process provides a relationship and communications base from which the client can develop under-

[1] E. L. Tolbert, *Introduction to Counseling,* 2nd ed. (New York: McGraw-Hill Book Company, 1972), p. 9.

[2] Garth J. Blackham, *Counseling: Theory, Process and Practice.* (Belmont, Calif.: Wadsworth Publishing Company, 1977), p. 7.

[3] Bruce Shertzer and Shelley C. Stone, *Fundamentals of Counseling,* 2nd ed. (Boston: Houghton Mifflin Company, 1974), p. 20.

[4] William C. Cottle and E. M. Downie, *Preparation for Counseling,* 2nd ed. (Englewood Cliffs, N.J.: Prentice-Hall, Inc., 1970), p. 1.

[5] Buford Stefflre and W. Harold Grant, *Theories of Counseling,* 2nd ed. (New York: McGraw-Hill Book Company, 1972), p. 15.

standings, explore possibilities, and initiate change. In this setting, it is the skill of the counselor which makes positive outcomes possible. The counselor's skills and knowledge provide the appropriate framework and direction that maximizes the client's potential for positive results. Untrained and unskilled helpers, regardless of their best intentions, cannot duplicate the functions of the professional counselor.

THEORIES OF COUNSELING

Having previously suggested that the various definitions of counseling differ little in actual meaning, one might assume that all counselors function similarly in like situations; that, like so many robots, we would all respond similarly, interpret client information in the same manner and agree on desired outcomes in specific counseling situations. Thus, a chapter on counseling techniques might read like a Betty Crocker Cook Book in which recipes were specified for the kinds of situations and the kinds of outcomes desired for these situations. Of course, nothing could be further from the truth! As definitions vary in counseling, the approaches that professional counselors use vary even more. While the variety in these approaches may, at times, confuse the beginning student and the general public as well, it is fair to say that unlike Betty Crocker recipes, there are a variety of proven approaches for the providing of counseling services to various populations. These approaches are usually distinguished and described under their theoretical labels.

In the previous chapter a brief explanation of the term theory was presented. While hopefully that explanation has not been forgotten by now, we would like to present some further discussion as we seek to relate theory to the practice of counseling. Theoretical models for counseling have their origins in the values and beliefs of individuals who, in turn, have converted these into a philosophy and a theoretical model for counseling. These values and beliefs form a rationale for what one does, how one does it, and under what circumstances.

As Brammer notes

> theorizing refers to a rational rather than a feeling function. Helpers need a guiding theory to help them make sense of the complex helping process. Of course, people can help others . . . without a thought about theory, but if they are going to work systematically in a helping function, they need some "hooks" on which to hang their experiences and some frame of reference for gaining perspectives on their work and improving their services.[6]

---

[6] Lawrence M. Brammer, *The Helping Relationship: Process and Skills,* 2nd ed. (Englewood Cliffs, N.J.: Prentice-Hall, Inc., 1979), p. 150.

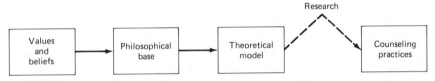

Figure 9–1.
Bridging the gap from theory to practice. *June G. Shane, Harold G. Shane, Robert L. Gibson, and Paul F. Munger,* Guiding Human Development: The Counselor and the Teacher in the Elementary School *(Worthington, Ohio: Charles A. Jones Publishing Company, 1971), p. 215.*

Of course, for the established theories, research has played an important part in bridging the gap through verifying or "proving" theoretical premises. This progress from values to practice may be noted in Figure 9–1.

In the next section of this chapter, brief descriptions of some of the popular counseling theories will be presented. It should be stated, however, that these and other recognized theories in the field of counseling provide only a base that the practicing counselor will modify and adjust in order to suit the unique situation in which he or she functions and the unique personality which he or she is. In other words, every counselor evolves his/her own unique counseling style, but in this process he or she is guided by his/her knowledge and understanding of the acceptable and researched models available to his or her professional field.

Psychoanalytic Theory

For beginning counselors, psychoanalytical theory is more important to study from an historical perspective rather than as a model for adoption. The psychoanalytical approach requires extensive training, so it is presented here for informational purposes only.

> Psychoanalysis historically has had three different meanings. First, it is a system of psychology derived from Sigmund Freud which stresses particularly the role of the unconscious and of dynamic forces in psychic functioning; second, it is a form of therapy which uses primarily free association and relies on the analysis of transferences and resistance; and third, it is sometimes used to differentiate the Freudian approach from neo-Freudian approaches within the field of psychoanalysis proper.[7]

Psychoanalytic theory views the structure of personality as separated into three major systems: the id, ego, and superego. Hereditary factors are represented by the id, which functions in the inner world of one's personality

---

[7] Reuben Fine, "Psychoanalysis," in *Current Psychotherapies,* ed. by Raymond Corsini (Itasca, Ill.: F. E. Peacock Publishers, Inc., 1973), p.1.

and is thus largely unconscious. The id is usually viewed as the original system of personality which is inherent and present at birth. Many believe that the id is ruled by the "pleasure principle" and thus, it seeks to avoid tension and pain, seeking, instead, gratification and pleasure. As Corey notes, it is "the spoiled brat of personality."[8]

The ego is viewed as the only rational element of the personality. The ego also has contact with the world of reality. Because of this contact with reality it controls consciousness and provides realistic and logical thinking and planning.

The superego represents the conscience of the mind and operates on a principle of moral realism. It represents the moral code of the individual, usually based on one's perceptions of the moralities and values of society. As a result of its role, the superego in a sense is responsible for providing rewards, such as pride and self-love, and punishments, such as feelings of guilt or inferiority to its owner.

In this triangle, the superego, because it resides largely in the subconscious, is most aware of the id's impulses and seeks to direct the ego to control the id. As a result, psychoanalytic theory views tension, conflict, and anxiety as inevitable in humans and that human behavior is therefore directed toward reduction of this tension. In the psychoanalytical context, then, the reduction of tension becomes a major goal of counseling. Because personality conflict is present in all people, nearly everyone can benefit from professional counseling.

In conclusion, much of classic psychoanalytic theory is based on three major and fairly popular assumptions about human nature.

> The first of these is that the initial five years of an individual's development are the most crucial and largely determine the adult behavior of the individual, regardless of whether that behavior is considered normal or abnormal. Second, the sexual impulses of an individual act as key determinants of behavior. Sexual impulses are generally interpreted to mean the need for each individual to gratify all bodily pleasures. A third assumption is that much of an individual's behavior is controlled by unconscious determinants.[9]

Client-centered

Client-centered counseling is another historically significant and influential theory. This theory was originally developed and described by Carl R. Rogers as a reaction against what he considered the basic limitations of psychoanaly-

---

[8] Gerald Corey, *Theory and Practice of Counseling and Psychotherapy* (Monterey, Calif.: Brooks/Cole Publishing Company, 1977), p. 11.

[9] James C. Hansen and Richard R. Stevic, and Richard W. Warner, Jr., *Counseling: Theory and Process*, 2nd ed. (Boston: Allyn & Bacon, Inc., 1977), p. 33.

sis. As a result of his influence, this particular approach is often referred to as "Rogerian counseling."

> Essentially, the client-centered approach is a specialized branch of humanistic therapy that highlights the experiencing of a client and his or her subjective and phenomenal world. The therapist functions mainly as a facilitator of personal growth by helping the client discover his or her own capacities for solving problems. The client-centered approach puts great faith in the client's capacity to lead the way in therapy and find his or her own direction. The therapeutic relationship between the therapist and the client is the catalyst for change; the client uses the unique relationship as a means of increasing awareness and discovering latent resources that he or she can use constructively in changing his or her life.[10]

In understanding the client-centered approach to counseling, it is helpful to be aware of the personality basis for this theory, as presented by Rogers in the form of nineteen propositions. The lead statements for each of these propositions are as follows:

1. Every individual exists in a continually changing world of experience of which he is the center.
2. The organism reacts to the field as it is experienced and perceived. This perceptual field is, for the individual, "reality."
3. The organism reacts as an organized whole to this phenomenal field.
4. The organism has one basic tendency and striving—to actualize, maintain, and enhance the experiencing organism.
5. Behavior is basically the goal-directed attempt of the organism to satisfy its needs as experienced, in the field as perceived.
6. Emotion accompanies and in general facilitates such goal-directed behavior, the kind of emotion being related to the seeking versus the consummatory aspects of the behavior, and the intensity of the emotion being related to the perceived significance of the behavior for the maintenance and enhancement of the organism.
7. The best vantage point for understanding behavior is from the internal frame of reference of the individual himself.
8. A portion of the total perceptual field gradually becomes differentiated as the self.
9. As a result of interaction with the environment, and particularly as a result of evaluational interaction with others, the structure of self is formed—an organized, fluid, but consistent conceptual pattern of perceptions of characteristics and relationships of the "I" or the "me," together with values attached to these concepts.
10. The values attached to experiences and the values which are a

---

[10] Gerald Corey, op. cit., p. 55

part of the self structure, in some instances, are values experienced directly by the organism, and in some instances are values introjected or taken over from others, but perceived in distorted fashion, *as if* they had been experienced directly.

11. As experiences occur in the life of the individual, they are either (a) symbolized, perceived, and organized into some relationship to the self; (b) ignored because there is no perceived relationship to the self-structure; (c) denied symbolization or given a distorted symbolization because the experience is inconsistent with the structure of the self.

12. Most of the ways of behaving which are adopted by the organism are those which are consistent with the concept of self.

13. Behavior may, in some instances, be brought about by organic experiences and needs which have not been symbolized. Such behavior may be inconsistent with the structure of the self, but in such instances the behavior is not "owned" by the individual.

14. Psychological maladjustment exists when the organism denies to awareness significant sensory and visceral experiences, which consequently are not symbolized and organized into the gestalt of the self-structure. When this situation exists, there is a basic or potential psychological tension.

15. Psychological adjustment exists when the concept of the self is such that all the sensory and visceral experiences of the organism are, or may be, assimilated on a symbolic level into a consistent relationship with the concept of self.

16. Any experience which is inconsistent with the organization or structure of self may be perceived as a threat, and the more of these perceptions there are, the more rigidly the self-structure is organized to maintain itself.

17. Under certain conditions, involving primarily complete absence of any threat to the self-structure, experiences which are inconsistent with it may be perceived, and examined, and the structure of self revised to assimilate and include such experiences.

18. When the individual perceives and accepts into one consistent and integrated system all his sensory and visceral experiences, then he is necessarily more understanding of others and is more accepting of others as separate individuals.

19. As the individual perceives and accepts into his self-structure more of his organic experiences, he finds that he is replacing his present value *system*—based so largely upon introjections which have been distortedly symbolized—with a continuing organismic valuing process.[11]

In the counseling relationship, six conditions account for personality change in the client. These are as follows:

---

[11] Carl R. Rogers, *Client-Centered Therapy* (Boston: Houghton Mifflin Company, 1965), pp. 483–524.

1. Two people (a therapist and a client) are in psychological contact.[12]
2. The client is experiencing a state of anxiety, distress, or incongruence.
3. The therapist is genuine (truly himself or herself) in relating to the client.
4. The therapist feels or exhibits *unconditional positive regard* for the client.
5. The therapist exhibits *empathetic understanding* of the client's frame of reference and conveys this understanding to the client.
6. The therapist *succeeds* to a minimum degree in communicating empathetic understanding and unconditional positive regard to the client.[13]

Some of the changes expected from a successful utilization of the client-centered approach are the following:

The person comes to see himself differently.

He accepts himself and his feelings more fully.

He becomes more self-confident and self-directing.

He becomes more the person he would like to be.

He becomes more flexible, less rigid, in his perceptions.

He adopts more realistic goals for himself.

He behaves in a more mature fashion.

He changes his maladjustive behaviors, even such a long-established one as chronic alcoholism.

He becomes more acceptant of others.

He becomes more open to the evidence, both to what is going on outside of himself, and to what is going on inside of himself.

He changes in his basic personality characteristics in constructive ways.[14]

Thus, it may be noted the client-centered model is optimistic or positive in its view of humankind. Clients are viewed as being basically good and possessing the capabilities for self-understanding, insight, problem solving, decision making, change, and growth.

The counselor's role is viewed as that of a *facilitator* and *reflector*. The counselor facilitates a counselee's self-understanding and clarifies and reflects

---

[12] Carl R. Rogers, "The Conditions of Change from a Client-Centered Viewpoint," in *Sources of Gain in Counseling and Psychotherapy,* edited by B. G. Berenson and R. R. Carkhuff (New York: Holt, Rinehart and Winston, 1967), p. 73.

[13] Carl R. Rogers, "A Theory of Therapy, Personality and Interpersonal Relationships as Developed in the Client-Centered Framework," in *Psychology: A Study of Science,* Vol. 3, edited by S. Koch (New York: McGraw-Hill Book Company, 1959).

[14] Carl R. Rogers, "Significant Learning: In Therapy and In Education," *Educational Leadership,* **16:**232 (1959).

back to the client his or her own expressed feelings and attitudes. Information giving for problem solving in a client-centered context is not usually considered as a counselor responsibility. The client-centered counselor also would not seek to direct the mediation of the counselee's "inner world," but, rather, would seek to provide a climate in which the counselee could bring about change in himself or herself.

In recent years, the label of *self-theory* has been increasingly used instead of the traditional client-centered, nondirective, or Rogerian labels. This has probably resulted from the emphasis on enhancement of self, the capacity of one's self, self-actualization, and self-perceptions. Regardless of one's choice of label, this theory, originated by Dr. Rogers, continues to exert its influence on the field of counseling.

Behavioral

Behavioral theory and conditioning can be traced directly from Pavlov's nineteenth century discoveries in classical conditioning. Later important foundations for the behavioral approach were discovered from the system of psychology called behaviorism, founded by an American psychologist John B. Watson, and expressed initially in his article "Psychology as the Behaviorist Views It."[15]

Significant research and publications on the subject were conducted by Watson, Thorndike, and others, but it was not until B. F. Skinner systematically refined and developed his prinicples of behaviorism that the behavioral theory moved toward its current popularity. The behaviorist views behavior as a set of learned responses to events, experiences, or stimuli in the individual's life history. The behaviorist believes that behavior can be modified by providing appropriate learning conditions and experiences. The experimental origins of the behaviorist's approach explain his/her indifference to concepts that cannot be empirically observed or measured. Thus, rather than concern himself/herself with the emotional dynamics of behavior characteristics of the insight approaches of either Freudians or Rogerians, the behaviorist focuses on specific behavioral goals, emphasizing precise and repeatable methods.

For the behaviorist, counseling involves the systematic use of a variety of procedures that are intended specifically to change behavior in terms of mutually established goals between a client and a counselor. The procedures employed encompass a wide variety of techniques drawn from knowledge of learning processes. Current leaders in behavioral psychology, John D. Krumboltz and Carl Thoreson, place these procedures into four categories, as follows:

---

[15] John B. Watson, "Psychology as the Behaviorist Views It," *Psychological Review,* **20:**159–170 (1913).

1. *Operant Learning.* This approach is based on the usefulness of reinforcers and the timing of their presentation in producing change. Reinforcers may be concrete rewards or expressed as approval or attention.
2. *Imitative Learning.* This approach facilitates acquisition of new responses by exposure to models performing the desired behaviors.
3. *Cognitive Learning.* This technique fosters learning of appropriate responses by simply instructing the client how he may better adapt.
4. *Emotional Learning.* Involves substitution of acceptable emotional responses for unpleasant emotional reactions, using techniques derived from classical conditioning.[16]

Behaviorists also believe that stating the goals of counseling in terms of behavior that is observable is more useful than goals that are more broadly defined, such as self-understanding or acceptance of self. This means that counseling outcomes should be identifiable in terms of overt behavior changes. Krumboltz suggests three criteria for counseling goals, as follows:

1. The goals of counseling should be capable of being stated differently for each individual client.
2. The goals of counseling for each client should be compatible with, though not necessarily identical to, the values of his counselor.
3. The degree to which the goals of counseling are attained by each client should be observable.[17]

Three examples of behavioral change appropriate to counseling are the altering of behavior that is not satisfactory; the learning of the decision-making process; and problem prevention. Krumboltz suggests that the consequences of the behavioral statements of counseling goals would include the following:

1. Counselors, clients and citizens could more clearly anticipate what the counseling process could, and could not, accomplish.
2. Counseling psychology would become more integrated with the mainstream of psychological theory and research.
3. The search for new and more effective techniques of helping clients would be facilitated.
4. Different criteria would have to be applied to different clients in assessing the success of counseling.[18]

Blackham and Silberman suggest an operant paradigm consisting of six steps as follows:

[16] John D. Krumboltz and Carl B. Thoreson, *Revolution in Counseling: Implications of Behavioral Science* (Boston: Houghton Mifflin Company, 1966), pp. 13–20.
[17] John D. Krumboltz, "Behavioral Goals for Counseling," in Gary S. Belkin, *Counseling Directions in Theory and Practice,* (Dubuque, Iowa: Kendall/Hunt Publishing Co., 1976), pp. 172–173.
[18] Ibid., pp. 175–176.

1. Identify and state the behavior to be changed in operational terms.
2. Obtain a baseline of the desired target behavior.
3. Arrange the situation so that the target behavior will occur.
4. Identify potential reinforcing stimuli and events.
5. Reinforce the desired target behavior or successive approximations of it.
6. Evaluate the effects of the treatment procedure by maintaining records of change in the target behavior.[19]

Counselors utilizing behavioral theory assume that the client's behavior is the result of his/her conditioning. The counselor further assumes that each individual reacts in a predictable way to any given situation or stimulus, depending on what he or she has learned.

Finally, the goal of behavioral decision-making counseling is obviously the making of a decision. Behavioral counselors assume that a favorable outcome is more likely if the client engages in a number of preparatory behaviors prior to choosing. The counselor's major tasks are to stimulate and reinforce these client behaviors.[20]

Rational Emotive Therapy

As is often the case, an individual, for instance, Carl R. Rogers, is associated with the formulation and development of a theory, client-centered therapy. A comparatively recent example is the rational emotive therapy movement, developed by Albert Ellis. This theory is based on the assumption that individuals have the capacity to act in either a rational or irrational manner. Rational behavior is viewed as effective and potentially productive, whereas irrational behavior results in unhappiness and nonproductivity. Ellis assumes that many types of emotional problems result from irrational patterns of thinking. This irrational pattern may begin early in life and be reinforced by significant others in the individual's life, as well as by the general culture and environment. According to Ellis, people with emotional problems develop belief systems that lead to implicit verbalizations or self-talk resting on faulty logic and assumptions. And what an individual tells himself is intimately related to the way he feels and acts.

The basic foundation of Ellis's theorizing is contained in his A B C D E paradigm. In this paradigm,

A refers to an external event to which a person is subjected. *B* refers to a sequence of thoughts or self-verbalizations in which the person engages in response to the external event. *C* connotes the feelings and

[19] Garth J. Blackham and A. Silberman, *Modification of Child and Adolescent Behavior,* 2nd ed. (Belmont, Calif.: Wadsworth, 1975).

[20] John J. Horan, *Counseling for Effective Decision Making.* (North Scituate, Mass.: Duxbury Press, 1979), p. 119.

behaviors that result from *B*. *D* indicates the therapist's attempt to modify the sequence of thoughts or self-verbalizations. *E* refers to the presumed affective and behavioral consequences resulting from intervention by the therapist.[21]

The main purposes of R.E.T. counseling are to (1) demonstrate to the client that self-talk is the cause of disturbance and (2) re-evaluate this self-talk in order to eliminate it and subsequent illogical ideas.[22]

In summary,

R.E.T. is an approach to counseling that is based on the assumption that most people in our society develop many irrational ways of thinking. These irrational thoughts lead to irrational or inappropriate behavior. Therefore, counseling must be designed to help people recognize and change these irrational beliefs into more rational ones. The accomplishment of this goal requires an active, confrontive, and authoritative counselor who has the capacity to utilize a whole variety of techniques.[23]

The R.E.T. therapist does not believe that a personal relationship between the client and counselor is a prerequisite to successful counseling. In the relationship the counselor is viewed more as a teacher and the client as a student. As a result, procedures may include not only teaching and related activities such as reading or other assignments, but also questioning and challenging, even confrontation tactics, contracts, suggestions, and persuasion. Corey notes that this model has been applied to not only individual therapy, but "ongoing group therapy, marathon encounter groups, brief therapy, marriage and family therapy, sex therapy, and classroom situations. The approach is applicable to delinquents and criminals and to clients with moderate anxiety, neurotic disorders, character disorders, psychosomatic problems, and sexual dysfunctions. It is most effective with those who can reason well and who are not seriously disturbed."[24]

Reality Therapy

Another current and increasingly popular theory of counseling is that of reality therapy, largely developed by William Glasser. Glasser's approach is a fairly straightforward one, which places confidence in the counselee's ability to deal with his/her needs through a realistic or rational process. "From a reality therapy standpoint, counseling is simply a special kind of

[21] Garth J. Blackham, op. cit., p. 152.

[22] John J. Pietrofesa, Alan Hoffman, Howard H. Splete, and Diana V. Pinto, *Counseling: Theory, Research, and Practice* (Chicago: Rand McNally & Company, 1977), p. 75.

[23] James C. Hansen, Richard R. Stevic, and Richard W. Warner, Jr., op. cit., p. 209.

[24] Gerald Corey, op. cit., p. 90.

teaching or training that attempts to teach an individual what he should have learned during normal growth in a rather short period of time."[25]

Glasser and Zunin suggest that reality therapy is

applicable to individuals with behavioral and emotional problems as well as any individual or group seeking either to gain a success identity for themselves and/or to help others toward this same goal. Focusing on the present and on behavior, the therapist guides the individual to enable him to see himself accurately, to face reality, to fulfill his own needs, without harming himself or others. The crux of the theory is personal responsibility for one's own behavior, which is equated with mental health.[26]

Reality therapy focuses on present behavior and, consequently, does not emphasize the client's past history. When utilizing this approach, the counselor functions as a teacher and a model. "Reality therapy is based on the premise that there is a single psychological need that is present throughout life: the need for identity, which includes a need to feel a sense of uniqueness, separateness, and distinctiveness. The need for identity, which accounts for the dynamics of behavior, is seen as universal among all cultures."[27]

Reality therapy is based on the anticipation that the client will assume personal responsibility for his or her well-being. The acceptance of this responsibility, in a sense, helps the individual to achieve autonomy or a state of maturity whereby he or she relies on his or her own internal support. Whereas many of the counseling theories suggest that the counselor function in a noncommital way, reality therapists praise clients when they act responsibly and indicate disapproval when they do not. Reality therapy has

direct implications for school situations. Glasser first became concerned about children's learning and behavior problems while he was working with delinquent girls at the Ventura School for Girls of the California Youth Authority. He noted the almost universal history of school failure among these girls, and this finding led him to the public schools as a consultant. Glasser (1965) developed the concepts for helping children in problem solving that he described in his book *Reality Therapy.*

As he continued his work in the public elementary schools, he became convinced that the stigma of failure permeated the atmosphere in most schools and had a damaging effect on most children in schools. The elimination of failure in the school system and the prevention, rather than merely the treatment, of delinquency became two of his goals.

---

[25] James C. Hansen et al., op. cit., p. 199.

[26] William Glasser and Leonard M. Zunin, "Reality Therapy," in *Current Psychotherapies,* ed. by Raymond Corsini (Itasca, Ill.: F. E. Peacock Publishers, 1973), p. 287.

[27] Gerald Corey, op. cit., p. 158.

Glasser (1969) believes that education can be the key to effective human relating, and, in his book *Schools Without Failure,* he proposed a program to eliminate failure, emphasize thinking instead of memory work, introduce relevance into the curriculum, substitute discipline for punishment, create a learning environment where children can maximize successful experiences that will lead to a success identity, create motivation and involvement, help students develop responsible behavior, and establish ways of involving the parents and the community in the school.[28]

In summary, the reality approach "is an active, directive, didactic, cognitive behavior-oriented therapy. The contract method is often used, and when the contract is fulfilled, therapy is terminated. The approach can be both supportive and confrontational. 'What' and 'how,' but not 'why' questions are used."[29] It is important to make a plan through which the client can improve his or her behavior. This plan should lead to behavior that enables the client to gain satisfaction and, even at times, favorable recognition as well.

Transactional Analysis

Transactional analysis is a cognitive-behavioral approach that assumes the individual has the potential for choosing and for redirecting or reshaping his or her own destiny. It is designed to help a client review and evaluate early decisions and to make new, more appropriate choices.

Transactional analysis (TA) places a great deal of emphasis on the ego, which, from a TA viewpoint, consists of three states: parent, adult, and child.

"The first step of any prospective counseling relationship is for the counselor to observe and begin the classification of ego states, one reason being that a counseling contract—even in a crisis situation—can be made only with the adult ego state. The first step in establishing a TA group is the teaching of the recognition of ego states."[30]

An essential technique in TA counseling is the contract that precedes each counseling step. This contract between counselor and counselee is a way of training or preparing people to make their own important decisions.

Dusay and Steiner (1971) state that the contract must meet the following requirements:

1. Both the counselor and the client, through Adult-Adult transactions, must mutually agree on the objectives.

---

[28] Ibid., p. 167.

[29] Ibid., p. 99.

[30] John Mellecker, "Transactional Analysis for Non-TA Counselors," in Gary S. Belkin, *Counseling: Directions in Theory and Practice* (Dubuque, Iowa: Kendall Hunt, 1976), p. 199.

2. The contract must call for some consideration. The counselor gives professional skill and time as his consideration. In some agency situations the client gives money, in others he signs a contract that commits his time and effort as his consideration.
3. The contract defines the competencies of both parties. On the part of the counselor, it means stating that he does have the skill to help with this problem; on the part of the client, it means that he is of mind and age sound enough to enter the contract.
4. Finally, the objective(s) of the contract must be legal and within the ethical limits adhered to by the counselor.[31]

In addition to the contract technique, TA also utilizes questionnaires, life scripts, structural analysis, role playing, analysis of games and rituals, and "stroking." Although not a counseling technique, TA sessions are tape-recorded in their entirety.

At each stage of counseling the decision to go ahead is squarely up to the counselee. (This is the way the counselor protects himself or herself from implications that the counseling is being forced on the counselee.) The counselor may specify conditions to his/her participation in contracts, such as requiring the counselee to define, in advance, what advantage might ensue from their joint effort.

Transactional analysis, of course, focuses on the individual, but it is a procedure for counseling individuals within a group setting. TA counselors feel that the group setting facilitates the process of providing feedback to the individual about the kind of transactions in which he/she engages. The counseling group, then, represents a microcosm of the real world. In this setting, the individual group members are there to work on their own objectives and the counselor is there in the role of the group leader.

Gestalt Counseling

Gestalt psychology is defined by Webster as "psychology based on the theory that physical, psychological, and biological events do not occur through the summation of separate elements, as sensations or reflexes, but through formed patterns of these integrated units which function singly or in interrelation; configurationism. Each of these patterns is called a *gestalt.*"[32] Gestalt counselors believe that individuals always act to organize stimuli into total pictures or wholes. Several principles that have been developed to explain this process are as follows.

Principle of closure: When we perceive a figure that is incomplete, our mind acts to finish the figure and perceives it as complete.

---

[31] James C. Hansen, et al., op. cit., pp. 105–106.
[32] *Webster's New Collegiate Dictionary.* (Springfiled, Mass.: G & C. Merriam Company, 1956), p. 348.

Principle of Proximity: The relative distance of stimuli from each other within the perceptual field determines how they are seen.

Principle of Similarity: The similarity of stimuli in the perceptual field causes us to group them together.[33]

Each of these three principles illustrates how the human mind seeks to make sense from the vast array of stimuli in the phenomenal field by pulling things together. The important point . . . is that the stimuli only have meaning as they are organized in the mind by the individual."[34]

Passons (1975) lists eight assumptions about the nature of man that act as the framework for Gestalt counseling:

1. Man is a composite whole who is made up of interrelated parts. None of these parts, body emotions, thoughts, sensations, and perceptions can be understood outside the context of the whole person.
2. Man is also part of his own environment and he cannot be understood apart from it.
3. Man chooses how he responds to external and internal stimuli; he is an actor on his world, not a reactor.
4. Man has the potential to be fully aware of all his sensations, thoughts, emotions, and perceptions.
5. Man is capable of making choices because he is aware.
6. Man has the capacity to govern his own life effectively.
7. Man cannot experience the past and the future, he can only experience himself in the present.
8. Man is neither basically good nor bad.[35]

Gestalt counseling has as its major objective the integration of the individual. In popular terminology, this might be called "getting it all together." In order to achieve this togetherness, the counselor seeks to increase the individual's awareness. As a result, the counselor functions in a way that provides his/her client an atmosphere conducive to client discovery of his or her needs, what he/she has lost because of environmental demands, and a setting in which he/she can experience the necessary discovery and growth.

To facilitate this process, counselors utilize the most important tool they have: themselves. A counselor, fully aware of herself in the now, engages the client in a here and now interaction. She does not interpret, probe, preach about reality; rather, she interacts with the client in the now. In sum, the Gestalt counselor must view himself as a catalyst that acts in whatever ways necessary to help the client increase his own awareness."[36]

[33] James C. Hansen, et al., op. cit., pp. 142–143.
[34] Ibid., p. 143.
[35] Ibid., pp. 145–146.
[36] Ibid., p. 153.

Eclectic Counseling

The eclectic approach to counseling is one of long-standing tradition and equally long-standing controversy. It originally provided a safe, middle-of-the-road theory for those counselors, primarily in school settings, who neither desired nor felt capable of functioning as purely directive or nondirective counselors. Defenders of the theory, on the other hand, suggested eclecticism as an approach that allowed each individual to construct his or her own theory by drawing on established theories. It has often been suggested that the eclectic counselor can choose the best of all counseling worlds.

Tolbert notes several assumptions appropriate to the eclectic approach:

> One of the most critical assumptions has to do with the effect of the counselor as a person in the counseling relationship. If one's counseling is viewed as a "personal trait" (Lister, 1964; Shoben, 1966), and it seems that it should be, then an approach is unique for the individual counselor and tied to his way of relating to others. To take this a step further, it may be inferred that he could not expect to help others unless his counseling approach were, in fact, a utilization of himself as a real person in a human relationship.
>
> A second assumption is that the counselor has a thorough knowledge of the necessary ingredients for personal theory building. These are himself, existing counseling approaches, theories of learning and personality development, and perceptions of others. Without these, it is difficult to conceive of any kind of meaningful and consistent approach being developed.
>
> A third assumption has to do with the underlying consistency of the counselor in interpersonal relations. In developing a personal theory, could the counselor include different sorts of basic attitudes and methods—to use an extreme example, could he be "democratic" at some times and "autocratic" at others? Arbuckle (1966) points out that: "If . . . what are called methodologies are actually qualities of the individual counselor, it is difficult to see how the counselor could be eclectic" (p. 229). But an *eclectic orientation* is quite different from an eclectic counseling approach: "There is a vast difference, however, between an eclectic *orientation,* which surely every professional counselor should have, and without which there will be provincialism or even downright ignorance of counseling, and an eclectic *method of counseling*" (Arbuckle, 1966, p. 231). The counselor should be consistent in his basic approach to others; he should have, however, a broad knowledge of counseling approaches. This concept of eclecticism is apparent in Arbuckle's (1966) illustration: "The consistency of the client-centered counselor, for example, comes simply because he has found, eclectically and pragmatically, that this is the means of operation in which he is comfortable, and in which he is most effective" (p. 232).
>
> Lister (1967) takes the same position in describing the possibilities of "theoretical eclecticism": "The primary advantage of theoretical

eclecticism is that it enables the counselor to work out for himself an internally consistent, coherent rationale for his counseling behavior . . . He may develop a point of view more personally meaningful than any existing orthodox position . . . He may conceptualize the counseling process in a way that meshes comfortably with his own life style" (pp. 288–291). This suggests that the counselor would desirably have a consistency in human relations, in contrast to the "technical eclectic" who concentrates on selecting "techniques" that seem to work but have no sound theoretical framework (Lister, 1967).

A final assumption is that a counselor is capable of developing a personal style that is better for him than other formal approaches. An eclectic counselor makes this assumption, implicitly or explicitly. He should be aware, however, that his approach may have serious deficiencies which he does not realize and which he does nothing to correct (Lister, 1967).[37]

Brammer and Shostrom also note that each counselor and psychotherapist must ultimately develop a point of view that is uniquely his or her own. They then go on to state that

Developing one's own view is a very demanding lifelong task. In addition to knowing current theories of personality structure and behavior change, the counselor must know his own assumptions about the nature of man and the process of knowing, his own values and views of the good life, and his model of the mature well-functioning person. This goal is accomplished through self-study of client-counselor relationships and personal therapeutic experiences resulting in increased self-understanding. Then one puts these pieces together into a unified system which is comfortable and effective for himself in his particular setting. Finally, he tests the ideas in practice and formulates hypotheses which can be tested experimentally. The results are incorporated into his system, or they produce revisions in the system. This is a continuous process.[38]

Brammer, Shostrom, and Hogan suggests that

a particular therapist's specific parameters can be identified and profiled hierarchically at each developmental level. At each of the following developmental levels the growing therapist would probably show a significantly different profile.

1. *General Level.* He is heavily influenced by the parameters of his teacher or supervisor and they are superimposed on his general psychological background.

[37] E. L. Tolbert, op. cit., p. 79.
[38] Lawrence M. Brammer and Everett L. Shostrom, *Therapeutic Psychology,* 2nd ed. (Englewood Cliffs, N.J.: Prentice-Hall, Inc., 1968), p. 32.

2. *Personalized Level.* He adapts his original training and further study to his own personality, evolving a more *personalized* parametric approach.
3. *Stylized Level.* Through his training and experience, he *commits* himself to selected stylized *parameters* which combine with his personality into an unique gestalt or *style.*
4. *Expressive Level.* He goes beyond his personal style to create unique parameters which he is confident are worth sharing professionally and worth risking critical evaluation by his colleagues.[39]

GOALS OF COUNSELING

Let us now contrast the goals of the various theoretical approaches to counseling and therapy, as shown in Table 9–1. Additional discussion of goal setting will be presented later in this chapter.

THE COUNSELING PROCESS

Having briefly introduced some of the popular counseling theories, let us now move on to examine the translation of these theories into action. This "action" is frequently referred to as the counseling process. This process is usually specified by a sequence of interactions or steps. Although various authors will conceptualize these stages or phases differently with differences usually resulting from different theoretical models, there is considerable agreement that initially the process is concerned with relationship establishment, followed by some method of problem identification and patterns of exploration leading to planning for problem solution and remediation, and concluding with action and termination. For example, Brammer specifies eight stages: entry, clarification, structure, relationship, exploration, consolidation, planning, and termination.[40] Blackham identifies the stages in the counseling process as follows: problem identification and relationship establishment stage; exploration and analysis stage; implementation stage; and termination stage.[41] A brief description of each of these stages follows.

Relationship Establishment

As often stated in definitions, counseling is a relationship. Further, it is defined as a helping relationship. It therefore follows that if it is to be a relationship

[39] Ibid., p. 30.
[40] L. M. Brammer, *The Helping Relationship: Process and Skills* (Englewood Cliffs, N.J.: Prentice-Hall, Inc., 1973).
[41] Garth J. Blackham, op, cit., pp. 187–212.

Table 9–1.
Goals of Therapy

Psychoanalytic therapy	To make the unconscious conscious. To reconstruct the basic personality. To assist the client in reliving earlier, past experiences and working through repressed conflicts. Intellectual awareness.
Client-centered therapy	To provide a safe climate conducive to client self-exploration so that the client can recognize blocks to growth and experience aspects of self that were formerly denied or distorted. To enable the client to move toward openness to experience, greater trust in self, willingness to be a process, and increased spontaneity and aliveness.
Behavior therapy	To eliminate the client's maladaptive behavior patterns and assist the client in learning constructive patterns. Behavior change. Specific goals are selected by the client. Broad goals are broken into precise subgoals.
Rational-emotive therapy (RET)	To eliminate the client's self-defeating outlook on life and assist the client in acquiring a more tolerant and rational view of life.
Reality therapy	To guide the client toward learning realistic and responsible behavior and developing a "success identity." To assist the client in making value judgments about behavior and in deciding on a plan of action for change.
Gestalt therapy	To assist the client in gaining awareness of moment-to-moment experiencing. To challenge the client to accept responsibility of taking internal support as opposed to external support.
Transactional analysis (TA)	To assist the client in becoming a script-free, game-free, autonomous person who is capable of choosing how he or she wants to be. To assist the client in examining early decisions and making new decisions based on awareness.

Source: Gerald Corey, *Theory and Practice of Counseling and Psychotherapy* (Monterey, Calif.: Brooks/Cole Publishing Company, 1977), p. 192.

that is helpful, the counselor must take the initiative in the initial interview to establish a climate conducive to mutual respect, trust, free and open communication, and understanding in general of what the counseling process involves.

Within a formal context, Brammer notes that this relationship takes the form of an interview—a structured helping relationship contributed to by many variables. Figure 9–2 illustrates these variables.

Although responsibility will later shift increasingly to the client, at this stage the responsibility for the counseling process rests primarily with the counselor. Among the techniques the counselor may use are those designed to relieve tensions and open communication. Both the counselor's attitude and verbal communications are significant to the development of a satisfactory

Figure 9–2.
The helping relationship in the interview. *Lawrence M. Brammer,* The Helping
Relationship: Process and Skills *(Englewood Cliffs, N.J.: Prentice-Hall, Inc., 1973),*
p. 45.

relationship. In the latter instance, all of the counselor's communication skills
are brought into play. These include attentive listening, understanding, and
feeling with the client. As Egan points out, the counselor's goal in this stage
is attending—"to attend to the other both physically and psychologically."[42]

Among the factors that are important in the establishment of this coun-
selor-client relationship are positive regard and respect, accurate empathy,
and genuineness. These conditions imply counselor openness, an ability to
understand and feel with the client, and valuing the client. As Hackney
and Cormier note, this constructive

> counselor-client relationship serves not only to increase the opportunity
> for clients to attain their goals, but also serves as a potential model
> of a good interpersonal relationship, one that clients can use to improve
> the quality of their other relationships outside the therapy setting.[43]

Counselors must keep in mind that the purpose of a counseling relationship is to meet, insofar as possible, client needs (not counselor needs). The
counseling process within this relationship seeks to assist the client in assuming
the responsibilities for his or her problem and its solution. As Okun notes

> a helping relationship that benefits the helpee is a two-way mutual
> learning process between two (or more) people. The relationship is
> dependent for its effectiveness upon the helper possessing the skill to
> communicate his or her understanding of the helpee's feelings and behav-
> iors and the ability to apply appropriate helping strategies in order to
> facilitate the recipient's self-exploration, self-understanding, problem-
> solving, and decision-making, all of which lead to constructive action
> on the part of the helpee.[44]

[42] Gerard Egan, *The Skilled Helper: A Model for Systematic Helping and Interpersonal Relating*
(Monterey, Calif.: Brooks/Cole Publishing, 1975), p. 30.
[43] Harold Hackney and L. Sherilyn Cormier, *Counseling Strategies and Objectives,* 2nd ed. (Englewood Cliffs, N.J.: Prentice-Hall, Inc., 1979), p. 8.
[44] Barbara F. Okun, *Effective Helping: Interviewing and Counseling Techniques* (North Scituate,
Mass.: Duxbury Press, 1976), p. 16.

The establishment of a relationship that is seen as helpful to the client must be achieved early in the counseling process, inasmuch as this will often determine whether or not the client will continue.

Eisenberg and Delaney suggest the essential goals of the initial counseling interview are as follows:

For the Counselor:

Stimulate open, honest, and full communication about the concerns needing to be discussed and the factors and background related to those concerns.

Work toward progressively deeper levels of understanding, respect, and trust between self and client.

Provide the client with the view that something useful can be gained from the counseling sessions.

Identify a problem or concern for subsequent attention and work.

Establish the "gestalt" that counseling is a process in which both parties must work hard at exploring and understanding the client and his or her concerns.

Acquire information about the client that relates to his or her concerns and effective problem resolution.

For Most Clients:

Stimulating self-examination.

Generating some specific task for the client to do, or some specific issue to think about before the next counseling session.[45]

Problem Identification and Exploration

Once an adequate relationship has been established, the client will be more receptive to the discussion and exploration in depth of his or her concern. At this stage, the client assumes more responsibility, because it is his or her problem and it is his or her willingness to communicate as much of the nature of the problem to the counselor that will determine to a large extent the assistance the counselor can give.

During this phase, the counselor continues to exhibit attending behavior and may place particular emphasis on such communication skills as para-phrasing, clarification, perception checking, or feedback. The counselor may question the client, but the questions are stated in such a way as to facilitate the continued exploration of the client's concern. Questions that would embarrass, challenge, or threaten the client are avoided. During this stage, the

---

[45] Sheldon Eisenberg and Daniel J. Delaney, *The Counseling Process*, 2nd ed. (Chicago: Rand McNally College Publishing Company, 1977), p. 75.

counselor is seeking to distinguish between what might be called surface problems and those that are more complex. He/she is also seeking to determine if the stated problem is, in fact, the concern that has brought the client to the counselor's attention. During this stage, some counselors may utilize appraisal techniques such as standardized tests for problem diagnosis. Subproblems of the problem may also be identified. During this stage, the client not only explores his or her experiences and behaviors, but also may reveal feelings and the relationship of his or her concern to the way he or she is living life in general. The counselor, on the other hand, is seeking to secure as much relevant data as possible and to integrate it into an overall picture of the client and his or her concern. The counselor also shares these perceptions with the client. A goal of this stage is for both the counselor and the client to perceive the problem and its ramifications similarly. Another goal of the counselor during this stage is to help the client develop a self-understanding that recognizes the need for dealing with his or her concern—the need for change and action.

Obviously, this is a busy stage of the counseling process. As Blackham notes

Much of the real work of counseling takes place in the second stage, where exploration and client analysis become intensive. Facilitative conditions are created that enable clients to explore and understand the basis of their problems, and procedures are formulated to resolve them. Some problem-solving activity may be initiated, but the bulk of this activity, along with the implementation of change procedures, takes place in stage three.

The goals and guidelines for this stage are as follows:

1. Explore and analyze each problem area.
2. Specify client problems behaviorally and state them in a form that makes them possible to resolve. Problems are stated in terms of client behavior that can be learned or changed in the context of the person's present life circumstances.
3. Analyze each problem in terms of variables that influence or maintain it. For example, if the client has a behavior or interpersonal problem, identify the significant people in the client's life and analyze the interactions or contingencies (stimulus-response-consequence relationships) that maintain the inappropriate response.
4. Determine the severity of client problems and make arrangements for referral if they are beyond the counselor's competence.
5. Arrange client problems in terms of priorities; decide which problem will be worked on first.
6. Extend the facilitative conditions that best promote problem exploration, client understanding, and problem-solving activity.
7. Recognize and deal effectively with transference, countertransference, and resistance.

8. Formulate procedures that will resolve client problems effectively or promote the desired behavior change.[46]

Successful counseling and therapeutic outcomes are not only a function of method and counselor's characteristics. Client problems and characteristics may also play an important role. Both clinical experience and research seem to suggest that counseling prognosis tends to be more positive under the following conditions:

1. Client problems are recent rather than long-standing, and the client has some expectation of improvement.
2. The symptoms the client exhibits and the degree of distress or anxiety present are handicapping or incapacitating.
3. The client voluntarily seeks help and is willing to explore problems and invest time and effort to change.
4. The client has normal intelligence or higher, has adapted reasonably well in the past, and his present family or circumstances of living do not negate or jeopardize counseling or change efforts.
5. The client's problem has no hereditary, constitutional, or endocrine basis.
6. The client's problems or symptoms do not produce major secondary gains. That is, the client's nonadaptive behavior should not provide excessive personal gratification or be intentionally encouraged or reinforced by significant others.
7. The client has experienced some satisfying interpersonal relationships in the past with parents or parent figures and is able to form an appropriate relationship to the counselor.[47]

Planning for Problem Solving

Once the counselor has determined that all relevant information regarding the client's concern is available and understood and once the client has accepted the need for doing something about his or her problem, the time is ripe for developing a plan to solve or remediate the concern of the client.

At this point, effective goal setting becomes the vital part of the counseling activity. Indicated here are seven specific criteria for judging effective goal setting in counseling.

1. Mutual agreement on goals is vital.
2. Goal specificity promotes goal achievement.
3. On-target goals are relevant to the self-defeating behavior of the goal setter.
4. Effectively set goals are achievable and success-oriented.
5. Effectively set goals are quantifiable and measurable.
6. Effectively set goals are behavioral and observable.

---

[46] Garth J. Blackham, op. cit., pp. 201 and 203.
[47] Ibid., pp. 196–197.

7. Goals have been effectively structured when a client understands them and can restate them clearly.[48]

Dyer and Vriend go on to suggest that the counselor can ask the following evaluative questions:

Am I helping this client to set goals that are: (a) High in mutuality? (b) Specific in nature? (c) Relevant to the client's self-defeating behavior? (d) Achievable and success-oriented? (e) Quantifiable and measurable? (f) Behavioral and observable? (g) Understandable and repeatable?[49]

In the further development of this plan, the counselor recognizes that the client will frequently not arrive at basic insights, implications, or probabilities as fast as the counselor will. However, most counselors will agree that it is better to guide the client toward realizing these understandings himself, rather than just telling the client outright. To facilitate the client's understanding, the counselor may use techniques of repetition, mild confrontation, interpretation, information, and, obviously, encouragement.

The outcome of this process is aimed at identifying as many of the possible solutions, projecting the consequences of each solution, and the final setting of priorities of these by the client.

Solution Application and Termination

In this final stage, the responsibilities are clear-cut. The client has the responsibility for applying the determined solution, and the counselor, for determining the point of termination. In the first instance, the counselor has a responsibility to encourage the client's acting on his or her determined problem solution. During the time that the client is actively engaged in applying the problem solution, the counselor will often maintain contact as a source of follow-up, support, and encouragement. The client may also need the counselor's assistance in the event things do not go according to plan. Once it has been determined, however, that the counselor and the client have dealt with the client's concern to the extent possible and practical, the process should be terminated. As noted before, this responsibility is primarily the counselor's, although the client has the right to terminate at any time. The counselor usually gives some indication that "the next interview should just about wrap it up," and may conclude with a summary of the main points of the counseling process. Usually, the counselor will leave the door open for the client's possible return in the event unexpected additional assistance is needed. Because counseling is a learning process, the counselor hopes that the client

---

[48] Wayne W. Dyer and John Vriend, "A Goal-Setting Checklist for Counselors," *Personnel and Guidance Journal,* **55:**470–471 (Apr. 1977).
[49] Ibid., p. 471.

has not only learned to deal with this particular problem, but has also learned problem-solving skills that will decrease the probability of the client's need for further counseling in the future.

SPECIAL COUNSELING SITUATIONS

Counselors in both school and nonschool settings deal with a variety of individual problems and concerns. Because increasing attention is being given to certain problem areas, it seems appropriate to note several of these "special" counseling situations. These include alcohol and drugs, sex, marriage, retirement and aging, women, and minorities.

Alcohol and Drug Abuse

Increases in the use of alcohol and drugs and the ill effects of the abuse of these substances are well publicized. Let us examine the counselor's role in the variety of community and rehabilitation agencies and school settings that either seek to prevent or engage in the treatment of these abuses.

In discussing the counselor's role, Belkin suggests the entire scope of activities and program may be divided as follows:

1. Preventive
   a. Understanding the problem.
   b. Creating a drug education program.
   c. Making available to students adequate information.
2. Therapeutic
   a. Working with drug users.
   b. Maintaining ongoing patterns of facilitative communication.
3. Administrative and legal
   a. Cooperating with systemwide efforts.
   b. Working with the community.
   c. Maintaining communication and feedback with law enforcement authorities.[50]

The school counselor should be actively involved in all three phases of this work. In the preventive phase, as the key mental health professional working in the school, he should have a thorough and well-grounded understanding of the drug problem. He should also be engaged in a continual interaction with teachers, sharing his understanding, learning from them, and helping to implement within the school a viable drug education program.[51]

---

[50] Gary Belkin, *Practical Counseling in the Schools* (Dubuque, Iowa: William C. Brown Company, Publishers, 1975), p. 349.
[51] Ibid., p. 349.

In working in community treatment centers, Page and associates indicates that

> it is important for professional counselors to consider several things when a treatment center is established in an agency or a community setting. A concrete working philosophy developed by the staff, and a staff committed to this philosophy, are mandatory. Staff training sessions need to be conducted before residents enter the program. A constructive and cooperative liaison with the sponsoring agency should be developed. Means to facilitate staff communication need to be initiated. A plan to foster positive public relations can prevent many problems. It is important to formulate an effective way to evaluate the success of the program.[52]

In many programs, both individual and group counseling are used. In some settings, counseling teams have been found to be effective for group counseling. It is also obviously important that counselors who work with drug and alcohol abuse have more than a superficial knowledge of the causes, symptoms, and potential outcomes of the problem. Further, in many individual situations, medical treatment may be needed, and referral or "teaming" with a psychiatrist may be necessary.

Sex and Marriage

Human sexuality interests and activities increase as youths progress along the educational continuum. Counselors will be confronted with initial concerns resulting from dating and other heterosexual relationships; however, by late adolescence, petting, arousal, and premarital coitus have created concerns for many. Certain common youth problems are an outgrowth of these sexual activities. They include concerns over birth control methods, pregnancy and abortion, value conflicts, frustrations and anxieties, the fear of venereal disease, and the sexual functioning of the male or female. Homosexuality is also a concern of some. Its more open recognition is resulting in more youth being willing to discuss their concerns or activities of a homosexual nature. The elementary school counselor must recognize that adult-child sexual relationship possibilities require his consideration of appropriate approaches for educational and preventive purposes, the verification of actual incidence, and how such incidents should be handled.

Masturbation, an activity in which most youth engage, is also a source of concern to many youth. The school counselor should not be primarily concerned with the extent of the practice, but rather, with its effects.[53]

---

[52] Richard C. Page, Mae Smith, and Patricia Beamish, "Establishing a Drug Rehabilitation Center," *Personnel and Guidance Journal,* **56**:183 (Nov. 1977).

[53] Marianne H. Mitchell, *The Counselor and Sexuality* (Boston: Houghton Mifflin Company, 1973), p. 37.

As the individual reaches young adulthood and progresses into maturity, his or her sexual concerns may become intertwined with marital considerations and later marital adjustment problems. Birth control and childbearing are also sexual concerns of the young married. Similarly, unmarried, but sexually active individuals are concerned with the prevention of pregnancy, abortion, and venereal disease. The older adult faces sexual problems in terms of the adequacy and frequency of his or her sexual activities.

Mitchell identifies twelve principles of counseling for sexual adjustment and development, as follows:

1. Counseling for human sexuality requires a recognition that such problems do exist.
2. Sexual development is a natural phase of human development.
3. Human sexuality is an important aspect of interpersonal relationships.
4. Counseling for human sexuality requires appropriate attention to a planned program of communication, coordination, and information.
5. Counseling for human sexuality requires adequate preparation.
6. Counseling for human sexuality requires a tolerant personal attitude toward human sexuality.
7. In counseling for human sexuality, the counselor must reaffirm the principle of confidentiality.
8. In counseling for human sexuality, the counselor must demonstrate a trust and belief in his counselee and his worth as a person.
9. The counselor should expect a wide variety of sexual concerns and activities among his clients.
10. It is important that the counselor develop those skills which he must employ to encourage his counselees to discuss freely their feelings, attitudes, and activities of a sexual nature.
11. In counseling for human sexuality, the counselor must recognize the limits of his responsibility.
12. The counselor is concerned with assisting youth to use sex positively.[54]

Although sex and marriage is the heading for this section, this is not to suggest that all marital problems are sexually related, or that all sexual concerns occur within the marriage relationship. Marital counseling is becoming a specialized area with its own professional organizations, The American Association of Sex Educators, Counselors and Therapists, and the American Association for Marriage Counseling.

Women

In recent generations, considerable attention has been focused upon the effects of sex role stereotyping with its detrimental effects, particularly on women.

[54] Ibid., pp. 38–43.

Although various federal and state legislation has sought to stimulate legal equality of the sexes, there is abundant evidence that women are still encountering problems in achieving their sex-role identity and career destinies without the impediments of sexual bias. In the area of career decision making alone, Feller noted that

> from early infancy onward, such sex-role stereotyping has profound effects on the manner in which the individual perceives herself/himself in relation to the environment. Self-concepts, values, attitudes, interests, needs, and goals all develop in response to the influence of sex-role differentiation (or equality).[55]

Maccoby and Jacklin (1974) pointed out that some of the most common sex-role stereotypes accepted within American society are as follows:

1. Females are more susceptible to persuasion than males.
2. Females have lower self-esteem.
3. Females excel in rote-learning and simple repetitive tasks, while males perform better in tasks that require higher-learning cognitive processing and the inhibition of previously learned responses.
4. Males are more analytic.
5. Females are more affected by heredity; males, by the environment.
6. Females lack achievement motivation.
7. Females are more fearful, timid, and anxious.
8. Males are more active; females are passive.
9. Males are more competitive.
10. Males are dominant; females are dependent.
11. Females are more compliant.
12. Females demonstrate more nurturing behavior.
13. Females are more emotional.
14. Males are more aggressive.
15. Females have greater verbal ability; males have greater mathematical ability.[56]

According to the extensive research review reported by Maccoby and Jacklin, only two* of these stereotypes have been supported by empirical evidence; however, all have popular support in American society. Thus, the counselor's role in counseling women is often further complicated by not only the woman's perception of what is appropriate for her, but also society's suggestion that her opportunities are limited by her sex. Counselors must be particularly alert not to reinforce these biases through sexist behavior or

---

[55] Jill L. Feller, "Impact of Sex-Role Stereotypes and Biases on the Vocational Development and Counseling of Women," unpublished manuscript (Bloomington, Ind.: Indiana University, 1978).

[56] E. E. Maccoby and C. N. Jacklin, *The Psychology of Sex Differences* (Stanford, Calif.: Stanford University Press, 1974).

* Numbers 14 and 15 are supported by research.

verbalization. With increasingly greater numbers of women seeking counseling, especially in periods of career planning and decision making, there is a need to be alert that sexist counseling does not limit their career opportunities.

Rawlings and Carter suggest the following guidelines for nonsexist counseling:

1. The therapist is aware of her/his own values.
2. There are no prescribed sex-role behaviors.
3. Sex-role reversals in life-style are not labeled pathological.
4. Marriage is not regarded as any better an outcome of therapy for a female than for a male.
5. Females are expected to be as autonomous and assertive as males; males are expected to be as expressive and tender as females.
6. Theories of behavior based on anatomical differences are rejected.
7. The therapist does not use the power of her/his position to subtly reinforce or punish clients for exhibiting "appropriate" or "inappropriate" feminine or masculine behaviors.
8. Diagnoses are not based on a client's failure to achieve culturally prescribed sex-role behaviors.
9. Sex-biased testing instruments are not used.[57]

As Ohlsen states

The counselor has the responsibility to help girls understand their own values, abilities, aptitudes, interests, to point out employment trends; to encourage examination of the woman's role, counselors must exhibit respect for female clients' rights to do what they believe is best for them.[58]

Minorities

In the past two decades, special attention has also been focused on the societal and legal rights of minority members of our society. Stimulated by the Civil Rights movement of the 1960s and the social activism of various groups during that period, society became increasingly aware of the plight and disadvantages imposed upon minorities. In attempting to correct these inequities, especially within the educational system, counselors were often expected to assume significant roles. However, in many instances, counselors failed to perceive the differences in perceptions, values, and cultural heritages that characterized minority group members in the society. As a result, counselors often failed to relate effectively to and meet the needs of the minority client.

As Ridley notes

[57] E. I. Rawlings and D. K. Carter, (eds.) *Psychotherapy for Women: Treatment toward Equality* (Springfield, Ill.: Charles C. Thomas, Publisher, 1977), pp. 51–53.
[58] Merle M. Ohlsen, *Guidance Services in the Modern School,* 2nd ed. (New York: Harcourt Brace Jovanovich, Inc., 1974), p. 320.

Evidence of differential treatment offered to minority-group clients is indicated by several major factors: (a) the types of treatment provided, (b) the duration of the treatment experience, and (c) the attitudes of the therapist and client toward the movement and outcome of the therapeutic endeavor. Historically, these inequities have been attributed to racism in the profession, and even though old treatment paradigms utilized in the past have given way to new therapeutic modalities, a comprehensive review of the literature suggests that the consequences in terms of racism remain essentially unchanged—the preferential treatment of majority-group clients over minority-group clients.[59]

Recognizing the problem, the question must be raised, "what can counselors do to interact effectively in the counseling relationship with minority counselees" (assuming the counselor is not a minority member). Belkin suggests that the counselor's understanding of nine special situations that he found commonly expressed by minority group members in a New York City school system will enable them to understand better and interact more effectively with the minority group client. These nine needs are as follows:

1. The Minority Group Client (MGC) needs to feel that he is perceived as an individual, rather than only as a member of a group.
2. The MGC wants to be able to retain his own identity as well as to function within the context of the larger society.
3. The MGC may tend to perceive the white counselor as being white above all other perceptions. This implies that whatever general stereotypical feelings about whites he has will be projected onto the counselor.
4. The MGC needs a sense of social mobility; he wants to be able to feel that he has an opportunity to rise above his present station in life. Often this hope has been tempered by the realization of the severe restraints that poverty imposes upon social advancement.
5. The MGC wants the emotional freedom to be able to express his own prejudices toward white people. He wants to be able to feel that the white counselor will not be overly threatened by this expression.
6. The MGC wants the school, through its curriculum, its teachers, and its rules to relate to his world rather than to the world of whitey.
7. The MGC sees things happening around him over which he feels no control. He wants to be better able to control his world, and thus his own destiny, but he is lacking many of the educational and psychological tools necessary for doing so.
8. The MGC often has less opportunity than his white counterpart

---

[59] Charles R. Ridley, "Cross-Cultural Counseling: A Multivariate Analysis," *Viewpoints in Teaching and Learning,* journal of the School of Education, Indiana University, **54**:43 (Jan. 1978).

to discuss home and family life problems. His loyalty to his family may deter him from discussing these with an outsider.

9. The MGC may see the school as the primary social institution (which he considers oppressive and nonresponsive), and be inclined to act out his rage and anger within the school environment.[60]

Obviously, understanding alone will not accomplish the task. The counselor must learn to communicate both verbally and nonverbally in a manner and style that is recognizable and comfortable for the client. The counselor must convey his/her own acceptance and respect for the minority client and the counselor must genuinely feel this respect if he/she is to successfully convey it.

Older Adults

While much has been written about the greening of America, we are being increasingly made aware of the graying of America. As our population grows older and lives longer and more actively, we identify another special population for counseling services.

As Blake and Peterson noted, "when facts about the life conditions of older people are added to the facts of numbers of people involved, the apparent needs for counseling and service opportunities for counselors seem obvious."[61]

From data available, they then drew eleven conclusions regarding the counseling of the aged, as follows:

1. Since the older old people (those over 75 years of age) are the fastest increasing part of the 65+ population, the demands for physical health services will be very great. These are the most expensive services, and the bulk of available funds for older people is most likely to go in that direction, rather than for retirement adjustment or other such programs oriented more toward the younger old. Since the physical needs are more obvious, counseling-type needs may require more action from counseling organizations if they are to be recognized and counselors' potential contributions better known.

2. When facts about the geographical distribution of older people are considered, we can see that all communities will have some older residents. (Even if there is an apartment building or block that has no older residents, there are almost certain to be many sons and daughters of older people. Some of these sons and daughters have concerns for their parents and often are involved in

---

[60] Gary F. Belkin, op. cit., p. 369.

[61] *Counseling the Aged: A Training Syllabus for Educators.* Special Training project on Counseling the Aged, American Personnel and Guidance Association, 1607 New Hampshire Avenue, N.W., Washington, D.C. 20009. Mary L. Ganikos (ed. and directors), 1979. "Module I: Demographic Aspects of Aging: Implications for Counseling" by Richard Blake and David Peterson.

very serious problems related to them.) Demographic data or living patterns also suggest that some areas have proportionately more older people than other areas and have different demographic trends. This suggests a need for identification of local data for planning in relation to local situations; over-reliance on national data or trends may be quite inappropriate.

3. Since the life expectancy of men is less than that of women, the potential clientele, generally speaking, will be women. The concerns of older women need special emphasis in the training of counselors and the design of service delivery. The greater number of older women may make it relatively easy to obtain funding for women-oriented programs. On the other hand, there is a considerable number of older men, and counseling as well as other service groups should guard against the neglect of these persons who might otherwise become a forgotten minority within a minority.

4. Services for "lonely" persons, or those living alone, are especially likely to have female clientele. There are more older women than men, and more of the older men are married than older women. This is because men tend to marry younger women, and more older men remarry than do older women. Proportionately, there are more older single women than men.

5. Most counseling for older people will be through public rather than private fee services. This is even more true of the older population than it is for the rest of the adult population and results from the substantially worsened financial condition of older people in general.

6. Existing counseling services such as the employment service or vocational rehabilitation can expect their client populations to be increasingly older. This suggests the possible need for additional aging-specific training of counselors in these programs. Such training may be needed for increased self-awareness of beliefs and values, possible special counseling techniques, referral sources, and possibly other factors particular to working with older people.

7. Counseling programs aimed at serving the general population of older persons can expect most potential clients to be physically able to travel to the service. But no program for older people can be truly inclusive unless it also has a capacity for having home delivery of service and a capacity for providing transportation assistance for those who require it. Five per cent of the noninstitutionalized older population is homebound and another fourteen per cent needs some human or mechanical aid in getting about.

8. The age to which older persons, on the average, can expect to live is greater than that for persons just born or that of the population in general. Data on life expectancy at birth are not appropriate for use with older persons. Counselors can better assist middle-aged or older clients in life planning by using the most relevant demographic data available. Counselors can help allay the mis-

taken beliefs about life expectancy that some older clients or their families may have.

9. Demographic data differ substantially between sexes and among racial groups. This implies that at least in some instances sex- and race-specific data are more helpful for clear understanding than general data. General demographic data are not always accurate in reflecting the condition of specific subgroups within the population, and counselors sometimes need group-specific data.

10. In all respects except age itself, older people are as different from each other as from any other group. In fact, the differences between people may be accentuated with age and the indicators of central tendency less meaningful. In wealth and health, for example, the differences among the old are the most extreme of any age group. Only among the old are found both newlyweds and couples who have been married for 60 years. Counselors are accustomed to viewing people as individuals, but there is no group for which this is more essential than for the extremely diverse older population.

11. Mental health problems of older adults are of such magnitude that the best hope for substantial improvement is to change the general psychosocial milieu in which we age. This suggests that counselors should be social activists working against factors such as ageism that mitigate against mental health. It also suggests a training role for professional counselors fostering an improved quality of relationships between older persons and those with whom they are in contact; children, friends, neighbors, and providers of all kinds of services. The level of self-help within the community of older persons can be raised by using appropriately prepared counselors as trainers for large numbers of peer counselors.[62]

Counselors will have the opportunities to meet, primarily through community services, the needs of another distinct and worthy segment of our population. Counselors working with older clients must again exhibit acceptance, openness, and respect of clients and their values. Even the oldest client must be permitted to look ahead and plan for a different future if this is the client's desire.

SUMMARY

Counseling is the heart of the counselor's activity. Although there is general agreement in broadly defining counseling, a variety of theoretical concepts have emerged over the years. Traditional approaches such as psychoanalytic and client-centered theories are still popular, but in recent generations, be-

---

[62] Ibid., pp. 23–24.

havioral, rational-emotive therapy, and reality theories have attracted their followings. However, as noted in concluding our discussion of theory, counselors may still opt for the eclectic approach, one that gives the option of selecting from any and all the existing theories.

The counseling process initially focuses upon relationship establishment, then seeks to identify and explore the client's problem with the objective of establishing client goals. The process then proceeds to the planning and problem-solving stage and, finally, to the applying of the solution and termination of the counseling relationship. Although these stages tend to blend one into the other, they serve as a guide to a logical sequence of events for the counseling process.

In recent generations, increasing attention has been given to the counselor's responsibility and need for special preparation in dealing with special populations and special problems.

As Kennedy suggests

for most who can learn to listen to others and can employ psychological counseling techniques successfully, the task of being a professional counselor is not an achievement but a never-ending process.[63]

[63] Eugene Kennedy, *On Becoming a Counsellor: A Basic Guide for Non-Professional Counsellors* (Dublin: Gill and Macmillan Ltd., 1977), p. 336.

Group Guidance **10**
and Counseling

INTRODUCTION

The rugged individualist has been extolled over the years in American history. The sagas and accomplishments of Daniel Boone, Davey Crockett, "Wild Bill" Hickcock, Wyatt Earp, Buffalo Bill, Susan B. Anthony, Charles Lindbergh, and others have been told and retold, and, in recent years, nearly all have been further immortalized by TV series recalling their feats. We still pay certain homage today to the "lone wolf" who makes it on his/her own, or ignores the system, or shuns the spotlight and public acclaim he/she has earned. Perhaps one of the reasons we so admire the rugged individualist is that we recognize it is almost impossible to go it alone in today's group-oriented, group-dominated, and group-processed society.

Suggestions of the influence and dependence on groups may result from an examination of the individual's functioning in today's society. Such an examination leads to the following conclusions:

1. Humans are group-oriented. People are meant to complement, assist, and enjoy each other. Groups are natural for these processes to occur.
2. Humans seek to meet most of their basic and personal-social needs through groups, including the need to know and grow mentally; thus, groups are a most natural and expeditious way to learn.

3. Consequently, groups are most influential in how the individual grows, learns, and develops behavioral patterns, coping styles, values, career potentials, and adjustment techniques.

For the counselor, teacher, and others who work with groups in leadership, facilitative, and teaching capacities, it can further be assumed that

1. An understanding of the influences and dynamics of groups can help further assessments and understandings of the individuals.
2. An understanding of the organization and utilization of groups can help in the teaching and guidance of others.
3. Group counseling may be more effective for some individuals and some situations than individual counseling.

DEFINITIONS AND EXPLANATIONS

In any study of group guidance and counseling, particularly of an introductory nature, it is important at the onset to clarify and define the various labels that have come into popular usage in the areas of group guidance and counseling.

Any attempt to clarify and define various terms common to the study of group guidance and counseling requires a definition or explanation of what is meant by the term *group*. Webster's defines a group as "two or more figures forming a design or a unit in a design; an assemblage of persons or things forming a separate unit, a cluster, an aggregation; an assemblage of objects having some relationship, resemblance, or common characteristic."[1]

However, within and across the professional disciplines engaged in the study and practice of groups, there are wide variations in defining a group. To narrow the definition of group for discussion here, it should be noted that counseling groups are characterized by interaction. They are functional or goal-oriented groups. Aggregate groups without interaction of the members are not functioning groups.

Going beyond interaction, Delamater,[2] in analyzing the definitions of several authors, noted three characteristics that recur as defining properties, as follows:

1. Interaction.
2. Perception.
3. Interdependence.

[1] *Webster's New Collegiate Dictionary* (Springfield, Mass.: G. & C. Merriam Company, 1956), p. 366.
[2] John Delamater, "A Definition of Group," *Small Group Behavior,* 5:36–41 (Feb. 1974).

Following his analysis of formal definitions and a systematic study of the variables employed in small group research, Delamater suggested (tentatively) that

A comprehensive definition of 'group' can be formulated in terms of the following properties: interaction between individuals, perceptions of other members and the development of shared perceptions, the development of affective ties, and the development of interdependence or roles.[3]

Interaction, as employed here, refers to face-to-face contact between persons in which each individual's behavior is affected by the behavior of others. Thus, imagined associations, considered by some as "reference group" phenomena, are not included.

Perception refers not only to the fact that we perceive those with whom we interact in an immediate sense, but also to the perceptions which each member develops concerning group norms, perceptions which are typically shared . . . It also refers to perceptions of the personalities of each of the other members, which may or may not be shared.

By *affective ties* are meant the positive and negative feelings which each member develops vis-a-vis other members as he interacts with them. These emotional reactions are partly influenced by how the others perform their roles, whether their behavior meets group norms. But an often stronger determinant is how the individual perceives the personalities of others, what he views them to be like as individuals. To the extent that affective reactions are due to such personal factors, they are less likely to be shared, to be common to other group members.

Interdependence can be viewed as basically interdependence with respect to the completion of some task(s) or goal achievement. This interdependence is the basis of the group, since members are attempting to achieve something which would be harder or impossible to achieve as individuals.[4]

Counselors and guidance workers may view various group activities as occurring at three levels. These may be identified as the guidance level, the counseling level, and the therapy level. In brief, the levels may be defined as follows.

Group Guidance. Group guidance may be viewed as group activities that focus on providing information and/or experiences through a planned and organized group activity. Examples of group guidance activities are orientation groups, career exploration groups, and college visitation days. Gazda[5] notes

---

[3] Ibid., p. 36.
[4] Ibid., pp. 39–40.
[5] George M. Gazda, *Group Counseling: A Developmental Approach* (Boston: Allyn & Bacon, Inc., 1971).

that group guidance is organized to prevent the development of problems. The content could include educational, vocational, personal, or social information, with a goal of providing students accurate information that will help them make more appropriate plans and life decisions.

Group Counseling. Group counseling may be viewed as routine adjustment and/or developmental experiences provided in a group setting. Group counseling focuses on assisting counselees to cope with their day-to-day adjustment and developmental concerns. Examples might focus on behavior modification, developing personal relationship skills, concerns of human sexuality, values or attitudes, or career decision making.

Gazda[6] suggests that group counseling can be growth engendering insofar as it provides participation incentives and motivation to make changes that are in the clients' best interests. On the other hand, it is remedial for those individuals who have entered into a spiral of self-defeating behavior, but who are, nevertheless, capable of reversing the spiral with counseling intervention.

Group Therapy. Therapy groups provide intense experiences for individuals with serious adjustment, emotional, and/or developmental needs. Therapy groups are usually distinguished from counseling groups by both the length of time and the depth of the experience for those involved. In chart form (Figure 10–1), these levels may be viewed as follows:

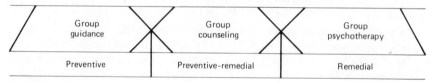

Figure 10–1.
Relationship among group guidance, group counseling, and group therapy.
George M. Gazda, Group Counseling: A Developmental Approach *(Boston: Allyn & Bacon, Inc., 1971), p. 9.*

Ohlsen[7] notes that whereas counselors devote most of their time to helping clients learn to recognize and cope early with self-defeating behaviors and to master developmental tasks, psychotherapists devote most of their time to remediation for emotionally disturbed persons.

Gazda's continuum, describing relationships among the group processes, is a clarifying one and is presented in Figure 10–2.

[6] Ibid., p. 8.
[7] Merle M. Ohlsen, *Group Counseling,* 2nd ed. (New York: Holt, Rinehart and Winston, 1977), p. 5.

Preventive and Growth Engendering	Preventive-Growth Engendering-Remedial	Remedial
Group guidance	Group counseling T-groups Sensitivity groups Organization-development groups Encounter groups Systematic human relations training groups	Psychotherapy groups

Figure 10–2.
Relationships among the group processes. *George M. Gazda,* Group Counseling: A Developmental Approach, *2nd ed. (Boston: Allyn & Bacon, Inc., 1978), p. 13.*

T-Groups. T-groups are derivatives of training groups. They represent the application of laboratory training methods to group work.

> Golembiewski and Blumberg (1970) indicate that the T-group may be considered a laboratory in the following ways: (1) It attempts to create a miniature society; (2) It is geared toward working with processes that emphasize inquiry, exploration, and experimentation with behavior; (3) It is oriented toward assisting its members to learn; (4) It stresses developing a psychologically safe atmosphere to facilitate learning; and (5) Group members determine what is to be learned, even though a trainer is usually available for guidance.[8]

T-groups are relatively unstructured groups in which the participants become responsible for what they learn and how they learn it. This learning experience also usually includes learning about how people function in groups and about one's own behavior in groups. A basic assumption appropriate to T-groups is that one learns more effectively when he/she establishes authentic relationships with others.

Sensitivity Groups. In actual practice, the label sensitivity group appears to be applied so frequently and broadly as to be almost meaningless. In a more technical sense, however, a sensitivity group is a form of T-group that

---

[8] James C. Hansen, Richard W. Warner, and Elsie M. Smith, *Group Counseling: Theory and Process* (Chicago: Rand McNally, 1976), p. 79.

focuses on personal and interpersonal issues, upon the personal growth of the individual. There is an emphasis in sensitivity groups on self-insight, which means that the central focus is not the group and its progress, but, rather, the individual.

Encounter Groups. Encounter groups are also members of the T-group family, although they are more therapy-oriented. These intensive, small group experiences, according to Eddy and Lubin (1971), emphasize

> personal growth through expanding awareness, exploration of intra-psychic as well as interpersonal issues, and release of dysfunctional inhibitions. There is relatively little focus on the group as a learning instrument; the trainer takes a more active and directive role; and physical interaction is utilized. Other modes of expression and sensory exploration such as dance, art, massage, and nudity have been tried on occasion as part of the encounter experience.[9]

Rogers defines an encounter group as one that stresses personal growth through the development and improvement of interpersonal relationships via an experiential group process. Such groups seek to release the potential of the participant. Rogers notes that

> In an intensive group, with much freedom and little structure, the individual will gradually feel safe enough to drop some of his defenses and facades; he will relate more directly on a feeling basis (come into a basic encounter) with other members of the group; he will come to understand himself and his relationship to others more accurately; he will change in his personal attitudes and behavior; and he will subsequently relate more effectively to others in his everyday life situation.[10]

Extended encounter groups are often referred to as marathon groups. The marathon encounter group uses an extended block of time in which massed experience and accompanying fatigue are used to break through the participants' defenses.

Mini-groups. Although technically two or more people can constitute a group, the use of the term *mini-group* has become increasingly popular in recent years to denote the smaller than usual counseling group. A mini-group usually consists of one counselor and a maximum of four clients. Because of the smaller number of participants, the potential exists for certain advantages resulting from the more frequent and direct interaction of its members. Mercurio and Weiner (1975) noted that

[9] W. B. Eddy and B. Lubin, "Laboratory Training and Encounter Groups," *Personnel and Guidance Journal,* **49**:627–628 (1971).

[10] Carl R. Rogers, "The Process of the Basic Encounter Group," in *Challenges of Humanistic Psychology,* ed. by James F. T. Bugenthal (New York: McGraw-Hill Book Company, 1967).

because of the increased dynamics that seem to occur in a group of this limited size, members of the mini-group are less able to withdraw or hide, and interaction seems to be more complete and responses fuller. . . . mini-groups may either function as the singular treatment focus or be used in conjunction with individual counseling.[11]

Group Process and Group Dynamics. Two terms commonly used in describing group activities are *process* and *dynamics.* Although often used interchangeably, they do have different meanings when used to describe group counseling activities. The beginning counseling student should note that *group process* is the continuous, ongoing movement of the group toward achievement of its goals. It represents the flow of the group from its starting point to its termination. It is a means of identifying or describing the stages through which the group passes.

Group dynamics, on the other hand, refers to the social forces and interplay operative within the group at any given time. It is descriptive of the interaction of a group, which may include a focus on the impact of leadership, group roles, and membership participation in groups. It is a means of analyzing the interaction between and among the individuals within a group. Group dynamics is also used on occasion to refer to certain group techniques such as role playing, decision making, rap sessions, and observation.

GROUP GUIDANCE ACTIVITIES

In a broad, general context, group guidance is probably as old as formal schooling. Good teachers through the years have used groups for what today would be called pupil guidance purposes. Group guidance activities have been designed to provide to students in groups information or experiences beyond those associated with the day-to-day learning activities in the classroom. These activities have been additionally planned to provide information, skill-building, opportunities for personal growth and development, orientation, and assistance in decision making.

Values

Over the years certain values have been attributed to group activities of a guidance nature, as follows:

Facilitating Personal Development. Certain experiences which lead to personal development can take place only in the group setting. These include

---

[11] John M. Mercurio and Michael Weiner, "The Mini-Group in Counseling," *Personnel and Guidance Journal,* **54**:227 (Dec. 1975).

the opportunity to learn and play certain roles, such as group leader, group follower or member, the development of patterns of cooperation with others, and the learning of group communication skills.

Stimulation of Learning and Understanding. As Lifton[12] has noted, it is fairly well accepted that clients will incorporate information when the information is presented in a way that enables them to use the facts with a minimum of transfer until they are secure enough to allow themselves to perceive the situation broadly, and when they have perceived that the information is necessary to achieve a goal important to them. He then points out that in group settings people are seeking two kinds of information: that about themselves and their relationships with others; and information about the external world. Group guidance activities are important in providing learning and understanding relevant to career and career decision making, educational planning and decision making, and personal-social adjustments and decision making.

Advantages of Group Interaction. By actively participating in groups organized for guidance purposes, individuals have the opportunity to broaden their scope of understanding regarding the subject or purpose for which the group is organized. Additionally, participants should grow in their understanding of group interactions and dynamics as well as understanding their own behavior in groups.

Economy. Although groups should not be organized for guidance purposes solely on the basis of economy, it must be recognized that where effectiveness in terms of outcome is not lessened, the saving of both counselors' and clients' time through the use of groups can be of considerable value.

Organization

All of us have experienced being participants in some type of group activity, social or otherwise, that has been organized on the spur of the moment. Occasionally these unanticipated activities have been enjoyable or worthwhile, but probably more often, they have resulted in confusion, uncertainty, perhaps even frustration, and have been considered a waste of time. The popularity of group guidance activities has, in some instances, led to their scheduling without appropriate preparation, but that is not and should not be the pattern. If group guidance activities are to achieve their potential, a great deal of consideration and organization must go into their planning, conducting, and evaluation. The following guidelines may be helpful.

   Determining that there is a need for group guidance. All too often group guidance activities are simply scheduled. On occasion, the scheduled activities

---

[12] Walter M. Lifton, *Groups: Facilitating Individual Growth and Societal Change* (New York: John Wiley & Sons, 1972), p. 251.

may be responding to an actual need. If we are to ensure their success, it must be determined beforehand that there is a need which a group shares in common and for which a guidance response is appropriate. Often, student questionnaires, problem surveys, or checklists administered to student groups will provide a factual basis for determining possible group guidance activities. Teachers and parents can also contribute to the determination of need through the use of such instruments.

Determining that group guidance is the most appropriate or effective response. Once needs have been determined, the counseling staff must identify those for which a group guidance activity would be appropriate, in contrast to group counseling or individual counseling, or perhaps even classroom instruction. It must be emphasized that group guidance focuses on providing information or experiences and is not designed for adjustment or therapy.

Determining the characteristics of the group. Once the nature of the group guidance activity has been established, certain group characteristics must be determined. Obviously, size of the group must be one consideration. Here, the counselor must determine what size group will be most appropriate for the activities planned and outcomes anticipated. Size will also have an influence on the operational format of the group. Format planning includes determining the types of activities of the group, length of time allotted for each group session, the number of sessions, and the setting. A final consideration affecting the group characteristics will be the role of the counselor. Will he/she be an active participant or an inactive observer who remains in the background once the group's activities are underway? Will he/she direct the group? Will he/she be a group arbitrator? What information will the leader provide the group? Will he/she assign roles or will his/her role evolve as the group progresses?

Establishing the group. Once the characteristics of the group have been determined, members may be selected. They may volunteer or they may be invited to participate. Invitation includes the right of the individuals to refuse participation. In establishing the membership of the group, it must be verified that the planned activity will respond to the need of the individual and that the structure or operational format will be comfortable for the group member. In large groups such as those organized for orientation purposes, college career days, or other special information purposes, this is not necessarily essential, but for smaller, intimate groups, it is an important consideration.

Monitoring the ongoing activities. Once the group has been established and the members oriented to its purpose and processes, the counselor or facilitator assumes the responsibility for keeping the group "on track." It is relatively easy, especially considering the participants' lack of experience and understanding of the group process, to deviate from the purposes of the group, to become bogged down in irrelevant discussions and activities, or to encounter personal factors that inhibit or impede the functioning of the group. The counselor must, therefore, be constantly on the alert to detect such symptoms and to utilize his/her skills to minimize these effects. The ongoing activities of the group are meaningful only as long as they promote the progress of the group and its members towards the end goals of the group.

Evaluating outcomes. The importance of evaluation in assessing the outcomes of groups cannot be overemphasized, and evaluation and the accountability process will be discussed in greater detail in Chapter 13. The goals or projected outcomes of the group must be stated in clear, objective, and measurable terms. The criteria for measuring goal achievement must be identified and stated, and data then collected which, when analyzed, will present an objective evaluation of outcomes. Such evaluations can assist counselors and others involved to determine which group guidance activities are most effective and which techniques within groups are most and least effective. Implications for group memberships, roles, and leadership may also result.

Examples of Group Guidance Activities

Group guidance activities, in school settings at least, may be separated into two broad categories according to size. Those involving large groups of students should be of potential value to the vast majority of the students in a designated group, such as a school, a class, all girls, or all college-bound. These would include such common large group guidance activities as college days, career days, and orientation programs. These activities emphasize providing information that may be useful in decision making and orientations that can be helpful in the individual's planning. They are usually designed to provide the participant direct contact with representatives of specific colleges and universities or careers, or, for school orientation programs, specific middle-junior or senior high schools. If these mass programs are to serve a group guidance purpose, the following are important considerations.

1. The activity should be based on some form of needs assessment that determines not only the extent of interest in the proposed activity, but also the nature or specifics of the group's interest.
2. The activity must be carefully planned with great attention given to detail. A "rule of thumb" for planning large group guidance activities is that the larger the group, the longer and more detailed the planning.
3. The activity must be evaluated. Any large group activity will consume a staggering number of total student hours (for example, 1,000 students participating in a five-hour career day program represents 5,000 student participation hours), not to mention the time demand on staff, faculty, and outside participants. It must be determined if such a commitment of time is worthwhile.

Small group guidance activities, in broad general terms, may be viewed as those designed for specific outcomes, which cater to the needs of smaller subgroups within the total population served by the school or agency counseling and guidance program. These activities may focus on providing information for decision making and planning purposes, activities for personal development purposes, and assistance for educational adjustments. Small group guidance activities can emphasize smaller components or follow-up activities for the larger college, career, or orientation programs. Other specific examples are guidance groups organized to develop job-seeking and interviewing skills, how to study techniques, assertiveness training, career education, values clarification activities, discussion groups, and experiences in nonverbal communications.

GROUP COUNSELING

More than eighty years ago, the psychologist William James wrote,

> We are not only gregarious animals liking to be in sight of our fellows, but we have an innate propensity to get ourselves noticed and noticed favorably, by our kind. No more fiendish punishment could be devised, were such a thing physically possible, than that one should be turned loose in society and remain absolutely unnoticed by all the members thereof.[13]

James, as well as others, have noted over the years, the importance of human relationships in meeting basic needs and influencing the personality development and adjustment of the individual. For most individuals, the vast majority of these relationships are established and maintained in a group setting, and for many, daily routine adjustment problems and developmental needs also have their origins in groups.

Counseling, as a facilitative science, has a helping relationship base, which must also be a human relationship. Because the most frequent and common human relationship experiences occur in groups, groups also hold the potential to provide positive developmental and adjustment experiences for many individuals. The following paragraphs examine some of the potential values of group counseling and how these values are realized. The careful selection of participants and formations of groups and the skillful utilization by the counselor of appropriate group techniques are also discussed.

Values of Group Counseling

Group counseling is not a team sport. The goal is not to have a winning group. The goal of group counseling is the achievement of the goals, the

---

[13] William James, *The Principles of Psychology,* Vol. 1 (New York: Henry Holt, 1890), p. 293.

meeting of the needs, and the providing of an experience of value to the individual members who comprise the group. The following are some of the opportunities that may be provided by group counseling.

1. Exploration, with the reinforcement of a support group, of one's developmental and adjustment needs, concerns, and problems, may be provided. Groups can provide a realistic social setting where the client can interact with peers who not only are likely to have some understanding of the problem or concern that the client brings to the group, but will, in many instances, also be sharing the same or a similar concern. The counseling group can provide the sense of security needed by the group members to spontaneously and freely interact and to take risks, thus promoting the likelihood that the needs of each of the members will be touched upon and that the resources of peers will be utilized. The old saying that "misery loves company" may in fact provide a rationale for group counseling. One is more comfortable in sharing a problem with others who have similar experiences and may also be more motivated to change under these conditions.

2. Group counseling may provide the client an opportunity to gain insights into his or her own feelings and behavior. Yalom (1975), in discussing the group as a social microcosm, states that

a freely interactive group, with few structural restrictions, will, in time, develop into a social microcosm of the participant members.[14]

He then goes on to point out that, given enough time in the group setting, clients will begin to be themselves, to interact with others, and to create the same interpersonal universe they have experienced, including the display of maladaptive, interpersonal behavior to the group. Yalom notes that corrective emotional experiences in groups may have several components, including the following:

Reality testing which allows the client to examine the incident with the aid of consensual validation from other members.

A recognition of the inappropriateness of certain interpersonal feelings and behavior or of the inappropriateness of certain avoided interpersonal behaviors.

The ultimate facilitation of the individual's ability to interact with others more deeply and honestly.[15]

As the client gains new insights into his/her own behaviors and feelings as a result of his/her interactions with members of the counseling group,

---

[14] Irvin D. Yalom, *The Theory and Practice of Group Psychotherapy* (New York: Basic Books, Inc., 1975), p. 29.
[15] Ibid, p. 28.

influences on self-concept formation may also occur. Because of the significant influence of self-concept in one's personal-social adjustment, perception of school and career decision making, the opportunity to bring about positive change in self-concept through new insights provided by the group counseling experience is a value not to be overlooked.

3. Group counseling provides clients an opportunity to develop positive, natural relationships with others. The personal interactions that take place within the group counseling structure provide an excellent and continuous opportunity for the group member to experiment with and learn to manage his/her interpersonal relations. This includes the developing of sensitivities to others, their needs, and feelings. It also provides opportunities to learn of the impact one's behavior has on others. Thus, through the group process and its interactions and sharing of experiences, the client may learn to modify earlier behavior patterns and seek new, more appropriate behaviors in situations that require interpersonal skills.

4. Group counseling provides opportunities for the client to learn responsibility to self and others. Becoming a member of a counseling group implies the assumption of responsibilities. Even when there are initial tendencies to avoid the assumption of responsibility for one's behavior, for contributions to the group's interactions, or one's "assignment" within the group, these avoidance techniques will usually fade away as group relationships develop and group goals are established.

Selection of Group Members

All of us have had experience in organizing groups. When we select group members for a social occasion we pick out good ole Charlie because he is a laugh a minute; Diane, because she gets along with everybody; Harry in case we need some serious conversation and Olga, because she is a good listener. On the other hand, if the purpose of the group is a more serious one, such as planning a neighborhood park, we might choose Rosalie because of her "know-how" with flowers and shrubbery; Jim because he is a landscaping expert; Jane because of her architectural skills and Jerry because of her proven fund-raising abilities. In each instance, individuals are usually selected because they can contribute something to the group and its interaction. Although group counseling focuses upon the need of the individual, the importance of group membership to the achievement and adjustments of individuals in the group cannot be overestimated. Group member selection is one key to a successful counseling group. The following are possible criteria for the selection of group members: (1) common interest; (2) volunteer or self-referred; (3) willingness to participate in the group process; and (4) ability to participate in the group process.

A popular criterion for group selection may be a common interest of the potential members in a similar problem, concern, or issue. Dinkmeyer and Caldwell[16] (1970) note that

> The homogeneous group, centered around a common problem or feeling, may possess a sense of unit in their mutual concerns, but also, they may lack the opportunity to react to normal youngsters who do not suffer from their handicap. As will be shown later, those in a predicament need to be able to gain insight from others who are competent in the area where they are lacking. In the beginning process of selection, however, some thought should be given to those most in need of resolving a particular kind of problem, then the rest of the group can be built around that focus. However, there should be enough of a heterogeneous makeup to provide varied feedback to the members. Homogeneous groups can only be so on a particular variable. To select groups upon the basis of a common problem is a crisis-oriented approach rather than a developmental one, and not usually workable. It is the *interaction,* not the problem, that is important. Further, a group above all needs to be *balanced* so that no one factor or type of individual is too dominant to allow free interaction.[17]

A number of authors—(Wagner[18] (1976); Bates and Johnson[19] (1972); and Ohlsen[20] (1977)—suggest that the best group member is a self-referred group member. Group counseling should be an option chosen by the group participants. Choice guarantees the protection of the client's rights and further enhances his/her motivation for counseling should he/she decide to be in a counseling group.

On the other hand, Ohlsen (1977) suggests

> Many clients who at first appear to be poor bets (and have not volunteered) can become good treatment risks when the treatment is described for them; their questions about it are answered; they are encouraged to explore alternative sources for help; they are permitted to decide for themselves whether to participate; and they accept the responsibility for convincing themselves and their counselor that they can discuss their problems openly, define precise behavioral goals, and encourage fellow clients to learn desired new behaviors. Perhaps even the reluctant client, including the resisting type, can be helped when he or she is included in a group in which most clients are strong enough to prevent [him/her] from interfering with the development of (or from destroying)

---

[16] Don C. Dinkmeyer and Charles E. Caldwell, *Developmental Counseling and Guidance: A Comprehensive School Approach* (New York: McGraw-Hill Book Company, 1970).

[17] Ibid., pp. 148–149.

[18] Carol A. Wagner, "Referral Patterns of Children and Teachers for Group Counseling," *Personnel and Guidance Journal,* 55:90 (Oct. 1976).

[19] M. M. Bates and C. D. Johnson, *Group Leadership* (Denver: Love, 1972).

[20] Merle M. Ohlsen, op. cit., 1977.

therapeutic group norms. If, however, [one] is to profit from counseling, [he/she] must not be forced to participate.[21]

Dinkmeyer and Caldwell suggest in the selection of potential group participants that the following questions might be proposed as a basis for determining selections:

1. Do you have a concern or difficulty you want to discuss in the group?
2. Are you willing to talk about it?
3. Are you willing to *listen* and to *help* others?[22]

In some instances, potential group members may lack the ability or desire to communicate with others or to relate to and assist others. From a temperament viewpoint, not everyone will be a suitable group member. In short, an individual must possess certain abilities or aptitudes if he/she is to profit from the group experience and contribute to it as well.

Hardy and Cull,[23] noting that there are any number of procedures used by counselors to form a group, suggested that inviting clients to participate once the counselor has become familiar with the individual and his/her concerns, is a procedure that is by far the most realistic and professionally sound. They then go on to suggest that the invitation to join the group will

be extended, or not, only after a personal interview with the prospective group member, with the emphasis in the interview being on what the student may gain through this kind of experience. The counselor explains the student's role, that of giving help to members in the group as well as receiving help from the group members and the counselor, should he decide to participate. Confidentiality with respect to the content of the group sessions should be stressed, and the prospective group member will need to commit himself to maintaining strict confidentiality for the duration of the group sessions, as well as after the group has terminated.[24]

It is further noted that by using this interview invitation approach,

the counselor has (1) made an assessment of the probable needs of the students who comprise the group; (2) assessed the probable contributions the student will make to the group; (3) set the parameters with respect to the personality composition of the group; (4) ascertained the probable extent to which each student would benefit from the group

[21] Ibid., pp. 20–21.
[22] Don C. Dinkmeyer and Charles E. Caldwell, op. cit., p. 149.
[23] Richard E. Hardy and John G. Cull, *Group Counseling and Therapy Techniques in Special Settings* (Springfield, Ill.: Charles C. Thomas, Publisher, 1974).
[24] Ibid., p. 9.

experience; and (5) established in his mind the probable goals for the group.[25]

Setting Goals

Few of us would set out on a journey by packing our suitcase, getting into our car, and driving out of town by following the first car in front of us. Many are reluctant to go shopping without a list, or to order a meal in a restaurant without reading the menu, or take a vacation without plans. Although the thought of being such a free spirit is intriguing at times, most persons would prefer to have definite goals in mind and to plan for their achievement.

Most of us have few undirected, nongoal-oriented activities in our typical everyday plan of action. Those who work with groups frequently, whether in teaching or other capacities, can well predict the outcome if one were to appear before such a group with the question, "how would you like to spend your time today?" At worst, chaos would result, and at best, considerable time would be lost before determining how the group could best utilize the time available.

Goal setting is no less important in group counseling than in any other activity that seeks to be meaningful. The early identification of goals in group counseling will facilitate the group's movement toward a meaningful process and outcomes. These goals are most readily identified and implemented when they are specified in behavioral terms. Ryan notes

Goal-setting in group counseling is the process of setting goals to implement the group counseling process. Goal-setting is accomplished by defining group goals and subgoals, which are implemented in individual behavioral objectives, and by ordering the objectives according to priority needs and contribution to the group goals.[26]

Ohlsen also notes

Most counselors have general goals for their treatment, but they are not sufficient. Precise, behavioral goals are needed to focus a client's attention and energy on learning desired new behaviors. Genuine participation in the development of the goals [is] necessary for a client to develop acceptance of the goals and the commitment required to sustain his efforts when he might be tempted to stop. Criteria for appraising growth with reference to each goal also enhance further growth.[27]

[25] Ibid., p. 10.

[26] T. Antoinette Ryan, "Goal Setting in Group Counseling," in *Counseling Effectively in Groups,* ed. by John Vriend and Wayne W. Dyer (Englewood Cliffs, N.J.: Educational Technology Publications, 1973).

[27] Merle M. Ohlsen, op. cit., p. 101.

The establishment of these goals of the group should be an expression and extension of individual members' own personal desires.

In group discussion and counseling alike, participants in most instances would select the problem or problem area to be discussed and proceed then to examine them by reference to problem-solving techniques— that is, how the goal may or may not be obtained. In group discussion, a common goal is absolutely essential, for without it, acceptance of values and procedures may never reach a consensus. In problem solving through group discussion, one may find a slight tendency for the needs of individuals to become somewhat subservient to the goals of the group, whereas in group counseling, individual needs merit prime importance.[28]

Group Leadership

In his recent book, *Leadership*, James M. Burns refers to the activity of leadership as "that most observed and least understood phenomenon,"[29] a viewpoint that few would dispute. The nature and quest for leadership at all levels and across all settings has been a continuing challenge to humankind. However, Burns' suggestion that "true leaders emerge from, and always return to, the wants and needs of their followers,"[30] appears to have some relevance for leaders of counseling groups.

An earlier (1972) and similar theme was suggested for group counseling leaders by Bates and Johnson who noted that

a counseling group draws definition from its leader. It will be only as good as the leader, as good as his skills and as good as the being of the leader himself. A person may be competent in the technical aspects of group leadership, but if he himself is not a "good" human being, his groups can become destructive . . . it is important that he (the leader) is a nourishing human being. Such a nourishing leader thrives on joyous human interaction and is a self-nourisher who will generate his own enrichment rather than feeding off group members. In other words, the group counselor's primary concern is the welfare of all the clients which comprise the group and it is to this and this end only that he directs his skills and energies.[31]

Within this framework of the group counselor as a leader-member nourisher, what are the leadership responsibilities or functions? Helen Driver,[32]

---

[28] Bernard C. Kinnick, "Group Discussion and Group Counseling Applied to Student Problem Solving," *The School Counselor* **15**:350–356, (1968).

[29] James M. Burns, *Leadership* (New York: Harper & Row, Publishers, 1978).

[30] Doris Kearns Goodwin, "True Leadership," interviewing James M. Burns, *Psychology Today* (Oct. 1978), p. 48.

[31] Marilyn M. Bates and Clarence D. Johnson, op. cit., p. 43.

[32] Helen I. Driver, *Counseling and Learning Through Small Group Discussions* (Madison, Wis.: Monona Publications, 1958), pp. 100–102.

an early leader in the group counseling movement, suggested (1958) leadership techniques for the group counselor as

1. Support; giving commendation; showing appreciation.
2. Reflection: mirroring feelings.
3. Clarification: making meanings clear, showing implications of an idea.
4. Questioning: bringing out deeper feelings, inviting further response.
5. Information: providing data for examination, serving as a resource person, teaching.
6. Interpretation: explaining the significance of data, using analogy.
7. Summary: asking for client summary first, pointing out progress, alternatives.[33]

In recommending co-leadership for counseling groups, Bates and Johnson specified four responsibilities of leadership as traffic directing (helping members become aware of behaviors that facilitate or inhibit open communications), modeling, acting as interaction catalyst, and as communications facilitator.[34]

Rutan and Alonso[35] suggested guidelines to help group leaders become more aware of ongoing process issues occurring in group meetings as

1. Building an hypotheses. It may be helpful for the counselor to speculate about possible outcomes and reactions in advance. Such speculation may help the leader to become better prepared to function in his/her role as a group leader.
2. Take your time. The old saying that "haste makes waste" is one that group leaders should keep in mind. It is important to guard against responding too quickly and attempting to move a group too rapidly toward possibly erroneously preconceived goals.
3. Note the beginning. Initial behavior and words of individuals comprising the group can be of particular significance as well as possibly forecasting the theme that the group will follow.
4. Think analogies. It is important for the group leader to also be aware of the covert meanings of group discussions and actions. Observable behavior may often be analogous to deeper, more hidden content.
5. Keep the presenting problem and client background in mind at all times. It is important that the group leader not lose track of the context within which each individual functions and views his problem. Thus, an understanding of each group member's background assists the counselor in keeping appropriate perspectives.

---

[33] Ibid., pp. 100–102.
[34] Marilyn M. Bates and Clarence D. Johnson, op. cit., p. 61.
[35] J. Scott Rutan and Anne Alonso, "Some Guidelines for Group Therapists," *Group,* Vol. 2, No. 1 (Spring 1978).

6. Formulate a summary. It is often suggested that the counselor begin identifying materials for a final summary statement from the very beginning of each meeting. The nature of the summary statement can be significant, too, in making effective transition between meetings, as well as in the final termination of the group.

The group counselor, in the leadership role, must also take on the responsibility when the occasion dictates, of intervening in the group interaction. Such interventions, whether initiated by the counselor or by group members, help to keep the group participants goal-oriented. Vriend and Dyer suggest that the group counselor can productively take responsibility for initiating or causing an intervention when:

1. A group member speaks for everyone.
2. An individual speaks for another individual within the group.
3. A group member focuses on persons, conditions, or events outside the group.
4. Someone seeks the approval of the counselor or a group member before and after speaking.
5. Someone says, "I don't want to hurt his feelings, so I won't say it."
6. A group member suggests that his problems are caused by someone else.
7. An individual suggests that "I've always been that way."
8. An individual suggests, "I'll wait, and it will change."
9. Discrepant behavior appears.
10. A member bores the group by rambling.[36]

Ohlsen[37] noted the group counselor's facilitative behaviors as:

1. Developing readiness.
2. Relationship building.
3. Relationship maintenance.
4. Problem identification.
5. Definition of counseling goals.
6. Definition of criteria to appraise client's growth.
7. Resistance.
8. Countertransference.
9. Feedback.
10. Termination.

An examination of these suggestions for group leadership indicates the group counselor's responsibility for the structure, conduct, and general overseeing of the group sessions. It should also be mentioned that the conscientious

---

[36] John Vriend and Wayne W. Dyer, *Counseling Effectively in Groups* (Englewood Cliffs, N.J.: Educational Technology Publications, 1973), pp. 171–182.
[37] Merle M. Ohlsen, op. cit., p. 39.

group counselor does not involve himself/herself in group activities beyond his/her depth of professional preparation. Group counseling emphasizes factors of associations, rather than deep emotional disturbances. The counselor's depth of psychological understanding and his/her skill in group dynamics are individual considerations in the level of group counseling that he or she undertakes. For those counseling groups that focus on specific and narrow concerns, such as family relations, human sexuality, or substance abuses, it is obviously desirable that the counselor-leader have some special understanding of the topic.

GROUP PROCESS

The elements of the group counseling process share much in common with those identified with individual counseling. These may be separated into their logical sequence of occurrence as follows:

The Establishment of the Group

The initial group time is used to acquaint the new group membership with the format and processes for the group, to orient them to such practical considerations as frequency of meetings, duration of group, and length of group meeting time. Additionally, the beginning session is used to initiate relationships and open communications between the participants. The counselor also may use beginning sessions to answer questions that clarify the purpose and processes of the group. The establishment of the group is a time to prepare members for meaningful group participation and to set a positive and promising group climate.

   The group counselor must remember that in the initial group sessions the general climate of the group may be a mixture of uncertainty, anxiety, and awkwardness. It is not uncommon for group members to be unfamiliar with one another and uncertain regarding the process and expectancies of the group. As Gruen noted

> they are, therefore, fearful about whether they may eventually be excluded because they may not "fit in." Furthermore, they are concerned about who else is to be included or excluded. In this way, they can figure out the group boundaries and then learn whom to attend to and whom to ignore. Members are apt to watch others as well as themselves for clues about proper behavior that invites acceptance by the group and especially by the leader. Since the group and the whole therapy climate is uniquely new to them, they want to be safe and secure. They do not want to create waves or stand out as potentially unacceptable. Hence, they discuss "safe topics"—if they talk at all—such as the weather or events outside the group. Many of these topics

were acceptable in the (social) groups they have known in the past. If they talk about their problems at all, they will initially do so in a stereotyped way.[38]

It is important for the counselor to take positive steps to reduce the initial anxieties of group members. If the counselor is to be successful in this endeavor,

the counselor must be genuine or congruent in the relationship. He must not display a facade nor play a role, but must behave exactly as he feels. He not only means what he says, but also matches what he feels to what he is expressing—behavior, feelings, and attitudes that exist within him. This is the only way the relationship can have reality for the group member.

Another facilitative condition in the relationship is the counselor's experiencing an empathic understanding of the member's world and being able to communicate this to the member. The counselor senses the feelings and personal meanings that the individual is experiencing. When he is able to perceive these as they seem to the group member and can successfully communicate some of this understanding to him, this condition is fulfilled.

A good counseling relationship requires that the counselor experience a warm, positive, accepting attitude toward the client. Although this is listed last, it probably is the first element that the counselor must be able to communicate to the group member. It means that he accepts the individual as a person and cares for him in a nonpossessive way as a person with potentiality. The counselor respects him and gives him positive regard. The more the positive regard is unconditional, the more effective and safer the relationship will be.[39]

Identification (Group Role and Goal)

Once an appropriate climate has been established that at least facilitates a level of discussion, the group may then move toward a second, distinct stage—that of identification. In this stage, a group identity should develop, the identification of individual roles should emerge, and group and/or individual goals be established. These may all emerge simultaneously or develop at different paces. They are, however, significant at this stage of the group counseling process. It is also important to make operational the group counseling goals.

Group goals are operationalized when broad statements of intent for the group are analyzed into cognitive, affective, and behavioral dimen-

---

[38] Walter Gruen, "The Stages in the Development of a Therapy Group: Tell-Tale Symptoms and Their Origin in the Dynamic Group Forces," *Group,* 1:13 (Spring 1977).
[39] James C. Hansen, Richard W. Warner, and Elsie M. Smith, op. cit., pp. 373–374.

sions, which in turn can be described as behavioral objectives for individual members. Behavioral objectives include specific, pertinent, obtainable, measurable, and observable behavior that will result from planned intervention. She [referring to T. A. Ryan] suggests that operationalizing group goals has four advantages that increase the likelihood of counseling success: (1) operationalized goals produce more homogeneity in the group's shared interest; (2) operationalized goals contribute to more realistic expectations; (3) operationalized goals lead to more highly motivated members because they know what they are working for; (4) operationalized goals make the group members more interdependent as they are able to see how goals for other members fit into their objectives as well.[40]

Hansen, Warner, and Smith point out that

there are certain problems in the process of goal setting for a group. The importance of a particular group goal for any individual in the group may be influenced by his individual needs. Obviously, goal setting is a part of the counseling process which must be accomplished jointly by the counselor and the group members. If a counselor establishes the goals for the group, he may not be aware of the individual subgoals. Other members in the group may not be aware of each other's individual goals underneath the umbrella of the general goal for the group. The extent to which group goals implement personal goals will vary from time to time throughout the group. Despite these difficulties involved in the goal setting process, however, it is one of the most important aspects to success in group counseling.[41]

It is also important for counselors to be aware of the probable, or, at least possible, conflict and confrontation during this stage of the group's development. Some writers (Yalom[42] 1975) labelled this second phase as the "conflict, dominance-rebellion stage." It is a time when

the group shifts from preoccupation with acceptance, approval, commitment to the group, definitions of accepted behavior, and the search for orientation, structure, and meaning to a preoccupation with dominance, control, and power. The conflict characteristic of this phase is between members or between members and the leader. Each member attempts to establish for himself his preferred amount of initiative and power, and gradually a control hierarchy, a social pecking order, is established.[43]

---

[40] Ibid., p. 375.
[41] Ibid., p. 375.
[42] Irvin D. Yalom, op. cit.
[43] Ibid., p. 306.

Hansen and colleagues describe this second stage as one in which the group members manifest their dissatisfaction with the operation of the group. It is a period of time following the initial acquaintance period when

members are frequently frustrated in their attempts to evolve new patterns of behavior through which to work toward group goals. The discrepancy between individuals' real selves and their stereotyped images of the group may lead to conflict. Group members may challenge others' reactions to them and insist on their own rights. Some conflict may erupt when certain issues are discovered to be more complex than the group members originally perceived. The process of conflict and confrontation also occurs as group members begin to perceive and experience difficulty implementing changes in behavior.[44]

It should also be noted

in many counseling groups Stage Two may not emerge early or may be avoided completely unless there is enough commitment to the group so that the members will risk open confrontation. In fact, the conflict may not be expressed openly but through passive resistance. The members may remain silent rather than confront each other or the counselor. Open conflict and confrontation is not often seen in group counseling conducted in school settings or other short-term counseling situations in which the counselor is perceived as an authority figure.

Without working through this phase and establishing appropriate norms of behavior, only a superficial level of cohesiveness can develop. As the group members work through their differences of opinions about appropriate behavior for each other and the counselor, they are able to accept the real person rather than the stereotyped image. This can lead to a greater feeling of identity with the group. It is important to recall that even when the group moves into a cohesive stage, it may regress to periods of conflict and confrontation.

The necessity for working through the stage of conflict and confrontation cannot be emphasized too strongly. For groups to evolve from a superficial to a more truly effective level of functioning, this painful and difficult period must be experienced and dealt with successfully.[45]

When conflicts and confrontations, as previously described, do occur, a more cohesive group usually emerges, with resulting increased openness in communication, consensual group action and cooperation, and mutual support among the members.

---

[44] James C. Hansen, Richard W. Warner, and Elsie M. Smith, op. cit., p. 386.
[45] Ibid., pp. 391–392.

Productivity

In the third stage of the group's development, a clear progression towards productivity is noted. As the group has achieved some degree of stability in its pattern of behaving, the productivity process can begin. Too, because the members are now more deeply committed to the group, they may be ready to reveal more of themselves and their problems in living.

This is the period of problem clarification and exploration, usually followed by an examination of possible alternate solutions.

> The established group now directs itself toward individual as well as group goals, attempting to produce something of a general and lasting value. In a counseling group the task may be to develop insight into personal and interpersonal processes and to affect constructive personality change.[46]

The emphasis of this stage is on recognizable progress toward the group's and individual members' goals. In this process, however, each group member is exploring and seeking his/her own understanding of self, situation, and problem or concern, and each member develops his/her own plan integrating these understandings. The three subphases of this stage may be viewed as (1) assessment, (2) understanding, and (3) planning. The group structure tends to be functional.

Although group strategies may be selected by the group for any and all of these phases, it is important that they make sense to each member in terms of his/her individual needs. The counselor may note that progress is being made when progress can be seen. Of course, progress is not always constant during this time, and occasionally regression, stagnation, or even confusion may occur. Thelen notes that

> Whenever the group does not know what it is doing, it ought to stop and find out. This does *not* mean that the group ought to argue over its objectives, but rather, that it ought to describe to itself what it is doing. In unclear situations, there is actually discrimination against the participation of some members. When a person knows what the group is doing, then he also knows how to participate, and if he does not participate, it is reasonable to assume that he has nothing to contribute. But when a person does not know what the group is doing, he does not know how to participate, and he is blocked. Therefore, with every change in the nature of the group's activity, it is well to be sure the member roles are redefined.[47]

---

[46] Ibid., p. 406.
[47] Herbert A. Thelen, *Dynamics of Groups at Work* (Chicago: University of Chicago Press, 1954), p. 288.

It is also on these occasions that the counselor is alert to prevent process problems from handicapping progress and group achievement. Often, a simple reminder by the counselor of the stated goals or objectives of the group can prevent activities or discussions that tend to sidetrack individuals or the group as a whole from maintaining progress. However, because of the relationships and the group climate previously established, groups should overcome these difficulties and regain their productivity. As Hansen and colleagues have noted

> Because interpersonal bonds are strong, evaluation, criticism, discussion, and re-evaluation can be undertaken. The group directs itself to members as objects since subjective relations have been established. Members view individual behavior in the group with greater objectivity. They show a greater ease in making decisions and more flexibility in controlling group processes. Because they have learned to relate to others as social entities, role structure is not an issue. Members can adopt and play roles that will enhance the effectiveness of the group.[48]

During this phase, the problem or concern should be clarified to everyone's satisfaction and ownership should be verified. This clarification includes a thorough understanding of the nature of the problem and its causes. It is only when this has been achieved that resources for problem solutions can be realistically examined. This phase may be successfully concluded when all possible solutions have been considered and examined in terms of their consequences. These solutions should be practical or capable of being realized (obtainable), and the final choice of a solution should be made only after appropriate considerations and discussion. It should be emphasized that this is not the time for snap judgments and hurried commitments. At this point, then, the group members have examined themselves and the problem as it applies to them and have explored these considerations in considerable depth; have looked at possible solutions and their consequences; have determined the course of action that appears most appropriate; and are ready to move into the next stage, one in which they will try out or experiment with their chosen solution. In this process, they have, by making their own decisions, also established their ownership of the problem and the chosen solution.

Realization

At the point at which the members of the group recognize the inappropriateness of past behaviors and begin to try out their selected solutions or new behaviors to implement in practice their decisions, progress is being made toward realization of their individual goals. At this time, responsibility has

---

[48] James C. Hansen, Richard W. Warner, and Elsie M. Smith, op. cit., p. 407.

been established with the individual member to act upon his/her decision. The counselor encourages the sharing of individual experiences and goal achievement *both* within and outside the group. Although general success with the new behaviors may provide sufficient reinforcement for many individuals to continue, for others a support base of "significant others" outside the group should now be developed to facilitate a maintenance of the change once the counseling group is terminated. In school settings, counselors might, for example, consult with parents and teachers to implement this strategy.

Termination

Most of us have experienced occasions of regret and even sorrow when temporary groups to which we have belonged reach the breaking-up point. Regardless of the purpose for which the group is organized, we may try to prolong its eventual dissolution by promising get-togethers, planning social activities, and in general agreeing that "this has been too much fun to let it end." On many such occasions, casual strangers have become the best of friends in relatively short periods of time, and the threatened termination of the relationships is at least psychologically resisted.

For these same reasons, members may resist the termination of a counseling group. The very nature of counseling groups, with their emphasis on interpersonal relationships, open communication, trust, and support, promises the development of a group that the membership may want to continue indefinitely. It is, therefore, important from the very beginning that the group counselor emphasize the temporary nature of the group and establish, if appropriate, specific time limitations. The counselor also reminds the group, as the time approaches, of the impending termination. This does not mean that the counselor alone is responsible for determining the termination point of a group. Although the counselor may, of course, assume this responsibility, termination may also be determined by the group members or by the group members and the counselor together.

Termination, like all other phases or stages of the group counseling experience, also requires skill and planning on the part of the counselor. Termination is obviously most appropriate when the group goals and goals of the individual members have been achieved and new behaviors and/or learnings have been put into practice in everyday life outside the group. The group will also be ready to terminate when, in a positive sense, it has ceased to serve a meaningful purpose for the members. Under less favorable circumstances, groups may be terminated when their continuation promises to be nonproductive, harmful, or when group progress is slow, and long-term continuation might create overdependency on the group by its members.

Individuals may be terminated from a group at any time during the group's existence. Individuals who are disruptive, who seriously handicap the other members, who may be more effectively assisted through individual counseling, or who personally desire to terminate are not uncommon subjects for individual terminations. Group counselors should be aware that this is a common happening, especially in the beginning stages of a group, when several members may voluntarily terminate. It is important that the counselor accept this as a matter of course and refrain from exerting pressure on such individuals to remain in the group. At the same time, however, the counselor may indicate his/her willingness to see the individual(s) on an individual basis.

The point of terminiation is a time for review and summary by both counselor and clients. With some groups, time will be needed to work through the feelings of the members regarding termination. Even though strong ties may have developed and there are pressures from the group to extend the termination time, those pressures must be resisted, and the group must be firmly, though gently, moved toward the inevitable termination.

SUMMARY

Today's society is group-oriented, and each person belongs to a variety of groups. These groups serve a variety of purposes, and in them one plays a variety of roles. Because of the group orientation of humankind, group guidance and counseling have become increasingly recognized as a means of assisting individuals in meeting their adjustment and developmental needs in both school and nonschool settings. These group activities are distinguished by the nature of their concern and the type of group experience provided. Group guidance activities are primarily confined to school settings with an emphasis on providing information or experiences helpful in decision making. Group counseling tends to focus on routine adjustments and developmental needs or problems of individuals, whereas group therapy provides an intense experience that may last for a considerable length of time for individuals with serious adjustment, emotional, or developmental needs. The counselor's role and leadership is important to the success and accomplishment of both guidance and counseling groups. The group counselor must also be skillful and aware of the steps through which the group process moves. This process begins with the selection of members and the initial establishment of the group as a group; the identification of group goals; the clarification and exploration of the group and its individual members' problems and/or concerns; the exploration of solutions and consequences; decision making regarding solutions; implementation of the decision; and, finally, termination and evaluation.

The Counselor As 11
Developmental and
Educational Consultant

INTRODUCTION

A network television news program on February 13, 1979, carried the report that a group of big business executives were going to offer their consulting services to small businesses to aid their (the small businesses) survival chances. In this newscast these business people were referred to as "consultants"—a term so common in that context that the newscaster did not bother to define it. The term *consultant* is familiar to the general public as applied to the medical, legal, and business worlds. A consultant is usually an expert in a field who consults with or offers professional expertise to others both within and outside the profession. In fact, so common is the activity in the business world that we frequently hear such humorous definitions of a consultant as "anyone fifty miles from home with a briefcase;" or, "one who pulls in, pops off, and pulls out."

Consultation as a mental health and educational activity is less well recognized and understood, although mental health consultation has a long tradition in the healing arts. Consultation in its application to counseling as a mental health activity in schools has been even less widely recognized and defined. Most of the attention prior to the 1970s given to consultation as a school counseling and guidance activity seemed to suggest that it was primarily appropriate for the elementary school only. Such articles as Abbe, "Consultation to a School Guidance Program,"[1] Crocker, "Depth Consultation with Parents,"[2] Eckerson and Smith, "Elementary School Guidance: The Consultant,"[3] and Faust, "The Counselor as a Consultant to Teachers,"[4] dealt with consultation in elementary school guidance programs. Some of the popular basic guidance texts of the 1950s and 1960s such as Jones, *Principles of Guidance,*[5] Hutson, *The Guidance Function in Education,*[6] Crow and Crow, *An Introduction to Guidance,*[7] Ohlsen, *Guidance: An Introduction,*[8] and Froehlich, *Guidance Services in Schools*[9] made no mention of consultation as a school counseling activity.

In discussing consultation in *The Counselor-Consultant in the Elementary School,* Faust noted

> Although counseling has been described and researched for many years, this is not true of consultation. The latter has been practiced for as many years as counseling, if not longer, but the literature is strangely sparse in its treatment of this role.[10]

Faust goes on to note that

> Counseling and consultation differ in several ways. These primary difences can be found in (a) focus and (b) the kinds of relationships that are developed within the employing school. The consultant focuses on some unit external to the consultee. In the case of a consultant to a teacher, the external unit may be a child, instructional method, course content, etc.[11]

[1] A. E. Abbe, "Consultation to a School Guidance Program," *Elementary School Journal,* Vol. 61 (1961).

[2] E. C. Crocker, "Depth Consultation with Parents," *Young Children,* Vol. 20 (1964).

[3] Louise Eckerson and Hyrum Smith, *Elementary School Guidance: The Consultant* (reprint of three articles in *School Life*), U.S. Department of Health, Education and Welfare, Office of Education (1962).

[4] Verne Faust, "The Counselor as a Consultant to Teachers," *Elementary School Guidance and Counseling,* Vol. 1, No. 2 (Mar. 1967).

[5] Arthur J. Jones, *Principles of Guidance,* 5th ed. (New York: McGraw-Hill Book Company, 1963).

[6] Percival W. Hutson, *The Guidance Function in Education* (New York: Appleton-Century-Crofts, 1958).

[7] Lester D. Crow and Alice Crow, *An Introduction to Guidance,* 2nd ed. (New York: American Book Company, 1960).

[8] Merle M. Ohlsen, *Guidance: An Introduction* (New York: Harcourt Brace Jovanovich, Inc., 1955).

[9] Clifford P. Froehlich, *Guidance Services in Schools,* 2nd ed. (New York: McGraw-Hill Book Company, 1958).

[10] Verne Faust, *The Counselor-Consultant in the Elementary School* (Boston: Houghton Mifflin Company, 1968), p. 32.

[11] Ibid., p. 32.

A second major difference between consultation and counseling is found in the kinds of relationships established outside the consultation and counseling settings. Since in consultation the chief focus is on a unit external to the self of the consultee, the personal risk is not as great as it is in counseling, where internal units (the person of the counselee) receive a majority of attention. Personal investment, exposing one's personal self, is not as extensive in consultation. Therefore, risk is not as great, and the consultee need not invest as much trust in the counselor. The consultant is freer to move in many of the normal, day-to-day competitive environments of school personnel.[12]

Caplan, in a book on mental health consultation oriented to community-industrial models,[13] restricted his use of the term *consultation* to

the process of collaboration between two professional persons: the consultant, typically the specialist, and the consultee, who requests the consultant's help with some professional problem which he or she is having difficulty solving and which is seen as within the consultant's area of specialized competence. The professional problem may involve the management or treatment of one or more of the clients of the consultee, or the planning or implementation of a program to cater to such clients. Caplan uses the concept of *client* to denote the lay person who is the primary focus of the consultee's professional practice, such as the teacher's student, the psychologist's, psychiatrist's, or social worker's patient, the minister's parishioner, or the lawyer's client.[14]

Caplan's definition of consultation is further restricted to those professional interactions in which the consultant has no direct responsibility for the client and the responsibility for implementing any remedial plan developed through the course of the consultation remains with the consultee. This type of consultation is aimed not only at helping the consultee with the particular problem under scrutiny, but also at increasing the general level of the consultee's competence in this area. While this definition of consultation is obviously applicable to any kind of professional work, Caplan restricts his discussion to work in the mental health field, that is, the promotion of mental health, and the prevention, treament and rehabilitation of mental disorders.[15]

Although these early definitions focused upon consultation in community agencies, industrial settings, and the elementary school, in the past decade consultation as an appropriate counselor activity in any setting, including secondary schools and higher education institutions, has developed rapidly.

[12] Ibid., p. 33.
[13] G. Caplan, *The Theory and Practice of Mental Health Consultation* (New York: Basic Books, Inc., Publishers, 1970).
[14] Leonard D. Goodstein, *Consulting with Human Service Systems* (Reading, Mass.: Addison-Wesley Publishing Co., Inc., 1978), p. 23.
[15] Ibid., pp. 23–24.

This is evidenced by two consecutive special issues of the American Personnel and Guidance Association's journal, *The Personnel and Guidance Journal* (February and March 1978), dealing with the counselor's role and function as a consultant at all educational levels as well as in community mental health settings and by an increasing number of textbooks dealing with the topic at all educational levels. Let us, therefore, proceed to examine some of the roles and models for consultation.

MODELS FOR CONSULTATION

The increase in popularity and demand for consultation services has resulted in the development or identification of a variety of models or styles appropriate to the consultation process. Although differences exist among authorities in the area of consultation in terms of the organization or categorization of theories or systems for providing consultation services, similarities are far more prevalent than differences.

A traditional model that highlights the basic consultation process is a *triadic model,* as suggested by Tharp and Wetzel. In this model, consultation services are offered indirectly through an intermediary to a target client or clients. The model illustrated in Figure 11–1 is described as a consultative triad, in which all effects proceed

> to the target via the *mediator,* none directly from consultant to target.
> This analysis describes functional positions, not the people who occupy
> those positions. For example, any number of individuals occupying
> any number of social roles might serve as mediator: father, teacher,
> sister, minister, mother, employer, friend, and psychotherapist. Indeed,
> the same is true of the functions of either consultant or target.[16]

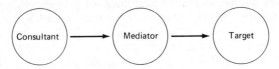

Figure 11–1.
The consultative triad. *R. G. Tharp and R. Wetzel,* Behavior Modification in the Natural Environment *(New York: Academic Press, Inc., 1969).*

Four popular consultation models, as identified by Kurpius,[17] suggest the counselor-consultant can function effectively by providing a direct service

[16] Clyde A. Parker, Ed. *Psychological Consultation: Helping Teachers Meet Special Needs* (Minneapolis: University of Minnesota, Leadership Training Institute, 1975), p. 137.
[17] De Wayne Kurpius. "Consultation Theory and Process: An Integrated Model," *Personnel and Guidance Journal,* Vol. 56, No. 6 (Feb. 1978).

to a client identified by another party, by prescribing a solution to a specific problem identified by a consultee, by assisting others in developing a plan for problem solution, and by taking direct responsibility for defining a problem and proposing a solution. These functions are organized by Kurpius into four consulting modalities as follows:

Provision Mode

The provision mode of consultation is commonly used when a potential consultee finds himself confronted with a problem for which he or she may not have the time, interest or competence to define objectively, to identify possible solutions, or to implement and evaluate the problem-solving strategy. Consequently, a consultant is requested to provide a direct service to the client, with little or no intervention by the consultee after the referral is accepted.

Prescriptive Mode

Sometimes consultees experience unusual work-related problems for which they request special help. Even though competent and motivated to solve the problem directly, the consultees may lack confidence in their own intervention strategy or may lack certain specific knowledge and skills for carrying out a given problem-solving plan.

In these situations, the consultee is often in need of a resource person (consultant) to support the diagnosis and treatment plan already developed by the consultee or to explore additional alternatives for defining and solving a specific problem.

There are other times, however, when a consultee is looking for an exact "prescription" to ameliorate a specific problem. While the prescriptive mode is quite appropriate for many situations, here are four questions that should be answered jointly by the consultant and consultee: (a) Has all the information needed to define and solve the problem been shared and is [it] accurate? (b) Has the plan prescribed by the consultant been accepted by the consultee and will it be implemented as designed? (c) Who will evaluate the "process" and "outcomes" associated with the prescriptive plan—the consultant, the consultee, or both? (d) Will adjustments in the prescription, if needed, be requested by the consultee?

Collaboration

When following the collaboration mode the consultant's goal is to facilitate the consultee's self-direction and innate capacity to solve problems. As a result, the consultant serves more as a generalist than a technical expert. His major efforts are directed toward helping people develop a plan for solving problems. Hence he acts as a catalyst and "reality tapper," helping consultees to share observations, concepts, and proven practices. He also helps consultees examine forces that are facilitative or debilitative in both the immediate and larger environments.

Mediation Mode

Mediation is uniquely different from the other three modes of consultation in which the *consultee* initiates the contact and requests help for solving a problem. In mediation, it is the *consultant* who recognizes a persisting problem, gathers, analyzes, and synthesizes existing information, defines the problem, decides on the most appropriate intervention, and then calls together the persons who have direct contact with the problem and have the greatest potential to influence a desired change.[18]

Schein organizes the consultation process into three models with assumptions as follows:

Model 1: Purchase of Expertise

The core characteristic of this model is that the client has made up his or her mind on what the problem is, what kinds of help are needed, and to whom to go for this help. The client expects expert help and expects to pay for it, but not to get involved in the process of consultation itself.

In order for this model to work successfully, the following assumptions have to be met, however.

1. That the client has made a correct diagnosis of his or her own problem.
2. That the client has correctly identified the consultant's capabilities to solve the problem.
3. That the client has correctly communicated the problem.
4. That the client has thought through and accepted the potential consequences of the help that will be received.

In summary, this model of consultation is appropriate when clients have diagnosed their needs correctly, have correctly identified consultant capabilities, have done a good job of communicating what problem they are actually trying to solve, and have thought through the consequences of the help they have sought. As can be seen, this model is "client intensive," in that it puts a tremendous load on the client to do things correctly if the problem is to be solved. If problems are complex and difficult to diagnose, it is highly likely that this model will not prove helpful.

Model 2: Doctor-Patient

The core of this model is that the client experiences some symptoms that something is wrong but does not have a clue as to how to go about figuring out what is wrong or how to fix it. The diagnostic process itself is delegated completely to the consultant along with the obligation to come up with a remedy. The client becomes dependent upon the

[18] Ibid., p. 335.

consultant until such time as the consultant makes a prescription, unless the consultant engages the client in becoming more active on his or her own behalf. Several implicit assumptions are the key to whether or not the doctor-patient model will in fact provide help to the client.

1. That the client has correctly interpreted the symptoms and the sick "area."
2. That the client can trust the diagnostic information that is provided by the consultant.
3. That the "sick" person or group will reveal the correct information necessary to arrive at a diagnosis and cure, i.e., will trust the doctor enough to "level" with him or her.
4. That the client has thought through the consequences, i.e., is willing to accept and implement whatever prescription is given.
5. That the patient/client will be able to remain healthy after the doctor/consultant leaves.

In summary, the doctor-patient model of consultation highlights the dependence of the client on the consultant both for diagnosis and prescription and thus puts a great burden on the client to correctly identify sick areas, accurately communicate symptoms, and think through the consequences of being given a prescription.

Model 3: Process Consultation

The core of this model is the assumption that for many kinds of problems that clients face, the *only* way to locate a workable solution, one that the client will accept and implement, is to involve the client in the diagnosis of the problem and the generating of that solution. The focus shifts from the content of the problem to the process by which problems are solved, and the consultant offers "process expertise" in how to help and how to solve problems, not expertise on the particular content of the client's problem. The consultant does not take the problem onto his or her own shoulders in this model. The "monkey always remains on the client's back," but the consultant offers to become jointly involved with the client in figuring out what is the problem, why it is a problem, why it is a problem right now, and what might be done about it. This consulting model is not a panacea appropriate to all problems and all situations. It also rests on some specific assumptions that have to be met if the model is to be viewed as the appropriate way to work with a client.

1. That the nature of the problem is such that the client not only needs help in making an initial diagnosis but would benefit from participation in the process of making that diagnosis.
2. That the client has constructive intent and some problem-solving ability.
3. That the client is ultimately the only one who knows what form of solution or intervention will work in his or her own situation.
4. That if the client selects and implements his or her own solution, the client's problem-solving skills for future problems will increase.

How does the consultant implement the process consultation model? The basic principle is to get into the client's world and see it initially from the client's perspective. This usually means paying attention to the "task process"—and how the problem is defined, how the agenda is set, how information is gathered, how decisions are made, all the activities that make up the "problem-solving process."[19]

Also in the February 1978 special issue of the *Personnel and Guidance Journal,* Werner discussed consultation in a community mental health agency. For this setting he described six possible models, as follows:

Client-Centered Case Consultation

The goal is to enable the consultee to deal more effectively with the client's problems and to improve the consultee's functioning with similar problems in the future.

Consultee-Centered Case Consultation

The goal is to collaboratively identify consultee problems in dealing with the client and to collaboratively develop the consultee's skills repertoire in dealing effectively with similar problems in the future.

Program-Centered Administration Consultation

The goal is to enable the consultee to deal more effectively with specific problems encountered in developing and providing a mental health program and to improve the consultee's functioning with similar problems in the future.

Consultee-Centered Administrative Consultation

The goal is to collaboratively identify consultee problems that have been generated in developing and providing a mental health program and to collaboratively develop the consultee's skill repertoire in dealing effectively with similar problems in the future.

Community-Centered Ad Hoc Consultation

The goal is to enable the ad hoc consultee to deal more effectively with community problems encountered in the development of a temporary program for increasing the competency of the community.

Consultee-Centered Ad Hoc Consultation

The goal is to collaboratively identify the ad hoc consultee problems that have been generated in the ad hoc consultee development in the provision of a temporary community program for increasing the competency of the community.[20]

[19] Edgar H. Schein, "The Role of the Consultant: Content Expert or Process Facilitator?" *Personnal and Guidance Journal,* **56:**340–342 (Feb. 1978).

[20] John L. Werner, "Community Mental Health Consultation with Agencies," *Personnel and Guidance Journal,* **56:**366 (Feb. 1978).

Regardless of one's choice of consultation models, consultants can function as readily in a developmental role as in a preventative role. Faust, among others, in support of this view, suggests *developmental consultation* as a process that focuses on how people function, learn, or change in facilitating ways. "It also takes the next step: to devise learning environments and ways of behavior which generally emerge out of decisions that are based on the universal nature of humankind."[21]

THE CONSULTATION PROCESS

To further understand how counselors function effectively in their consulting role, let us next examine briefly the nine stages of the consulting process, as identified by Kurpius.

Stage 1. Preentry. Clarifying the consultant's values, needs, assumptions and goals about people and organizations, specifying an operational definition of consultation and assessing the consultant's skills for performing as a consultant.

Stage 2. Entry. Defining and establishing the consultation relationship, roles, ground rules and contract, including statement of presenting problem.

Stage 3. Gathering Information. Gathering of additional information as an aid to clarifying the presenting problem.

Stage 4. Defining the Problem. Utilizing the assessment information in order to determine the goals for change.

Stage 5. Determination of the Problem Solution. Analyzing and synthesizing of information in search of the best solution to the problem as presently stated.

Stage 6. Stating Objectives. Stating desired outcome that can be accomplished and measured within a stated period of time and within specified conditions.

Stage 7. Implementation of the plan. Implementing of the intervention following the guidelines clarified in the preceding steps.

Stage 8. Evaluation. The monitoring of the ongoing activities (process evaluation) culminating with the measuring of the final outcomes (outcome evaluation).

Stage 9. Termination. Agreeing to discontinue direct contact with the consultant, keeping in mind the effects of the consulting process are expected to continue.[22]

[21] Parker, op. cit., p. 237.
[22] Kurpius, op. cit., p. 337.

These nine stages suggest that effective consultation draws on an organized and systematic process in which each step logically leads to the next. Consultants will also frequently find it helpful to their consultees to identify these stages as guidelines for the process they will be sharing and as a means of keeping the activity "on track."

SKILLS FOR CONSULTATION

As with all counseling and guidance activities, certain special skills are needed if the counselor is to function effectively as a consultant in either school or agency settings. Dinkmeyer and Carlson suggested that counselor training for consultation should be based on the counselors building skills so that they can perform the following competencies:

1. Understand the purposive nature of behavior and develop skills of observation and interpretation that will facilitate problem solving.
2. Apply theories of learning to specific learning difficulties of students, that is, learning disabilities.
3. Understand and apply idiographically logical consequences and other corrective procedures for concerns presented by teachers and parents.
4. Demonstrate the ability to communicate effectively to develop effective helping relationships.
5. Demonstrate the basic group leadership competencies: structuring, universalizing, feedback, formulation of tentative hypotheses, encouraging, task setting, and commitment.
6. Understand management by objectives and be able to establish hierarchies, a plan of action, and assessment procedures needed for a systematic change.
7. Demonstrate competence in a brief, diagnostic student interview to determine the purposive nature of the individual's behavior.
8. Demonstrate effectiveness in individual teacher consultation.
9. Demonstrate effectiveness in individual parent consultation.
10. Demonstrate effectiveness in administrator consultation.
11. Develop and facilitate productive consultation groups with teachers (i.e., the consultation group collaborates, consults, clarifies, confronts, develops commitments, and is confidential).
12. Develop and facilitate effective parent education with parents.
13. Develop and facilitate productive consultation groups with parents.
14. Demonstrate knowledge and use processes and materials of the psychological or affective education programs in the classroom.[23]

[23] Don Dinkmeyer and Jon Carlson, "Consulting: Training Counselors to Work with Teachers, Parents, and Administrators," *Counselor Education and Supervision Journal,* **16:**173–174 (Mar. 1977).

CONSULTATION IN SCHOOL SETTINGS

In school settings, counselors who function in a consulting role are, in effect, giving their special expertise to teachers, school administrators, and other appropriate personnel. In this role, they become a resource professional for the developmental or adjustment needs involving third parties, usually students. For the counselor to function effectively as a consultant in the educational setting, one must possess special knowledge or skills appropriate to the consulting need. Among the relevant skills the counselor can bring to consulting with teachers and other educational providers and planners are the following:

1. An understanding of human growth and development, the problems and processes of adjustment, and the needs of the individual as he goes through those processes.
2. An understanding of psychological or affective education in the classroom, and a concern for its importance.
3. An understanding and skills in promoting communications and other desirable human relationship skills.
4. Training in the assessment of individual characteristics and skills in relating these assessments to the development of the individual's potential.
5. Special knowledge of educational and career development and opportunities.
6. An ability to communicate, counsel, and consult with parents, fellow educators, and the community.
7. An understanding of group processes and skills useful in facilitating group motivation and change.[24]

In addition, to function effectively as a consultant, the counselor must have a background of understanding of the individual or group with whom he/she is consulting, the target population for the consulting, and the characteristics of the school in which the consulting is taking place. The counselor-consultant should also be knowledgeable regarding contributing, external environmental factors. Too,

> the consultation function, like the counseling function, is based on communication and human interaction. The relationship between the consultant and the consultee is basic. Acceptance, trust, and understanding are essential.[25]

---

[24] Robert L. Gibson, "The Counselor As Curriculum Consultant," *American Vocational Journal,* **48**:51–54 (Oct. 1973).

[25] Harold L. Munson, *Foundations of Developmental Guidance* (Boston: Allyn & Bacon, Inc., 1971), p. 158.

As a consultant, the school counselor has the potential to engage in a wide range of activities or roles. In discussing these roles, Faust suggested a hierarchy of first and second level of consulting roles as follows:

First Level:

1. Consultation with groups of teachers.
2. Consultation with the individual teacher.
3. Consultation with groups of children.
4. Consultation with the individual child.

Second Level:

5. Consultation in curriculum development.
6. Consultation with administrators.
7. Consultation with parents.
8. Consultation with school personnel specialists (psychologists, social workers, psychometrists, curriculum supervisors, nurses, psychiatrists).
9. Consultation with community agencies (family service, child guidance clinic, family physician, high school counselors, private psychotherapists, etc.).[26]

Some specific examples of these activities are suggested in Table 11–1.

Table 11–1.
Consulting Activities Counselors Perform

With Administrators	With Teachers	With Parents
1. Plan a schoolwide educational assessment program. 2. Identify children with special needs. 3. Facilitate community and parent-school relations.	1. Identify and analyze deficiencies in the academic and psychological development of children. 2. Develop skill in understanding child behavior, in classroom management, and in conducting parent-teacher conferences. 3. Develop remedial or prescriptive programs for individuals and groups. 4. Help develop more effective teaching strategies. 5. Help teachers develop effective career education programs.	1. Facilitate positive school-parent relationships. 2. Enhance parent understanding of children's development, abilities, and difficulties. 3. Help parent to modify child learning and behavior problems. 4. Conduct parent education groups.

Source: **Garth J. Blackham,** *Counseling: Theory, Process and Practice* **(Belmont, Calif.: Wadsworth Press, 1977), p. 361.**

[26] Verne Faust, op. cit., p. 34.

Consulting with Teachers

As mentioned previously, the teacher is the key individual and most populous professional in school settings at any level. In consultation in schools, then, the counselor must assume that he/she will most frequently consult with teachers individually or in groups. This probability is further highlighted by the fact that teachers have the most frequent contacts with pupils and that the developmental and adjustment needs of their pupils are often expressed in classroom groups. Counselors may effectively assist teachers as consultants to individualize classroom instruction.

School counselors are also experienced in collecting, organizing, and synthesizing data on individual students and in interpreting this information to identify individual differences. Through these activities, they sharpen their understanding of the individual in terms of his/her aptitudes, interests, values, personal growth, health, and ability to adjust.[27]

Further, the effects of Public Law 94–142, requiring all children categorized as handicapped to be placed in regular educational programs to the fullest extent possible, will result in a wider diversity in the characteristics and abilities of classroom groups. As Aubrey notes,

> The consequence will be a significant change in the social system of most classrooms and a need for many physical and social alterations. As currently trained, it is doubtful if any educators are sufficiently prepared for these changes. Yet, who will teachers turn to when in trouble?
>
> In addition to mainstreaming and the enormous problems this will pose for classroom socialization and adaptation, Public Law 94–142 will provide parents with rights and prerogatives never granted before. The law will allow any parent the right to demand a complete diagnostic workup on their child, and in addition, the right to appeal the school's appraisal. Also, schools will be held accountable for prescriptive contracts made between school and parents extending over the duration of the school year and clearly outlining the complete learning sequence for a given child.[28]

As Aubrey suggests, the counselor has a significant consultant role to play in assisting teachers specifically and the educational system generally in implementing this act.

As consultant in identifying and utilizing appropriate instructional resources: The classroom teacher is obviously the most knowledgeable about resources appropriate to his subject matter, but the counselor

---

[27] Robert L. Gibson, op. cit., p. 51.
[28] Roger F. Aubrey, "Consultation, School Interventions, and the Elementary Counselor," *Personnel and Guidance Journal,* **56**:355 (Feb. 1978).

can nonetheless be profitably consulted on those occasions when specialized occupational and educational information is needed to make a class more meaningful. He can also be consulted to identify out of school resources and experiences relevant to student's learning needs. And his insights can be helpful in the development of materials and methodologies that will enable counselors and teachers to work together in special educational activities with vocational students.[29]

As consultant in the development of a classroom environment conducive to learning: The counselor's expertise in human behavior and development theory combined with the teacher's knowledge of instructional methods and materials is the basis for an excellent team effort in the crucial task of planning and establishing a productive learning environment.[30]

A basic principle of effective consultation is that the recipients must believe that they need it. Teachers and others will neither seek out nor be receptive to the counselor as a consultant if they see no value or rationale for such assistance. Many teachers, like counselors, do not understand or accept the counselor as a consultant. In each situation it is therefore important for the counselor to communicate and demonstrate his or her role as an effective consultant. Too,

in educational systems, more often than not, the clients do not know what they are looking for and, indeed, should not be expected to know. All they know is that something is wrong. An important part of the consultation process is to help such clients (teacher, administrator, department) define the problem, then decide what kind of help is needed or warranted and what consultation approach would be most useful and acceptable.[31]

The Counselor As a Consultant to the School Administrator

The school counselor can also make significant consultation contributions to the educational leadership of the school and the school system. The counselor has the capacity to gather data descriptive of the characteristics of the student population and their needs, which, in turn, can provide useful information for educational planning and management.

The counselor's understanding of the process and characteristics of human growth and development enables him or her to relate and to provide special counsel regarding the special needs of individuals and groups of pupils on occasion.

---

[29] Gibson, op. cit., p. 51.
[30] Ibid., p. 54.
[31] Garth J. Blackham, op. cit., p. 390.

Consulting with Parents

The counselor can effectively consult with parents on various occasions. Many of these occasions would focus on promoting parent understanding of pupil characteristics and their relationships to pupil behavior and school achievement. Consultation can also assist parents in coping with or modifying pupil behaviors on occasion. The counselor may also serve as a consultant to interpret school programs to parents.

The Counselor As a Curriculum Consultant

Federal legislation specifying the counselor's role and importance in implementing programs of career education and education of the handicapped have already suggested that it is time for the school counselor to function actively as a consultant for curriculum development and management. In an instructional sense, the school counselor is not, of course, a curriculum specialist. However, when the curriculum is viewed as the sum of educational experiences the school proposes to provide, it follows that the counselor, because of his or her professional commitment to the total development of each student, should be actively involved, regardless of legislative mandates in curriculum planning.

Several specific examples of this function might view the counselor as follows:

As a consultant in matters related to the career interests and concerns of students: Comprehensive assessments of student career interests provide a basis for expanded and relevant curriculum offerings. Nor should the important area of avocational interests be overlooked. A combination of educational and avocational opportunities often provides an experience which maintains student interest and motivation. The counselor should assume major responsibility to identify and interpret these interests and concerns to all educators involved. Assessment of student interest must be translated into action, however, and it is at that point that many opportunities for curriculum development are left to founder in the sea of academic indifference.[32]

As consultant in matters relating to the career development needs of all students: Related to the vocational interests of students, but worth singling out, are the developmental needs of all students as they prepare for entry and progression in the world of work. Students at all grade levels need opportunities to test, compare, develop, and experience skills, concepts, roles and values as they relate to work. They need to learn to appreciate the value of all honest work and to understand the educational prerequisites for entering various careers. The more actively youth can explore and test out their abilities, interests, and work styles (espe-

[32] Robert L. Gibson, op. cit., p. 51.

cially in true, work-type situations), the more insight they will gain for later decision making.[33]

School counselors and curriculum planners have a joint responsibility to see that these important aspects of the student's total development are not left to chance. In this regard, it should be noted that curricular consultation frequently points out the need for curricular change. Because the school counselor's responsibilities involve him/her with both teachers and administrators, he/she is in a position to facilitate their cooperation and interaction in promoting curricular change. Such change usually involves the prerequisites of (1) identification of the need for change, (2) a willingness on the part of those involved to consider change, and (3) the development and acceptance of a plan for change.

SUMMARY

Booz/Allen and Hamilton noted in an advertisement in the *Chicago Tribune* March 18, 1979, that firms use their consulting services for such activities as "provide planning and strategy guidance; provide an economic and technical review of their R & D programs; perform economic and technical evaluations as they relate to proposed government regulations; provide technical marketing assistance in the chemical processing, agribusiness, engineering materials and medical fields; recommend process modifications as part of an economic evaluation/justification study."

In this same issue of the *Tribune,* other firms described their consulting services and still other firms advertised positions for consultants. These classified advertisements are only surface indications that consultation is a recognized and ongoing activity in the business world. Consultation has also been a recognized mental health activity for a number of years although not nearly as well publicized as its business counterpart. There are also consulting firms that specialize in educational matters.

However, consultation as an activity of school counselors, especially at the secondary school level, is a relatively recent development. This has led to an examination of various models appropriate to the consultation process and of their adaptation to counselor use. Kurpius organized these into four modalities of provision, prescriptive, collaborative, and remediation. Schein organized the process into three models: purchase of expertise, doctor-patient, and process consultation. Werner described six possible agency models as client-centered case consultation; consultee-centered case consultation; program-centered administration consultation; consultee-centered administrative consultation; community-centered ad hoc consultation; and consultee-centered ad hoc consultation.

[33] Ibid., p. 51.

Regardless of model choice, the counselor-consultant must recognize that he/she is involved in a process that provides structure and direction for his/her consultation efforts. It is naive to think that knowledge and/or experience in itself qualifies one to consult. An understanding of the process of consultation and the acquisition of the skills for consultation are prerequisites to success as a consultant. These are usually initiated through special courses in consultation.

The qualified school counselor will have many opportunities to consult with faculty, administrative staff, parents, and student groups. It is important to keep in mind, however, that consultation must be wanted—must be requested—if it is to take place. Even when requested, the counselor-consultant should proceed with tact and understanding. After all, no one likes to be "told off"—even by experts!

Program Management, 12
Development, and
Leadership

INTRODUCTION

Through the centuries, a great deal has been written about the importance of management, leadership, and development to success in the worlds of business and government. The business world has long studied and contrasted the successes and failures of corporations large and small and the techniques or styles of management that have accounted for their achievements or lack of them. Leadership has played a role in the rise and fall of nations, management is important in government effectiveness and fiscal soundness, and development is crucial in many countries, even in these modern times.

In this century, the "art" of school administration in education, hospital administration in medicine, and personnel administration in business and the armed services have become areas for specialization. Despite a general recognition of the importance of management, leadership, and development to any organized enterprise, little attention has been given, in terms of formal preparation at least, to the "art" of developing and managing counseling programs in various settings. The complex multi-goals required of most schools, school systems, public agencies, and institutions emphasize the need for development and management of counselor programs and accountability to the public. Accountability means the providing of objective evidence to prove that counselors are successfully responding to identified needs. Such evidence requires recording and writing, and, perhaps, computations and tables. However, all too often those preparing to enter the profession and practice of counseling naively assume that the practice of therapy precludes any involvement with such mundane matters as program management, including administration. This is not to suggest that paper work replace people work or that it should be an equal priority. However, prospective counselors should be aware of the prospects and significance of program management, leadership, and development. Let us first define these terms.

Management: Those activities that facilitate and complement the daily, ongoing functions of the counseling staff. These include such administrative activities as recording and reporting, budgetary planning and control, facility management, and provisions for support personnel and resources.

Development: Includes needs assessment for program planning, research, evaluation, and the establishment of program accountability. Also presumes planning for program improvement.

Leadership: The providing of positive direction and motivation for personnel and program improvement. Primarily, *but not exclusively,* the responsibility of the professional designated as the chief management person for a specified unit. (Program, office, department, clinic.)

UNDERSTANDING PROGRAM MANAGEMENT AND DEVELOPMENT

Beginning counselors might view the prospects of program management and development responsibilities and the likelihood of being involved in the administering of an ongoing program as not only remote, but also as potentially undesirable. Let us therefore advance some of the reasons for counselors possessing minimal understanding of management, development, and leadership.

"Administrivia" and You and Your Job

A common complaint throughout all organizations today and perhaps throughout history concerns the inroads made upon professional time by "administrivia" activities. Administrative responsibilities are a fact of life for all functioning professionals, including counselors in all settings. It would, in fact, appear that one cannot provide a vital service without recording the fact that he/she has. Because one cannot avoid all responsibilities for program administration, management, and development, at any level, it will be beneficial if from the beginning of your professional activities as a counselor you have some minimal understandings of these matters and how you may best respond.

Once one recognizes the inescapable presence of administrative, management, and program development responsibilities, one must make a decision to work against this part of the system, to work for it, or to sit in the middle and see what happens. According to one survey of school principals' perceptions of counselors and their assumption of administrative responsibilities,[1] it would appear that most counselors in school settings, at least, prefer to drift with the tide. Recognizing the inevitability of administrative responsibilities, what can one do to discharge these responsibilities as expeditiously and effectively as possible? The following are suggestions gleaned from informal interviews with successful program managers and administrators in various settings.

Be Organized. To be organized means, among other things, having a place for everything and everything in its place. This keeps you from wasting time in search and find operations. Being organized also means planning the use of your time. This includes the maintaining of a daily calendar that allows sufficient time for each task for which you are responsible. Because it is not always possible to estimate the exact amount of time a counseling interview may consume, it is better to allocate too much rather than too little time on one's calendar. Implicit in organization is an efficient filing and record-keeping system that allows ready access of items as needed. Files should contain all necessary and relevant information but should be periodically purged of outdated and nonuseful materials. Although neatness is not necessarily a guarantee of organization, there appears to be a relationship between a neat office and a well-organized office.

Do It Right the First Time. Much administration seems to focus upon the preparation of reports, the maintenance of records, and the organizing of data. As previously indicated, increasing emphasis on accountability has further accentuated the necessity of gathering objective data supporting the counseling enterprise. It is important to take time to understand exactly what it is you have to report and how it is to be reported. If you don't understand it, don't hesitate to ask for help if you need it. Don't waste your time and someone else's by doing it wrong the first time. You must also demand accuracy of yourself in the completing of any report or record and in the organizing of data. Long and cumbersome documents encourage guessing on the part of respondents. Other reports, especially those of an evaluative nature, may tempt one to fake or "fudge" a bit on the responses. The single word of advice is "don't." In addition to the risk of being embar-

---

[1] R. L. Gibson, "School Administrator Opinions of School Guidance Programs," unpublished study, Indiana University, 1976.

rassed by someone noting your inaccuracies, you risk the more dangerous possibility of important decisions being made on the basis of inaccurate and irresponsible data.

Do It on Time.   Assuming that you have been convinced to do your reporting and recording accurately, don't detract from your administrative responsibilities by being late. Usually, there is a reason that certain data are required at certain times for certain decisions. Your delays can handicap this process, especially when your colleagues have all responded on time. On those rare occasions when an emergency prevents the completion of a responsibility on time, it is important to give it the most immediate priority for completion at the earliest opportunity to avoid a domino effect in which every activity down the line will also be subject to tardiness.

Plan Your Own Time.   All of us on occasion will come up against constraints on our time. By simply walking down the halls in almost any setting we can hear comments such as "all I ever do is go to meetings" or "all I get done is answer the phone" or "if people would just stop dropping in unannounced" or "I don't seem to have any time to myself any more." Time frustration seems to occur with all of us. Thus, the use and control of time are critical in one's efficient functioning, both in administration and in counseling, and also have an impact on one's morale. The objective of planning your time is to make the most of it and, at the same time, to leave you enough freedom and flexibility so you do not feel that the clock is your boss. In order to do this, there are several considerations. One is to do the things you do at the times when you do them best. For example, some may find they are most efficient in the preparation of reports if they do them the first thing in the morning. Others may find it desirable to use the first hour or so at work to complete the waking-up process with a second cup of coffee. It is also important to do the things we do where we do them best. This may mean that for certain of our administrative responsibilities we may want to get away to some private little corner where we are uninterrupted. On the other hand, we may wish an informal setting for conferences with colleagues. In planning the use of our time, it is important that we understand ourselves in relationship to where and how we function best. We adapt our time commitment to our working style.

Do It Neatly.   The effects of doing it right and doing it on time may still be lost if an interpreter is needed to translate what you have done. If you are among those grown adults whose handwriting has steadily regressed since kindergarten days, you must develop some set alternative, such as typing or printing, in preparing written reports for others. Lack of neatness can also detract from the impressions or impact of reports. A report that looks as if it had been done and re-done a dozen times may also be more subject to scrutiny and questions by superiors.

Suggestions for functioning effectively also include some don'ts.

Don't Let It Spoil Your Day. Although not everyone may enjoy the challenges of recording and reporting, such tasks should be accepted as inevitable responsibilities that will not be facilitated by constant complaints. The frequent suggestion of many administrators is that you do it and forget it.

Don't Expect to Understand the Need for Every Report. Frustrations frequently occur when one fails to see a rationale for the kind of data that are needed. Allied with this is the fact that we may also not understand why it has to be done "their" way instead of our "better way." When something is requested by your immediate supervisor, you are more likely to understand the need than if it is requested by the upper management, several layers removed. However, there will inevitably be occasions when reports are requested from afar that will challenge all that is rational. Again, do it and forget it.

Don't Be Tempted to Become an Administrator. In some settings, counselors appear to receive their largest number of "brownie points" from their superiors by meeting their administrative responsibilities. It therefore becomes a natural temptation to overemphasize that aspect of the job. A common complaint of many counselors is that they spend too much of their time in administrative activities. Many school administrators claim that counselors spend too much of their time in administrative activities. The major responsibility of a counselor in any setting, with the possible exception of a program director, is to counsel. This should be the counselor's major, time-consuming activity. Although it is important to meet one's administrative responsibilities efficiently and effectively, that does not imply they overshadow in importance or time the primary reason for which one is hired as a counselor.

As an aid to help those who may be reluctant to move from disorganization to organization, the following score pad (Table 12–1) will enable you to play the time game. It may help individuals develop an awareness of their personal time management styles.

Program Management

Program Management as a process seeks to provide structure, order, and coordination of those activities for which it is responsible. This information, of course, will function at varying levels. For example, in educational systems, the Board of Education, the school superintendent, and his or her offices represent top management. The school principal and his or her assistants

Table 12–1.
The Time Game Score Pad

Hour	What did I do?	Had I planned to do it?*	How well did I do it?**	Did I do it with a positive attitude?***	Comments to self****
8 A.M.					
9 A.M.					
10 A.M.					
11 A.M.					
12 noon					
1 P.M.					
2 P.M.					
3 P.M.					
4 P. M.					
5 P.M.					

    * 5 points if you had planned to do it.
      3 points if you had planned to do it because it was overdue.
      0 points if you hadn't planned to do it.
      −3 points if you hadn't planned to do it but it was an unexpected requirement
         that had a higher priority than what you had planned.
   ** Score yourself on a scale of 0 to 5.
 *** 3 points if you did it with enthusiasm.
      2 points if you did it with a positive attitude.
      1 point if you did it and then forgot about it.
      0 points if you did it and then worried about it.
      −1 point if you did it with frustration and/or anger.
      −5 points if you did it and it drove you to drink.
**** 1 point for each constructive suggestion.
      −1 point for statements using profanity.
Totals:
    1. Subtotal A + B + C + D.
    2. Subtract 5 points if you didn't take a lunch break.
    3. Subtract 10 points if you didn't take a lunch break for a second day in a row.
Object of the time game: To improve your score on a daily, weekly, and/or monthly
                   basis.

can be viewed as middle management, and program directors, such as the director of guidance, represent component or lower management.

Figure 12–1 represents this concept. Regardless of the levels of management, however, the overall objective remains the same—the facilitation of the goal achievement of the organization. It is important for counselors in various settings to note that the objectives of the counseling program must be consistent with and contribute to the achievement of the objectives of the institution of which it is a part. For example, in recent years, counselors working in school settings have been called upon to indicate the contributions they are making to the *education* of school-aged youth. Although education may be viewed broadly as all growth and development, it may be more

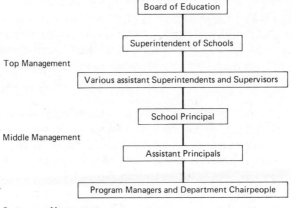

Figure 12–1.
Levels of educational management.

difficult for counselors to respond in those settings when education is viewed as a learning activity only. As previously noted,

> Helping "Harry High School" become a happy, well-adjusted (whatever this means) individual may be a commendable outcome of counseling; however, if, in the process or as a result, he does not become better educated or more effective as a student, the counseling program may be viewed by many as of questionable value to the educational institution.[2]

The responsibilities and activities of program management may vary according to levels and settings, but it is possible to identify two basic areas of functioning. The first deals with the managing of basic resources, such as personnel, budget, and facilities. The second focuses on organizing and facilitating such basic activities as coordination, communication, cooperation, decision making, and evaluation. The emphasis of discussions here will be on what is involved rather than on how one should do it. Following are some suggestions appropriate for entering counselors, who should also be aware that as one moves into management responsibilities, one's own style and techniques tend to emerge.

Managing Resources

Of all the resources that a program manager is called upon to utilize, the human resource is by far the most important. The manner in which this

[2] Robert L. Gibson, Marianne H. Mitchell, and Robert E. Higgins, *The Development and Management of School Programs* (Dubuque, Iowa: William C. Brown Company, Publishers, 1973).

resource is managed will largely determine the success or failure of the program and also whether the manager is a program leader or simply a program administrator. The program manager's initial responsibility in many instances will begin with staffing, and this will be a consistent consideration as long as there is staff turnover. Staff selection should minimally consider these four factors:

Qualifications. These are primarily but not exclusively based on training and experience in relationship to the expectancies of the position. In viewing one's training background, consideration should be given to not only the content of the training program, but also to when, where, and areas of specialization. Although academic achievements in themselves are not the sole criterion for performance on the job, one's academic achievements should not be completely ignored. There may be little difference in performance between the A and B student, but one should not anticipate that the C student will perform as well on the job as the A student.

When examining experience, program managers usually compare the type, amount, and success of previous experiences. Experience may not always be a factor, for many program managers are anxious to hire recent graduates who can bring new ideas, more up-to-date concepts, and, perhaps, needed youthful enthusiasm to their programs.

Staff Versatility. When the program manager has a staff to manage (at least one staff person other than himself/herself), providing for program versatility enters into staff selection. Differing backgrounds should provide a wider range of speciality skills. Too, it has frequently been noted that staffs of two or more should include one member of each sex and minority or cultural representation, as appropriate. Some range in age representation is important, especially in institutional and community settings, and the old schoolboy network (hire all graduates from the same school) should not be perpetuated at the expense of program versatility.

Adaptability. Another consideration that is often overlooked in staffing is the adaptability of a staff member to both the job setting and the community or area environment. The individual must not only like his/her job but it must like him/her. A staff member will function more effectively when there are congenial relationships among the staff as well as those with whom they come in frequent contact. This, of course, would include the clients that the staff is serving. It is not suggested that one form friendships with clients, but it is important to be able to relate to the client population, whether it is inner-city, suburban society, Appalachia poor, or Alaskan Eskimo. Staff members must also be able to adapt to the community or area environment that supports the job setting. It is highly unlikely that one can be unhappy in his/her community-home life and happy in his/her work life. The inability to adapt to a community environment can also have adverse effects on the public relations aspect of the counseling program. Once staffing decisions have been made and personnel are functioning on a job, management's responsibilities continue to be important. These include the following:

The Assignment of Responsibility.   Each staff member should have specific activities for which he/she is responsible and for which the staff member knows he/she is responsible. In assigning these responsibilities, the program manager seeks to capitalize upon the special skills, experiences, and personal characteristics of the staff member. It must be recognized that in some instances this will involve the delegation of some undesirable or less-favored tasks. Staff members must anticipate these as well as their share of the more rewarding activities. A good program manager will not delegate all the "donkey work" and keep only the "goodies" for himself/herself.

Provisions for Staff Development.   The fact that counselors are providing helping services and human support to others does not mean that counselors should or can function without the support of others. A program manager must see that staff members help and support each other and, additionally, receive help and support from beyond the counseling offices. Ways in which this may be accomplished include meaningful group work or committee assignments in which members share interest in a common problem or topic with other staff members and/or personnel outside the counseling staff. Obviously, part of this human support system is the program manager's personal interaction with each staff member.

Budget.   It is hardly possible to overemphasize the importance of budget and budget management in any setting today. Its import in any system of accountability is paramount. In effect, it enables the supporting public, whether they are taxpayers or donators, to see what they are paying for or if they are getting their money's worth. To the individual staff member, budgeting is often a mysterious, misunderstood, maddening and far-removed process that has a direct and undeniable relationship to staff morale. It is therefore important that staff members recognize the level at which their immediate program manager is involved and the extent of that involvement. It is also helpful to understand the level at which budgeting decisions, especially those affecting staff members, are made. In many settings, lower-level managers may be limited in their budget responsibilities to recommending and/or requisitioning from budgets established elsewhere. Crucial budget decisions, such as salaries and salary increments, staffing additions, and equipment purchases, tend to be made at middle- and upper-management levels. These real budget managers are usually involved in budgeting for personnel, including both professional and support staff; and services, such as consultants, communications, supplies, equipment, and travel. Budget decisions for capital improvements, such as new buildings or significant remodeling, are usually made at only the highest level of management.

One form of budgeting that has in recent generations become increasingly prevalent at even the lower levels of management involves program activities supported by federal or state grants. These are usually developed in response to mandated federal or state programs. These programs have specific objectives and procedures and a budget that is directly related and accountable to those procedures and objectives.

The likelihood of beginning counselors being involved in budget management is small, but the probability of some involvement in budget expenditures is considerable. Because mismanagement or misspent monies may become your personal expense, the following suggestions are pertinent:

Each budget item is related to an activity which in turn is related to a specific goal or objective of the organization. It is important to understand the reason for an expenditure. This also suggests that you spend only for those categories that are budgeted; for example, if professional travel is not provided for in a budget, you do not travel professionally by taking $500 from the supply item in the budget even if it isn't being spent and even if the travel is to a professional meeting.

Spend only what you have. Although one may on occasion overdraw a bank account, one is usually reminded quickly and makes amends before it becomes a bankruptcy disaster. However, all too frequently, when spending someone else's money, there is an inclination to be less concerned until it is too late. Remember, any spending in which you engage that is beyond the available budget will probably end up being your own personal expense.

Spend economically. The fact that you have a budget does not mean that the sky is the limit as long as you spend it for items in the budget and as long as you don't exceed the budget. Budget managers are expected to be good shoppers. This does not mean that you sacrifice quality for economy but that you get the most for your budgetary dollar. For example, on major purchases, such as typewriters, video equipment, and tape recorders, it is customary to obtain two or three estimates including those provided by traditional discount houses before determining the place of purchase. If the expenditure is for travel, recipients are usually expected to be aware of the various bargain travel fares and to travel regular or tourist class on common carriers. If private vehicles are used, mileage rates are usually established by federal, state, or local agencies.

Secure receipts. If you are involved in the spending of budgeted funds in any amount, reimbursement is only provided when there is proof of purchase. The only acceptable proof of purchase is a receipt for the goods or service obtained (showing the item, even if it is an elephant, is not considered proof of purchase).

Keep a running account. It is important to anyone who has responsibility for any budget or segment of one to know *exactly* what has been expended and what remains at any given point during the duration of the budget. This means keeping a daily, if necessary, running account of debits, credits, and balances.

Be aware of any unusual (or usual) legal or contract restraints. This point is perhaps most appropriate when individuals have budgetary responsibilities emanating from special contracts or grants. In such instances, budget managers, when in doubt, should consult the appropriate legal or contract authority before authorizing an expenditure.

Managing Facilities

The management of facilities takes on appropriate importance when one considers that persons spend more of their waking hours in their place of work than in their home or any other facility they frequent. Facilities are important in determining whether persons will have the opportunity to do the job they are hired to do in a manner in which they are capable of doing it. In large, complex institutions, facilities are often viewed as symbols that reflect the importance with which the operation is viewed. (It is thus inevitable that a school principal's office will always be a shade larger, at least, than the school counselor's; that the college president's office and decor will be considerably larger and more luxurious than that of the institution's most distinguished professor; etc., etc.) Facility concerns of program managers include the following:

Adequacy. Size, furnishings, and general decor, cleanliness and above all for counselors, privacy are determinants of the adequacy of one's work space. These factors tend to determine the atmosphere in which one works. During a recent university visitation, a dean of students, showing the offices of the university counseling center, remarked that he had $25,000-a-year counselors in $10,000 offices turning in $5,000-a-year performances. Those who have ever worked in dingy, dreary, ill-equipped and/or dirty facilities can recall the impact of these on their morale and subsequent performance. Yet, from time to time, high-level program managers seem to expect that as long as they are comfortable and their morale is good, it will spread to all levels regardless of working conditions.

Accessibility. An individual should not feel that he/she has already done a half-day's work just by getting to his/her office. Accessibility is not only important in terms of those clients it is intended to serve. Countless studies have noted that when university counseling centers or community agencies are situated in locations that are remote to the main populations they are intended to serve, their clientele does not materialize.

Individuality. Have you ever viewed the administrative offices of large-scale enterprises or business corporations, where dozens of employees have been provided identical cubicles and furnishings as so many similar mechanical parts in a precision machine? Such facilities provide little opportunity for the individual worker to assert his/her individuality. Counselors are constantly reminded of the uniqueness of the individual. It would, therefore, seem inconsistent with that theoretical framework to suggest that the individual counselor would not have enough flexibility in his/her personal office facilities to express his/her individuality.

Supplementary Space. Program managers also are responsible for the securing and management of supplementary facilities, such as conference rooms, resource or staff room, filing (security can be important here), storage and supply areas, reception area and support staff facilities.

Management by Objectives

Management by objectives has become increasingly popular in recent years. This system of management was first brought to public attention by Drucker in *A Practice of Management,* which described it as an industrial system. It was later described as a process by Odiorne

> whereby the superior and subordinate jointly identify goals, define individual major areas of responsibility in terms expected of them, and use these measures as guides for operating the contributions of each of its members.[3]

In recent years, this system has received increasing attention as an approach to management for counseling and other human service organizations and educational institutions. In an article describing management by objectives (MBO) for guidance and counseling services, Thompson and Borsari suggested that

> every pupil-personnel program staff should assess its unique strengths and weaknesses before attempting an MBO program. Among other things, the staff must consider whether it is primarily concerned with internal program improvements or external accountability, the leadership roles to be adopted, the support for evaluation from the entire school community, time and money expenditures, the use of the data, and the commitment to personal and professional change. Development of an effective MBO system has a profound effect on all the members of the pupil-personnel team. An MBO system requires that the staff work closely together in order to develop the goals and objectives men-

[3] G. S. Odiorne, *Management by Objectives* (Belmont, Calif.: Pitman Publishing Corporation, 1965), p. 55.

tioned. Therefore, an MBO system should be attempted only after the basic issues listed have been fully investigated.[4]

Then they noted, "while each MBO effort has its own qualities that reflect the uniqueness of its creators, a generalized process for efficient development may be suggested."[5]

In an abbreviated form, these processes (1) define long-range goals, or what the system wants to accomplish, and set the ideal limits toward which the organization's plan will direct its efforts; (2) formulate a needs assessment to focus priorities; and (3) establish departmental objectives. Each program's activities should clearly relate to one or more systems goals. The articulation of these activities and programs and the relationships to systems goals make up the departmental objectives. Then, (4) establish individual objectives. Each staff member must develop an individual plan to help the department achieve its objectives. Individual staff members should be given the freedom to select those strategies that will make the most of the individual's personal and professional strengths. Also, (5) develop action plans and assess feasibility of action plans (cost, time, personnel). Management by objectives requires the counselor to think about how he/she will achieve an objective and evaluate the activity. Counselor team members should evaluate their individual objectives in terms of how they affect client populations. Behavioral objectives keep the focus on the real test of counseling services—changes in the behaviors of clients. Finally, (6) implement action plans, monitor and evaluate operations; (7) review progress toward objectives; and (8) recycle.

The departmental objectives, activities, and their related evaluations are reviewed to direct rational decision making concerning program operation and modification.[6]

Thompson and Borsari suggested that the advantages demonstrated by the system occur in the development of goals, objectives, and measurable programs, improved feedback systems, and in personal development of the counseling staff. They caution that difficulties may occur because effective outcomes are sometimes difficult to describe and measure and because many human service specialists see management systems' accountability and evaluation as a threat to humanistic values and procedures. They suggest that commitment, time, patience, and a willingness to learn and change are prerequisites for both the individuals and the organizations involved in adopting a management by objectives strategy.

---

[4] Donald L. Thompson and Leonard R. Borsari, "An Overview of Management by Objectives for Guidance and Counseling Services," *The School Counselor*, 25 No. 3:174 (Jan. 1978).
[5] Ibid., p. 175.
[6] Ibid., p. 176.

Organizing and Facilitating Basic Activities

The program manager must also initiate and guide the organizing and facilitating of the basic activities of the counseling program. This does not mean the professional activities but, rather, the basic supporting activities that complement the professional services of the organization. These include the following:

Coordination. In even less than complex organizations, some degree of coordination is necessary to prevent overlapping, conflicting, or duplicating of activities. Coordination is necessary among activities and programs, both internally and externally.

Cooperation. Cooperation is a vital ingredient in both coordination and public relations. Program managers must encourage and demonstrate a willingness to work with others in such vital counselor activities as case studies, conferences, referrals, and consultation. As suggested previously, counselors should not hesitate to ask for help when they need it. Counselors should also be willing to give help when called upon by fellow professional colleagues or support personnel in other fields as well. Cooperation is one of the basic functions in establishing and maintaining positive professional connections.

Effective Communications. Communications often determine whether or not a program is managed efficiently or not. Counselors are usually well trained in the art of personal communication, but it is surprising how frequently the communication process breaks down within a program as well as with higher-level management and external agencies and organizations. Guidelines for effective communications in management suggest care must be taken that the personal touch is not lost as a result of using impersonal means to communicate, such as memos, policy statements, and directives. When it is necessary to use such impersonal means, there must be adequate personal follow-up to ensure that such communications are understood. In addition, communication must provide for some sort of feedback. Oral communication to large groups such as staff or faculty meetings must justify the time it consumes for the number of people present.

Evaluation. A program manager is responsible for ensuring the gathering of data that provides for systematic, ongoing evaluation of the program's activities. He/she also coordinates periodic and accreditation types of planning. At the individual staff member level, a program manager is responsible for evaluation of each member of the organization and communicating this evaluation to both the individual staff member and higher management.

Decision Making. Effective program management requires that someone be in charge. A program manager as the one in charge must have decision-making authority commensurate with the responsibilities of the decision. It is appropriate for program managers to share the decision thinking, but they cannot be expected to share all the decision making.

PROGRAM LEADERSHIP

Perhaps no single characteristic beyond the professional qualifications of the counseling staff is more significant to the success of the counseling operation than the quality of program leadership. It is desirable that counselors at least recognize those characteristics that tend to identify leaders and distinguish them from program administrators or managers. Most persons recognize the individual who is a true leader. A real leader is one who leads, not directs; real leadership gives priority to the benefit of the program and to those who are led, rather than to the leader. Some of the characteristics of program leadership include the following:

A Record of Success. Program leaders have good track records. They justify the old concept that success breeds success. Included in the program leader's win column is previous recognition as a successful and resourceful counselor. Too, the program leader is an extra competent professional. Program leadership for counseling programs can only be provided by professional counselors. It is anticipated that program leaders will contribute their competence and expert knowledge to the successful functioning of the counseling program, including an awareness of professional, ethical, and legal guidelines for the profession.

Inspires Confidence. A program leader inspires confidence in himself/herself and in the individual staff members. He/she does this by being supportive and also realistic. He/she expects the possible, but not the impossible. He/she gives and shares credit publicly so that others know of the successes of individual staff members.

Shares. The program leader shares the "ownership" of the operation. He/she develops a feeling of "us" rather than "me and you." Active ownership does not mean that the staff runs the operation. It means that the staff shares in the running of it. Sharing the ownership of the operation creates a feeling of belonging, of being on the team. Real leadership sees that no one feels left out. There are no in-groups and out-groups.

Motivates. All studies of leadership indicate that a common ingredient of leaders in nearly every setting is an ability to motivate others to achieve their potential, and perhaps at times, even exceed it. Although each leader has his/her different and own unique style, the evidence is present when one observes hard-working, achieving staff members.

Creates a Positive Atmosphere. A leader understands what makes life at the office liveable or one happy in one's work. He/she creates professional atmospheres conducive to accomplishment. This includes effective program organization, management, and administration.

Visibility. One cannot lead in absentia. Successful program leaders at all levels are those who are frequently and clearly visible to and available for interacting with their supporting staffs.

Forward Looking. Leadership demands planning for the future. Program leaders are insightful and future-oriented in their planning.

Decision Makers. Effective leadership not only accepts the decision-making responsibility and will make the hard decisions, but will also make the appropriate decision.

These characteristics can provide a checklist to identify potential counseling program leaders. As your authors noted in a previous publication,[7] program leaders are not likely to be chosen when the top management position is viewed as a consolation prize; a stepping stone for someone tagged to proceed up the organization; a political position to shore up support for top management; or as proof that the "Peter Principle"[8] really operates. This principle suggests that one is eventually promoted to his/her level of incompetence.

CONTRIBUTING TO PROGRAM DEVELOPMENT AND IMPROVEMENT

Upon joining a counseling staff, a counselor becomes committed and involved in the continuous process of program development and improvement. The effective development of any counseling program, whether in a school or institutional setting, is dependent first upon an accurate and continuous assessment of the needs of the target population to be served. Such needs assessment is the key to the successful development of goals and objectives. The accurate assessment of needs is critical in establishing and maintaining program relevance and as a basis for program accountability and evaluation. The needs assessment activity, which can range from a simple to a complex process, is concerned with two data bases, as follows:

1. Target population assessment. This data gathering seeks to establish factually the needs of the target population that the counseling program

---

[7] Robert L. Gibson, Marianne H. Mitchell, and Robert E. Higgins, op. cit., 1973.

[8] Laurence I. Peter and Raymond Hull, *The Peter Principle* (New York: Wm Morrow & Co, 1959).

has been established to serve. These data will also influence priorities among these needs.

2. Environmental assessment. This is the gathering of factual data that facilitate the counseling program's understanding of the setting from which the target population comes and within which the program functions.

Target population assessment provides a factual basis for a program's goals and objectives, and environmental assessment provides a factual basis for the procedures whereby a program achieves its goals and objectives. The personal needs are the internal factors that initiate, direct, and sustain the program's activities, whereas the environmental characteristics provide the depth of understanding for more effectively responding to the needs.

Two approaches to needs assessment are presented as examples. Although these both illustrate needs assessment for educational settings, they are equally appropriate, with minor modifications, for other counseling settings. The first example illustrates a relatively simple approach and was designed by the Department of Public Instruction, State of Indiana.[9]

Step 1. Identify and list all populations to be served. To assess the guidance needs of the school and community, representatives from the following populations might be included in data collection:

Pupils.
Teachers.
Principals and other administrators.
Parents.
Pupil Personnel Service staff.

To assure an adequate representation from each of these groups, the counselor might identify the population(s) to be served in terms of the following characteristics:

Ethnic composition.
Socioeconomic strata.
Political factors.
Grade level.
Educational expectations.

Step 2. Collect data using a systematic approach that is designed to identify guidance-related needs and to identify whether current guidance practices are appropriate to these needs. Frequently used methods for collecting data include questionnaires, interviews, brainstorming sessions, school and community records, and follow-up studies. Various other methods may be developed. Also, the entire population may be

---

[9] Frank DiSilvestro, *The Application of the Planning, Programming, Budgeting System (PPBS) Concept to Counseling and Guidance Services,* (Indianapolis: Indiana State Department of Public Instruction, 1974).

surveyed, or a sample may be assessed, such as a stratified random sample.

Step 3. Develop a system for utilizing the collected data. The counselor will compile, classify, and analyze the data collected. The data will be used in determining guidance priorities.

A more complex approach is that suggested by the Department of Health, Education and Welfare (1975), in which the strategy of needs assessment was described as follows:

   (i)   The overall concept of educational needs assessment defines an educational need as the difference between the current status of the learner and the desired learner outcomes.

  (ii)   The assessment strategy includes both long- and short-range goals.

 (iii)   The strategy includes specific activities which have been designed to achieve each objective included in the strategy.

 (iv)   The strategy includes a time frame for accomplishing each activity.

  (v)   The strategy is sufficiently constructed so as to consider all the required elements.

 (vi)   Student learning goals are established for the purpose of determining children's needs through the educational needs assessment.

 (vii)   The student learning goals are behaviorally stated and representative of cognitive, affective, and psychomotor learning.

(viii)   The student learning goals are sufficiently definitive to make them measurable objectives for student learning.

 (ix)   The strategy includes the elementary and secondary grade levels which will be assessed.

  (x)   The strategy includes provisions for collecting data about student learning objectives into three categories:

    (a)   Perceptions of the community (including those in business and industry), educators, and the learners regarded as relevant and important to attaining these objectives;

    (b)   Criterion-based test instruments to determine the extent to which student learning objectives have been achieved; and

    (c)   Relevant demographic data about the learners.

 (xi)   The strategy includes provisions for a data sample from which validity can be determined; i.e., evidence that what is measured is that which purports to being measured.

 (xii)   The strategy includes provisions for a data sample from which reliability can be determined; i.e., that measurement is being performed accurately and consistently.

(xiii)   The needs assessment strategy includes provisions for collecting appropriate information on specific sub-populations.

(xiv) The strategy includes provisions to assure that the data collected are manageable and current.

(xv) The instruments which are designed to collect data have been tested thoroughly on a pilot basis.

(xvi) Procedures for analyzing data have been thoroughly tested to determine if all data collected can be appropriately utilized and treated.

(xvii) The conclusions drawn from the interpretation of data can be supported.

(xviii) There are logical and defensible procedures established for determining the criticalness of educational needs identified by data for the State as a whole and for each distinct area of the state.

(xix) A listing of critical educational learner needs which are representative of cognitive, affective, and psychomotor learning is given.[10]

The Needs Assessment Survey

As previously indicated, the assessment of the needs of the target population is a technique for factually establishing program goals and objectives. Such an assessment directly involves the target population or a sampling thereof, as well as critical support populations. For example, a school guidance program would not only gather data from students, but would also survey parents, teachers, and others who had frequent and direct contact with the student population. The direct involvement of these populations is usually secured through questionnaires and/or structured interviews. Figure 12–2 presents an example of a simple questionnaire used in student needs assessment and completed not only by students, but support populations as well.

In addition to questionnaire and interview data, other sources such as school and community records will provide data that substantiate or identify the needs of potential clients. Environmental assessment seeks to establish the characteristics of program and population setting through identifying the characteristics of the environment's population, economics, and geography. Community assessment may be facilitated through the use and development of certain data planning instruments, as may be noted in Figures 12–3 and 12–4. Typical sources from which the previously suggested data may be gathered are noted in Figure 12–4. Figure 12–3 shows how to identify community leaders in the categories noted. Figure 12–4, on the other hand, is a checklist designed to guide the information seeker to common sources of community information. The form is not intended to record data, but only to provide a guide to possible sources.

---

[10] *The Federal Register,* **40:**51025, No. 212 (Nov. 3, 1975).

Person filling out form:	Rankings: Check one for each question below					Additional Response
_____ Student						
_____ Parent	Very Important	Quite Important	Moderately Important	Somewhat Important	Not Important At All	In your opinion is this service being provided?
_____ Teacher						
_____ Business Person						(check one)
1. How important is it for the student to be able to discuss personal problems with the school counselor?						yes ___ no ___
2. How important is it for the school counselor to provide career information?						yes ___ no ___
3. How important is it for the school counselor to provide information concerning colleges, trade schools, or the armed services?						yes ___ no ___
4. How important is it for the counselor to show the relationship between education and careers?						yes ___ no ___
5. How important is it for the counselor to provide assistance to the student in job placement upon graduation?						yes ___ no ___
6. How important is it for the counselor to discuss with the student which courses he will take in school?						yes ___ no ___
7. How important is it for the counselor to work with students who are failing or dropping out?						yes ___ no ___
8. How important is it for the counselor to lead small group discussions on current student problems?						yes ___ no ___
9. How important is a guidance program in a high school?						yes ___ no ___
10. What other services for students do you think the school counselor should provide? (Please write in the space below and on the back.)						yes ___ no ___

Figure 12–2.
Needs identification questionnaire.

Identifying Priorities and Developing Program Relevancy

The needs assessment data that may be gathered through the previously described procedures provide direction for the determining of goals and priorities and the development of counseling program objectives that are relevant and meaningful to the target population and setting. The initial procedure is a simple listing of goals and priorities, first as perceived by the target population. These then may be slightly reordered, as verified by immediate support population, and then slightly reordered again, once these base data

Community: _____   _____

Survey dates: _____   _____

Survey team: _____   _____

_____   _____

_____ 1. Political leadership

_____

_____

_____ 2. Governmental (nonpolitical) leadership

_____

_____ 3. Educational leadership
(School board members, superintendents, principals,
_____ education association or union officials)

_____ 4. Major religious denominations
(ministers, priests, rabbis)

_____

_____ 5. Minority group (or groups) leadership

_____

_____ 6. Judicial system
(Chief of police, juvenile judge, lawyers, county sheriff, probationary officials)

_____ 7. Business/commercial/industrial leadership
(Presidents (in residence) of local corporations, plant managers, owners of
_____ prominent local businesses)

_____ 8. Labor organization leadership

_____

_____ 9. Youth leadership
(Student council members, athletic standouts, social club or gang leadership)

_____

_____ 10. Civic leadership
(Officials of civic clubs, volunteer organizations)

_____ 11. Other (indicate status and representation)

_____   _____

_____   _____

_____   _____

Figure 12–3.
Community survey checklist (interview schedule).

Community: _____   _____

Survey dates: _____   _____

Survey team _____   _____

_____   _____

_____

_____ 1. Census data

_____ 2. News media analysis

_____ 3. Board of education (minutes of) meetings

_____ 4. Annual reports of schools

_____ 5. County government data

_____ 6. City government data

_____ 7. Employment agencies

_____ 8. Church board reports

_____ 9. Chamber of Commerce data

_____ 10. Geographic data

_____ 11. Ecological-environmental data

_____ 12. Other significant data (list sources)

_____

_____

_____

_____

Note: If data are not available, place notation "NA" in blank at left of
item. Otherwise, when data are collected, place a "√."

Figure 12–4.
Community survey checklist (data collection).

are supplemented by secondary populations and sources. In the school setting, the students would represent the target population, and teachers and parents, the immediate support population. Supplementary or secondary population would include community personnel and data from student and other relevant records. This process leads to a tentative prioritizing of needs. A final reordering is established by eliminating any needs that may not be the professional responsibility of the counseling program or may require resources beyond those available to the counseling program. The final outcome of this process is the establishment of working priorities in a hierarchical order, which are then translated into goals and objectives.

The translation of priorities into goals and objectives requires their being stated in written terms. The goals of a program are typically described in broad, general terms that may not be tied to specific time constraints. On the other hand, the program objectives must be stated in objective, measurable terms and related to a time frame. Objectives are designed to describe desired performances and should contribute to the achievement of a program goal and the meeting of one or more specifically identified needs. Of course, the assessment of needs and the establishment of related goals and objectives are not, in and of themselves, a guarantee of program relevancy. A needs assessment only establishes an awareness of what a counseling program should consider in planning the utilization of its resources. The real criteria of program relevancy will result from the degree of understanding and concern and the appropriateness of the plan of action developed and executed by the counseling staff. An effective plan of action will reflect many, if not all, of the following characteristics:

It should be developmental. Program planning should be developmental, indicating immediate, intermediate, and long-range program goals. As a starting point, it may be appropriate to envision an ultimate, utopian program for the setting for which it will be designed and, once having established these long-range goals, determine those priorities that should be given immediate attention, those that may need attention within the next several years, and those that the program ultimately hopes to accomplish.

Programs should never reach the point where they function simply to maintain the status quo. Programs should at all times be developmental, for development implies continuous growth and improvement.

It should have a logical, sequential pattern of development. The development of any program usually proceeds from a foundation which seems appropriate to subsequent development. As previously suggested, the appropriate foundation from which planning proceeds are its needs and readiness assessment and their relationship to the resources at hand.

It should be flexible. Counseling programs must be flexible in order to meet the changing needs of youth and other client populations. This suggests also that initial planning for program development must be limited to that which can be reasonably achieved. Programs that are overly ambitious in their design allow little room for alternate or unexpected opportunities. A part of flexibility in planning should be the identification of possible problems and alternate procedures for goal achievement.

It should give a high priority to communication, coordination, and cooperation. Like the other components of program development, these activities should not be left to chance. It is important, for example, that there be a plan for communicating the development of the school guidance program to faculty members individually and in groups, as well as to students, parents, and others.

Cooperation with other programs and individuals is important if the program is to anticipate the need for reciprocal cooperation. In communicating with the various relevant groups and individuals in the community, different approaches must be utilized that recognize the uniqueness and differences of these individuals and groups. For example, techniques for communicating with youth would certainly be different in many ways than those that are effective with adults and related professionals. Often in recent years, counseling programs increasingly fail to communicate their mission clearly and effectively to others, resulting in many questioning the need for such programs. Coordination and cooperation failures have also adversely affected the positive image which counseling programs seek to portray.

It should provide a basis for resource employment. An adequate plan for program development provides a logical basis for personnel assignment, budget development, and resource allocation and utilization. This means that the plan must be a clear and concise one in which the relationships between program goals, the activities for achieving these goals, and the personnel and other resources needed to accomplish them can be readily recognized.

The program director must be a resource coordinator. Program planning must therefore take into account those resources that may be available for program development and goal accomplishment. An inventory of possible resources becomes, therefore, an important activity in planning for program development.

Any plan for program initiation and development must include provisions for program accountability or evaluation. The evaluation component of a developmental plan provides a built-in mechanism for program accountability, development, and improvement.

THE COUNSELOR AND THE LAW

During recent years few aspects of education at any level have remained untouched by judicial and legislative activities. Increasingly, managers of school guidance programs and counselors have become aware of the legal implications of their activities, and the legal restrictions, and even legal conflicts with their professional conscience. This increased legal intervention is an outgrowth of a dramatic increase in litigation and attending legislation during the past twenty-five years. McCarthy, in addressing both of these points, stated

Alexis de Tocqueville has noted that all important social issues in America eventually become judicial issues. This observation is verified in the field of education, as litigation in this arena has increased dramatically in recent years. Before 1850, education was mainly ignored by both federal and state courts. Thus, practices at the local level were left largely unquestioned whether or not they conflicted with the Federal Constitution. From 1850 until 1950 education became firmly established as a state responsibility, and most adjudication during this period took place in state courts. Prior to 1954, slightly more than 100 cases involving education had been initiated in federal courts. However, since 1954 well over 1,000 cases concerning education have been litigated at the federal level, with many going all the way to the United States Supreme Court. During the past few decades the federal courts have assumed a more prominent role in ensuring that the individual's constitutional rights are protected and balanced against the interests of the state. This increasing reliance on the federal judiciary is indicative of the growing public dissatisfaction with efforts of legislative bodies to effect reform in public education.[11]

She also pointed out

The increasing national interest in exploring the internal operations of schools to guarantee that the rights of children are not arbitrarily impaired also has been reflected in recent congressional legislation which has addressed certain aspects of the school's duty toward the child. The Family Rights and Privacy Act has placed restrictions on school officials' former power to indiscriminately record data about students. In addition, procedural safeguards are now required before the school can release a student's personal files. Thus, the rationale that a certain practice is "in the best interest of education" can no longer justify educational policies that arbitrarily interfere with the individual's personal liberties. Also, Title IX of the Educational Amendments of 1972 is causing some changes in the organization and administration of public schools. Title IX requires schools to eliminate discriminatory practices based on sex regarding admission policies, employment, and athletics. It is conceivable that federal legislation will continue to become more explicit in establishing standards for school policies, perhaps even in the area of instructional program adequacy.[12]

However, despite the increased public interest in both judicial and legislative activities with direct legal implications for schools, a study by Zirkel[13] indicated that school leadership is abysmally ignorant of the operational dictates of Supreme Court decisions affecting education. The fact that this study was limited to Supreme Court decisions further highlights the general lack of knowledge among educators of their legal responsibilities and legal restraints.

Counselors cannot afford to be "legally ignorant." They must understand the law and its implications in arenas of counselor concern and function. These include acts or practices which might be viewed as discriminatory,

---

[11] Martha M. McCarthy, *School Law: A Growing Concern,* Teacher Education Forum, Division of Teacher Education, Bloomington, Ind.: Indiana University, **4:**1 (Jan. 1976).
[12] Ibid.
[13] Perry A. Zirkel, "A Test on Supreme Court Decisions Affecting Education," *Phi Delta Kappan* (Apr. 1978), p. 521.

compromising the constitutional and other legal rights as prejudicing the opportunities of individuals. In these regards, note some of the legal implications for counselors of Title IX, The Buckley Amendment, and Education for the Handicapped Children Act.

The Counselor and Title IX

Title IX of the Education Amendments of 1972, which took effect in July 1975, provides that

> no person . . . shall on the basis of sex, be excluded from participation in, be denied the benefits of, or be subjected to discrimination under any education program receiving federal financial assistance.

Some of the provisions that are of particular interest to counselors are as follows:

A recipient shall not provide any course or otherwise carry out any of its education program or activity separately on the basis of sex. This includes shop and home economics courses.

With respect to physical education courses, institutions were to comply with the requirements as expeditiously as possible, but in no event later than one year from the effective date of the regulation at the elementary level and three years from the effective date at the secondary and post-secondary levels. Students may be grouped by ability in physical education classes and activities as long as ability is assessed by objective standards developed and applied without regard to sex. Students may be separated in physical education classes during participation in contact sports.[14]

Nearly half of all the girls now enrolled in vocational education are enrolled in consumer and homemaking courses which do not prepare them for employment. The courses of study which do train for employment—and in which girls predominate—offer training in only 33 different occupations. In contrast, courses of study in which boys predominate offer training for paid employment in 95 different occupations. When girls do enroll in programs leading to paid employment, it is most often in areas such as office education or health services which offer relatively poor pay and relatively poor prospects for advancement. Many girls limit their own opportunities because they and their parents often approach vocational education with a narrow vision of what is appropriate and many schools have reinforced these notions with their own discriminatory policies. Schools have barred girls from certain courses

[14] Harold H. Negley, Superintendent, *PPS Newsletter,* Indiana State Department of Public Instruction, Vol. 3, No. 2 (Dec. 1975).

of study outright and guided them away from other traditionally male fields through recruitment, admission, and counseling practices which discouraged girls' enrollment when it did not directly forbid it. The major issue in vocational education is whether girls are going to be as capable of supporting themselves as boys with the same level of education. If this is to be accomplished, a lot of past practices need to be changed.[15]

Title IX requires the school to assure itself that any outside agencies, business organizations, or individuals with whom it cooperates do not discriminate against its students on the basis of sex. This might be in cooperative education, work-study programs, apprenticeships or job placement. If the outside party refuses to give that assurance—or gives it but continues to discriminate—the school is required to end its cooperation.[16]

The counselor can no longer cooperate with an outside agency, organization or individual that wishes to discriminate against students on the basis of sex. What that boils down to is that if an employer is seeking a boy for summer employment, the counselor may not refer only one sex. For a counselor to be genuinely effective in counteracting stereotypes, the counselor will need to do more than simply not discriminate. An active attempt to expand options and opportunities is required. While Title IX does not require this kind of activity from the counselor, it is the kind of help most girls need to get past their own built-in stereotypes.[17]

No club which is school sponsored can be limited to a single sex. Outside organizations which receive significant assistance from the school must also be nondiscriminatory, UNLESS they meet very strict criteria set up by Title IX to exempt youth service organizations such as the Girl Scouts and Campfire Girls. In order to be exempt the sponsoring organization must: be single sex; be a voluntary youth service organization; have a membership mostly under 19 years of age; and be tax exempt.[18]

More than one million teenagers become pregnant each year. We all need to be concerned that in teenage pregnancy, which involved two sexes to begin with, discrimination is most often directed against just one sex. More than half of all female dropouts leave school because of pregnancy. Eighty per cent of the young women who become pregnant for the first time at age 17 or younger NEVER complete high school. Teenage mothers are less likely than other mothers to be working and

---

[15] *Cracking the Glass Slipper: Peer's Guide to Ending Sex Bias in Your Schools,* Holly Knox, Project Director, the NOW Legal Defense and Education Fund, 1977.
[16] Ibid.
[17] Ibid.
[18] Ibid.

more likely to be receiving Aid to Dependent Children. Their critical lack of education certainly plays a part in this.[19]

Under Title IX the pregnant student has the same rights and responsibilities as any other student. Solely because of pregnancy, she:

a. may not be expelled from school;
b. may not be required to attend a special school for pregnant students;
c. may not be barred from any program, course (including physical education or extra curricular activity, including competing for, or receiving, any award, honor or elective office);
d. may not be required to take special courses in child care or related topics unless those courses are required of every other student in the school;
e. may not be required to leave school at a certain time before the birth of the child or required to remain out of school for a certain length of time afterwards;
f. may not be required to furnish notes from her physician that she is able to continue or re-enter a course of study unless such notes are required of all students (e.g., to tell when they intend to leave for surgery; or after an illness, to say that they are strong enough to return).[20]

The Counselor and the Buckley Amendment

Few legislative actions have had the impact upon the practice of counseling and the attending record keeping than the Buckley Amendment. Prior to the passage in 1974 of the Family Educational Rights and Privacy Act (FERPA) as it is titled (or the Buckley Amendment as it is commonly referred to), counselors derived most of their directions for their professional functioning from the ethical guidelines provided by their professional associations. In this regard, the American Personnel and Guidance Association Ethical Standards suggested that

> Records of the counseling relationship including interview notes, test data, correspondence, tape recordings and other documents are to be considered professional information for use in counseling, and they are not part of the public or official records of the institution or agency in which the counselor is employed. Revelation to others of counseling material should occur only upon the express consent of the counselee.[21]

Although ethical standards were not in themselves legally binding, there are numerous instances, beginning with the case of Cherry versus the Board

[19] Ibid.
[20] Ibid.
[21] "Ethical Standards," American Personnel and Guidance Association, *Guidepost,* **17**:156–157 (July 4, 1974).

of Regents of the State of New York in 1942, that suggested courts might use professional ethical codes as guidelines for making judicial decisions. In the case of record keeping and confidentiality, however, the passage of the Buckley Amendment became the single most important guideline for professional conduct with regard to student records and related activities.

> The FERPA stipulates that the parents of unemancipated minor students have ". . . the right to inspect and review any and all official records, files and data directly related to their children, including all material that is incorporated into each student's cumulative record folder and intended for school use or to be available to parties outside the school or school system, and specifically including but not necessarily limited to identifying data, academic work completed, level of achievement (grades, standardized achievement scores), attendance data, scores of standardized intelligence, aptitude and psychological tests, interest inventory results, health data, family background information, teacher or counselor ratings and observations, and verified reports of serious recurrent behavior patterns."[22]

Recognizing the conflict or, as they put it, ethical standards squeeze, Getson and Schweid suggested the following steps for school counselors to protect their counselees and students:

> First, review all existing records to assure that there is no material that predates FERPA that would violate implied or stated guarantees of privacy to the child. Second, remove all material that, because of its technical nature or vocabulary, may be inappropriate for use by lay persons. Retain only materials that can be expressed in a form unlikely to be misinterpreted. Third, initiate a policy of maintaining only records that can be reviewed with parents without threat to the welfare of a counselee. Fourth, be sure that counselees understand the legal limitation of the privacy afforded the counseling relationship relative to the rights of parents to inspect official records. Fifth, initiate a study of the full implications of the conflict between the FERPA and APGA's Ethical Standards. There may be safeguards to the right to privacy of the student implicit in FERPA of which we who are not lawyers are not aware. Sixth, if there is a clear or probable conflict between the FERPA and APGA's Ethical Standards, initiate action to change the act, the standards, or both. It would seem that, as a minimum, a provision should exist within the act that withholds from anyone except public authorized investigative bodies information under study.[23]

[22] Russell Getson and Robert Schweid, "School Counselors and the Buckley Amendment-Ethical Standards Squeeze," *The School Counselor,* **24**:57 (Sept. 1976).
[23] Ibid., pp. 57–58.

Because school counselors as well as counselors in other educational settings are frequently called upon to write letters of recommendation for college admissions and/or employment, it should be noted that the Buckley Amendment implications are clear that

Unless the educator is specifically informed otherwise, he or she should assume that the student may have access to letters of recommendation. The student can be requested to sign a waiver, so that he or she will not have such access. However, unless such a waiver is signed, the student can be defended, both factually and professionally. In general, educators are on relatively safe ground when writing letters of recommendation if the following conditions are met:

1. Letters of recommendation are an expected, normal, and integral part of one's duties and responsibilities.
2. Letters are sent only to second parties (not published), who can be expected to have a reasonable interest in and concern for the person in question.
3. Letters are factual, free of malice, and reasonably objective.
4. Letters are in response to a request.[24]

St. John and Walden suggest three recommendations:

First, it is recommended that professional educators consult with an attorney, preferably one conversant with educational matters, or with the school district's legal counsel, on all matters regarding confidential communications. Second, it is recommended that school districts and state departments of education cooperatively develop detailed guidelines to assist all school personnel in protecting student confidences and to respect the confidentiality of communications consistent with state and federal statutes. Third, it is recommended that the various professional organizations develop specific and up-dated codes of ethics related to this area.[25]

School Counselors and Public Law 94–142

Another act of importance to school counselors is the Education for All Handicapped Children Act (PL 94–142) of November 1975. This law guarantees the rights of all children, regardless of the severity of the handicap, to a free, appropriate education. The law further establishes a formula for providing financial aid to states and local school districts, based on the number of handicapped children receiving special education plus related services. It is this latter activity—related services—that provides for counseling by a

[24] Walter D. St. John and John Walden, "Keeping Student Confidences," *Phi Delta Kappan* (June 1976), p. 683.
[25] Ibid., p. 683.

certified counselor. In noting the implications of this act for counselors, Humes noted that

> while the role of the counselor in the implementation of PL 94–142 will vary from district to district and in part will be contingent on the availability of other specialized personnel and whether the counselor has an elementary or secondary assignment, it is difficult to conceive of any situation in which a counselor will have no role to play. Some of the possible ranges of responsibility are
>
> 1) participation in team meetings.
> 2) development of the IEP [Individual Educational Plan].
>
> (IEP—The core of the law is the concept of the IEP. An IEP, which is to be reviewed annually, must be developed for each handicapped child. The content of the IEP must include the present level of functioning, annual goals, short-term measurable objectives, and specific educational services required by the child.)
>
> 3) monitoring progress.
> 4) parental counseling.
>
> (A section of the law that is overlooked, partly because of its traditional neglect in American public education and partly because of the ambiguous nature of the language in the statute, is the requirement for parent counseling. Parent counseling may have a variety of meanings. Parent counseling suggests a possible range of services from psychiatric assistance to advice about academic offerings and may occur in an outside agency or within the school. A conservative approach would suggest that parent counseling should occur in the school setting and satisfy the definition of counseling as opposed to therapy. If we accept this assumption, the logical person to satisfy this need would be the counselor.)
>
> 5) extracurricular planning
> 6) classroom consulting
> 7) inservice training
>
> (While it is reasonable to assume that in the early stages counselors will be the recipients of in-service training along with other pupil personnel services workers, it would be a reasonable assumption that in the middle-to-later stages of implementation the counselor will become one of the providers of in-service training.)
>
> 8) record keeping.[26]

Finally, we should note that counselors have, on occasion, been defendents in criminal action. As Burgum and Anderson suggest, the counselor

[26] Charles W. Humes II, "School Counselors and PL 94–142," *The School Counselor,* 25:193–195 (Jan. 1978).

may unwittingly risk criminal liability leading to one of four possible criminal charges:

Accessory to a crime after the fact.

Encouraging an illegal abortion.

Co-conspirator in civil disobedience.

Contributing to delinquency of a minor.[27]

Although the counselor is honor-bound to protect the integrity and promote the welfare of his client, he also has an obligation to society at large. No area of counselor activity poses greater prospect of conflict and trouble for the counselor than when a student-client is guilty of a crime. Accessory after the fact is generally defined as "one who, knowing a felony to have been committed, receives, relieves, comforts, or assists the felon, or in any manner aids him to escape arrest or punishment."

Three elements must exist to render one an accessory after the fact:

1. A felony must have already been committed.
2. The person charged as an accessory must have knowledge that the person he is assisting committed the felony.
3. The accessory must harbor or assist the felon.

The first condition—that the felony be completed—is required because if the felon is given aid during commission of a crime the person helping him becomes a principal and not an accessory after the fact. Knowledge on the part of the defendant that a crime was committed is necessary to a charge of being an accessory after the fact. But one cannot escape guilt by merely claiming lack of knowledge. Knowledge, like intent, is a matter of fact which can be proven by inference from all facts and circumstances developed at trial. And a defendant must be able to counter any evidence that he did have knowledge of a crime. Different types of conduct can constitute sufficient "assistance" to produce judgment that the person giving such assistance was, indeed, an accessory after the fact.

Generally, evidence that a person helps to hide a felon, lends him money, gives advice, provides goods, offers transportation, blocks the path of pursuers, and, in some cases, gives false information tending to mislead the authorities has been held sufficient to sustain conviction as accessory after the fact. However, it would be inaccurate to say that just any affirmative assistance or relief would automatically result in charges that one has been an accessory. Even those acts just enumerated have not always been held sufficient to justify conviction.[28]

[27] Thomas Burgum and Scott Anderson, *The Counselor and the Law* (Washington, D.C.: American Personnel and Guidance Association Press, 1975), p. 88.
[28] Ibid., pp. 89–91.

SUMMARY

Much of the success of any counseling program will be dependent upon how the program is managed, developed, and led. As educational and community institutions have become more complex in their organizational and operational structure, the necessity for special preparation of program leaders in terms of managing resources, coordinating and facilitating activities, and providing personnel motivation has become increasingly self-evident. This chapter has also noted the importance of counselors informing themselves of the legal implications and restrictions on their professional activities.

Accountability, Evaluation, and Research 13

INTRODUCTION

The mere mention of the activities of accountability, evaluation, and research is said on frequent occasion to strike fear into the hearts of any honest and able practitioner. To mention all three of these as topics for a chapter should suffice to bring out all the traditional fears associated with these activities. These include (1) the fear of being held responsible, regardless of intervening variables, for one's activities; (2) the fear of being judged by criteria determined externally over which one has no control; (3) the fear of being judged by unrealistic standards and expectancies; (4) the fear of being required, in the case of research, to master difficult mathematical formulae that one feels he/she will never use again; (5) the fear of being expected to understand and possibly even apply the results of research studies written by researchers to impress other researchers; and (6) the fear, or assumption, that evaluation is never intended to be positive.

Many of these fears will diminish to mere myths when one learns to appreciate the values and advantages of accountability, evaluation, and research for the practitioner in the school or agency setting.

DEFINITIONS

Although textbooks and many periodical articles have been published dealing with the separate topics of accountability, evaluation, and research, this chapter will present an overview that stresses the relationships between accountability, evaluation, and research. Let us then distinguish among these terms.

In defining accountability, the American Association of School Administrators National Academy for School Executives notes in its *Administrators Handbook on Educational Accountability* that a clear-cut definition of the term is complicated.

> For example, the term appears in the literature frequently with three senses. First is its uncritical usage as synonymous with *responsibility*. A second usage is more critical, suggesting an obligation to explain or account for the disposition of tasks entrusted to an individual. The third sense appears in the form of a partially defined concept peculiar to education—*educational accountability*. This usage conveys the notion that the schools and the educators who operate them be "held to account" (i.e., held both responsible and answerable) for what they produce as "educational outcomes" (i.e., for what students learn.)
>
> Before education borrowed the term and inflated it with its own meanings, accountability expressed a relationship between the occupants of roles that control institutions, the "holders of power"—or stewards— and those who possess the formal power to displace them—reviewers. The scope of this form of accountability includes everything— *everything*—those who hold formal powers of dismissal (the reviewers) find necessary in making their major decision. This decision is whether to continue or to withdraw their confidence in those officeholders held to account (the stewards). From this role relationship, a simple definition of accountability follows: "the requirement on the occupant of a role, by those who authorize that role, to answer for the results of work expected from him in that role."[1]

Leon Lessinger, often referred to as the "father of accountability" for the impetus given this movement during his tenure as Commissioner of Education, defines accountability as responsibility for something, to someone, with predictable consequences for the desirable and understandable performance of the responsibility. In education, accountability means the continuing assessment of the educational achievement of pupils in a school system, the relating of levels of achievement attained to the state and community's educational

---

[1] *An Administrator's Handbook on Educational Accountability,* prepared for American Association of School Administrators National Academy for School Executives, American Association of School Administrators, Arlington, Virginia, 1973, pp. 5–6.

goals and expectations to the parents, teachers, taxpayers, and citizens of the community.[2]

Evaluation has been defined variously by Lessinger and others as the "process of assessment or appraisal of value; the comparison of desired outcomes (objectives) with the actual progress made in actual accomplishments."[3]

Others have defined evaluation as "the task of establishing desired objectives; collecting and organizing information to assess the accomplishment of objectives; judging the adequacy of accomplishments, and making decisions for improving programs;"[4] or "the process of delineating, obtaining, and providing useful information for judging decision alternatives."[5] Indiana University Evaluation Center defined evaluation as

a disciplined system for helping decision makers: a continuous evaluation is a continuous assessment concerned with answering decision-making questions.[6]

Gibson noted that the

process of evaluation seeks to provide objective evidence of a program's performance through an assessment of progress towards program objectives. The evidence collected through this process then becomes valuable as a basis for future program planning and decision making. As such, a planned and conscientious program evaluation is essential to the continuous improvement of school guidance programs.[7]

A definition of evaluation from the National Institute of Mental Health suggests as a working definition that

Program evaluation is a systematic set of data collection and analysis activities undertaken to determine the value of a program to aid management, program planning, staff training, public accountability, and promotion. Evaluation activities make reasonable judgments possible about

---

[2] Leon Lessinger and associates, *Accountability: Systems Planning in Education* (Homewood, Ill.: ETC Publications, 1973).

[3] Ibid, p. 236.

[4] H. E. Wysong, "Accountability: Foiled Fable or Solution?" *Impact,* 2:33 (1972).

[5] D. L. Stufflebeam, W. J. Foley, W. J. Gephart, E. G. Guba, R. L. Hammond, H. O. Merriman, and M. M. Provos, *Educational Evaluation and Decision Making* (Bloomington, Ind.: Phi Delta Kappan Study Committee on Education, 1971), p. 40.

[6] Carl B. Smith and Roger Farr, *Evaluation Training Package,* 2nd ed. (Bloomington, Ind.: Measurement and Evaluation Center in Reading Education, Indiana University, 1971), p. 1.

[7] Robert L. Gibson, *Career Development in the Elementary School* (Columbus, Ohio: Charles E. Merrill Publishing Company, 1972), p. 70.

the efforts, effectiveness, adequacy, efficiency, and comparative value of program options.[8]

A final, easily understood definition views

Evaluation as the determination of the worth of a thing. It includes obtaining information for use in judging the worth of a program, product, procedure, or objective, or the potential utility of alternative approaches designed to attain specified objectives.[9]

A common definition views research as organized scientific efforts that seek the advancement of knowledge. Galfo suggests that "research implies a systematic study of variables in order to determine if and or how they may be related to one another."[10] Oetting and Hawkes note that research is

aimed at the advancement of scientific knowledge. There is no need for research to be immediately useful or practical and there can be great concern for making sure that the exact relationship between independent and dependent variables is known.[11]

Research is the activity aimed at obtaining generalizable knowledge by contriving and testing claims about relationships among variables or describing generalizable phenomena. This knowledge, which may result in theoretical models, functional relationships, or descriptions, may be obtained by empirical or other systematic methods and may or may not have immediate application.[12]

ACCOUNTABILITY

A study of reference books in education published prior to 1970, such as Good's *Dictionary of Education,* will disclose entries for accounting and accountant, but not for accountability. It is safe to say that all such books published in the future will devote space to this concept. Accountability has become the "in" word in education and judging solely from the sheer volume of books, articles, editorials and speeches

---

[8] Homer J. Hagedorn, Kenneth J. Beck, Stephen F. Neubert, and Stanley H. Werlin, *Working Manual of Simple Program Evaluation Techniques For Community Mental Health Centers* (Rockville, Md.: Arthur D. Little, Inc., for National Institute of Mental Health, 1976), p. 3.
[9] Blaine R. Worthen and James R. Sanders, *Educational Evaluation: Theory and Practice* (Worthington, Ohio: Charles A. Jones, 1973), p. 19.
[10] Armand J. Galfo, *Interpreting Educational Research,* 3rd ed. (Dubuque, Iowa: William C. Brown Company, Publishers, 1975), p. 8.
[11] E. R. Oetting and F. J. Hawkes, "Training Professionals for Evaluative Research," *Personnel and Guidance Journal,* **52**:435 (1974).
[12] Blaine R. Worthen and James R. Sanders, op. cit., p. 19.

published since 1969, it seems safe to say that *The Washington Post* may be correct in its designation of education as entering an "age of accountability."[13]

While accountability has been becoming a byword in education, its popularity has also spread to other tax-supported governmental institutions and agencies, including mental health agencies. Thus, with the possible exception of private practice, the likelihood is great that counselors will be employed in settings in which they will be expected to be accountable—to provide factual evidence of their accomplishments related to their costs.[14]

A Positive View of Accountability

Recognizing that many helping professionals have negative attitudes or, at the least, uneasy feelings about accountability, let us accentuate the positive. Baker,[15] in his "Argument for Constructive Accountability," noted five positive aspects of accountability.

a. *Skill acquisition:* Whatever accountability system one uses, certain specific skills are required of the participants. Acquisition of such skills may increase one's satisfaction and confidence. Satisfaction with one's level of competence is associated with knowledge of specific skills possessed. Confidence in one's capacity to encounter new tasks, such as those related to an accountability system, increases with acquisition of new skills. Among those skills that may be acquired or improved through attention to an accountability system are the ability to envision and develop a system; developing data collection instruments; analyzing data; reporting results; making decisions based on acquired results; making plans for future actions based upon acquired results; and applying those plans to a real life setting.

b. *Program improvement:* Conscientious counselors are constantly searching for ways to improve their services. Finding useful sources of evaluative information about the existing services is a universal problem for these people. An accountability system offers the solution to this universal need because data acquired from the accountability activities may be used as the basis for program improvement. As a result, data are used constructively.

c. *Positive results:* Results acquired through an accountability system may be complimentary. Prospects of acquiring complimentary outcomes from accountability studies need to be emphasized more

---

[13] Leon Lessinger & Associates, op. cit., p. 6.

[14] Gibson, Robert L., Unpublished report. Counseling and Annual Guidance Committee. North Central Association of Colleges & Schools, 1977.

[15] Stanley B. Baker, "An Argument for Constructive Accountability," *The Personnel and Guidance Journal,* **56**:53–55 (Sept. 1977).

than is presently the case . . . Such results provide intrinsic rewards for the counselor because awareness of consumer satisfaction or of successful program outcomes provides the counselor with a feeling of satisfaction and accomplishment.

d. *A process rather than an event:* A systematic, ongoing model incorporates the accountability activities and other planned enterprises with a minimum amount of drudgery and maximum efficiency.

e. *Rewards for a job well done:* The ultimate outcome for an accountability system, it seems, is to reward extrinsically those who have demonstrated that their accomplishments are extraordinary. . . . The reward system is viewed as the ultimate outcome because it completes the unfinished accountability model.[16]

Krumboltz[17] also noted that "the potential advantages warrant counselors' efforts to construct a sound accountability system for themselves." Such an accountability system would enable counselors to:

Obtain feedback on the results of their work.

Select counseling methods on the basis of demonstrated success.

Identify students with unmet needs.

Devise shortcuts for routine operations.

Argue for increased staffing to reach attainable goals.

Request training for problems requiring new competencies.

How would counselors benefit from a sensible accountability system? By learning how to help clients more effectively and efficiently, counselors would obtain:

More public recognition for accomplishments.

Increased financial support.

Better working relationships with teachers and administrators.

Acknowledged professional standing.

The satisfaction of performing a constantly improving and valued service.[18]

It is clear from the statements of Baker, Krumboltz, and others that conscientious counselors, dedicated to improving their skills and serving their clientele as effectively and efficiently as possible, have little to fear and much to gain from a system that will be their ally. Accountability may, at last, provide the ultimate proof that programs of counseling and guidance, both in and out of schools, can make a positive difference.

---

[16] Ibid., pp. 53–55.

[17] John D. Krumboltz, "An Accountability Model for Counselors," *The Personnel and Guidance Journal,* **52:**639–646 (June 1974).

[18] Ibid., pp. 639–646.

Developing Accountability in Counseling and Guidance Programs

Krumboltz identified seven criteria to be met if an accountability system is to produce the desired results. These were identified as follows:

1. In order to define the domain of counselor responsibility, the general goals of counseling must be agreed to by all concerned parties.
2. Counselor accomplishments must be stated in terms of important observable behavior changes by clients.
3. Activities of the counselor must be stated as costs, not accomplishments.
4. The accountability system must be constructed to promote professional effectiveness and self-improvement, not to cast blame or punish poor performance.
5. In order to promote accurate reporting, reports of failures and unknown outcomes must be permitted and never punished.
6. All users of the accountability system must be represented in designing it.
7. The accountability system itself must be subject to evaluation and modification.[19]

Although there is no best single approach to developing an accountability model, most programs seem to focus upon some form of needs assessment out of which program objectives are identified and perhaps arranged as to priorities, which, in turn, lead to program activity planning and an accounting for and evaluation of the outcomes. An example of developing an accountability program is described in the *American Association of School Administrators Handbook*. The four phases of this planning are described as follows:

Phase 1. Preliminary Planning

The aim of the preliminary planning phase is to determine informally whether it is feasible to consider some form of accountability. It represents a feasibility study seeking a decision whether to move into Phase 2 or to drop the matter from consideration for the present. Probably only a few key people need to be involved at this point. In framing an answer, it is expected that (a) each of the imperatives offered will have been duly considered, and (b) a positive decision to move ahead to Phase 2 is regarded as "tentative."

Phase 2. Formal Planning

The purpose of Phase 2 is twofold:

a. To place before the community and staff two questions: what *does* our school do? and what *should* it be doing?

---

[19] Ibid., pp. 640–641.

b. To bring together an appropriate group of persons to work on these questions by (1) examining the extant data (for what they say and, sometimes shocking, for what they fail to say): (2) considering alternative ways to meet the questions; and (3) of major importance, developing a consensus of the goals and objectives of an educational program.

Phase 3. Program Implementation

The major concern of Phase 3 centers on the task of further developing the staff and implementing the particular program (e.g., basic reading competency). By now, the major dimensions of the program will have been formed: through the needs assessment, specific problem areas will have been identified; a preliminary and then formal change strategy to involve people in the review of needs, the framing of general goals and performance objectives, and the design of the program will have been employed; and presumably, a generally supportive climate (in terms of attitudes, financial support, realistic time constraints, etc.) will have been established (negotiated?) through community and staff involvement.

Table 13–1.
A Process for Developing an Accountability Program

Phase 1: Preliminary Planning
Assess needs (critical).
Develop a preliminary change strategy (critical).
Consider the use of technical assistance and management systems (optional).
Make decision to move, or not to move, to Phase 2.

Phase 2: Formal Planning
Involve community/staff (critical).
  Repeat needs assessment (optional).
  Repeat change strategy development (optional).
Develop goal consensus and performance objectives (critical).
Consider plan-program-budget system (optional).
Make decision to move, or not to move, to Phase 3.

Phase 3: Program Implementation
Develop program staff (critical).
Implement program procedures (critical).
Consider
  Performance contracting (internal and/or external) (optional).
  Network monitoring (optional).
Reach predetermined completion points of program efforts.

Phase 4: Rendering the Account
Evaluate program (critical).
Report the results (critical).
Use an educational program auditor (optional).
Determine level of confidence (critical).
Certify the nature of results (critical).

Source: *An Administrator's Handbook on Educational Accountability* (Arlington, Va.: American Association of School Administrators, 1973), p. 47.

Phase 4. Rendering the Account

The final phase of the program deals with taking a close look at the efforts and reporting the results in accordance with the plan adopted in Phase 2.[20]

A summary way of viewing the development of this accountability program is shown in Table 13–1.

EVALUATION

Everyone everyday constantly seeks ways to improve many daily routine chores, whether it is trying a new toothpaste or a different breakfast cereal or taking a new route to work. In a sense, people constantly evaluate many daily decisions and activities. People are also involved, usually unofficially, in many external evaluations of the local newspaper, a current TV program, the decisions of Congress, and the teachers, courses, and textbooks with which children come in contact. Just as these evaluations are a part of the process of improving daily living and/or exercising a right to express one's opinions, the more formal, structured evaluations of one's professional activities and organizations should also receive daily and constant attention. As the critics of both education and counseling have so frequently and constantly pointed out in recent years, justifiably or not, evaluative evidence and activities appear to be either missing or misleading at best.[21]

Evaluation: A Process for Professional Improvement

One often reads or hears about the teacher with thirty years' teaching experience but with no mention of the quality of that experience. Experience does not, in and of itself, guarantee improvement and quality. Professionals must have as their own personal-ethical goal the constant and critical evaluation of their professional performance. A lack of evaluation often leads to mediocrity or failure to reach one's full potential in terms of what professionals might accomplish for clients, students, or others they serve. Evaluation, then, for counselors in a variety of settings and for other professionals, is first and foremost a process for professional improvement, a process in which one gathers objective, performance-oriented data on a systematic and nonbiased basis. These data one then utilizes as information that leads to constantly improving, upgrading, and updating one's professional performance.

[20] *An Administrator's Handbook on Educational Accountability,* op. cit., pp. 35–44.
[21] Marianne H. Mitchell, Unpublished paper. Annual Counseling and Guidance Workshop. (Indiana University, June, 1976).

Evaluation: Providing Information for Decision Makers

Amidst the changing concepts of evaluation in recent decades, one of the most popular among evaluation experts is the view of evaluation as a process for providing information for decision makers. A leader in this decision-management approach to evaluation, D. L. Stufflebeam, developed the CIPP (context, input, process, product) evaluation model. This model affirms that "evaluation is the process of delineating, obtaining, and providing useful information for judging decision alternatives"[22] and suggests several key points as follows:

1. Evaluation is performed in the service of *decision making;* hence, it should provide information which is useful to decision makers.
2. Evaluation is a cyclic, continuing *process* and, therefore, must be implemented through a systematic program.
3. The evaluation process includes the three main steps of delineating, obtaining, and providing. These steps provide the basis for a methodology of evaluation.
4. The delineating and providing steps in the evaluation process are *interface* activities requiring collaboration between evaluator and decision maker, while the obtaining step is largely a *technical* activity which is executed mainly by the evaluator.[23]

Thus, evaluation is also viewed as a process that can provide decision makers at all levels with objective data, which will assist them in determining the relative value of competing alternatives and which will immeasurably improve their probability of making the "right decision."

Evaluation: Other Functions

The wide range of evaluation purposes may seem to rival that of the political party platforms of "promising something for everybody!" Although that is not the intent, it is important to recognize some of the values of this activity. Examples of these additional functions of evaluation are as follows:

1. Verifies or rejects practices by providing evidence as to what works and what doesn't, or the degree to which an activity seems to be effective. This also tends to lead to the avoidance of meaningless innovations and unproven fads.
2. Measures improvement by providing evidence on a continuous basis so that both rate and level of progress may be ascertained.

[22] Daniel L. Stufflebeam, et al., *Educational Evaluation and Decision Making* (Itasca, Ill.: F. E. Peacock Publishers, Inc., 1971).
[23] Ibid.

3. Enhances probability of growth by providing a basis for improvements in the operation and its activities.
4. Builds credibility—by the very nature of the activity, evaluation suggests a continuous search for better ways of doing things; a constant quest for improvement; a willingness to put efforts on the line and take a look at "how we're doing!"
5. Provides for increased insights—by the fact of examining our own or an organization's functioning, we become more knowledgeable and understanding about this functioning; more aware of influencing factors and potential consequences.
6. Increases and improves participation in decision making—because evaluation involves everyone within the organizational structure, the process, by necessity, involves them in the outcomes, which in turn *should* bring about the participation of all such personnel in the planning of new directions and in implementing the findings.
7. Places responsibilities—by identifying "who is responsible for what and when," evaluation stimulates linkages between specific individuals and specific activities. It decreases the probability of everyone claiming responsibility for the successes and no one claiming the failures.
8. Provides a rationality for the enterprise by improving overall accountability, including evidence of accomplishments and growth.

Principles of Evaluation

Because evaluation is a process for appraising the value or effectiveness of a program or activity, it is most effective when conducted within a framework of guiding principles. Six of these are discussed in the following paragraphs.[24]

Effective evaluation requires a recognition of program goals. Before any meaningful program of evaluation can be undertaken, it is essential that the goals or objectives of that program be clearly identified. These objectives provide indications of program intent, which form the basis for subsequent planning and procedures. The objectives of the program should be stated in clear and measurable terminology. This principle suggests that school guidance programs be evaluated on the basis of "how well it is doing what it set out to do."

Effective evaluation requires valid measuring criteria. Once program goals are clearly defined, valid criteria for measuring progress towards those goals must be identified. The development of such criteria is crucial if the evaluation is to be both valid and meaningful. For example, if an annual program goal for a junior community college guidance program would be to provide each entering student with a series of three career interviews with a counselor, the measuring criteria could be a simple count indicating the percentage of

---

[24] Robert L. Gibson, op. cit., pp. 70–72.

students who did, in fact, have such an opportunity. If, on the other hand, the program goal was to provide each student with "a broadening of his career understanding," the measuring criteria would be less obvious and might be dependent on a further refinement of what is meant by "career understanding." In other words, vaguely stated goals and vaguely stated criteria lessen the effectiveness of program evaluation.

Effective program evaluation is dependent on valid application of the measuring criteria. As discussed in the previous paragraph, valid criteria for measuring progress toward the program's stated goals must be established. It is not sufficient, however, to merely establish criteria. Their ultimate validity will depend on their valid application. This implies that effective evaluation of all counseling programs should involve, in each instance, individuals who are professionally competent in both evaluation techniques and understandings of such counseling programs. Too often, effective evaluation criteria are dissipated in the hands of evaluators who have, at best, only a superficial knowledge of appropriate role and functions of guidance programs.

Program evaluation should involve all who are affected. Evaluation of the school guidance program should involve those who are participants in or affected by the program. This would include, in addition to the guidance staff, faculty members, and administrators, students and their parents, and, on appropriate occasion, members of the community or supporting agencies. The major contribution to effective evaluation must come from those who have a first-hand knowledge or involvement in the program. External evaluators from governmental agencies, accrediting associations, or other educational institutions can, of course, be helpful, but those should not be the sole bases of evaluation.

Meaningful evaluation requires feedback and follow-through. The evaluation process and the evaluation report are not in and of themselves of great value. It is only when the results are used for program improvement and development that the evaluation process takes on meaning. This presumes, then, that the results of any program evaluation are made available to those concerned with the program management and development. It also presumes that the program manager and his or her staff will use these results for future program planning, development, and decision making.

Evaluation is most effective as a planned, continuous process. Inasmuch as pupil guidance is a continuous process, the assessment of such a program is most effective when planned as a continuous process. This means that there are specific plans and designated responsibilities for both the ongoing evaluation of a program's progress and the more extensive annual or semi-annual reviews.

Evaluation emphasizes the positive. Frequently, evaluation is viewed as a threatening process aimed at ferreting out hidden weaknesses and spotlighting "goofs." If program evaluation is to produce the most meaningful results possible, it must be conducted in a spirit that is positive, that is aimed at facilitating program improvement, and that emphasizes strengths as well as weaknesses.

Methods of Evaluation

Before-and-After Method.   This method of evaluation seeks to identify the progress that takes place in a program's development as a result of specific program activities over a given period of time. For example, an objective of a school guidance program might be to provide each student a weekend work experience during his/her junior year. At the beginning of the school year, before the program, one could presume that none had had this experience. At the end of the year, after the program, the number who actually participated would give some indication of goal achievement.

Comparison Methods.   The "how-do-we-compare" process makes evaluations on the basis of comparing one group against another or against the norm of a number of groups. Different techniques for achieving the same goal can also be evaluated by this comparative method. For example, a secondary school in Bloomington, Indiana, might note that it has a pupil-counselor ratio of 1 to 258, compared to the norm for 200 midwestern secondary schools of 1 to 418. Such a comparison would indicate, of course, that the Bloomington school system is making more adequate provisions for high school counseling personnel than most other school systems in the Midwest.

The "How-Do-We-Stand" Method.   This particular method is based on the identification of desirable program outcomes and related characteristics and criteria. From these criteria, rating scales, checklists, and questionnaires may be developed and used to indicate the degree to which a program measures up. For example, evaluative criteria or checklists utilized by most accrediting associations and many state departments of education reflect this approach. Although this approach to evaluation may locally ignore appropriate objectives and sometimes unique and innovative practices, it does provide guidelines that enable guidance programs to be compared with generally accepted standards.

An example of a simple checklist that could be used with appropriate modifications to evaluate an elementary or secondary school guidance program might include some of the items shown in Table 13–2.

Procedures for Evaluation

The evaluation process usually involves a series of activities in a sequence, which approximates the following.

Identification of goals to be assessed. The first step establishes the parameters, or limits, for the evaluation. Evaluation can focus on the total guidance program or on only one or several particular objectives. These program objectives should be stated in clear, concise, specific, and measurable terms. Broadly stated goals (for example, "to facilitate the adjustment of the student body of J. J. Jenkins High School") are much more difficult to measure than, for example, a specifically stated goal, such as, "to provide each student in Penny Junior High School a yearly scheduled opportunity to discuss his/her career planning with a school counselor."

Development of an evaluation plan. Once the objectives for evaluation have been established, the identification and validation of criteria appropriate for measuring the program's progress toward these objectives follows. In the previous example, a simple, yet valid, criterion would be an indication of the percentage of the Penny Junior High School students who actually did have a scheduled career-planning interview with a school counselor. This example is illustrative of the principle that measuring criteria should also be stated in specific and objective terms. The overall evaluation plan, in addition to specifying the kinds of data to be collected, should also specify how it will be collected, when, and by whom. This plan must also give attention to how the data will be organized and reported, and to whom. Finally, such a plan should conclude with provisions for utilizing the findings for future program development.

Application of the evaluation plan. After an acceptable evaluation plan has been designed, its validity is then dependent on the manner in which it is carried out. Once again we stress the importance of adequate planning and a positive approach, utilizing evaluators who possess the necessary understanding and competency. Timing is also important because some aspects of a program can only be appropriately evaluated in a "longitudinal" sense, whereas other specific activities need an "immediately after" assessment.

Utilization of the findings. Evaluation as an activity is in itself of little value. It is in the application of the findings that the real worth of evaluation lies. Through the process of evaluation, programs can ascertain their strengths and weaknesses. The resulting insights may then provide directions for future program improvement. The utilization of these findings, however, cannot be left to mere chance. There must be planning, with specific responsibilities for the utilization of the findings, and subsequent follow-up to establish the degree to which the evaluation recommendations have been fulfilled.

Evaluation for Community Mental Health Counseling Programs

As with educational programs, including those of counseling and guidance in schools, community mental health center programs have also felt pressures to conduct systematic program evaluations, partly as the result of the increasing demands of the federal government to verify program efficiency and effectiveness in community mental health centers. In this regard, Public Law

Table 13–2.
Checklist to Evaluate a Guidance Program

	Yes	No
1. The objectives of the school guidance program are stated and understood by		
(a) guidance staff		
(b) faculty		
(c) administration		
(d) parents.		
2. These objectives are consistent with the overall educational objectives of the institution.		
3. There is a planned program for achieving the guidance objectives.		
4. The planning of this program cooperatively involved		
(a) guidance staff		
(b) faculty		
(c) administration		
(d) parents and/or community personnel.		
5. The program itself involves		
(a) guidance staff		
(b) teaching faculty		
(c) community resource personnel.		
6. The school guidance program is under the direction of a trained and certified school counselor.		
7. The professional staff of the school guidance program is composed of trained and certified school counselors.		
8. The school guidance program makes provisions for pupils to		
(a) receive regular periodic interpretations of their school guidance records, including standardized test results		
(b) identify and practice good study habits		
(c) understand the relationship between educational preparation and the career opportunities		
(d) integrate career information with subject matter knowledge		
(e) participate in special career development activities		
(f) participate in special human relationship development activities		
(g) participate in small group counseling		
(h) have individual counseling with a school counselor.		
9. The guidance program makes provisions for		
(a) working cooperatively with faculty in providing appropriate informational and developmental activities for pupils		
(b) assessing school-community resources for guidance		
(c) parental conferences		
(d) resource materials for teacher, pupil, and parent use.		
10. The guidance program is evaluated on a regular basis.		
11. This evaluation involves		
(a) guidance staff		
(b) school administration		
(c) faculty		
(d) pupils		

Table 13–2 Cont.
Checklist to Evaluate a Guidance Program

	Yes	No
(e) others (consultants, parents, community resource personnel).	————	————
12. The results of evaluation are utilized for program planning and improvement.	————	————
13. The achievements and activities of the program are reported regularly to		
(a) the school administration	————	————
(b) faculty	————	————
(c) parents	————	————
(d) interested and involved community personnel.	————	————

94–63, The Community Mental Health Centers Amendments of 1975, requires community mental health to allocate not less than 2 per cent of their previous year's operating budgets for the conducting of program evaluation. The law mandates three general types of evaluation, as follows:

1. Quality assurance of clinical services.
   Each center is to establish an ongoing quality assurance of its clinical services.
2. Self-evaluation
   Each center will collect data and evaluate its services in relation to program goals and values and to catchment area needs and resources. "The data shall consist of (a) Cost of center operations; (b) Patterns of use of services; (c) Availability, awareness, acceptability, and accessibility of services; (d) Impact of services upon the mental health of residents of the catchment area; (e) Effectiveness of consultation and education services; (f) The impact of the Center on reducing inappropriate institutionalization."[25]

3. Residents' review:

   Each center will at least annually publicize and make available all evaluation data of the type listed above to residents of the catchment area. In addition, it will organize and publicize an opportunity for citizens to review the Center's program of services in order to assure that services are responsive to the needs of residents of the catchment area.[26]

[25] *A Working Manual of Simple Program Evaluation Techniques for Community Mental Health Centers,* National Institute of Mental Health, U.S. Department of Health, Education and Welfare, 1976, p. 6.
[26] Ibid., p. 7.

RESEARCH

It must be acknowledged that research has an unpopular image. It is appropriate to recognize some of the frequently stated reasons for this unpopularity.

Most research seems to ignore the common problems and everyday needs of practitioners.

Most research reports are written in a manner that limits their interpretation and hence their application by practitioners.

Research activities and resulting research reports rarely "excite the imagination."

The research monies made available by federal and state agencies are "cornered" by universities and private research and development corporations.

Research is too time-consuming and has very few "rewards" for most practitioners.

All of these concerns may have some basis in fact, as Goldman, in his Introduction to *Research Methods for Counselors,* notes.

> From 1969 to 1975 I was editor of the *Personnel and Guidance Journal.* I resolved from the beginning that we would publish only those articles that had something to say to counseling practitioners, that we were a reader's not a writer's journal. We found almost no research manuscripts during those years that satisfied that criterion; quite a few research reports were received, especially in the earlier years, but almost every one of them either was so technical that it could not be truly understood except by very research-sophisticated people, or was so limited in its implications that it really had nothing to offer the practicing counselor. . . . I came to the realization that the problem was not "research" as a general idea but rather the *kinds* of research that have predominated in our field. I became convinced that the kinds of research methods and the kinds of research studies that prevail in the field are largely inappropriate or inadequate for most of the kinds of knowledge and insight counselors require in their daily work.[27]

Although many concur with Goldman's concerns, it should be pointed out that research can provide (1) positive outcomes; (2) some clarifying research definitions; and (3) research can be carried out by even beginning practitioners within a simple framework of research procedures.

---

[27] Leo Goldman, ed. *Research Methods for Counselors* (New York: John Wiley & Sons, Inc., 1978), pp. 4–5.

Positive Outcomes of Research

For general practitioners in counseling and other helping professions, the most positive general outcome of "practitioner research" is the improvement of one's professional skills and understanding. Research can provide answers to professional questions, dilemmas, and failures. Research enables practitioners to become better at their "art." It can enable us to verify what works and what doesn't and, if pursued, why. It can eliminate much of the guesswork, "hunch," and uncertainty from practices. Engaging in practical research can increase our insights and deeper understandings of ourselves, our profession, and relationships between the two. Our own research can help us as individual professionals become better at what we do.

Too, practitioner's research tends to focus on "local" problems or concerns and may, therefore, have opportunities to provide results that are immediately applicable. The opportunities to "make a positive difference" in one's job environment can be challenging. Further, even if practitioners tend to focus on local concerns in their research activities, that still gives them the opportunities to make contributions to their profession; to exchange their ideas and findings with other similar local settings and other interested professionals. Presentations and discussions at local, state, and national conferences give the local researcher further opportunity to share findings, explore with other professionals the implications of the results, and possibly expand the interpretation of the research findings.

Finally, research can be interesting. Any new experience, learning of new knowledge, or finding an answer to an old problem can be stimulating. Research only becomes "dull" and meaningless to researchers when they investigate topics or problems that are to them dull and meaningless. Identify a professional question (problem or concern) that you would personally like answered, and set out to find the answer. You may find it a surprisingly exciting quest, and you may then agree that research can be one of the most exciting and rewarding professional activities.

Some Definitions

Basic Research. Basic research may be viewed as that which is concerned or conducted solely for the purpose of theory development or the establishing of general principles. In educational and other settings, basic research provides the theory which, in turn, produces implications for solving problems.

Applied Research. Applied research provides data to support theory through applying or testing the theory and evaluating its usefulness in problem solving.

Action Research. Action research is designed to solve problems through the application of scientific method. For example,

Action research provides a systematic framework in which the practicing counselor, therapist, or other professional in the helping field can solve problems and determine the effectiveness of his or her work. Action research provides a model for the evaluation of the effectiveness of an individual, a single program or a totality of guidance services.[28]

Historical Research.

Historical research involves studying, understanding, and explaining past events. The purpose of historical research is to arrive at conclusions concerning causes, effects or trends of past occurrences which may help to explain present events and anticipate future events.[29]

Galfo discusses four types of historical methods as follows:

1. Cross-checking pieces of evidence against each other.
2. Establishing authorship of a document by comparative study.
3. Investigations of chronological events.
4. Word and language interpretation.[30]

Descriptive Research. Descriptive research seeks to test hypotheses or answer questions concerning the present. Three common types of descriptive studies are surveys, case studies, and comparative studies.[31]

Experimental Research. Experimental research experiments with different variables in order to predict what will occur in the future under a given set of conditions.

Experimental educational research has been derived from the laboratory method often used in the natural sciences. In its most elementary form, the experimental method of science is based upon two assumptions regarding variables which may be identified in the phenomenon under investigation:

1. If two situations are equal in every respect except for a factor present in one of the situations, any difference which appears between the two situations can be attributed to the factor. This statement is referred to as the "law of the single variable."
2. If two situations are not equal but it can be demonstrated that none of the variables are significant in producing the phenomenon under investigation; or if significant variables are made equal, any difference occurring between the two situations after the introduction of a new variable to one of the systems can be attributed to

---

[28] Ibid., p. 80.
[29] L. R. Gay, *Educational Research: Competencies for Analysis and Application* (Columbus, Ohio: Charles E. Merrill Publishing Company, 1976), p. 9.
[30] Armand J. Galfo, op. cit., p. 15.
[31] Ibid., p. 15.

the new variable. This statement is referred to as the "law of the only significant variable."

The purpose of establishing experimental-control conditions, thus, is to create a situation in which the effect of a single variable can be studied.[32]

Pilot Study. A pilot study is a preliminary trial of research methods and instruments prior to the development of the final research plan.

Hypotheses. Hypotheses are predictions regarding the probable outcome of a research study which, in turn, form a basis for goals and procedures to achieve these goals.

Sampling. Sampling is a research technique for selecting a specified number of people from a defined population as representative of that specific population.

The Research Process

Some research undoubtedly requires complex, sophisticated research skills. However, much valuable information can be obtained through research that meets the requirements of scientific inquiry but does not require a high level of research skill. As noted by Cramer, "Elegance of design is not the ultimate test of the adequacy of research. The test is whether the objectives of the researcher are furthered and whether these objectives turn out to be useful."[33]

Thus, the following examination of research procedures is not intended to provide a basis for undertaking research, but, rather, to provide a better understanding of the basic factors involved in conducting research. It is hoped it will encourage practitioners to consider and become involved in relatively unsophisticated research investigations.

The first step in undertaking educational research is the identification of a researchable problem—a need for information. Whatever stimulates your interest or curiosity or arouses doubts in you may be a basis for the identification of a research problem. Most of us experience a constant and continuing need for information in our daily jobs. We wonder about the adequacy or effectiveness of our techniques, the various characteristics of our clients, and the nature of client needs. If we decide to initiate research in the area of techniques, we might simply seek to determine the kinds of information needed for justifying present practices or developing more effective and functional ones.

A second step in most research in education is to review or survey previous research and writings relevant to the possible research topic. The purposes of this review are (1) to see if adequate answers have already been

---

[32] Ibid., pp. 17–18.
[33] Stanley H. Cramer, et al., *Research and the School Counselor* (Boston: Houghton Mifflin Company, 1970).

found to the questions the researcher has in mind; (2) to gain a better under-standing of the nature of the problem; and (3) to gain insights regarding approaches that might be used to efficiently attain the outcomes desired. Although in the past this particular step may have been one that discouraged many from considering research activities, the developing computer capacities of libraries with their various information retrieval systems enable even the neophyte researcher to have in hand, in a short period of time, a computerized printout of relevant research and writings, usually summarized for conve-nience.

The third step is to identify specifically the nature of the information desired, or to formulate the specific research problem. The problem should be stated fully and precisely in objective terminology in a complete grammati-cal sentence.

> One way to test your statement as a problem is to determine if it is written in such a way that anyone anywhere could read it, understand it, and react to it without the benefit of your presence.[34]

The beginning researcher should also be aware that within the main problem there may be logical subcomponents, identified as subproblems.

> By being solved separately these sub-problems resolve the main problem piecemeal. By looking at the main problem through its sub-problems, the researcher frequently gets a more global view of the problem. Think of a problem, therefore, in terms of its component sub-problems. Rather than make a frontal attack upon the entire problem, divide and conquer it in small segments.[35]

The fourth step in the research process is to determine the kinds of information needed to permit sound conclusions about the issue (or issues) in question. In this step, the previously stated problem and related subprob-lems are now viewed through questions or logical constructs, called hypothe-ses. Hypotheses are assumptions made regarding the problem or its solution that provide the researcher some direction for the gathering of facts that will provide the most valid answers. For example, a research investigation may be attempting to determine why a school has an unusually high dropout rate. It could be hypothesized that there are several possibilities for this dropout rate, as follows: (1) students are not interested in school; (2) students lack the ability to continue in school; (3) students are under economic pressure to leave school and obtain a job. Thus, each of these assumptions or hypotheses would provide some direction or basis for identifying facts, which would

---

[34] Paul D. Leedy, *Practical Research: Planning and Design* (New York: Macmillan Publishing Co., Inc., 1974), p. 49.
[35] Ibid., p. 51.

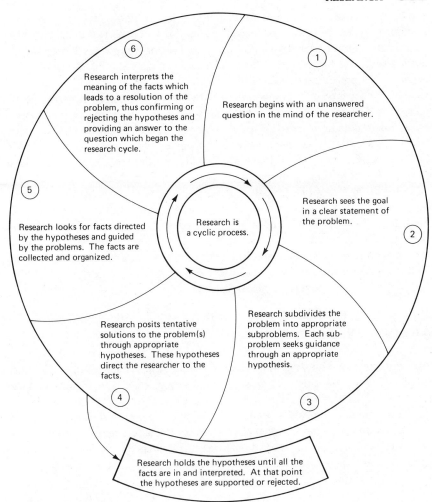

Figure 13–1.
The research process. *Paul D. Leedy,* Practical Research: Planning and Design *(New York: Macmillan Publishing Co., Inc., 1974), p. 8.*

enable the investigator to determine factually why the majority of students are leaving school.

Having determined the kinds of information needed, in the fifth step, the researcher determines what procedures are most appropriate for collecting and analyzing the data. In this stage, the population or sample to be used and the means by which it is to be selected are determined, as are instruments and other data-collecting tools appropriate for the questions or hypotheses that have been stated. In this fifth step, the researcher seeks to determine the most appropriate sampling procedures and the most appropriate, efficient, and effective instruments and/or techniques for gathering the data needed in order to respond to the hypotheses as completely and as validly as possible.

Once the types of information needed and the procedures and instruments needed for collecting this information have been determined, the sixth step is the actual collection of the data.

In the seventh step, the collected data are systematically organized and analyzed. The method of data analysis should be determined prior to the collection of data in order to ensure that the suggested treatment is appropriate to the data collected and the manner in which it is organized. Depending on the research design developed in step five of this sequence, the analysis may be no more than a simple mathematical or elementary statistical one.

Beginning practitioners can still engage profitably in research activities by simply recognizing their limitations in the design of their study. In the final step, the research findings are interpreted and conclusions drawn, which may lead to the resolving or answering of the problems. Here the previously stated hypotheses are either confirmed or rejected and answers are provided to the questions that initiated the research activity.

Figure 13–1 depicts the research process.

SUMMARY

Accountability, evaluation, and research are all responsibilities of counseling programs and counselors in any setting. Although each is a distinct activity in its own right, the interrelationships are evident. Further, all three activities hold promise for the advancement of the professional and the profession. Accountability provides a model or method for the assessment of professional achievements. Evaluation enables one to gather evidence regarding the quality of a program's performance. Research enables one to advance the scientific knowledge in a field.

Bibliography

Abbott, Langer and Associates. *Compensation in the Guidance and Counseling Field.* Park Forest, Ill.: 1977.

American Association of School Administrators. *An Administrator's Handbook on Educational Accountability.* Prepared for American Association of School Administrator's National Academy for School Executives. Arlington, Va. 1973.

Anastasi, Anne. *Psychological Testing,* 4th ed. New York: Macmillan Publishing Co., Inc., 1976.

Arbuckle, Dugald S. *Counseling and Psychotherapy: An Existential-Humanistic View,* 3d ed. Boston: Allyn and Bacon, Inc., 1975.

Beers, Clifford. *A Mind That Found Itself.* New York: Longmans Green and Company, 1908.

Belkin, Gary S. *Practical Counseling in the Schools.* Dubuque, Iowa: William C. Brown Company, Publishers, 1975.

————, ed., *Counseling: Directions in Theory and Practice.* Dubuque, Iowa: Kendall/Hunt Publishing Company, 1976.

Benjamin, Alfred. *The Helping Interview,* 2d ed. Boston: Houghton Mifflin Company, 1974.

Bennett, Lawrence A., and Thomas S. Rosenbaum. *Counseling in Correctional Environments.* New Vistas in Counseling Series vol. 6. New York: Human Sciences Press, 1978.

Berenson, B. G., and R. R. Carkhuff, eds. *Sources of Gain in Counseling and Psychotherapy.* New York: Holt, Rinehart and Winston, Inc., 1967.

Bernard, Harold W. *Principles of Guidance,* 2d ed. New York: Thomas Y. Crowell Company, 1977.

Blackham, Garth J. *Counseling: Theory, Process and Practice.* Belmont, Calif: Wadsworth Publishing Company, Inc., 1977.

———, and Silberman. *Modification of Child and Adolescent Behavior,* 2d ed. Belmont, Calif: Wadsworth Publishing Company, Inc., 1975.

Bloom, Benjamin S. *Human Characteristics and School Learning.* New York: McGraw-Hill, Inc., 1976.

Bolles, Richard N. *What Color Is Your Parachute?* Berkeley, Calif.: Ten Speed Press, 1976.

Brammer, L. M. *The Helping Relationship: Process and Skills,* 2d ed. Englewood Cliffs, N.J.: Prentice-Hall, Inc., 1979.

Bruce, Alice. *The Guidance Function.* Highland Park, N.J.: Essence Publications, 1977.

Burks, Herbert M., Jr., and Buford Stefflre. *Theories of Counseling,* 3rd ed. New York: McGraw Hill, Inc., 1979.

Buros, Oscar K., ed. *Tests in Print II: An Index to Tests, Test Reviews and the Literature on Specific Tests.* Highland Park, N.J.: Gryphon Press, 1974.

Calia, Vincent F., and Raymond L. Corsini. *Critical Incidents in School Counseling.* Englewood Cliffs, N.J.: Prentice-Hall, Inc., 1973.

Campbell, David. *If You Don't Know Where You Are Going, You'll Probably End Up Somewhere Else.* Niles, Ill.: Argus Communications, 1974.

Caplan, G. *The Theory and Practice of Mental Health Consultation.* New York: Basic Books, Inc., Publishers, 1970.

Carkhuff, Robert R., and B. G. Berenson. *Beyond Counseling and Therapy.* New York: Holt Rinehart and Winston, Inc., 1967.

———. *Helping and Human Relations:* vols. 1 and 2. New York: Holt, Rinehart and Winston, Inc., 1969.

———, and William A. Anthony. *The Skills of Helping: An Introduction to Counseling Skills.* Human Resource Development Press, Inc., Box 863, Dept. M65, Amherst, Mass. 01002 1979.

Corey, Gerald. *Theory and Practice of Counseling and Psychotherapy.* Monterey, Calif.: Brooks/Cole Publishing Company, 1977.

———, Marianne Schneider Corey, and Patrick Callanan. *Professional and Ethical Issues in Counseling and Psychotherapy.* Monterey, Calif.: Brooks/Cole Publishing Company, 1979.

Cormier, William H., and L. Sherilyn Cormier. *Interviewing Strategies for Helpers: A Guide to Assessment, Treatment and Evaluation.* Monterey, Calif.: Brooks/Cole Publishing Company, 1979.

Corsini, Raymond, ed., 2d ed. *Current Psychotherapies.* Itasca, Ill.: F. E. Peacock Publishers, Inc., 1979.

Crites, John O. *Vocational Psychology.* New York: McGraw-Hill Book Company, 1969.

Crozier, Colin. *Moral Values Clarification.* Toronto, Ontario, Canada: Ministry of Education, 1975.

Dinkmeyer, Don, and W. L. Pew. *Adlerian Counseling and Psychotherapy.* Monterey, Calif.: Brooks/Cole Publishing Company, 1978.

Dodson, Laura S. *Family Counseling: A Systems Approach.* Muncie, Ind.: Accelerated Development, 1977.

Dollard, John, and N. E. Miller. *Personality and Psychotherapy.* New York: McGraw-Hill, Inc., 1966.

Dye, H. Allan, and Harold Hackney. *Gestalt Approaches to Counseling.* Boston: Houghton Mifflin Company, 1975.

Egan, Gerard. *The Skilled Helper: A Model for Systematic Helping and Interpersonal Relating.* Monterey, Calif.: Brooks/Cole Publishing Company, 1975.

————. *Interpersonal Living: A Skills Contract Approach to Human-Relations Training in Groups.* Monterey, Calif.: Brooks/Cole Publishing Company, 1976.

Eisenberg, Sheldon, and Daniel J. Delaney. *The Counseling Process,* 2d ed. Chicago: Rand McNally College Publishing Company, 1977.

————, and Lewis E. Patterson. *Helping Clients with Special Concerns.* Chicago: Rand McNally College Publishing Company, 1979.

Ellis, Albert. *A Guide to Rational Living.* Englewood Cliffs, N.J.: Prentice-Hall, Inc., 1961.

Farwell, Gail F., Neal R. Gamsky, and Phillipa Mathieu-Coughlan, eds. *The Counselor's Handbook.* New York: Intext Educational, 1974.

Faust, Verne. *The Counselor-Consultant in the Elementary School.* Boston: Houghton Mifflin Company, 1968.

Foster, Betty. *Teaching Children Moral Values Through Hominological Counseling.* Pueblo, Colo.: Nationwide Press, 1977.

Foxley, Cecelia H. *Nonsexist Counseling: Helping Women and Men Redefine Their Roles.* Dubuque, Iowa: Kendall/Hunt Publishing Company, 1979.

Frankl, Viktor. *Man's Search for Meaning.* New York: Washington Square Press, 1963.

Gazda, George M. *Human Relations Development.* Boston: Allyn and Bacon, Inc., 1973.

————. *Group Counseling: A Developmental Approach,* 2d ed. Boston: Allyn and Bacon, Inc., 1978.

George, R. L., and T. S. Cristiani. *Theories, Methods and Processes of Counseling and Psychotherapy.* Englewood Cliffs, N.J.: Prentice-Hall, Inc., 1981.

Gibson, Robert L. *Career Development in the Elementary School.* Columbus, Ohio: Charles E. Merrill Publishing Company, 1972.

Goldman, Leo, ed. *Research Methods for Counselors.* New York: John Wiley & Sons, Inc., 1978.

Goodman, Joel, ed. *Turning Points: New Developments, New Directions in Values Clarification.* Saratoga Springs, N.Y.: Creative Resources Press, 1978–1979.

Goodstein, Leonard D. *Consulting with Human Service Systems.* Reading, Mass.: Addison-Wesley Publishing Co., Inc., 1978.

Gordon, Sol. *Sexuality Today and Tomorrow.* N. Scituate, Mass.: Duxbury Press, 1976.

Gray, H. Dean, and Judy A. Tindall. *Peer Counseling: In-Depth Look at Peer Helping.* Muncie, Ind.: Accelerated Development Press, Inc., 1978.

Gysbers, Norman C., Harry N. Drier, Jr., and Earl J. Moore, eds. *Developing Careers in the Elementary School.* Columbus, Ohio: Charles E. Merrill Publishing Company, 1973.

Hansen, James C., Richard W. Warner, and Elsie M. Smith. *Group Counseling: Theory and Process.* Chicago: Rand McNally & Company, 1976.

————, Richard R. Stevic, and Richard W. Warner, Jr. *Counseling: Theory and Process,* 2d ed. Boston: Allyn and Bacon, Inc., 1977.

Hansen, L. Sunny, and Rita S. Rapoza. *Career Development and Counseling of Women.* Springfield, Ill.: Charles C Thomas, Publisher, 1978.

Hardy, Richard E., and John G. Cull. *Group Counseling and Therapy Techniques in Special Settings.* Springfield, Ill.: Charles C Thomas, Publisher, 1974.

Harmin, Merrill, Howard Kirschenbaum, and Sidney B. Simon. *Clarifying Values Through Subject-Matter.* Minneapolis: Winston Press, 1973.

Harmon, Lenore W., Janice M. Birk, Laurine E. Fitzgerald, and Mary Faith Tanney, eds. *Counseling Women.* Monterey, Calif.: Brooks/Cole Publishing Company, 1978.

Hart, Gordon M. *Values Clarification for Counselors.* Springfield, Ill.: Charles C Thomas, Publisher, 1978.

Hawley, Robert C., and Isabel L. Hawley. *Human Values in the Classroom: A Handbook for Teachers.* New York: Hart Publishing Company, Inc., 1975.

Hennessey, Thomas C., ed. *Value Moral Education: The Schools and the Teachers.* New York: Paulist Press, 1979.

Herr, Edwin L., and Stanley H. Cramer. *Career Guidance Through the Life Span.* Boston: Little Brown & Company, 1979.

Holland, John L. *Making Vocational Choices: A Theory of Careers.* Englewood Cliffs, N.J.: Prentice-Hall, Inc., 1973.

Hollis, J. W., and R. A. Wantz. *Counselor Education Directory, 1980.* Muncie, Ind.: Accelerated Development, Inc., 1980.

Hoppock, Robert. *Occupational Information,* 4th ed. New York: McGraw-Hill, Inc., 1976.

Horan, John J. *Counseling for Effective Decision-Making.* N. Scituate, Mass.: Duxbury Press, 1979.

Howe, Leland W., and Mary Martha Howe. *Personalizing Education: Values Clarification and Beyond.* New York: Hart Publishing Company, Inc., 1975.

Hyde, Janet Shibley. *Understanding Human Sexuality.* New York: McGraw Hill Book Company, 1979.

Hyman, Herbert H. *Education's Lasting Influence on Values.* Chicago: University of Chicago Press, 1979.

Isaacson, Lee E. *Career Information in Counseling and Teaching.* Boston: Allyn and Bacon, Inc., 1974.

Ivey, Allen E., and Jerry Authier. *Microcounseling: Innovations in Interviewing, Counseling, Psychotherapy and Psychoeducation,* 2d ed. Springfield, Ill.: Charles C Thomas, Publisher, 1978.

Johnson, M. Clemens. *A Review of Research Methods in Education.* Chicago: Rand McNally & Company, 1977.

Kirschenbaum, Howard. *Advanced Value Clarification.* LaJolla, Calif.: University Associates, 1977.

Kniker, Charles R. *You and Values Education.* Columbus, Ohio: Charles E. Merrill Publishing Company, 1977.

Koberg, Don, and Jim Bagnall. *Values Tech: The Polytechnic School of Values.* Wm. Kaufmann, Inc., One First Street, Los Altos, Calif. 94022 1976.

Krumboltz, John D., and Carl B. Thoreson. *Revolution in Counseling: Implications of Behavioral Science.* Boston: Houghton Mifflin Company, 1966.

———, and C. E. Thoreson. *Counseling Methods.* New York: Holt, Rinehart and Winston, Inc., 1976.

Lamb, H. Richard and Associates. *Rehabilitation in Community Mental Health.* San Francisco: Josey-Bass, Inc., Publishers, 1971.

Lessinger, Leon and Associates. *Accountability: Systems Planning in Education.* Creta D. Sabine, ed. Homewood, Ill.: ETC Publications, 1973.

Lewis, Judith A., and Michael D. Lewis. *Community Counseling.* New York: John Wiley & Sons, Inc., 1977.

Lippitt, Gordon, and Ronald Lippitt. *The Consulting Process in Action.* LaJolla, Calif.: University Associates, 1978.

Loughary, John W., and Theresa M. Ripley. *Second Chance, Everybody's Guide to Career Change.* Eugene, Oreg.: United Learning Corporation, 1975.

McCary, James L. *McCary's Human Sexuality,* 3d ed. New York: D. Van Nostrand Company, 1978.

Maslow, Abraham H. *Toward a Psychology of Being,* 2d ed. New York: D. Van Nostrand Company, 1968.

Mitchell, Marianne H. *The Counselor and Sexuality.* Boston: Houghton Mifflin Company, 1973.

Muro, James J., and Don C. Dinkmeyer. *Counseling in the Elementary and Middle Schools.* Dubuque, Iowa: William C. Brown Company Publishers, 1977.

Norris, Willa, et. al. *The Career Information Service,* 4th ed. Chicago: Rand McNally & Company, 1979.

Obermann, C. Esco. *A History of Vocational Rehabilitation in America.* Minneapolis: T. S. Denison & Company, Inc., 1965.

Ohlsen, Merle M. *Guidance Services in the Modern School,* 2d ed. New York: Harcourt Brace Jovanovich, Inc., 1974.

————. *Group Counseling,* 2d ed. New York: Holt, Rinehart and Winston, Inc., 1977.

Okun, Barbara F. *Effective Helping: Interviewing and Counseling Techniques.* N. Scituate, Mass.: Duxbury Press, 1976.

Osipow, Samuel H. *Theories of Career Development.* New York: Appleton-Century-Crofts, 1973.

Parsons, Frank. *Choosing a Vocation.* Boston: Houghton Mifflin Company, 1909.

Peters, Herman J., and James C. Hansen. *Vocational Guidance and Career Development: Selected Readings,* 3rd ed. New York: Macmillan Publishing Co., Inc., 1977.

Pietrofesa, John J., George E. Leonard, and William Van Hoose. *The Authentic Counselor,* 2d ed. Chicago: Rand McNally & Company, 1978.

————, Alan Hoffman, Howard H. Splete, and Diana V. Pinto. *Counseling: Theory, Research and Practice.* Chicago: Rand McNally & Company, 1978.

Prediger, D. J., J. D. Roth, and R. J. Noeth. *Nationwide Study of Student Career Development: Summary of Results.* The American College Testing Program Research and Development Division, Number 61, November 1973.

Raths, Louis E., Merrill Harmin, and Sidney B. Simon. *Values and Teaching.* Columbus, Ohio: Charles E. Merrill Publishing Company, 1966.

Rogers, Carl R. *Counseling and Psychotherapy.* Cambridge, Mass.: The Riverside Press, 1942.

————. *Client-Centered Therapy.* Boston: Houghton Mifflin Company, 1965.

————. *Carl Rogers on Encounter Groups.* New York: Harper & Row Publishers, Inc., 1970.

Schlossberg, Nancy K., and Alan D. Entine. *Counseling Adults.* Monterey, Calif.: Brooks/Cole Publishing Company, 1977.

———— et al. *Perspectives on Counseling Adults: Issues and Goals.* Monterey, Calif.: Brooks/Cole Publishing Company, 1978.

Shertzer, Bruce, and Shelley C. Stone. *Fundamentals of Counseling,* 3d ed. Boston: Houghton Mifflin Company, 1980.

———— and ————. *Fundamentals of Guidance,* 3d ed. Boston: Houghton Mifflin Company, 1976.

Shertzer, Bruce, and James D. Linden. *Fundamentals of Individual Appraisal: Assessment Techniques for Counselors.* Boston: Houghton Mifflin Company, 1978.

Shulman, Lawrence. *The Skills of Helping: Individuals and Groups.* Itasca, Ill.: F. E. Peacock Publishers, Inc., 1979.

Simon, Sidney B., Leland M. Howe, and Howard Kirschenbaum. *Values Clarification: A Handbook of Practical Strategies for Teachers and Students.* New York: Hart Publishing Company, Inc., 1972.

Smith, Maury. *A Practical Guide to Value Clarification.* LaJolla, Calif.: University Associates, 1977.

Stewart, Norman, et al. *Systematic Counseling.* Englewood Cliffs, N.J.: Prentice-Hall, Inc., 1978.

Super, Donald E. *The Psychology of Careers.* New York: Harper & Row Publishers, Inc., 1975.

Thompson, Charles L., and William A. Poppen. *Guidance Activities for Counselors and Teachers.* Monterey, Calif.: Brooks/Cole Publishing Company, 1979.

Toffler, A. *Learning for Tomorrow.* New York: Vantage Books, 1974.

Tolbert, E. L. *Introduction to Counseling,* 2d ed. New York: McGraw-Hill Book Company, 1972.

————. *Counseling for Career Development.* Boston: Houghton Mifflin Company, 1974.

————. *An Introduction to Guidance.* Boston: Little, Brown and Company, 1978.

Vriend, John, and Wayne W. Dyer, eds. *Counseling Effectively in Groups.* Englewood Cliffs, N.J.: Educational Technology, 1973.

Walz, Garry R., and Libby Benjamin. *Transcultural Counseling: Needs, Programs and Techniques.* New York: Human Sciences Press, 1978.

Wedding, Dan, and Raymond J. Corsini, eds. *Great Cases in Psychotherapy.* Itasca, Ill.: F. E. Peacock Publishers, Inc., 1979.

Wrenn, C. Gilbert. *The Counselor in a Changing World.* Washington, D.C.: American Personnel and Guidance Association, 1962.

————. *The World of the Contemporary Counselor.* Boston: Houghton Mifflin Company, 1973.

Yalom, Irvin D. *The Theory and Practice of Group Psychotherapy,* 2d ed. New York: Basic Books, Inc., Publishers, 1975.

Zaccaria, J. *Theories of Occupational Choice and Vocational Development.* Boston: Houghton Mifflin Company, 1970.

Appendices

Appendix A
Summary of School Counselor Certification Requirements

Summary of School Counselor Certification Requirements

States

Courses	AL	AZ	AK	CA	CO	CT	DE	DC	FL	GA	HA	ID	IL	IN	IA	KS	KY	LA	ME	MD	MA	MI	MN	MS	MO
Introductory Guidance; philosophy, principles, history	X		X			X	X	X	X			X	X	X		X	X	X	X	X	X		X		X
Counseling; techniques, theory	X		X			X	2 req.	X	X			X	X	X			X	X	X	X	X		X	X	X
Appraisal; testing, appraisal, analysis	X		X			X	X	X	X			X	X	X		3 req.	X	X	X	X	X		X	X	X
Group	X		X					X						X		X*	X	X*	X						
Occupational-education information; career, vocational guidance	X		X*			X	X	X	X			X	X	X		X*	X	X	X	X	X		X	X	X
Program development: organization & admin., management & leadership	X		X*			X	X	X				X		X		X	X							X	
Practicum			X			X	X	X	X		X	X	X	X	X	X	X	X	X	X	X	X	X	X	X
Internship																									
Other		**	**			**	**	**	**							**	**	**	**	**			**		**

*For secondary only   ** Other courses required vary considerably from state to state; frequently, required "other" courses include mental hygiene, human growth and development, and research methods.

Source.

Data was compiled from Elizabeth H. Woellner, *Requirements for Certification,* 42nd ed. (Chicago: The University of Chicago Press, 1977).

Courses	MT	NB	NV	NH	NJ	NM	NY	NC	ND	OH	OK	OR	PA	RI	SC	SD	TN	TX	UT	VT	VA	WA	WV	WI	WY
Introductory Guidance; philosophy, principles, history			X					X	X	X	X				X		X				X		X	X	
Counseling; techniques, theory			X		X			X	X	X	X				X	X	X				X		X	X	
Appraisal; testing, appraisal, analysis			X		X			X	X	X					X	X	X				X		X	X	
Group			X		X					X							X				X			X	
Occupational-education information; career, vocational guidance			X		X				X	X	X				X	X	X				X			X	
Program development: organization & admin., management & leadership									X							X	X								
Practicum			X			X	X	X	2 sem.	X	X				X	X	X				X		X	X	
Intership															X										
Other										**	***				***		**						**	**	

Appendix B
The Unique Role
of the Elementary
School Counselor*

RATIONALE

Consistent with the philosophy of education, elementary school counseling concerns itself with children in the developmental process of maximizing their potential. The elementary counselor works within the educational framework and the child's total environment to enable each child to arrive at an identity and learn to make choices and decisions that lead to effective functioning as a worthwhile being.

Particular attention and time need to be given in the educational program of young children to provide training and opportunities to learn decision-making skills. Individuals make the choices and decisions that ultimately determine their behavior and their learning. Elementary school counselors, because of their specialized training, provide service and leadership in this area as it is integrated into the total school experience.

Elementary guidance and counseling builds upon the belief that human beings must have continuous experience of challenge, achievement, and suc-

---

* This position paper describes the unique role of the elementary school counselor. It was approved by the American School Counselor's Association Governing Board, August 1977.

This is a revision of the statement published in *Elementary School Guidance and Counseling,* March 1974, Vol. 8, No. 3.

cess. The school creates situations in which children find themselves needed and wanted by others. Teachers can demonstrate to pupils that they matter as individuals and are accepted as they are, by their teacher as well as by their peers. The teacher plays the primary role in working with children and the counselor aids the teacher in making education more meaningful to each child with the implementation of an appropriate guidance and counseling program.

OBJECTIVES

As an elementary school guidance and counseling program is composed of more than a professional counselor, it is imperative that our objectives represent all of the various populations. We are then able to communicate more clearly our responsibilities and goals and the manner in which they relate to the total education and environment of the child.

I. *For individual children* (age-appropriate):
   A. To be able to identify themselves by description, likes, dislikes, interests, skills, and similar concern.
   B. To be able to define their role in the family, school setting, neighborhood, and community.
   C. To have a positive feeling of self and be able to verbalize self-feelings in a straightforward, comfortable manner without fear of nonacceptance.
   D. To be able to recognize their own shortcomings and accept their limitations, then proceed to work toward improvement as goals are set.
   E. To be acceptant of other people and be able to identify and work toward solving conflicts in relationships.
   F. To feel good about learning and working and, when distress occurs, be able to use appropriate skills of problem-solving and decision-making to reach a level at which they are able to cope.
   G. To have interest in the future and engage in some fantasizing of possible life roles.
   H. To have a realistic understanding of the interrelatedness of people and the world of work and services and the part that the child, other members of the family and acquaintances play in it.
II. *For teachers, administrators, and parents in the child's life*
   A. To understand and accept the child's self-concept and work toward determining with them positive changes; then to provide guidance and support as each child endeavors to make those changes.
   B. To relate to the child as a worthwhile human being, so that the child can use acceptable and appropriate relationship behavior.

    C. To provide teaching, experiences, and opportunities for learning decision-making skills and grant the child the dignity to live with and learn from mistakes without criticism and ridicule, or without "taking over" the decision making.

    D. To seek help for themselves when necessary in order to provide the most effective learning environment for the child.

III. *For the counselor*

    A. To be a congruent human being comfortable in both personal and professional life to the extent that the counselor can function for the best interest of those served.

    B. To accept each person (child and adult) in the professional environment, with all accompanying feelings and behaviors, and help the counselee with unique training and skills to define needs and concerns.

    C. To provide the guidance and counseling appropriate and acceptable for the counselee.

    D. To be able to identify changes and objectives reached by counselees and interpret them to others.

    E. To serve as an advocate for the child within the adult structure of the school and community.

Appendix C
The Unique Role of the Middle/Junior High School Counselor*

There is a unique role for the middle/junior high school counselor, and there has been an increasing need to develop a position paper to describe this role. This position paper was originally authored by Mary K. Ryan, Middle/Junior High School Vice President for ASCA, 1972–73. The original paper has since been modified by incorporating suggestions and recommendations made by practicing school counselors. This position paper has now been officially recognized and accepted by the American School Counselor Association Governing Board.

The middle/junior high school counselor recognizes the commonalities of the role and function with those of the elementary and secondary work settings. However, since early adolescents or transecents have special physical, emotional, and social needs, services specifically related to middle/junior high school students must be established. To ensure the fullest development of each child's talents and capabilities, an effective guidance program must recognize the many physiological and psychological differences of adolescents in grades five through nine.

* This paper was approved by ASCA Governing Board, August 1977. It appeared in *Elementary School Guidance and Counseling,* Vol. 12, No. 2, February, 1978, p. 203.

COUNSELING

In serving as a facilitator of self-development, the middle/junior high school counselor should provide an individual counseling environment for all students to help them gain an understanding of themselves and find an identity. Emphasis on individual counseling does not rule out the benefits obtained from group sessions or peer counseling. The capable middle/junior high school counselor will utilize all techniques in helping students objectively evaluate their present and future lives. The counselor recognizes that a successful developmental guidance program with such a learner-centered base depends upon cooperative efforts of the total learning team.

SCHOOL STAFF

To improve the educational climate and foster personal and social development of the counselee, it is incumbent upon the counselor to share his expertise with the teachers. Through individual conferences, case conferences, inservice training, and as an integral part of the team, the counselor can assist the staff in becoming increasingly aware of and sensitive to the needs of the early adolescent. The counselor should supply necessary personal data, interpret test results, and help resolve value conflicts.

Teachers, with their close, everyday student contact, have significant opportunities to affect the students' self concepts. Cooperation is not only essential but beneficial to the counselor and to the staff, since both are working toward the same goal—i.e., enabling the student to reach his full potential.

The counselor may assist administrators in ascertaining that the curriculum is meeting the needs of all students, that discipline is a positive nature, and that quality integrated services are provided.

PARENT INVOLVEMENT

Maintaining open lines of communication with parents, in either individual or group settings, should maximize the students' social as well as academic adjustment. This counselor responsibility, applicable to all age groups, is particularly pertinent in the middle/junior high school, since adolescents are striving for independence and are reaching a level of maturity and socialization that causes them to question environmental pressures.

The counselor's role in parental consultation includes such activities as interpreting test results, acquainting parents with school policy and procedures, making parents aware of in-school and out-of-school referral agencies, as well as assisting through direct instruction in parental understanding of child growth and development.

COMMUNITY CONTACT

Since the general public has been oriented to thinking of guidance counselors as [a] means of obtaining college admissions and vocational information, it is mutually advantageous for the community to have an understanding of all guidance functions as they relate to this work setting.

Contact with community social, civic, and professional organizations is essential for maximizing student welfare. In order to facilitate community understanding [of] the middle/junior high school guidance program, the counselor has a responsibility to share the guidance program with the public through the newsletter, handbooks, newspaper articles, radio, and television.

The citizens' involvement in defining community needs will ensure support for the counselor's endeavors in planning a complete guidance program. Untapped resources will be forthcoming from the public to assist the counselor in becoming a change agent in promoting improved human relations. Prevention of problems for the impressionable early-teenagers should be an outcome of the combined school and community interest.

OTHER AREAS OF SPECIAL RESPONSIBILITY

Orientation to junior and senior high schools, educational placement, career development, and group activities to promote greater self-direction, particularly in value formulation and decision making, are all areas with special implications for the middle/junior high school counselor.

A well-rounded middle/junior high school guidance program addresses itself to the social, emotional, and physical uniqueness of the early adolescent and aims to promote a high level of self-understanding and self-direction in each individual student.

It is hoped that this position paper will assist in strengthening the position of the middle/junior high school counselors. Counselors are encouraged to make use of this position statement whenever appropriate.

Appendix D
Role Statement:
The Role of the Secondary
School Counselor*

The purposes of this article are to identify and to clarify the role of the secondary school counselor as it is perceived by ASCA members and to commit to public record certain philosophic tenets and essential operational conditions entailed.

PROFESSIONAL RATIONALE

As members of the educational team, secondary school counselors believe that each child possesses intrinsic worth and inherent and inalienable rights and that each child is the focus of the educational process. No other country in the world devotes so much attention to the individual student. Schools in all societies are concerned with the transmission of cultural heritages and with the socialization of youth. In the United States, schools also emphasize the individual and individual needs and desires. Guidance in schools is a phenomenon of the United States and is, as one phase of pupil-personnel services, a unique and integral part of the total school program.

The following role statement is a revision of that which appeared in the May 1974 issue of *School Counselor*. The statement was formulated by the 1976–77 ASCA Governing Board. It appeared in *The School Counselor*, Vol. 24, No. 4, March, 1977, p. 228.

Counselors believe that most students, given the experience of an accepting, nonevaluating relationship, will make intelligent decisions. When effective, school counseling functions as a continuous process to assist students by identifying and meeting their needs in the educational, vocational, and personal-social domains. Although personal counseling is a major function of the guidance staff, other responsibilities and involvements include, but are not limited to, staff consultation, parental assistance, student self-appraisal, educational-vocational information and planning, referral to allied community agencies, and public relations.

Guidance is a function of every member of the educational team, but the school counselor has the primary responsibility for leadership. Guidance assists students to understand themselves by focusing attention on their interests, abilities, and needs in relation to their home, school, and environment. Counseling assists students in developing decision-making competence and in formulating future plans. The school counselor is the person on the staff who has special training in assessing the specific needs of each student and in planning an appropriate guidance program in the educational, vocational, and personal-social domains.

Social changes bring new and different challenges to schools. New knowledge is constantly available. The effective school counselor, through training and retraining, remains informed and approaches each counseling situation realistically.

PROFESSIONAL RELATIONSHIPS

Counseling Relationships

Counseling relationships are based on the following principles:

It is the counselor's obligation to respect the integrity of the counselee and promote the welfare of the student being counseled.

Before entering the counseling relationship, the counselee should be informed of the conditions under which assistance may be received.

Counselors shall decline to initiate or shall terminate a counseling relationship when they cannot be of professional assistance.

The counseling relationship and information resulting from it must be kept confidential in accordance with the rights of the individual and the obligations of the counselor as a professional person.

Counselors reserve the right to consult with other competent professionals about the counselee.

Should the counselee's condition endanger the health, welfare, and/or safety of self or others, the counselor is expected to consult the appropriate responsible person. In some instances, referral of the counselee to a specialist may be desirable.

The Counselor's Relationship with the Student

Through the counseling relationship, the counselor seeks to help students to understand themselves in relation to the world in which they live. The counselor helps students to know themselves, to recognize their strengths and weaknesses, to establish values, and to learn how to make realistic and positive decisions. To accomplish these goals in the high school environment, the secondary school counselor

Sees students as individuals and acknowledges their right to acceptance as human beings.

Recognizes that each student's behavior is meaningful and represents the individual's attempt to develop within the environment as it is perceived.

Is available to all students and works with them in relation to their educational, vocational, and personal-social needs.

Creates an atmosphere in which mutual confidence, understanding, and respect result in a helping relationship.

The Counselor's Relationship with the Parent or Guardian

The school counselor serves as consultant to parents or guardians regarding the growth, educational and career planning, and development of the counselee. To accomplish this goal, the secondary school counselor

Accepts parents as individuals and acknowledges their uniqueness.

Approaches the conference in a courteous, professional, sincere, and nonjudgmental manner.

Respects the basic right and responsibility of parents to assist their children in decision making.

Conveys a sincere interest in establishing a helpful and cooperative relationship.

Assures parents of confidentiality about the information received.

The Counselor's Relationship with the Teacher

The counselor assists teachers to gain a better understanding of the plan for the educational, career, and personal-social development of the students. To accomplish this goal, the secondary school counselor

Views teachers as members of the guidance team.

Serves as interpreter of the school's guidance program to teachers and familiarizes them with the guidance services available.

Shares appropriate individual student data with teachers with due regard for confidentiality and assists the teachers in recognizing individual differences in students, as well as their needs in the classroom.

Assists teachers in making referrals to other appropriate school personnel, such as the remedial reading teacher, the school nurse, or the school's learning-disabilities specialist.

Supports teachers of vocational and/or cooperative programs offering students on-site work experience.

Cooperates with efforts of middle school, junior high school, and senior high school teachers to describe academic course work for the benefit of the student entering senior high school.

Maintains an objective and impartial view in teacher-student relationships, endeavoring to understand the problems that may exist and to assist in their solution.

Assists in the planning of classroom guidance activities and acts as a resource person for obtaining appropriate up-to-date materials and information.

Makes current information available to teachers about the myriad of career and job opportunities during and after high school.

Involves teachers in conferences with students and parents, promoting a better understanding of the student and the individual's development.

Develops a teacher-consultation program to help teachers with students who show discipline and learning problems in the classroom.

The Counselor's Relationship with the Administration

The work of the school counselor should contribute directly to the purpose of the school. To accomplish this goal, the secondary school counselor

Recognizes that the administrator is the major member of the guidance team whose outlook, leadership, and support create the atmosphere for success in important school services.

Serves as interpreter of the guidance program to the administration, familiarizing it with the guidance services available.

Works closely with the administration in planning, implementing, and participating in in-service training and other programs designed to maintain and promote the professional competency of the entire staff in curriculum development, in adapting learning activities to pupil needs, and in effecting positive student behavior.

Serves as liaison between the guidance staff and the school administration by preparing pertinent information regarding student needs and abilities or other data related to the guidance program and curriculum development.

Is aware that any statement on the role and function of the secondary school counselor does not supersede nor is it in direct conflict with legislation dealing with confidentiality, privileged communications, or contract agreements between counselors and boards of education.

The Counselor's Relationship with Significant Others

The counselor has professional responsibilities to a number of significant others as an effort is made to use all available community resources to assist the student. It is essential that a good working relationship be established and maintained with these community and area resources. To assure ongoing rapport with community and area resources, the secondary school counselor

Maintains good communication with the office of the probate judge and with law-enforcement agencies.

Maintains a cooperative working relationship with community and social agencies.

Consults with students' previous counselors in order to use valuable knowledge and expertise of former counselors.

Maintains a close and cooperative relationship with the admission counselors of post–high school institutions.

PROFESSIONAL RESPONSIBILITIES

The Counselor's Responsibility to the Student

In addition to specifying the counselor's professional relationships with the student, it is important to consider the counselor's personal responsibilities to the student. In a counseling relationship, the secondary school counselor

Demonstrates respect for the worth, dignity, and quality of the student's human rights.

Shows concern for and assists in the planning of the student's educational, career, personal, and social development.

Aids students in self-evaluation, self-understanding, and self-direction, enabling them to make decisions consistent with their immediate and long-range goals.

Assists students in developing healthy habits and positive attitudes and values.

Encourages students to participate in appropriate school activities with a view toward increasing effectiveness in personal and social activities.

Participates in the planning and design of research that may have beneficial results for counselees.

Assists students in the development of an awareness of the world of work and in the use of school and community resources.

Helps students to acquire a better understanding of the world of work through the acquisition of skills and attitudes and/or participation in work-related programs.

Encourages students to plan and use leisure-time activities and to increase personal satisfaction.

Clearly indicates the conditions under which counseling is provided with respect to privileged communication.

Assists in students' adjustment to senior high school, evaluates academic progress, and reviews graduation requirements.

Makes referral to appropriate resources whenever professional or role limitations curtail assistance.

Assists students in understanding their strengths, weaknesses, interests, values, potentials, and limitations.

The Counselor's Responsibility to the Parent or Guardian

The counselor holds conferences with parents or guardians about students' growth and development. Through individual or group conferences, the secondary school counselor

Provides parents or guardians with accurate information about school policies and procedures, course offerings, educational and career opportunities, course or program requirements, and resources that will contribute to the continuing development of counselees.

Makes discreet and professional use of information shared during conferences.

Shares information with parents or guardians and interprets pertinent data about counselees' academic records and progress.

Assists the parent or guardian in forming realistic perceptions of the student's aptitudes, abilities, interests, and attitudes as related to educational and career planning, academic achievement, personal-social development, and total school progress.

Interprets the guidance program of the school to the parent or guardian and familiarizes him or her with the guidance services available.

Involves the school's guidance staff with parent or guardian groups.

Involves the parent or guardian in the guidance activities within the school.

The Counselor's Responsibility to the Staff

In a democratic society, the school's basic purpose is the education and development of all students toward individual fulfillment. To carry out this important responsibility, the secondary school counselor

Works with all members of the school staff by providing appropriate information, materials, and consultation assistance in supporting teacher efforts to understand better the individuality of each pupil.

Contributes to curriculum development and cooperates with administrators and teachers in the refinement of methods for individualized learning.

Contributes to the development of a flexible curriculum to provide a meaningful education for each student.

Acts as the coordinator in the school's program of student appraisal by accumulating meaningful information and interpreting this to students, parents, and the professional staff.

Uses modern technology, techniques, and paraprofessional personnel to disseminate educational and career information.

Assists in research related to pupil needs by conducting studies related to the improvement of educational programs and services.

Assists students in planning programs of educational and vocational training consistent with their goals.

Coordinates the use of services available beyond those the counselor can provide by making appropriate referrals and by maintaining a cooperative working relationship with community specialists.

Serves the school's program of public relations by participating in community groups and by furnishing information regarding guidance programs to the media.

Acts as a consultant to administrators, to teachers, and to significant others by sharing appropriate individual student data, identifying students with special needs, suggesting materials and procedures for a variety of group-guidance experiences, and participating in in-service training programs.

Implements student articulation between junior high school and high school and high school and post–high school experiences.

Accepts professional obligations related to school policies and programs.

Participates in the planning, development, and evaluation of the guidance program.

The Counselor's Responsibility Regarding the Community

The secondary school counselor has a professional responsibility to have accurate information about current community programs, including knowledge of such services as health clinics, planned-parenthood clinics, volunteer programs, cooperative programs, apprenticeship of labor organizations, Chamber of Commerce programs, and other community agencies' programs.

The Counselor's Responsibility to the Profession

ASCA presumes that the professional identity of the school counselor must be derived from unique training and service. To assure continued professional growth and contributions to the profession, the secondary school counselor

Has an understanding of his or her own personal characteristics and their effects on counseling relationships and personal-social encounters.

Is aware of his or her level of professional competence and presents it accurately to others.

Continues to develop professional competence and maintains an awareness of contemporary trends inside and outside the school community.

Fosters the development and improvement of the counseling profession by assisting with appropriate research and participating in professional association activities at the local, state, and national levels.

Discusses with related professional associates (counselors, teachers, and administrators) practices that may be implemented to strengthen and improve standards or conditions of employment.

Prepares meaningful, objective, and succinct case reports for other professional personnel who are assisting students.

Discusses with other professionals situations related to their respective discipline in an effort to share unique understanding and to elicit recommendations to assist counselees further.

Enhances the image of counselors and of other related professionals by positive references in communicating with students, parents, and the community.

Maintains constant efforts to adhere to strict confidentiality of information concerning counselees and releases such information only with the signature of the counselee and/or parent or guardian.

Becomes an active member of ASCA and state and local counselor associations in order to enhance professional growth.

The Counselor's Responsibility to Self

Beyond the counselor's responsibility to the profession is a further responsibility to self. To meet the responsibilities deemed significant to self, the secondary school counselor is expected to

Maintain a strict adherence to the concept and practice of confidentiality and recognize the right to share such information only with a signed release.

Be well informed on current theories, practices, developments, and trends.

Use time primarily for guidance and counseling and strive constantly to reduce the demands of clerical or administrative duties.

Become a professional individual and, in so doing, develop and maintain a well-rounded educational, social, and professional attitude.

Appendix E
The Role and Function of Post-Secondary Counseling*

Post-secondary counselors function in a wide variety of settings, such as vocational-technical, colleges and universities, community colleges, private agencies, governmental agencies, armed forces, proprietary institutions, and adult continuing education centers. Though they are an integral part of the total institution/agency staff and are members of the student services team, their major concern is with the normal developmental needs and concerns of students.

The primary role of post-secondary counselors is to assist individual students in acquiring information and developing attitudes, insights, and understanding about themselves and their environment, which are necessary for optimal growth and development. This is usually accomplished through the counseling relationship, either individually or in groups. It will also include consultation with teachers, administrators, and other significant adults. During these contacts, professional confidentiality is maintained.

Post-secondary counselors should be proficient in working with students, either individually or in groups, and in consultation activities, though the emphasis will vary depending on the particular setting in which one works. Their purpose, in all instances, is to help students understand themselves

* *The School Counselor,* May, 1974. Vol. 21, No. 5. p. 387.

in relation to the social, psychological, and economic world in which they live, to develop decision making competency, and to resolve special problems.

WORK WITH STUDENTS

Post-secondary counselors work with students in educational, career, and personal-social counseling. They also play a role in orientation to post-secondary education and in providing testing services. These functions may be performed individually or in groups. Though they are necessarily interrelated, they will be dealt with here as separate functions.

Orientation

Orientation is that process which assists both new and potential students to experience a successful entry into post-secondary education. The counseling staff should play a leadership role in the planning and implementation of this program. These functions are designed to assist students to:

Recognize and identify the kinds of difficulties that they may encounter during their enrollment.

Recognize procedures and processes that have an effect upon their progress.

Be aware of the counseling services.

Recognize the channels of communication they may utilize during their enrollment.

Provide informal exchange of ideas and/or experiences with a counselor.

Become aware of the total student services available.

Become aware of information regarding curricula, career information, transfer information, etc.

Reduce anxiety related to entrance into a new or unknown environment.

Become acquainted with some of their fellow students as an initial base for the development of interpersonal relationships.

Individual Student Counseling

Educational Counseling. By helping students relate their previous school records, test scores, ability, achievement, aptitude, and work and life experiences to their expressed feelings and ambitions, a counselor is able to provide help in the selection of programs or classes which are appropriate for the student's existing life goals.

Career Counseling. The counselor provides the opportunities for students to develop a basis for career decision making by helping them consider the following:

Background information discussion of past experiences that provides a basis for future career decision making.

Personal career needs—detailed consideration of work and life-style values and priorities as they relate to each other.

Self-concept—exploration of how students see themselves physically and intellectually, as well as in interpersonal relations.

Level of functioning—discussion of reality factors such as academic attainment, test information, including vocational and interest testing, and special abilities that are necessary for career decision making.

Career information and exploration—utilizing various media that provide information about careers.

Career planning and summary—summarization of all data with assistance in short- and long-term planning for a career.

Personal-Social Counseling. Through individual counseling, students are assisted toward actualizing their potential. The counselor helps students to:

Adjust to immediate problems or situations.

Learn methods to use in dealing with future problems.

Develop a better understanding of themselves.

Accept and think positively about themselves.

Clarify alternatives open to them in their problem solving.

Verbalize problems pressing upon them.

Clarify their thoughts and actions.

Become aware of and seek assistance from appropriate referral sources.

Group Procedures

This function typically takes two forms, group counseling and group guidance. In practice the two forms are often interrelated.

Group Counseling. Groups are particularly effective with students who:

Are vocationally undecided.

Have study problems.

Have personal-social problems.

Are on academic probation or are having achievement or attendance problems.

Wish to improve their ability to direct their own lives.

Wish to become more effective in their interpersonal relationships.

Wish to increase their ability to understand themselves and others.

Group Guidance. This form of group process typically deals with the dissemination of information in the following areas:

Orientation of students and/or parents.

Academic problem solving.

Career information.

Educational information.

Summarization of guidance and counseling functions.

Testing

Testing services deal with the administration and scoring of tests and interpretation and evaluation of test information for students. This service includes:

Assisting with the placement of students into appropriate programs and courses.

Assisting students in their selection of educational and vocational goals.

Assisting students to develop an understanding of test results for their individual needs.

Referring students to agencies or test centers where special testing is available.

Providing test data for research and curriculum revision.

Providing a permanent or systematic recording procedure and storage for filing test scores.

Articulation

Articulation with other institutions, agencies, businesses, industries, labor, and government by a counselor will:

Help students in their plans for satisfying curriculum requirements.

Provide feedback from former students through follow-up programs to be utilized in curriculum evaluation.

Improve the articulation process by having counselors serve on local and state committees.

Aid in job development and job placement.

CONSULTANT TO FACULTY AND ADMINISTRATION

Post-secondary counselors serve as consultants to members of the faculty and administration. Counselors are part of the educational team. Their service and contribution to the faculty and administration is helpful in the following situations:

Discussing student needs related to curriculum and classroom functioning.

Interpreting student cumulative record information to faculty members as needed.

Helping them to identify and plan programs for students with special abilities and needs.

Serving as counselor-consultant or liaison to a particular department or division of the institution.

Reporting the results of follow-up visits to schools and industry.

Serving on faculty committees, particularly in the area of curriculum development.

Offering the counselor's expertise in various areas of classroom instruction, group dynamics, human relations, communication, study techniques, etc.

INSTITUTIONAL AND PROFESSIONAL RESEARCH

Post-secondary counselors should become involved in institutional and professional research in order to make certain that valid information is provided to the institution regarding:

Accountability of the counseling program.

Follow-up of graduates and former students.

Development of local norms for standardized tests where appropriate.

Special projects or programs.

Characteristics of students.

Occupational trends in the community, state, and nation.

PERSONAL AND PROFESSIONAL GROWTH

Post-secondary counselors should strive to grow personally and professionally through activities such as:

Attending staff meetings dealing with policies, procedures, or special topics.

Attending staff training sessions led by other staff members or outside consultants.

Attending local, state, and national workshops on topics related to counselors' activities.

Updating skills by taking courses related to counseling.

Attending local, state, and national conferences.

Joining and becoming actively involved in local, state, and national professional associations.

Supervising counseling interns.

Having access to professional supervision and consultation as needed.

Developing new and innovative counseling programs.

Visiting and working with local business and industry.

COMMUNICATION PROGRAM

Post-secondary counselors should provide an effective communication program regarding the nature of counseling and guidance services for students, faculty, administrators, and other interested individuals. This can be done through:

Speaking to community or local schools about the counseling program.

Providing counseling services to the local community.

Leading counseling groups or teaching courses in human development.

Maintaining close working relationships with counseling programs at all school levels.

Sponsoring or hosting counseling-related groups.

Visiting local businesses and industries to open communications regarding jobs, work trends, counseling function, and student preparation.

Serving on civic committees where counseling knowledge and skills can be of value.

Sponsoring meetings for local school counselors to increase their knowledge and understanding of career programs and services.

SUMMARY

In order for post-secondary counselors to function effectively, they must clearly understand their role as counselors. Their role within a particular institution should be firmly stated, as should their relationship to faculty, administrators, and other members of the student services team. This will enable them to function freely without interference from assignments or activities that are inappropriate. It will also enable counselors to become clearly accountable in their stated functions.

Appendix F
Ethical Standards of the American Personnel and Guidance Association*

PREAMBLE

The American Personnel and Guidance Association is an educational, scientific, and professional organization whose members are dedicated to the enhancement of the worth, dignity, potential, and uniqueness of each individual and thus to the service of society.

The Association recognizes that the role definitions and work settings of its members include a wide variety of academic disciplines, levels of academic preparation, and agency services. This diversity reflects the breadth of the Association's interest and influence. It also poses challenging complexities in efforts to set standards for the performance of members, desired requisite preparation or practice, and supporting social, legal, and ethical controls.

The specification of ethical standards enables the Association to clarify to present and future members and to those served by members the nature of ethical responsibilities held in common by its members.

The existence of such standards serves to stimulate greater concern by members for their own professional functioning and for the conduct of fellow professionals such as counselors, guidance and student personnel workers,

* American Personnel and Guidance Association, Washington, D.C., 1974.

427

and others in the helping professions. As the ethical code of the Association, this document establishes principles which define the ethical behavior of Association members.

SECTION A: GENERAL

1. The member influences the development of the profession by continuous efforts to improve professional practices, teaching, services, and research. Professional growth is continuous throughout the member's career and is exemplified by the development of a philosophy that explains why and how a member functions in the helping relationship. Members are expected to gather data on their effectiveness and to be guided by the findings.

2. The member has a responsibility both to the individual who is served and to the institution within which the service is performed. The acceptance of employment in an institution implies that the member is in substantial agreement with the general policies and principles of the institution. Therefore the professional activities of the member are also in accord with the objectives of the institution. If, despite concerted efforts, the member cannot reach agreement with the employer as to acceptable standards of conduct that allow for changes in institutional policy conducive to the positive growth and development of counselees, then terminating the affiliation should be seriously considered.

3. Ethical behavior among professional associates, members and nonmembers, is expected at all times. When information is possessed which raises serious doubt as to the ethical behavior of professional colleagues, whether Association members or not, the member is obligated to take action to attempt to rectify such a condition. Such action shall utilize the institution's channels first and then utilize procedures established by the state, division, or Association.

   The member can take action in a variety of ways: conferring with the individual in question, gathering further information as to the allegation, conferring with local or national ethics committees, and so forth.

4. The member must not seek self-enhancement through expressing evaluations or comparisons that are damaging to others.

5. The member neither claims nor implies professional qualifications exceeding those possessed and is responsible for correcting any misrepresentations of these qualifications by others.

6. In establishing fees for professional services, members should take into consideration the fees charged by other professions delivering comparable services, as well as the ability of the counselee to pay. Members are willing to provide some services for which they receive little or no financial remuneration, or remuneration in food, lodging, and materials.

When fees include charges for items other than professional services, that portion of the total which is for the professional services should be clearly indicated.

7. When members provide information to the public or to subordinates, peers, or supervisors, they have a clear responsibility to ensure that the content is accurate, unbiased, and consists of objective, factual data.

8. The member shall make a careful distinction between the offering of counseling services as opposed to public information services. Counseling may be offered only in the context of a reciprocal or face-to-face relationship. Information services may be offered through the media.

9. With regard to professional employment, members are expected to accept only positions that they are prepared to assume and then to comply with established practices of the particular type of employment setting in which they are employed in order to ensure the continuity of services.

SECTION B: COUNSELOR-COUNSELEE RELATIONSHIP

This section refers to practices involving individual and/or group counseling relationships, and it is not intended to be applicable to practices involving administrative relationships.

To the extent that the counselee's choice of action is not imminently self- or other-destructive, the counselee must retain freedom of choice. When the counselee does not have full autonomy for reasons of age, mental incompetency, criminal incarceration, or similar legal restrictions, the member may have to work with others who exercise significant control and direction over the counselee. Under these circumstances the member must apprise counselees of restrictions that may limit their freedom of choice.

1. The member's *primary* obligation is to respect the integrity and promote the welfare of the counselee(s), whether the counselee(s) is (are) assisted individually or in a group relationship. In a group setting, the member-leader is also responsible for protecting individuals from physical and/ or psychological trauma resulting from interaction within the group.

2. The counseling relationship and information resulting therefrom must be kept confidential, consistent with the obligations of the member as a professional person. In a group counseling setting the member is expected to set a norm of confidentiality regarding all group participants' disclosures.

3. If an individual is already in a counseling/therapy relationship with another professional person, the member does not begin a counseling relationship without first contacting and receiving the approval of that other professional. If the member discovers that the counselee is in another counseling/therapy relationship after the counseling relationship

begins, the member is obligated to gain the consent of the other professional or terminate the relationship, unless the counselee elects to terminate the other relationship.

4. When the counselee's condition indicates that there is clear and imminent danger to the counselee or others, the member is expected to take direct personal action or to inform responsible authorities. Consultation with other professionals should be utilized where possible. Direct interventions, especially the assumption of responsibility for the counselee, should be taken only after careful deliberation. The counselee should be involved in the resumption of responsibility for his actions as quickly as possible.

5. Records of the counseling relationship including interview notes, test data, correspondence, tape recordings, and other documents are to be considered professional information for use in counseling, and they are not part of the public or official records of the institution or agency in which the counselor is employed. Revelation to others of counseling material should occur only upon the express consent of the counselee.

6. Use of data derived from a counseling relationship for purposes of counselor training or research shall be confined to content that can be sufficiently disguised to ensure full protection of the identity of the counselee involved.

7. Counselees shall be informed of the conditions under which they may receive counseling assistance at or before the time when the counseling relationship is entered. This is particularly so when conditions exist of which the counselee would be unaware. In individual and group situations, particularly those oriented to self-understanding or growth, the member-leader is obligated to make clear the purposes, goals, techniques, rules of procedure, and limitations that may affect the continuance of the relationship.

8. The member has the responsibility to screen prospective group participants, especially when the emphasis is on self-understanding and growth through self-disclosure. The member should maintain an awareness of the group participants' compatibility throughout the life of the group.

9. The member reserves the right to consult with any other professionally competent person about a counselee. In choosing a consultant, the member avoids placing the consultant in a conflict of interest situation that would preclude the consultant's being a proper party to the member's efforts to help the counselee.

10. If the member is unable to be of professional assistance to the counselee, the member avoids initiating the counseling relationship or the member terminates it. In either event, the member is obligated to refer the counselee to an appropriate specialist. (It is incumbent upon the member to be knowledgable about referral resources so that a satisfactory referral

can be initiated.) In the event the counselee declines the suggested referral, the member is not obligated to continue the relationship.

11. When the member learns from counseling relationships of conditions that are likely to harm others, the member should report *the condition* to the responsible authority. This should be done in such a manner as to conceal the identity of the counselee.

12. When the member has other relationships, particularly of an administrative, supervisory, and/or evaluative nature, with an individual seeking counseling services, the member should not serve as the counselor but should refer the individual to another professional. Only in instances where such an alternative is unavailable and where the individual's condition definitely warrants counseling intervention should the member enter into and/or maintain a counseling relationship.

13. All experimental methods of treatment must be clearly indicated to prospective recipients, and safety precautions are to be adhered to by the member.

14. When the member is engaged in short-term group treatment/training programs, e.g., marathons and other encounter-type or growth groups, the member ensures that there is professional assistance available during and following the group experience.

15. Should the member be engaged in a work setting that calls for any variation from the [foregoing] statements, the member is obligated to consult with other professionals whenever possible to consider justifiable alternatives. The variations that may be necessary should be clearly communicated to other professionals and prospective counselees.

SECTION C: MEASUREMENT AND EVALUATION

The primary purpose of educational and psychological testing is to provide descriptive measures that are objective and interpretable in either comparative or absolute terms. The member must recognize the need to interpret the statements that follow as applying to the whole range of appraisal techniques including test and nontest data. Test results constitute only one of a variety of pertinent sources of information for personnel, guidance, and counseling decisions.

1. It is the member's responsibility to provide adequate orientation or information to the examinee(s) prior to and following the test administration so that the results of testing may be placed in proper perspective with other relevant factors. In so doing, the member must recognize the effects of socioeconomic, ethnic, and cultural factors on test scores. It is the member's professional responsibility to use additional unvali-

dated information cautiously in modifying interpretation of the test results.

2. In selecting tests for use in a given situation or with a particular counselee, the member must consider carefully the specific validity, reliability, and appropriateness of the test(s). "General" validity, reliability, and the like may be questioned legally as well as ethically when tests are used for vocational and educational selection, placement, or counseling.

3. When making any statements to the public about tests and testing, the member is expected to give accurate information and to avoid false claims or misconceptions. Special efforts are often required to avoid unwarranted connotations of such terms as IQ and grade equivalent scores.

4. Different tests demand different levels of competence for administration, scoring, and interpretation. Members have a responsibility to recognize the limits of their competence and to perform only those functions for which they are prepared.

5. Tests should be administered under the same conditions that were established in their standardization. When tests are not administered under standard conditions or when unusual behavior or irregularities occur during the testing session, those conditions should be noted and the results designated as invalid or of questionable validity. Unsupervised or inadequately supervised test-taking, such as the use of tests through the mails, is considered unethical. On the other hand, the use of instruments that are so designed or standardized to be self-administered and self-scored, such as interest inventories, is to be encouraged.

6. The meaningfulness of test results used in personnel, guidance, and counseling functions generally depends on the examinee's unfamiliarity with the specific items on the test. Any prior coaching or dissemination of the test materials can invalidate test results. Therefore, test security is one of the professional obligations of the member. Conditions that produce most favorable test results should be made known to the examinee.

7. The purpose of testing and the explicit use of the results should be made known to the examinee prior to testing. The counselor has a responsibility to ensure that instrument limitations are not exceeded and that periodic review and/or retesting are made to prevent counselee stereotyping.

8. The examinee's welfare and explicit prior understanding should be the criteria for determining the recipients of the test results. The member is obligated to see that adequate interpretation accompanies any release of individual or group test data. The interpretation of test data should be related to the examinee's particular concerns.

9. The member is expected to be cautious when interpreting the results of research instruments possessing insufficient technical data. The spe-

cific purposes for the use of such instruments must be stated explicitly to examinees.

10. The member must proceed with extreme caution when attempting to evaluate and interpret the performance of minority group members or other persons who are not represented in the norm group on which the instrument was standardized.

11. The member is obligated to guard against the appropriation, reproduction, or modifications of published tests or parts thereof without the express permission and adequate recognition of the original author or publisher.

12. Regarding the preparation, publication, and distribution of tests, reference should be made to:
    a. *Standards for Educational and Psychological Tests and Manuals,* revised edition, 1973, published by the American Psychological Association on behalf of itself, the American Educational Research Association, and the National Council on Measurement in Education.
    b. "The Responsible Use of Tests: A Position Paper of AMEG, APGA, and NCME," published in *Measurement and Evaluation in Guidance* Vol. 5, No. 2, July 1972, pp. 385–388.

SECTION D: RESEARCH AND PUBLICATION

1. Current American Psychological Association guidelines on research with human subjects shall be adhered to (*Ethical Principles in the Conduct of Research with Human Participants.* Washington, D.C.: American Psychological Association, Inc., 1973).

2. In planning any research activity dealing with human subjects, the member is expected to be aware of and responsive to all pertinent ethical principles and to ensure that the research problem, design, and execution are in full compliance with them.

3. Responsibility for ethical research practice lies with the principal researcher, while others involved in the research activities share ethical obligation and full responsibility for their own actions.

4. In research with human subjects, researchers are responsible for their subjects' welfare throughout the experiment, and they must take all reasonable precautions to avoid causing injurious psychological, physical, or social effects on their subjects.

5. It is expected that all research subjects be informed of the purpose of the study except when withholding information or providing misinformation to them is essential to the investigation. In such research, the member is responsible for corrective action as soon as possible following the research.

6. Participation in research is expected to be voluntary. Involuntary participation is appropriate only when it can be demonstrated that participation will have no harmful effects on subjects.

7. When reporting research results, explicit mention must be made of all variables and conditions known to the investigator that might affect the outcome of the investigation or the interpretation of the data.

8. The member is responsible for conducting and reporting investigations in a manner that minimizes the possibility that results will be misleading.

9. The member has an obligation to make available sufficient original research data to qualified others who may wish to replicate the study.

10. When supplying data, aiding in the research of another person, reporting research results, or in making original data available, due care must be taken to disguise the identity of the subjects in the absence of specific authorization from such subjects to do otherwise.

11. When conducting and reporting research, the member is expected to be familiar with and to give recognition to previous work on the topic, as well as to observe all copyright laws and follow the principle of giving full credit to all to whom credit is due.

12. The member has the obligation to give due credit through joint authorship, acknowledgement, footnote statements, or other appropriate means to those who have contributed significantly to the research, in accordance with such contributions.

13. The member is expected to communicate to other members the results of any research judged to be of professional or scientific value. Results reflecting unfavorably on institutions, programs, services, or vested interests should not be withheld for such reasons.

14. If members agree to cooperate with another individual in research and/ or publication, they incur an obligation to cooperate as promised in terms of punctuality of performance and with full regard to the completeness and accuracy of the information provided.

SECTION E: CONSULTING AND PRIVATE PRACTICE

Consulting refers to a voluntary relationship between a professional helper and help-needing social unit (industry, business, school, college, etc.) in which the consultant is attempting to give help to the client in the solution of some current or potential problem. When "client" is used in this section it refers to an individual, group, or organization served by the consultant. (This definition of "consulting" is adapted from "Dimensions of the Consultant's Job" by Ronald Lippitt, *Journal of Social Issues,* Vol. 15, No. 2, 1959.)

1. Members who act as consultants must have a high degree of self-awareness of their own values and needs in entering helping relationships that involve change in social units.

2. There should be understanding and agreement between consultant and client as to the task, the directions or goals, and the function of the consultant.

3. Members are expected to accept only those consulting roles for which they possess or have access to the necessary skills and resources for giving the kind of help that is needed.

4. The consulting relationship is defined as being one in which the client's adaptability and growth toward self-direction are encouraged and cultivated. For this reason, the consultant is obligated to maintain consistently the role of a consultant and to avoid becoming a decision maker for the client.

5. In announcing one's availability for professional services as a consultant, the member follows professional rather than commercial standards in describing services with accuracy, dignity, and caution.

6. For private practice in testing, counseling, or consulting, all ethical principles defined in this document are pertinent. In addition, any individual, agency, or institution offering educational, personal, or vocational counseling should meet the standards of the International Association of Counseling Services, Inc.

7. The member is expected to refuse a private fee or other remuneration for consultation with persons who are entitled to these services through the member's employing institution or agency. The policies of a particular agency may make explicit provisions for private practice with agency counselees by members of its staff. In such instances, the counselees must be apprised of other options open to them should they seek private counseling services.

8. It is unethical to use one's institutional affiliation to recruit counselees for one's private practice.

SECTION F: PERSONNEL ADMINISTRATION

It is recognized that most members are employed in public or quasi-public institutions. The functioning of a member within an institution must contribute to the goals of the institution and vice versa if either is to accomplish their respective goals or objectives. It is therefore essential that the member and the institution function in ways to: (a) make the institution's goals explicit and public; (b) make the member's contribution to institutional goals specific; and (c) foster mutual accountability for goal achievement.

To accomplish these objectives it is recognized that the member and the employer must share responsibilities in the formulation and implementation of personnel policies.

1. Members should define and describe the parameters and levels of their professional competency.

2. Members should establish interpersonal relations and working agreements with supervisors and subordinates regarding counseling or clinical relationships, confidentiality, distinction between public and private material, maintenance and dissemination of recorded information, work load, and accountability. Working agreements in each instance should be specified and made known to those concerned.
3. Members are responsible for alerting their employers to conditions that may be potentially disruptive or damaging.
4. Members are responsible for informing employers of conditions that may limit their effectiveness.
5. Members are expected to submit regularly to review and evaluation.
6. Members are responsible for in-service development of self and/or staff.
7. Members are responsible for informing their staff of goals and programs.
8. Members are responsible for providing personnel practices that guarantee and enhance the rights and welfare of each recipient of their service.
9. Members are expected to select competent persons and assign responsibilities compatible with their skills and experiences.

SECTION G: PREPARATION STANDARDS

Members who are responsible for training others should be guided by the preparation standards of the Association and relevant division(s). The member who functions in the capacity of trainer assumes unique ethical responsibilities that frequently go beyond that of the member who does not function in a training capacity. These ethical responsibilities are outlined as follows:

1. Members are expected to orient trainees to program expectations, basic skills development, and employment prospects prior to admission to the program.
2. Members in charge of training are expected to establish programs that integrate academic study and supervised practice.
3. Members are expected to establish a program directed toward developing the trainees' skills, knowledge, and self-understanding, stated whenever possible in competency or performance terms.
4. Members are expected to identify the level of competency of their trainees. These levels of competency should accommodate the paraprofessional as well as the professional.
5. Members, through continual trainee evaluation and appraisal, are expected to be aware of the personal limitations of the trainee that might impede future performance. The trainer has the responsibility of not only assisting the trainee in securing remedial assistance, but also screening from the program those trainees who are unable to provide competent services.

6. Members are expected to provide a program that includes training in research commensurate with levels of role functioning. Paraprofessional and technician-level personnel should be trained as consumers of research. In addition, these personnel should learn how to evaluate their own and their program effectiveness. Advanced graduate training, especially at the doctoral level, should include preparation for original research by the member.

7. Members are expected to make trainees aware of the ethical responsibilities and standards of the profession.

8. Training programs are expected to encourage trainees to value the ideals of service to individuals and to society. In this regard, direct financial remuneration or lack thereof should not influence the quality of service rendered. Monetary considerations should not be allowed to overshadow professional and humanitarian needs.

9. Members responsible for training are expected to be skilled as teachers and practitioners.

10. Members are expected to present thoroughly varied theoretical postions so that trainees may make comparisons and have the opportunity to select a position.

11. Members are obligated to develop clear policies within their training institution regarding field placement and the roles of the trainee and the trainer in such placements.

12. Members are expected to ensure that forms of training focusing on self-understanding or growth are voluntary, or, if required as part of the training program, are made known to prospective trainees prior to entering the program. When the training program offers a growth experience with an emphasis on self-disclosure or other relatively intimate or personal involvement, the member should have no administrative, supervisory, or evaluative authority regarding the participant.

13. Members are obligated to conduct a training program in keeping with the most current guidelines of the American Personnel and Guidance Association and its various divisions.

Revised 1974

Appendix G
Ethical Standards of Psychologists[1]

PREAMBLE

Psychologists[2] *respect the dignity and worth of the individual and honor the preservation and protection of fundamental human rights. They are committed to increasing knowledge of human behavior and of people's understanding of themselves and others and to the utilization of such knowledge for the promotion of human welfare. While pursuing these endeavors, they make every effort to protect the welfare of those who seek their services or of any human being or animal that may be the object of study. They use their skills only for purposes consistent with these values and do not knowingly permit their misuse by others. While demanding for themselves freedom of inquiry and communication, psychologists accept the responsibility this freedom requires: competence, objectivity in the application of skills and concern for the best interests of clients, colleagues, and society in general. In the pursuit of these ideals, psychologists subscribe to principles in the following areas: 1. Responsibility, 2. Competence, 3. Moral and Legal Standards, 4. Public Statements, 5. Confidentiality, 6. Welfare of*

---

[1] Approved by the Council of Representatives January 30, 1977. Reprinted from the APA "Monitor," March 1977. Source: *Biographical Directory of the American Psychological Association,* 1978 ed. (Washington, D.C.: APA).

[2] A student of psychology who assumes the role of a psychologist shall be considered a psychologist for the purpose of this code of ethics.

the Consumer, 7. Professional Relationships, 8. Utilization of Assessment Techniques, and 9. Pursuit of Research Activities.

PRINCIPLE 1. RESPONSIBILITY

In their commitment to the understanding of human behavior, psychologists value objectivity and integrity, and in providing services they maintain the highest standards of their profession. They accept responsibility for the consequences of their work and make every effort to insure that their services are used appropriately.

a. As scientists, psychologists accept the ultimate responsibility for selecting appropriate areas and methods most relevant to these areas. They plan their research in ways to minimize the possibility that their findings will be misleading. They provide thorough discussion of the limitations of their data and alternative hypotheses, especially where their work touches on social policy or might be construed to the detriment of persons in specific age, sex, ethnic, socioeconomic or other social groups. In publishing reports of their work, they never suppress disconfirming data. Psychologists take credit only for the work they have actually done.

    Psychologists clarify in advance with all appropriate persons or agencies the expectations for sharing and utilizing research data. They avoid dual relationships which may limit objectivity, whether political or monetary, so that interference with data, human participants, and milieu is kept to a minimum.

b. As employees of an institution or agency, psychologists have the responsibility of remaining alert to and attempting to moderate institutional pressures that may distort reports of psychological findings or impede their proper use.

c. As members of governmental or other organizational bodies, psychologists remain accountable as individuals to the highest standards of their profession.

d. As teachers, psychologists recognize their primary obligation to help others acquire knowledge and skill. They maintain high standards of scholarship and objectivity by presenting psychological information fully and accurately.

e. As practitioners, psychologists know that they bear a heavy social responsibility because their recommendations and professional actions may alter the lives of others. They are alert to personal, social, organizational, financial, or political situations or pressures that might lead to misuse of their influence.

f. Psychologists provide adequate and timely evaluations to employees, trainees, students, and others whose work they supervise.

PRINCIPLE 2. COMPETENCE

The maintenance of high standards of professional competence is a responsibility shared by all psychologists in the interest of the public and the profession as a whole. Psychologists recognize the boundaries of their competence and the limitations of their techniques and only provide services, use techniques, or offer opinions as professionals that meet recognized standards. Psychologists maintain knowledge of current scientific and professional information related to the services they render.

a. Psychologists accurately represent their competence, education, training, and experience. Psychologists claim as evidence of professional qualifications only those degrees obtained from institutions acceptable under the Bylaws and Rules of Council of the American Psychological Association.
b. As teachers, psychologists peform their duties on the basis of careful preparation so that their instruction is accurate, current and scholarly.
c. Psychologists recognize the need for continuing education and are open to new procedures and changes in expectations and values over time. They recognize differences among people, such as those that may be associated with age, sex, socioeconomic, and ethnic backgrounds. Where relevant, they obtain training, experience, or counsel to assure competent service or research relating to such persons.
d. Psychologists with the responsibility for decisions involving individuals or policies based on test results have an understanding of psychological or educational measurement, validation problems and other test research.
e. Psychologists recognize that their effectiveness depends in part upon their ability to maintain effective interpersonal relations, and that aberrations on their part may interfere with their abilities. They refrain from undertaking any activity in which their personal problems are likely to lead to inadequate professional services or harm to a client; or, if engaged in such activity when they become aware of their personal problems, they seek competent professional assistance to determine whether they should suspend, terminate or limit the scope of their professional and/ or scientific activities.

PRINCIPLE 3. MORAL AND LEGAL STANDARDS

Psychologists' moral, ethical and legal standards of behavior are a personal matter to the same degree as they are for any other citizen, except as these may compromise the fulfillment of their professional responsibilities, or reduce the trust in psychology or psychologists held by the general public. Regarding their own behavior, psychologists should be aware of the prevailing community standards and of the possible impact upon the quality of professional services provided by their conformity to or deviation from these standards. Psychologists are also aware of the possible impact of their public behavior upon the ability of colleagues to perform their professional duties.

a. Psychologists as teachers are aware of the diverse backgrounds of students and, when dealing with topics that may give offense, treat the material objectively and present it in a manner for which the student is prepared.

b. As employees, psychologists refuse to participate in practices inconsistent with legal, moral and ethical standards regarding the treatment of employees or of the public. For example, psychologists will not condone practices that are inhumane or that result in illegal or otherwise unjustifiable discrimination on the basis of race, age, sex, religion, or national origin in hiring, promotion, or training.

c. In providing psychological services, psychologists avoid any action that will violate or diminish the legal and civil rights of clients or of others who may be affected by their actions.

 As practitioners, psychologists remain abreast of relevant federal, state, local, and agency regulations and Association standards of practice concerning the conduct of their practice. They are concerned with developing such legal and quasi-legal regulations as best serve the public interest and in changing such existing regulations as are not beneficial to the interests of the public and the profession.

d. As researchers, psychologists remain abreast of relevant federal and state regulations concerning the conduct of research with human participants or animals.

PRINCIPLE 4. PUBLIC STATEMENTS

Public statements, announcements of services, and promotional activities of psychologists serve the purpose of providing sufficient information to aid the consumer public in making informed judgments and choices. Psychologists represent accurately and objectively their professional qualifications, affiliations, and functions, as well as those of the institutions or organizations with which they or the statements may be associated. In public statements providing psychological information or professional opinions or providing information about the availability of psychological products and services, psychologists take full account of the limits and uncertainties of present psychological knowledge and techniques.

a. When announcing professional services, psychologists limit the information to: name, highest academic degree conferred, date and type of certification or licensure. Diplomate status, address, telephone number, office hours, and, at the individual practitioner's discretion, an appropriate brief listing of the types of psychological services offered, and fee information. Such statements are descriptive of services provided but not evaluative as to their quality or uniqueness. They do not contain testimonials by quotation or by implication. They do not claim uniqueness of skills or methods unless determined by acceptable and public scientific evidence.

b. In announcing the availability of psychological services or products, psychologists do not display any affiliations with an organization in a manner that falsely implies the sponsorship or certification of that organization. In particular and for example, psychologists do not offer APA membership or fellowship as evidence of qualification. They do not name their employer or professional associations unless the services are in fact to be provided by or under the responsible, direct supervision and continuing control of such organizations or agencies.

c. Announcements of "personal growth groups" give a clear statement of purpose and the nature of the experiences to be provided. The education, training and experience of the psychologists are appropriately specified.

d. Psychologists associated with the development or promotion of psychological devices, books, or other products offered for commercial sale make every effort to insure that announcements and advertisements are presented in a professional, scientifically acceptable, and factually informative manner.

e. Psychologists do not participate for personal gain in commercial announcements recommending to the general public the purchase or use of any proprietary or single-source product or service.

f. Psychologists who interpret the science of psychology or the services of psychologists to the general public accept the obligation to present the material fairly and accurately, avoiding misrepresentation through sensationalism, exaggeration or superficiality. Psychologists are guided by the primary obligation to aid the public in forming their own informed judgments, opinions and choices.

g. As teachers, psychologists insure that statements in catalogs and course outlines are accurate and sufficient, particularly in terms of subject matter to be covered, bases for evaluating progress, and nature of course experiences. Announcements or brochures describing workshops, seminars, or other educational programs accurately represent intended audience and eligibility requirements, educational objectives, and nature of the material to be covered, as well as the education, training and experience of the psychologists presenting the programs, and any fees involved. Public announcements soliciting subjects for research, and in which clinical services or other professional services are offered as an inducement, make clear the nature of the services as well as the costs and other obligations to be accepted by the human participants of the research.

h. Psychologists accept the obligation to correct others who may represent the psychologist's professional qualifications or associations with products or services in a manner incompatible with these guidelines.

i.   Psychological services for the purpose of diagnosis, treatment or personal advice are provided only in the context of a professional relationship, and are not given by means of public lectures or demonstrations, newspaper or magazine articles, radio or television programs, mail, or similar media.

PRINCIPLE 5. CONFIDENTIALITY

Safeguarding information about an individual that has been obtained by the psychologist in the course of his teaching, practice, or investigation is a primary obligation of the psychologist. Such information is not communicated to others unless certain important conditions are met.

a.   Information received in confidence is revealed only after most careful deliberation and when there is clear and imminent danger to an individual or to society, and then only to appropriate professional workers or public authorities.

b.   Information obtained in clinical or consulting relationships, or evaluative data concerning children, students, employees, and others are discussed only for professional purposes and only with persons clearly concerned with the case. Written and oral reports should present only data germane to the purposes of the evaluation and every effort should be made to avoid undue invasion of privacy.

c.   Clinical and other materials are used in classroom teaching and writing only when the identity of the persons involved is adequately disguised.

d.   The confidentiality of professional communications about individuals is maintained. Only when the originator and other persons involved give their express permission is a confidential professional communication shown to the individual concerned. The psychologist is responsible for informing the client of the limits of the confidentiality.

e.   Only after explicit permission has been granted is the identity of research subjects published. When data have been published without permission for identification, the psychologist assumes responsibility for adequately disguising their sources.

f.   The psychologist makes provisions for the maintenance of confidentiality in the prevention and ultimate disposition of confidential records.

PRINCIPLE 6. WELFARE OF THE CONSUMER

Psychologists respect the integrity and protect the welfare of the people and groups with whom they work. When there is a conflict of interest between the client and the psychologist's employing institution, psychologists clarify the nature and direction of their loyalties and responsibilities and keep all parties informed of their commitments. Psychologists fully inform consumers as to the purpose and nature of an evaluative, treatment, educational or training procedure, and they freely acknowledge that clients, students, or participants in research have freedom of choice with regard to participation.

a. Psychologists are continually cognizant of their own needs and of their inherently powerful position *vis a vis* clients, in order to avoid exploiting their trust and dependency. Psychologists make every effort to avoid dual relationships with clients and/or relationships which might impair their professional judgment or increase the risk of client exploitation. Examples of such dual relationships include treating employees, supervisees, close friends or relatives. Sexual intimacies with clients are unethical.

b. Where demands of an organization on psychologists go beyond reasonable conditions of employment, psychologists recognize possible conflicts of interest that may arise. When such conflicts occur, psychologists clarify the nature of the conflict and inform all parties of the nature and direction of the loyalties and responsibilities involved.

c. When acting as a supervisor, trainer, researcher, or employer, psychologists accord informed choice, confidentiality, due process, and protection from physical and mental harm to their subordinates in such relationships.

d. Financial arrangements in professional practice are in accord with professional standards that safeguard the best interests of the client and that are clearly understood by the client in advance of billing. Psychologists are responsible for assisting clients in finding needed services in those instances where payment of the usual fee would be a hardship. No commission, rebate, or other form of remuneration may be given or received for referral of clients for professional services, whether by an individual or by an agency. Psychologists willingly contribute a portion of their services to work for which they receive little or no financial return.

e. The psychologist attempts to terminate a clinical or consulting relationship when it is reasonably clear that the consumer is not benefiting from it. Psychologists who find that their services are being used by employers in a way that is not beneficial to the participants or to employees who may be affected, or to significant others, have the responsibility to make their observations known to the responsible persons and to propose modification or termination of the engagement.

PRINCIPLE 7. PROFESSIONAL RELATIONSHIPS

Psychologists act with due regard for the needs, special competencies and obligations of their colleagues in psychology and other professions. Psychologists respect the prerogatives and obligations of the institutions or organizations with which they are associated.

a. Psychologists understand the areas of competence of related professions, and make full use of all the professional, technical, and administrative resources that best serve the interests of consumers. The absence of formal relationships with other professional workers does not relieve psychologists from the responsibility of securing for their clients the best possible professional service nor does it relieve them from the exercise of foresight, diligence, and tact in obtaining the complementary or alternative assistance needed by clients.

b. Psychologists know and take into account the traditions and practices of other professional groups with which they work and cooperate fully with members of such groups. If a consumer is receiving services from another professional, psychologists do not offer their services directly to the consumer without first informing the professional person already involved so that the risk of confusion and conflict for the consumer can be avoided.

c. Psychologists who employ or supervise other professionals or professionals in training accept the obligation to facilitate their further professional development by providing suitable working conditions, consultation, and experience opportunities.

d. As employees of organizations providing psychological services, or as independent psychologists serving clients in an organizational context, psychologists seek to support the integrity, reputation and proprietary rights of the host organization. When it is judged necessary in a client's interest to question the organization's programs or policies, psychologists attempt to effect change by constructive action within the organization before disclosing confidential information acquired in their professional roles.

e. In the pursuit of research, psychologists give sponsoring agencies, host institutions, and publications channels the same respect and opportunity for giving informed consent that they accord to individual research participants. They are aware of their obligation to future research workers and insure that host institutions are given adequate information about the research and proper acknowledgement of their contribution.

f. Publication credit is assigned to all those who have contributed to a publication in proportion to their contribution. Major contributions of a professional character made by several persons to a common project are recognized by joint authorship, with the experimenter or author who made the principal contribution identified and listed first. Minor contributions of a professional character, extensive clerical or similar nonprofessional assistance, and other minor contributions are acknowledged in footnotes or in an introductory statement. Acknowledgement through specific citations is made for unpublished as well as published material that has directly influenced the research or writing. A psychologist who compiles and edits material of others for publication publishes the material in the name of the originating group, if any, and with his/her own name appearing as chairperson or editor. All contributors are to be acknowledged and named.

g. When a psychologist violates ethical standards, psychologists who know first-hand of such activities should, if possible, attempt to rectify the situation. Failing an informal solution, psychologists bring such unethical activities to the attention of the appropriate local, state, and/or national committee on professional ethics, standards, and practices.

h. Members of the Association cooperate with duly constituted committees of the Association, in particular and for example, the Committee on Scientific and Professional Ethics and Conduct, and the Committee on Professional Standards Review, by responding to inquiries promptly and completely. Members taking longer than 30 days to respond to such inquiries shall have the burden of demonstrating that they acted with "reasonable promptness." Members also have a similar responsibility to respond with reasonable promptness to inquiries from duly constituted state association ethics committees and professional standards review committees.

PRINCIPLE 8. UTILIZATION OF ASSESSMENT TECHNIQUES

In the development, publication, and utilization of psychological assessment techniques, psychologists observe relevant APA standards. Persons examined have the right to know the results, the interpretations made, and, where appropriate, the original data on which final judgments were based. Test users avoid imparting unnecessary information which would compromise test security, but they provide requested information that explains the basis for decisions that may adversely affect that person or that person's dependents.

a. The client has the right to have and the psychologist has the responsibility to provide explanations of the nature and the purposes of the test and the test results in language that the client can understand, unless, as in some employment or school settings, there is an explicit exception to this right agreed upon in advance. When the explanations are to be provided by others, the psychologist establishes procedures for providing adequate explanations.

b. When a test is published or otherwise made available for operational use, it is accompanied by a manual (or other published or readily available information) that fully describes the development of the test, the rationale, and evidence of validity and reliability. The test manual explicitly states the purposes and applications for which the test is recommended and identifies special qualifications required to administer the test and to interpret it properly. Test manuals provide complete information regarding the characteristics of the normative population.

c. In reporting test results, psychologists indicate any reservations regarding validity or reliability resulting from testing circumstances or inappropriateness of the test norms for the person tested. Psychologists strive to insure that the test results and their interpretations are not misused by others.

d. Psychologists accept responsibility for removing from clients' files test score information that has become obsolete, lest such information be misused or misconstrued to the disadvantage of the person tested.

e. Psychologists offering test scoring and interpretation services are able to demonstrate that the validity of the programs and procedures used in arriving at interpretations are based on appropriate evidence. The public offering of an automated test interpretation service is considered as a professional-to-professional consultation. The psychologist makes every effort to avoid misuse of test reports.

PRINCIPLE 9. PURSUIT OF RESEARCH ACTIVITIES

The decision to undertake research should rest upon a considered judgment by the individual psychologist about how best to contribute to psychological science and to human welfare. Psychologists carry out their investigations with respect for the people who participate and with concern for their dignity and welfare.

a. In planning a study the investigator has the responsibility to make a careful evaluation of its ethical acceptability, taking into account the following additional principles for research with human beings. To the extent that this appraisal, weighing scientific and humane values, suggests a compromise of any principle, the investigator incurs an increasingly serious obligation to seek ethical advice and to observe stringent safeguards to protect the rights of the human research participants.

b. Responsibility for the establishment and maintenance of acceptable ethical practice in research always remains with the individual investigator. The investigator is also responsible for the ethical treatment of research participants by collaborators, assistants, students and employees, all of whom, however, incur parallel obligations.

c. Ethical practice requires the investigator to inform the participant of all features of the research that might reasonably be expected to influence willingness to participate, and to explain all other aspects of the research about which the participant inquires. Failure to make full disclosure imposes additional force to the investigator's abiding responsibility to protect the welfare and dignity of the research participant.

d.   Openness and honesty are essential characteristics of the relationship between investigator and research participant. When the methodological requirements of a study necessitate concealment or deception, the investigator is required to insure as soon as possible the participant's understanding of the reasons for this action and of a sufficient justification for the procedures employed.

e.   Ethical practice requires the investigator to respect the individual's freedom to decline to participate in or withdraw from research. The obligation to protect this freedom requires special vigilance when the investigator is in a position of power over the participant, as, for example, when the participant is a student, client, employee, or otherwise is in a dual relationship with the investigator.

f.   Ethically acceptable research begins with the establishment of a clear and fair agreement between the investigator and the research participant that clarifies the responsibilities of each. The investigator has the obligation to honor all promises and commitments included in that agreement.

g.   The ethical investigator protects participants from physical and mental discomfort, harm, and danger. If a risk of such consequences exists, the investigator is required to inform the participant of that fact, secure consent before proceeding, and take all possible measures to minimize distress. A research procedure must not be used if it is likely to cause serious or lasting harm to a participant.

h.   After the data are collected, the investigator provides the participant with information about the nature of the study and to remove any misconceptions that may have arisen. When scientific or human values justify delaying or withholding information, the investigator acquires a special responsibility to assure that there are no damaging consequences for the participant.

i.   When research procedures may result in undesirable consequences for the individual participant, the investigator has the responsibility to detect and remove or correct these consequences, including, where relevant, long-term after effects.

j.   Information obtained about the individual research participants during the course of an investigation is confidential unless otherwise agreed in advance. When the possibility exists that others may obtain access to such information, this possibility, together with the plans for protecting confidentiality, must be explained to the participants as part of the procedure for obtaining informed consent.

k.   A psychologist using animals in research adheres to the provisions of the Rules Regarding Animals, drawn up by the Committee on Precautions and Standards in Animal Experimentation and adopted by the American Psychological Association.

l.   Investigations of human participants using drugs should be conducted only in such settings as clinics, hospitals, or research facilities maintaining appropriate safeguards for the participants.

REFERENCES

Psychologists are responsible for knowing about and acting in accord with the standards and positions of the APA, as represented in such official documents as the following:

American Association of University Professors. Statement on Principles on Academic Freedom and Tenure. *Policy Documents & Report,* 1977, 1–4.

American Psychological Association. *Guidelines for Psychologists for the Use of Drugs in Research.* Washington, D.C.: Author, 1971.

American Psychological Association. *Principles for the Care and Use of Animals.* Washington, D.C.: Author, 1971.

American Psychological Association. Guidelines for conditions of employment of psychologists, *American Psychologist,* 1972, *27,* 331–334.

American Psychological Association. Guidelines for psychologists conducting growth groups. *American Psychologist,* 1973, *28,* 933.

American Psychological Association. *Ethical Principles in the Conduct of Research with Human Participants.* Washington, D.C.: Author, 1973.

American Psychological Association. *Standards for Educational and Psychological Tests.* Washington, D.C.: Author, 1974.

American Psychological Association. *Standards for Providers of Psychological Services.* Washington, D.C.: Author, 1977.

Committee on Scientific and Professional Ethics and Conduct. Guidelines for telephone directory listings. *American Psychologist,* 1969, 24, 70–71.

Appendix H
Education Amendments of 1974
Public Law 92–380[*]

TABLE OF CONTENTS

TITLE I—AMENDMENTS TO THE ELEMENTARY AND SECONDARY EDUCATION ACT OF 1965

* An Act to extend and amend the Elementary and Secondary Education Act of 1965, and for other purposes. *Source:* United States Code. Congressional and Administration News. 93rd Congress-Second Session, 1974. Volume I, Laws. Published by Government Publications, St. Paul, Minn. West Publishing Company.

(5)   Amendments relating to applications.

(6)   Amendments relating to participation of children enrolled in private schools.

(7)   Amendments relating to adjustments where necessitated by appropriations.

(8)   Amendments relating to allocation of funds within the school district of a local educational agency and program evaluation.

(9)   Technical amendments.

(10)   Provision with respect to additional authorizations for certain local educational agencies.

(b)   Effective date.

Sec. 102.   School library resources, textbooks, and other instructional materials.

Sec. 103.   Supplementary educational centers and services; guidance, counseling, and testing.

Sec. 104.   Strengthening State and local educational agencies.

Sec. 105.   Bilingual educational programs.

Sec. 106.   Statute of limitations.

Sec. 107.   Dropout prevention projects.

Sec. 108.   School nutrition and health services.

Sec. 109.   Correction education services.

Sec. 110.   Open meetings of educational agencies.

Sec. 111.   Ethnic heritage studies centers.

Furnishing Information

Sec. 512.   (a) Part C of the General Education Provisions Act is further amended by adding at the end thereof the following new section:

Responsibility of States to Furnish Information

Sec. 437.   (a) The Commissioner shall require that each State submit to him, within sixty days after the end of any fiscal year, a report on the uses of Federal funds in that State under any applicable program for which the State is responsible for administration. Such report shall—

(1) list all grants and contracts made under such program to the local educational agencies and other public and private agencies and institutions within such State during such year;

(2) include the total amount of funds available to the State under each such program for such fiscal year and specify from which appropriation Act or Acts these funds were available;

(3) with respect to the second preceding fiscal year, include a compilation of reports from local educational agencies and other public and private agencies and institutions within such State which

sets forth the amount of such Federal funds received by each such agency and the purposes for which such funds were expended;

(4) with respect to such second preceding fiscal year, include a statistical report on the individuals served or affected by programs, projects, or activities assisted with such Federal funds; and

(5) be made readily available by the State to local educational agencies and other public and private agencies and institutions within the State, and to the public.

(b) On or before October 15 of each year, the Commissioner shall submit to the Committee on Labor and Public Welfare of the Senate and to the Committee on Education and Labor of the House of Representatives an analysis of these reports and a compilation of statistical data derived therefrom.

(b) The amendment made by subsection (a) shall be effective upon enactment of this Act.

Protection of the Rights and Privacy of Parents and Students

Sec. 513. (a) Part C of the General Education Provisions Act is further amended by adding at the end thereof the following new section:

Protection of the Rights and Privacy of Parents and Students

Sec. 438. (a) (1) No funds shall be made available under any applicable program to any State or local educational agency, any institution of higher education, any community college, any school, agency offering a preschool program, or any other educational institution which has a policy of denying, or which effectively prevents, the parents of students attending any school of such agency, or attending such institution of higher education, community college, school, preschool, or other educational institution, the right to inspect and review any and all official records, files, and data directly related to their children, including all material that is incorporated into each student's cumulative record folder, and intended for school use or to be available to parties outside the school or school system, and specifically including, but not necessarily limited to, identifying data, academic work completed, level of achievement (grades, standardized achievement test scores), attendance data, scores on standardized intelligence, aptitude, and psychological tests, interest inventory results, health data, family background information, teacher or counselor ratings and observations, and verified reports of serious or recurrent behavior patterns. Where such records or data include information on more than one student, the parents of any student shall be entitled to receive, or be informed of, that part of such record or data as pertains to their child. Each recipient shall establish appropriate procedures for the granting of a request by parents for access to their child's records within a reasonable period of time, but in no case more than forty-five days after the request has been made.

(2) Parents shall have an opportunity for a hearing to challenge

the content of their child's school records, to insure that the records are not inaccurate, misleading, or otherwise in violation of the privacy or other rights of students, and to provide an opportunity for the correction or deletion of any such inaccurate, misleading, or otherwise inappropriate data contained therein.

(b) (1) No funds shall be made available under any applicable program to any State or local educational agency, any institution of higher education, any community college, any school, agency offering a preschool program, or any other educational institution which has a policy of permitting the release of personally identifiable records or files (or personal information contained therein) of students without the written consent of their parents to any individual, agency, or organization, other than to the following—

(A) other school officials, including teachers within the educational institution or local educational agency who have legitimate educational interests;

(B) officials of other schools or school systems in which the student intends to enroll, upon condition that the student's parents be notified of the transfer, receive a copy of the record if desired, and have an opportunity for a hearing to challenge the content of the record;

(C) authorized representatives of (i) the Comptroller General of the United States, (ii) the Secretary, (iii) an administrative head of an education agency (as defined in section 409 of this Act), or (iv) State educational authorities, under the conditions set forth in paragraph (3) of this subsection; and

(D) in connection with a student's application for, or receipt of, financial aid.

(2) No funds shall be made available under any applicable program to any State or local educational agency, any institution of higher education, any community college, any school, agency offering a preschool program, or any other educational institution which has a policy or practice of furnishing, in any form, any personally identifiable information contained in personal school records, to any persons other than those listed in subsection (b) (1) unless—

(A) there is written consent from the student's parents specifying records to be released, the reasons for such release, and to whom, and with a copy of the records to be released to the student's parents and the student if desired by the parents, or

(B) such information is furnished in compliance with judicial order, or pursuant to any lawfully issued subpoena, upon condition that parents and the students are notified of all such orders or subpoenas in advance of the compliance therewith by the educational institution or agency.

(3) Nothing contained in this section shall preclude authorized representatives of (A) the Comptroller General of the United States, (B) the Secretary, (C) an administrative head of an education agency or (D) State educational authorities from having access to student or

other records which may be necessary in connection with the audit and evaluation of Federally-supported education program, or in connection with the enforcement of the Federal legal requirements which relate to such programs: *Provided,* That, except when collection of personally identifiable data is specifically authorized by Federal law, any data collected by such officials with respect to individual students shall not include information (including social security numbers) which would permit the personal identification of such students or their parents after the data so obtained has been collected.

(4) (A) With respect to subsections (c) (1) and (c) (2) and (c) (3), all persons, agencies, or organizations desiring access to the records of a student shall be required to sign a written form which shall be kept permanently with the file of the student, but only for inspection by the parents or student, indicating specifically the legitimate educational or other interest that each person, agency, or organization has in seeking this information. Such form shall be available to parents and to the school official responsible for record maintenance as a means of auditing the operation of the system.

(B) With respect to this subsection, personal information shall only be transferred to a third party on the condition that such party will not permit any other party to have access to such information without the written consent of the parents of the student.

(c) The Secretary shall adopt appropriate regulations to protect the rights of privacy of students and their families in connection with any surveys or data-gathering activities conducted, assisted, or authorized by the Secretary or an administrative head of an education agency. Regulations established under this subsection shall include provisions controlling the use, dissemination, and protection of such data. No survey or data-gathering activities shall be conducted by the Secretary, or an administrative head of an education agency under an applicable program, unless such activities are authorized by law.

(d) For the purposes of this section, whenever a student has attained eighteen years of age, or is attending an institution of post-secondary education the permission or consent required of and the rights accorded to the parents of the student shall thereafter only be required of and accorded to the student.

(e) No funds shall be made available under any applicable program unless the recipient of such funds informs the parents of students, or the students, if they are eighteen years of age or older, or are attending an institution of postsecondary education, of the rights accorded them by this section.

(f) The Secretary, or an administrative head of an education agency, shall take appropriate actions to enforce provisions of this section and to deal with violations of this section, according to the provisions of this Act, except that action to terminate assistance may be taken only if the Secretary finds there has been a failure to comply with the provisions of this section, and he has determined that compliance cannot be secured by voluntary means.

(g) The Secretary shall establish or designate an office and review board within the Department of Health, Education, and Welfare for the purpose of investigating, processing, reviewing, and adjudicating violations of the provisions of this section and complaints which may be filed concerning alleged violations of this section, according to the procedures contained in sections 434 and 437 of this Act.

(b) (1) (i) The provisions of this section shall become effective ninety days after the date of enactment of section 438 of the General Education Provisions Act.

(2) (i) This section may be cited as the "Family Educational Rights and Privacy Act of 1974".

Protection of Pupil Rights

Sec. 514.   (a) Part C of the General Education Provisions Act is further amended by adding after section 438 the following new section:

Protection of Pupil Rights

Sec. 439.   All instructional material, including teacher's manuals, films, tapes, or other supplementary instructional material which will be used in connection with any research or experimentation program or project shall be available for inspection by the parents or guardians of the children engaged in such program or project. For the purpose of this section "research or experimentation program or project" means any program or project in any applicable program designed to explore or develop new or unproven teaching methods or techniques.

(b) The amendment made by subsection (a) shall be effective upon enactment of this Act.

Name Index

Loughary, John W., 399
Lubin, B., 300

M

McCarthy, Martha M., 362, 363
McCary, James L., 399
Maccoby, E. E., 288
McCully, C. Harold, 19, 56
Mace, David R., 183
McKenna, Bernard, 150
McKown, H. C., 28
McQueen, Mildred, 43
Mann, Horace, 5
Marland, Sidney P., 212
Maslow, Abraham, 31, 32, 248, 399
Mathieu-Coughlan, Phillipa, 397
Mayo, A. D., 5
Meares, Paula Allen, 76
Mehrens, William A., 163, 171
Mellecker, John, 273
Mercurio, John M., 300, 301
Merriman, H. D., 374, 381
Miles, Matthew B., 73
Miller, A. J., 223, 224
Miller, V. E., 397
Mitchell, Marianne H., 29, 35, 37, 240,
    241, 286, 287, 345, 354, 380, 399
Moni, Linda, 65
Moore, Barbara, 244
Moore, Earl J., 397
Moran, K. D., 83, 145
Morrill, Weston H., 62
Munger, Paul F., 12, 15, 33, 263
Munson, Harold L., 20, 332
Muro, James J., 399
Myers, Gail E., 141
Myers, Michele T., 141
Myers, R. A., 83
Myrick, Robert D., 65

N

Negley, Harold H., 364
Neubert, Stephen F., 375

Nitko, A. J., 177
Noeth, R. J., 43, 239, 399
Nolte, Mervin Chester, 149
Norris, Willa, 256, 399

O

Obermann, C. Esco, 14, 399
O'Brien, Bernard A., 89, 90
Odiorne, G. S., 350
Oetting, E. R., 62, 375
Ohlsen, Merle M., 239, 289, 298, 308,
    310, 313, 323, 399
Okun, Barbara F., 280, 399
Ornstein, Allan C., 149
Osipow, Samuel H., 399

P

Page, Richard C., 286
Parker, Clyde A., 325, 330
Parker, L. Allen, 214, 248, 249, 255, 256,
    257, 258, 259
Parker, Max, 96
Parnes, H. S., 229
Parsons, Frank, 8, 9, 10, 22, 34, 185, 211,
    399
Parsons, Talcott, 181
Pascal, Anthony H., 248
Passons, W. R., 275
Patterson, C. H., 182
Patterson, Lewis E., 397
Pavlov, Ivan P., 268
Peer, Gary G., 92
Peter, Laurence I., 354
Peters, Herman J., 181, 399
Peterson, David, 291
Peterson, James, 181, 182, 183, 188
Pew, W. L., 396
Phelps, R. J., 92
Pietrofesa, John J., 86, 88, 271, 399
Pine, Gerald J., 43
Pinto, Diana V., 271, 399
Poppen, William A., 400

Subject Index